FOUNTAIN SPRINGS UP IN THE DESERT, AT THE PRAYER

THE
LIVES OF THE FATHERS
OF THE
EASTERN DESERTS.

ST. MARY OF EGYPT.

BY THE REV. DR. CHALLONER.

New York:
D. & J. SADLIER & CO., 31 BARCLAY STREET
BOSTON : 128 FEDERAL STREET
MONTREAL, C. E. : COR. OF. ST. FRANCIS XAVIER AND NOTRE DAME STREETS
1863

THE LIVES

OF

THE FATHERS

OF THE

Eastern Deserts;

OR

THE WONDERS OF GOD

IN

THE WILDERNESS.

TO WHICH IS ADDED AN APPENDIX.

NEW-YORK:

D & J. SADLIER & Co. 31 BARCLAY-STREET

MONTREAL, C. E:
CORNER OF ST. FRANCIS XAVIER AND NOTRE-DAME STREETS.

176

CONTENTS.

APPENDIX.

PREFACE.

"THE SAINTS OF THE DESERT!" what a
subject to be brought before the minds of this
worldly-wise and self-worshipping generation!—
how can men and women who live but to indulge
their tastes, and fancies, and gratify their passions, understand or appreciate the antiquated
custom of crucifying the flesh, and macerating
the body by vigils and fasts, and giving up all
the fascinations of this world to devote the
whole being, heart, and soul to God from whom
it came?—" And then it is only the Catholics
who practise these things, or are at all influenced by such notions. It is only the Church
of Rome that inculcates such unnatural doctrines, and teaches people to forget themselves
and be as though they were not." Very true,
and it is only for Catholics that these pages

are expected to have any interest. We have no
idea of penetrating the depths of the burning
deserts, and entering the cavern or cell where
the solitary abides in uninterrupted commune
with his God, to lay bare the beautiful recesses—
the calm, untroubled depths of his super-human
soul—merely to expose them to the derision of
the unbeliever. The saints of the desert—the
religious of the cloisters—all the monastic orders whether active or contemplative are the
pride and glory of the Church—they are her
richest treasures—her chosen children, who sit
ever at her feet drinking in her divine precepts
and literally putting them in practice; they are
the blooming wreaths wherewith she crowns her
beloved Spouse, because they are His faithful
imitators, and her docile pupils. It is true—
very true—that the children of this world who
are wiser in their generation than the children of
light have little or nothing in common with these
saintly personages, and that in their eyes our
Anthonys, our Anselms, our Teresas, nay even
our Jeromes, our Gregorys, and our Basils bear

but a sorry figure—nay, the divine Precursor himself—the first of our solitaries—must seem little better than a fool, because he practised, to the very letter, this spirit of self-denial which the world cannot understand, but which the Church of God has ever inculcated, and still does inculcate.

This work of Dr. Challoner's has long been familiar to the Catholic public, and it is a very fair collection of the EMINENT SAINTS OF THE DESERT, but on looking over it recently, prior to its re-publication, it struck me that there were a few important omissions. I looked in vain for the lives of St. Jerome—St. Gregory Nazianzen, or his illustrious friend, St. Basil the Great, and knowing that some portion of the lives of each of those great saints was spent in solitude, I thought it would be an acceptable addition to the work to give the *monastic* lives of those three illustrious doctors, who have rendered and do still render such invaluable service to the Church. This portion of their lives I found in a French work entitled *Viès des*

Peres du desert, and it is with much pleasure that I now give their rightful place to these three great Fathers of the Oriental Church. As for the style of the translation I shall say nothing, for I had only to make the best of a bad bargain, as there was no style at all in the original. However, in a work of this kind, which is chiefly read by pious Christians, I have not much to dread from criticism, and with that conviction I proceeded in my task, being more anxious to do honor to the sainted memory of these great men—who may be truly called " pillars of the Church "—than to produce a finished piece of composition.

𝔐. 𝔄. 𝔥.

MONTREAL, July 1852

INTRODUCTION.

AMONGST the various departments of reading, none can be more interesting than that which records the actions of men who have rendered themselves illustrious by their wisdom, their heroism, or their eminent virtues. In the Lives of the Saints of the Oriental Deserts, the reader will find an heroism that exceeds the natural powers of man;—a wisdom, in comparison of which that of a Socrates or a Solon is but childishness (for wisdom becomes more or less estimable in proportion to the value of the objects that attract its attention); hence the virtues of the illustrious characters whose memoirs are the subject of the subsequent pages, as far surpass those of the most exalted characters of Pagan antiquity, as man in a state of nature is surpassed by the angelic spirits.

Many traits will be found in their lives that cannot accord with the enervated delicacy of modern ideas and habits, pre-occupied, as they unfortunately are, by the false maxims and vitiated manners of an age that labors to substitute a vain philosophy, the pander of every passion, in lieu of divine revelation, which not only commands and afford the means of their subjugation, but also invites us to erect on their ruins the fabric of evangelical perfection.

The Almighty has at all times inspired his servants with a conduct suitable to the exigencies of the age in which they lived, making them all to all, in order to gain all to himself. Reasonings and exhortations make but a feeble impression on ignorant or brutal men, accustomed to blood and pillage;—men who, as they had been trained up in the fatigues of war, and were always in the harness,—hardened in vicious habits and blinded by hereditary errors, would have esteemed ordinary austerities as to nothing; but when they witnessed an absolute contempt of all earthly comforts in an Antony, a Macarius, &c. the severe chastisements they inflicted on themselves, and their alacrity in assuaging the corporal as well as the spiritual necessities of others, which proceeded to such a length as even to do penance for them, what could they infer, but that they loved God and their neighbor with an ardor at once holy and invincible. With minds therefore deeply impressed with so edifying an exterior, they became more docile; and from listening to those whom they so greatly admired, at length became proselytes to the holy religion they professed. Thus St. Abraham, by his invincible patience and meekness under a series of the most cruel outrages for the space of three years, more than by his preaching, subdued the blindness and obstinacy of the Pagans near Edessa, who were at length obliged to acknowledge, "that the God whom he preached must be the true God, and the religion which taught him so much patience and charity, the true religion." Thus Theodoret witnessed Simon Stylites from his pillar receiving the abjuration of multitudes of Iberians, Armenians, Persians, and Saracens, who, in his presence, with a loud voice renounced their idols, and trampled them under foot. And thus barbarians and infidels of distant regions frequently invoked with success, protection amidst the dangers of the sea, in the name of the God of Theodosius.

But it is not in Pagan or barbarian nations only, that the lives of these illustrious men have contributed to promote the cause of God and virtue :—St. Chrysostom, who was no less distinguished for his learning and accomplishments, than for being the metropolitan of the Eastern Empire, recommends (Hom. 8. in Matt. 7. p. 128,) the reading the life of St. Antony, as replete with instruction and edification; and St. Augustin, in the eighth book of his Confessions, chap. 6, gives a minute detail of the conversion of two courtiers in the emperor's service, who had renounced the world by accidentally reading the life of St. Antony; and moreover attributes his own conversion in a great measure to the same cause.

There was a time when the bare testimonies either of St. Chrysostom or St. Augustin, would render any further arguments in favor of a work of this kind un-

necessary; but, unfortunately in an age wherein scep-
ticism and infidelity are so prevalent, the most venerable authority or incontestible evidence in support of
miraculous or supernatural events, whether of an ancient or modern date, will not always satisfy the weak
or temporising amongst those who consider themselves
of the number of the faithful—who generally listen
with indifference, or treat with disdain and derision,
the bare mention of a miracle; for stupidity itself will
on such occasions assume the office of censor, and aspire to wit, when tinctured by the buffoon philosophy
of Voltaire's school.

A distinguished modern, MONTESQUIEU, whose works
are supposed to have promoted the French Revolution,
imagines the spectres that tempted the otherwise as-
sailed St. Antony and others, to have been metaphor-
ical; whereas such a supposition, if admitted as a
truth, would not only invalidate the testimonies of SS.
Athanasius, Jerome, Cyril, &c. but even the holy
Scriptures themselves, Wisd. xvii. where it is said, that
during the Egyptian darkness, the infernal spirits increased the terror of the inhabitants by frightful apparitions; of whose existence even the Pagan poet
Virgil seems to have had some idea.

> Yet be not overbold,
> The slippery God will try to loose his hold;
> And various forms assume to cheat thy sight;
> And with vain images of beasts affright

With foamy tusks will seem a bristly boar,
Or imitate the lion's angry roar;
Break out in crackling flames to shun thy snare,
Or hiss a dragon, or a tiger stare;
Or with a wife thy caution to betray,
In fleeting streams, attempt to slide away.

Georg. B. iv

That the Almighty has, at certain periods, granted a limited power to the devil personally to tempt or torment the sons of men, either with a view to put the virtue of his chosen servants to a trial, and thereby afford them opportunities of triumphing over the powers of hell, or for other reasons best known to his ever just but inscrutable judgments, is evident from the testimonies of the scriptures both of the Old and New Testaments : as in the cases of Job,—our Saviour in the desert—the young man possessed by the devil ; and several other instances of the kind recorded by the Evangelists. Similar events have also frequently occurred in every age of the church, in countries emerging, or struggling to emerge, from Idolatry into Christianity through the missionary labors of apostolical men ;* for when Satan perceives kingdoms over which he had for so long a time exercised an almost unlimited control, on the point of being extricated from his dominion, it is then he exerts the utmost extent of his power to retain them under his subjection.

* See Butler's " Lives of the Saints." See also " Missiones Orientales," recue et imprime a Londres, ann. 1797.

In a word, whatever may appear supernatural to our readers, in the perusal of the lives of these holy solitaries, rests on the same credit and authority as the most ordinary and familiar circumstance related of them ; nor is any miraculous interposition of Providence enabling them to pursue a system of life, impossible to mere human efforts, that has not a parallel in the holy scriptures themselves : for example, if some of them fasted many weeks without any corporal sustenance [without referring to the forty days' fast of our Saviour in the desert], did not Elias and St. John the Baptist also fast in the same rigorous manner ? If St. Paul the first hermit was miraculously fed by a raven, was not the prophet Elias also fed in a like miraculous manner ? If a lioness saved the life of St. Malchus and his companion in a cave, and destroyed their vengeful pursuers, did not bears also rush from the woods to devour the wicked children who had derided and insulted the baldness of Elizeus the prophet ? But however wonderful and interesting the events here recorded of these venerable solitaries may appear, yet the sublime virtues which they practised are by far more deserving of our frequent contemplation. In profane history we often discover the most splendid actions of worldly heroes tainted by motives of pride, vanity, or self-interest : whereas we invariably find the heroes of the wilderness to have founded their greatness on the most profound humility, and absolute an nihilation of their own will, that they might the more implicitly conform in every action and circumstance of their lives to the holy will of God ; hereby exemplifying in themselves the character of a monk or anchoret as drawn by the celebrated Abbé Rancé, founder of the Abbey of La Trappe : "When," says he, "a soul relishes God in solitude, she thinks no longer on any thing but heaven—she forgets the earth, on which there is nothing that can please her—she burns with the fire of divine love, and sighing after God alone, regards death as her greatest advantage. Nevertheless, they will find themselves much deceived, who, on forsaking the world, imagine they shall advance towards God by straight paths, or roads sown with lilies and roses ; or that they have chosen a state in which they will find no difficulties to encounter that could disturb the tranquillity of their retreat, which the hand of God will not turn aside : on the contrary, they must be persuaded that temptations will every where pursue them ; that there is no time nor any place wherein they can be exempt from them ; that the peace which God promises is procured in the midst of tribulations, as rosebuds are found among thorns. God has not promised his servants that they should meet with no trials, but that with the temptation he will also give them the grace to overcome it. Heaven is offered us on no other condition : it is a kingdom of conquests, a prize of victory ; but, O God ! what a prize !!!"

LIVES

OF THE

SAINTS OF THE DESERTS.

---•◦•---

ST. JOHN THE BAPTIST.

Saint John the Baptist, the son of Zachary and Elizabeth, was sanctified and hallowed in his mother's womb, and even in the tender years of childhood received an inspiration to retire to the wilderness, where his holy life manifested the true effects of grace on a heart that has burst the bonds of the slavery of sin. St. John the Baptist was called by God to be the forerunner of his Divine Son, to usher him into the world, and to prepare mankind by penance to receive their great Redeemer, whom the prophets had foretold at a distance through every age from the beginning of the world; never ceasing to excite the people of God to faith and hope in him, by whom alone they were to be saved. The more the sublime function of this saint surpassed that of the Jewish legislator and of all the patriarchs and ancient prophets, the greater were the graces by which he was fitted for the same. Some of

the prophets had been sanctified from their birth : but
neither in so wonderful nor in so abundant a manner
as the Baptist.   In order to preseve his innocence
spotless, and to improve the extraordinary graces
which he had received, he was directed by the Holy
Ghost to lead an austere and contemplative life in the
wilderness, in the continual exercises of devout prayer
and penance, from his infancy till he was thirty years
of age.   How much does this precaution of a saint,
who was strengthened by such uncommon privileges
and graces, condemn the rashness of parents who ex
pose children in the slippery time of youth to the con-
tagious air of wicked worldly company, and to every
danger! or, who, instead of training them up in suitable habits of self-denial, humility, devotion, and reasonable application to serious duties, are themselves by
example and pernicious maxims the corruptors of their
tender minds, and the flatterers of their passions, which
they ought to teach them to subdue.

St. John cannot be commonly imitated by youth in
his total retreat from the world; but he teaches what
are the means by which they must study, according to
their circumstances, to sanctify that most precious age
of life; what they must shun, in what maxims they
ought to ground themselves, and how they are to form
and strengthen in themselves the most perfect habits
of all virtues.   Let them consider him as a special
pattern, and the model of innocence and of that fervor

with which they must labor continually to improve in
wisdom, piety, and every virtue. He is particularly
the pattern which those ought always to have before
their eyes, who are called by God to the ministry of
his altar, or of his word. Let no one be so rash as to
ntrude himself into the sanctuary before he has labored a long time to qualify himself for so high an
office by retirement, humility, holy contemplation, and
penance, and before the spirit of those virtues has
taken deep root in his soul. Saint John led a most
austere life in the wilderness conversing only with
God, till, in the thirtieth year of his age, he was perfectly qualified to enter upon the administration of his
office ; that being also the age at which the priests
and Levites were permitted by the Jewish law to begin
the exercise of their functions. The prophets had long
before described the Baptist as the messenger and
forerunner sent to prepare the way of the Lord, by
bringing men to a due sense of their sins, and to the
other necessary dispositions for receiving worthily their
Redeemer. Isaias and Malachy in these predictions
allude to harbingers and such other officers whom
princes upon their journeys sent before them, to take
care that the roads should be levelled, and all obstruc-
tions that might hinder their passage removed.

God, by a revelation, intimated to John his commission of precursor in the wilderness, and the faithful
minister began to discharge it in the desert of Judea

itself near the borders, where it was thinly inhabited,
upon the banks of the Jordan, towards Jericho,
Clothed with the weeds of penance, he announced to
all men the obligation they lay under of washing away
their iniquities with the tears of sincere compunction ;
and proclaimed the Messiah, who was then coming to
make his appearance among them.   He was received
by the people as the true herald of the most high
God, and his voice was, as it were, a trumpet sounding
from heaven to summon all men to avert the divine
judgments, and to prepare themselves to reap the benefit of the mercy that was offered them.   All ranks
of people listened to him, and, amongst others, came
many Pharisees, whose pride and hypocrisy, which
rendered them indocile, and blinded them in their
vices, he sharply reproved.   The very soldiers and
publicans or tax-gatherers, who were generally persons
hardened in habits of immorality, violence and injustice, flocked to him.   He exhorted all to works of
charity, and to a reformation of their lives, and those
who addressed themselves to him, in these dispositions, he baptized in the river.   The Jews practised
several religious washings of the body as legal purifi-
cations ; but no baptism before this of John had so
great and mystical a signification.   It chiefly represented the manner in which the souls of men must be
cleansed from all sin and vicious habits, to be made
partakers of Christ's spiritual kingdom, and it was an

emblem of the interior effects of sincere repentance ; but it differed entirely from the great Sacrament of Baptism which Christ soon after instituted, to which it was much inferior in virtue and efficacy, and of which it was a kind of type.

St. John's baptism was a temporary rite, by which men who were under the law were admitted to some new spiritual privileges, which they had not before, by him who was the messenger of Christ, and of his new covenant. Whence it is called by the fathers a partition between the law and the gospel. This baptism of John prepared men to become Christians, but did not make them so. It was not even conferred in the name of Christ, or in that of the Holy Ghost, who had not been as yet given. When St. John had already preached and baptized about six months, our Redeemer went from Nazareth, and presented himself, among others, to be baptized by him. The Baptist knew him by a divine revelation, and, full of awe and respect for his sacred person, at first excused himself, but at length acquiesced out of obedience. The Saviour of sinners was pleased to be baptized among sinners, not to be cleansed himself, but to sanctify the waters, says St. Ambrose, that is, to give them the virtue to cleanse away the sins of men. St. Austin and St. Thomas Aquinas think he then instituted the holy Sacrament of Baptism, which he soon after administered by his disciples, whom doubtless he had first baptized himself.

The solemn admonitions of the Baptist, attended with the most extraordinary innocence and sanctity, and the marks of his divine commission, procured him a mighty veneration and authority among the Jews, and several began to look upon him as the Messiah, who, from the ancient prophecies, was expected by all the nations of the East to appear about that time in Judea, as Suetonius, Tacitus, and Josephus testify. To remove all thoughts of this kind, he freely declared that he only baptized sinners with water in order to repentance and a new life; but that there was one ready to appear among them, who would baptize them with the effusion of the Holy Ghost, and who so far exceeded him in power and excellency, that he was not worthy to do for him the meanest servile office. Nevertheless, so strong were the impressions which the preaching and deportment of John made upon the minds of the Jews, that they sent to him a solemn embassy of priests and Levites from Jerusalem to inquire of him if he was not the Christ. True humility shudders at the very mention of undue honor; and the higher applause it meets with among men, the lower it sinks in a deep sense and sincere acknowledgment of its own baseness and unworthiness, and in the abyss of its nothingness; and in this disposition it is inflamed with a most ardent desire to give all praise

And glory to the pure gratuitous goodness and mercy of God alone. In these sentiments St. John *confessed, and did not deny : and he confessed, I am not the Christ.* He also told the deputies that he was *neither Elias nor a prophet.* He was indeed Elias in spirit; being the great harbinger of the Son of God ; and excelled in dignity the ancient Elias, who was a type of our saint. The Baptist was likewise eminently a prophet, and more than a prophet, it being his office not to foretell Christ at a distance, but to point him out present among men. Yet, far from pluming himself with titles and prerogatives, as pride inspires men to do, he forgets his dignity in every other respect only in that of discharging the obligations it lays upon him, and of humbling himself under the almighty and merciful hand of Him who had chosen and exalted him by his grace. Therefore, because he was not Elias in person, nor a prophet in the strict sense of the word, though, by his office, more than a prophet, he rejects those titles.

Being pressed to give some account who he was, he calls himself *the voice of one crying in the desert ;* he will not have men have the least regard for him, but turns their attentions entirely from himself, as unworthy to be named or thought of, and only bids them listen to the summons which God sent them by his mouth. A voice is no more than an empty sound ; it is a mere nothing. How eloquent does sincere hu mility render the saints to express the sentiments of their own nothingness! Like the Baptist, every preacher of God's word must be penetrated with the most feeling sense of his own baseness; must study always to be nothing himself and in his own eyes, whilst yet he exerts all his powers that God, the great All, may be known, loved, served, and glorified by all, and in all: he must be himself merely a voice, but a voice of thunder to awake in all hearts a profound sense of their spiritual miseries, and of the duties which they owe to God. This maxim St. Austin illustrates by the following simile drawn by the pagan mythologists: "It is related in the fables," says he, "that a wolf thought, from the shrillness of the voice, that a nightingale was some large creature, and, coming up and finding it to have so small a body, said: Thou art all voice, and art therefore nothing. In like manner let us be nothing in our own esteem. Let the world despise us, and set us at naught, provided we only be the voice of God and nothing more."

The Baptist proclaimed Jesus to be the Messias at his baptism; he did the same when the Jews consulted him from Jerusalem whether he was not the Messias: again, when seeing him come towards him the day following, he called him, *The Lamb of God;* also when his disciples consulted him about the baptism of Jesus, and on other occasions. He baptized first in the Jordan on the borders of the desert of Jadea : afterward, on the other side of that river, at a place called Bethania, or rather Bethabara, which word signifies House of the Passage or common ford ; lastly at Ennon, near Salim, a place abounding in waters, situated in Judea near the Jordan. In the discharge of his commission he was a perfect model to be imitated by all true ministers of the divine word. Like an angel of the Lord *he was neither moved by benedictions nor by maledictions,* having only God and his holy will in view. Entirely free from vanity or love of popular applause, he preached not himself, but Christ. His tenderness and charity won the hearts, and his zeal gave him a commanding influence over the minds of his hearers. He reproved the vices of all orders of men with impartial freedom, and an undaunted authority ; the hypocrisy of the Pharisees, the profaneness of the Sadducees, the extortion of the publicans, the rapine and licentiousness of the soldiers, and the incest of Herod himself.

The tetrarch Herod Antipas going to Rome in the sixteenth year of Tiberius, the thirty-third of Christ, lodged in his way at the house of his brother Herod Philip, and was smitten with love for his wife Herodias, who was niece to them both. He discovered to her his criminal passion, and she consented to leave her husband and marry him, upon condition that he first divorced his wife, who was daughter of Aretas, king of the Arabs. To this he readily agreed, and being returned from Rome in the following autumn, he considered how to rid himself of his wife. The princess having got intelligence of his resolution, made her escape, and fled to her father. By her voluntary retreat Herod Antipas saw himself at liberty, and, by a notorious infringement of all laws divine and human, married Herodias his sister-in-law, though she had children by her own husband Philip, his brother, who was yet living. St. John Baptist boldly reprehended the tetrarch and his accomplices for so scandalous an incest and adultery, and said to that prince : *It is not lawful for thee to take thy brother's wife.* Herod feared and reverenced John, knowing him to be a holy man ; and he did many things by his advice ; but, on the other hand, he could not bear that his main sore should be touched, and was highly offended at the liberty which the preacher took in that particular. Thus, whilst he respected him as a saint, he hated him as a censor, and felt a violent struggle in his own breast, between his veneration for the sanctity of the prophet, and the reproaches of his own conduct. His passion still got the better, and held him captive, and his flame was nourished by the flatteries of courtiers, and the clamors and artifices of Herodias, who, like an enraged infernal fury, left nothing unattempted to take away the life of him who durst impeach her conduct, and disturb her criminal pleasures and ambition. Herod, to content her, cast the saint into prison.

Josephus says, the servant of God was confined in the castle of Macherus, two leagues beyond the lake As- phaltites, upon the borders of Arabia Petræa. St. John, hearing in prison of Christ's wonderful works and preaching, sent two of his disciples to him for their information, not doubting but that Christ would satisfy them that he was the Messiah ; and that by his answers they would lay aside their prejudices, and join themselves to him.

Herod continued still to respect the man of God, frequently sent for him, and heard him discourse with much pleasure, though he was troubled when he was admonished by him of his faults. Herodias on the other hand, never ceased by her instigations to endeavor to exasperate him against the holy man, and to seek an opportunity to compass his destruction. An occasion at length fell out favorable to her designs. It was about a year since John the Baptist had been committed close prisoner, when He- rod, upon a return of his birthday, made a splendid entertainment for the principal nobility of Galilee, in the castle of Macherus. The dancing of Salome and other circumstances of this banquet are sensible proofs to what an infamous pitch of impudence, debauchery was carried in this impious court. To dance at ban- quets was looked upon among civilized nations which had any regard to rules of decency and temperance, as a base effeminacy, and an excess of softness and volup

tuousness, as it is called by Cicero, who clears the reputation of king Deiotarus from the aspersion of such
an indecency, because, being a man remarkable from
his youth for the gravity of his manners, he was incapable of such an extravagance.   That orator had before endeavored in the same manner to justify Muræna
from a like imputation.   When luxury and intemperance overran the Roman commonwealth, these maxims
of ancient severity still so far prevailed, that Tiberius
and Domitian, who will never pass for rigid reformers
of morals, turned patricians out of the senate for having
danced, and the former banished all the professed dan-
cers and comedians out of Rome, so incompatible with
purity of manners was a passion for dancing looked
upon.   This reflection leads us to form a judgment of
the extreme degeneracy of Herod's court, in which the
mirth and jollity of this feast was heightened by dancing.   Salome, a daughter of Herodias by her lawfu
husband, pleased Herod by her dancing, insomuch
that he promised her, with the sacred bond of an oath,
to grant her whatever she asked, though it amounted
to half of his dominions.   From this instance St. Ambrose and other fathers take occasion to show the
dangerous consequences of a passion for dancing, and
the depravity from which it often takes its rise.   Salome having received the above-said ample promise
made her by Herod, consulted with her mother what
to ask.   Herolias was so entirely devoured by lust

and ambition, as willingly to forego every other consideration, that she might be at liberty to gratify her passions, and remove him who stood in her way in the pursuit of her criminal inclinations. She therefore instructed her daughter to demand the death of John the Baptist, and her jealousy was so impatient of the least delay, for fear the tyrant might relent if he had time to enter into himself, that she persuaded the young damsel to make it part of her petition that the head of the prisoner should be forthwith brought to her in a dish. This strange request startled the tyrant himself, and caused a damp upon his spirits. He, however, assented, though with reluctance, as men often feel a cruel sting of remorse, and suffer the qualms of a disturbed conscience flying in their face and condemning them, whilst they are drawn into sin by the tyranny of a vicious habit, or some violent passion. We cannot be surprised that Herod should be concerned at so extravagant a petition. The very mention of such a thing by a lady, in the midst of a feast and solemn rejoicing, was enough to shock even a man of uncommon barbarity.

The evangelist also informs us, that Herod had conceived a good opinion of the Baptist as a just and holy man ; also that he feared the resentment of the people, who held the man of God in the highest veneration and esteem. Moreover, it was a constant rule or custom, that neither the prince's birthday, nor the

mirth of a public assembly and banquet, were to be
stained with the condemnation or execution of any
criminal whatever ; only favors and pardons were to
be granted on such occasions.   Flaminius, a Roman
general, was expelled the senate by the censors for
having given an order for beheading a criminal whilst
he was at a banquet.   Nevertheless, the weak tyrant,
overcome by his passion, and by a fond complaisance,
was deaf to the voice of his own conscience, and to
every other consideration ; and studied, by foolish
pretences, to excuse a crime which they could only
serve to exaggerate.   He alleged a conscience of his
oath ; though if it be one sin to take a wicked oath, it
is another to keep it ; for no oath can be a bond of
iniquity, nor can any one oblige himself to do what
God forbids.   The tyrant also urged his respect for
the company, and his fear of giving them scandal by
a perjury.   But how easy would true virtue and
courage have justified the innocent man to the satisfaction of all persons whom passion did not blind, and
have shown the inhumanity of an execution which
could not fail to damp the joy of the meeting, and
give offence to all who were not interested in the plot!
But the tyrant, without giving the saint a hearing, or
allowing him so much as the formality of a trial, sent
a soldier of his guard to behead him in prison, with an
order to bring his head in a charger, and present it to
Salome.   This being executed, the damsel was not

fraid to take that present into her hands, anu deliver
it to her mother. St. Jerome relates, that the furious
Herodias made it her inhuman pastime to prick the
sacred tongue with a bodkin as Fulvia had done Cicero's. Thus died the great forerunner of our blessed
Saviour, about two years and three months after his
entrance upon his public ministry, about the time of
the Paschal solemnity, a year before the death of our
blessed Redeemer.

Josephus, though a Jew, gives a remarkable testimony to the innocence and admirable sanctity of John,
and says, " He was indeed a man endued with all virtue
who exhorted the Jews to the practice of justice towards men, and piety towards God ; and also to baptism, preaching that they would become acceptable to
God, if they renounced their sins, and to the cleanness
of their bodies added purity of soul " This historian
adds, that the Jews ascribed to the murder of John
the misfortunes into which Herod fell. For his army
was soon after cut to pieces by Aretas, king of Arabia
Petræa, who, in revenge for the affront offered his
daughter, invaded his territories, and conquered the
castle of Macherus. When Caligula afterward conferred on Agrippa the title of king of Judæa, the ambitious Herodias being racked with envy, prevailed with
Herod Antipas to repair to Rome, in order to request
the like favor of the emperor. But Caligula had received a bad impression against him, being informed

by Agrippa that he was making a league with the
Parthians, and was provided with arms for seventy
thousand men.   Whereupon, instead of granting him
a crown, he deprived him of his tetrarchate, confiscated
his goods, and banished him and Herodias to Lyons
in Gaul, in the thirty-eighth year of the Christian era,
about four years after Christ had appeared before him
at Jerusalem, and been treated by him as a mock king.
Herod and Herodias died in great misery, as Josephus
assures us, probably at Lyons, though some moderns
say they travelled into Spain.   What Nicephorus
Calixti and other modern Greeks tell us, is not supported by any ancient voucher, that Salome going
over the ice in winter, the ice broke and let her in up
to the head, which by the meeting of the ice was
severed from her body.

The Baptist's disciples came and took away his
body, which they honorably interred.   Rufinus and
Theodoret inform us, that in the reign of Julian the
Apostate, the pagans broke open the tomb of St. John
the Baptist, which was at Sebaste or Samaria, and
burnt part of his sacred bones, some part being saved
by the Christians.   These were sent to St. Athanasius
at Alexandria.   Some time after, in 396, Theedosius
built a great church in that city, in honor of the Baptist, upon the spot where the temple of Serapis had
formerly stood, and these holy relics were deposited in
it, as Theophanes testifies.   But a distribution of some

portions was made to certain other churches , and the great Theodoret obtained a share for his church at Cyrus, and relates, that he and his diocess had received from God several miraculous favors, through the intercession of this glorious saint.   The Baptist's head was discovered at Emisa in Syria, in the year 453, and was kept with honor in the great church of that city ; till, about the year 800, this precious relic was conveyed to Constantinople, that it might not be sacrilegiously insulted by the Saracens.   When that city was taken by the French in 1204, Wallo de Sarton, a canon of Amiens, brought part of this head, that is, all the face, except the lower jaw, into France, and bestowed it on his own church, where it is preserved to this day. Part of the head of the Baptist is said to be kept in St. Sylvester's church, in Campo Marzo at Rome ; though Sirmond thinks this to be the head of St. John the Martyr of Rome.   Pope Clement VIII., to remove all reasonable doubt about the relic of this saint, procured a small part of the head that is kept in Amiens, for St. Sylvester's church.

This glorious saint was a martyr, a virgin, a doctor, a prophet, and more than a prophet.   He was declared by Christ himself to be greater than all the saints of the old law, the greatest of all that had been born of women.   All the high graces with which he was favored, sprang from his humility ; in this all his other virtues were founded.   If we desire to form ourselves upon so great a model, we must, above all things, labor to lay the same deep foundation. We must never cease to purge our souls more and more perfectly from all leaven of pride, by earnestly begging this grace of God, by studying with this saint, truly to know ourselves, and by exercising continual acts of sincere humility. The meditation of our own nothingness and wretchedness will help to inspire us with this saving knowledge; and repeated humiliations will ground and improve our souls in a feeling sense of our miseries, and a sincere contempt of ourselves.

ST. PAUL, THE FIRST HERMIT.

Abridged from his Life written by St Jerome

This Saint was born in the lower Thebais, a province of Egypt, in the third century, of Christian parents, who being wealthy in worldly riches took care to give him a liberal education, and to train him up both in the Greek and Egyptian literature; yet without any prejudice to his innocence, or christian piety; for which he was remarkable from his childhood; being always of a meek and humble disposition, and greatly fearing and loving his God. His parents dying when he was about fifteen years of age, left him their estate;

wnich he had not long enjoyed, when that bloody persecution, set on foot by the Emperor Decius (who employed all manner of torments to oblige the Christians to renounce Jesus Christ, and offer sacrifice to idols,) had reached Egypt and Thebais ; where it made many martyrs ; and drove many others into the deserts and mountains; where great numbers of them perished with hunger or sickness, or fell a prey to robbers and wild beasts ; as we learn from St. Denys, who was at that very time bishop of Alexandria, in his epistle to Fabius, bishop of Antioch. Upon this occasion Paul also withdrew himself to a remote country-house, designing to lie concealed there till the storm blew over : but his sister's husband, who was acquainted with the place of his retreat, conceived a resolution to betray him to the persecutors in hopes of possessing himself of his estate. The Saint being informed of his wicked resolution, quitted his country-house, and fled into the wilderness, where he purposed to pass his time till the danger was over. Here, as he advanced still further and further into the remoter parts of the desert, he came at last to a rocky mountain, at the foot of which he found a large den or cave ; and going in, he there discovered a kind of a spacious porch, open at the top to the heavens, but protected by an old palm-tree, which covered it with its spreading branches : near which there was a spring of clear water : and in a hollow part of the mountain, several cells or rooms,

which, by the instruments he found there, appeared to
have been formerly occupied by coiners. This place
the Saint judged to be very proper for his abode: and
embraced it as a dwelling assigned him by divine Providence for the remainder of his life. And thus he
who thought only at first to hide himself for a while
in the wilderness from the fury of the persecutors, was
by the design of God conducted thither, to be an in-
habitant for life, and the first that should dedicate,
and, as it were, consecrate, those deserts to divine love ;
by living there for so many years a perfect model of
an entire separation and disengagement from all ties
and affections of this world ; for the instruction and
encouragement of many thousands, who should, by
his example, in following ages, embrace a recluse or
eremitical life. Thus the malice of his brother-in-law,
by driving him away from his worldly possessions, became the occasion of his embracing a state of life, in
and by which his soul was daily more and more enriched with the treasures of divine grace, and placed
in the most effectual way to secure to himself immense
and everlasting treasures in the eternal possession of
his God. Upon which occasion we may admire and
adore the wonderful ways of the divine goodness,
which generally draws the greatest good, even the
sanctification and salvation of our souls, from what we
poor mortals apprehend as great evils ; more especially
from the crosses and sufferings of this life, and the loss

of those things which are apt to affect us too much,
to the prejudice of that love which we owe to God.

But who shall be able to relate the wonderful manner
of life our Saint here led, estranged from all conversation with mortals, perpetually addressing himself to
God, by prayer and contemplation, night and day; or
the continual progress he made every day in the love
of God, the true science of the Saints, and *that better
part which they have chosen with Mary, and which
never shall be taken from them?* It may suffice to
say, that the perfection which he attained to in divine
love, which is the true measure of all sanctity, was so
great and supereminent in the sight of God, as to exceed by far that of St. Antony, the wonder of all ages
for christian and religious perfection : and this, by the
testimony of God himself: but yet we are not to sup-
pose that, with all his sanctity, he could be exempted
in his solitude, no more than St. Antony was, from
the temptations and molestations of the common enemy, who, by the permission of God, is most troublesome to those who oppose him most ; though it all
turns in the end to their greater good, and his own
confusion. As to the food and raiment of St. Paul,
we learn from my author, who had his account from
the disciples of St. Antony, and they from their master
that he lived (at least for a good part of the time, til
God was pleased to provide for him in a miraculou.
manner,) on those dates which the palm-tree produ·

4

ced ; and drank of the water of the spring : and as for his clothing, he made himself a garment of the leaves of the same tree, woven together after the manner of a mat or a basket.   And lest this austerity of his life might seem to any one incredible, or a thing impossible, St. Jerome in his relation calls our Lord Jesus and his angels to witness, that he himself saw certain solitaries in that part of the desert of Syria which borders upon the Saracens ; one of whom had lived, shut up .for thirty years, upon barley bread alone and muddy water ; and another who had chosen for his mansion an old pit or cistern, where he had no other food to subsist on but five dry figs every day.

Our saint had now lived in his solitude to the age of one hundred and thirteen years , when St. Antony, who was then about ninety years old, was one day thinking with himself that no one amongst the religious of Egypt had penetrated further into those wildernesses than he had done.   Whereupon he was one night admonished in a dream, that there was one still further on in the desert much better than himself; and that he should make haste to visit him.   In compliance with this divine admonition, Antony set out at break of day in quest of this servant of God, with great confidence that he who had sent him forth, would conduct him to the place where he should find him.   Thus he spent two whole days, fatigued with the labor of the journey, and broiled by the heat of

an, which is violent in those sandy deserts, meeting with no creature the whole way, except two in
mon strous shape ; the one representing a *centaur*, half
man, and half a horse, and the other a *satyr*, made up
of a man and a goat : which whether they were phantoms and illusions of the enemy, or monsters bred in
those vast wildernesses, is uncertain. The Saint, when
he opposed to these frightful figures his usual arms,
the shield of faith and sign of the cross, neither of
them offered him any harm ; but on the contrary the
former, on being asked where the servant of God
dwelt, pointing towards the place, ran swiftly away,
and disappeared ; and the latter brought him some
dates for his food ; and being asked, who or what he
was ? delivered an intelligible answer, (by some supernatural power) with an acknowledgment of God,
and of Jesus Christ, his Son ; which gave the Saint
occasion to glorify our Lord, and to reproach the un-
believing city of Alexandria, which refused to acknowledge the true and living God, whom even beasts
adored, and worshipped these very beasts instead of
him. At which words of the Saint the monster fled
away with incredible speed, and was seen no more.

Antony having spent two nights watching in prayer,
at break of day on the third morning, he perceived a
wolf at a distance panting for thirst, going into a cavern at the foot of a mountain. Whereupon coming
up to the place after the beast was gone, he ventured

into the cave, advancing cautiously and silently in the
dark, till at length he perceived at some distance a
glimmering of light (from the opening from above
over the porch of the cell of the Saint,) upon which
in hastening forward he stumbled upon a stone, when
the noise gave occasion to St. Paul to shut his door,
and fasten it within.   Antony was now convinced that
he found the person whom he sought: and coming
up to the door earnestly begged for admittance, with
many tears, lying prostrate on the ground from morning till noon, (to teach us the necessity of fervor and
perseverance in prayer, if we would obtain what we
ask,) till at length the holy old man opened the door
to him.   Then after falling upon each other's neck,
embracing each other, and calling one another by
their proper names, as if they had been of long acquaintance, they joined in giving thanks to God.
When they had sat down together, Paul said to Antony, behold here the man whom thou hast taken so
much pains to seek, and who very speedily must return to dust: tell me, then, if thou pleasest, how mankind goes on ; what is the present state of the empire ;
are there any still remaining that worship devils, &c. ?—
Whilst they were discoursing on these matters, they
perceived a raven alighting upon one of the branches
of the palm-tree, which descending gently, dropped a
oaf of bread before them, and then flew away. Behold, said Paul, how our loving and merciful Lord has

sent us a dinner! There are now sixty years elapsed
since I have daily received from him half a loaf, but
upon thy coming, Christ hath been pleased to send his
soldier a double proportion. Then after praying and
thanksgiving, they sat down by the edge of the spring,
to take the meal which God hath sent them: but no
without an humble contention who should break the
loaf; which they at last decided by breaking it conjointly. After taking a moderate refreshment, they
laid themselves down to sip at the fountain: and then
returned to prayer and the praises of God, in which
they spent the evening, and the whole of the following
night.

The next morning Paul thus accosted Antony: "It
is a long time, brother, since I have known of your
dwelling in these regions: and the Lord long ago
promised me your company. But as my time is now
come to go to rest, (as I have always *desired to be
dissolved and to be with Christ,*) and my race being
finished, the crown of justice waits for me, thou art
now sent by the Lord to cover this body with ground,
or rather to commit earth to earth." Which when
Antony heard, breaking out into sighs and tears, he
began to entreat him not to leave him, but to take
him along with him for his companion in so happy a
journey. "Thou oughtest not," said Paul, "to seek
in this thy own interest, but what may be for the good
of others. It would be expedient indeed to thee to

lay down this load of flesh, and to follow the Lamb:
but it is necessary to the rest of the brethren, that
thou shouldest continue here, to instruct them by thy
example. Wherefore go, I beseech thee, if it be not
too much trouble, and bring hither the cloak which
was given thee, by bishop Athanasius, to wrap up my
body for its burial:" which, says St. Jerome, he asked,
not that he who for many years had used no other
clothing but the leaves of the palm-tree, cared much
whether his body was committed to the earth covered
or naked, but that Antony being absent when he died
might be less afflicted with his death. To which our
church historians add another reason, *viz.* that by his
desiring to be buried in the cloak of Athanasius (at
that time violently persecuted by the Arians, for the
Catholic faith of the Trinity,) he might bear testimony
to the cause of God and his truth, and declare to the
world his communion with his illustrious prelate, who
was then, and had been all his lifetime, one of the
principal champions of God and his church against
the Arian heresy.

Antony being astonished to hear him speak of Athanasius, and of the cloak (of which he could no otherwise have been informed but by revelation,) as if he
saw Christ himself in Paul, without making any further reply, kissed his hands with tears, and departing
from him, made the best of his way home to his own
monastery. Here his two disciples (Amathas and

Macarias,) asked him where he had been so long?
To whom he made no answer, but, "wo to me a
sinner, who deserve not to bear the name o. a religious
man! I have seen Elias: I have seen John in the
wilderness: I have seen with truth, Paul in paradise."
And thus without explaining himself any further, he
went into his cell, striking his breast, and taking up
the cloak. instantly hastened away without staying to
take any refreshment; having Paul continually in his
mind, and fearing, that which indeed happened, lest
Paul should die before he reached his cave. On the
second morning, when he had travelled for about three
hours, he saw the soul of Paul encompassed in great
glory ascending to heaven, attended with an innumerable multitude of angels and saints. At this sight,
falling down on the ground, he cried out lamenting
and mourning: "O Paul, why dost thou leave me?
why dost thou go without letting me salute thee?
too late, alas! have I come to know thee, and dost
thou depart from me so soon?" Then rising up he
went on the remaining part of the way, notwithstanding his great age, and his having been before greatly
fatigued, with such unaccustomed speed, that, as he
himself afterwards relates, he seemed rather to fly than
walk.

When he arrived and had entered into the cave, he
found the body of the Saint in the posture of one at
prayer, kneeling with uplifted hands; so that thinking

he might be yet alive, he knelt down to pray with
him. But not perceiving him to sigh, as he was accustomed at his prayers, he was convinced he was
dead. Wherefore weeping and embracing the dead
body, he wrapt it up in the cloak, and carried it out
singing hymns and psalms according to the christian
tradition. But here no small difficulty occurred, how
he should bury the body, having no spade or other
instrument to dig a grave: so that what to do he
knew not: to go back to his monastery, was three
days' journey; to stay where he was, was doing nothing. Whilst he remained in this perplexity, behold
two lions, from the remoter part of the wilderness,
came running with all speed towards him. At the
sight of them Antony was at first surprised; but presently recollecting himself in God, he shook off all fear,
and stood his ground till the beasts coming up to the
place, went and laid themselves down at the feet of
the deceased saint, and seemed, in their way, to lament
his death. Then going a little distance off, they began to scratch up the sandy ground with their claws,
and did not cease till they had made a hole big enough
to answer the purpose of a grave; which when they
had done, coming to Antony as it were for their wages,
wagging their ears and hanging down their heads,
they licked his hands and feet. The Saint conceivin
that in their mute way they craved his blessing, took
occasion to praise and glorify God, whom all his crea-

'ures serve ; and then prayed in this manner : " O
Lord, without whose disposition not a leaf falls from
the tree, nor a sparrow to the ground, give to them as
thou knowest best :" and so making them a sign with
his hand he sent them away. Then taking the dead
body of St. Paul, he laid it down in the grave which
they had made, and covered it with the earth ; and
so returned home, carrying with him the garment
made of the leaves of the palm-tree, which Paul had
worn (which for the remaining years of his life he
always put on upon the solemn festivals of Easter and
Pentecost,) and related all that he had seen and done
to his disciples, from whom St. Jerome had his account.

And here it may not be improper to reflect, with
this holy Doctor of the church in the conclusion of
his life of this Saint, on the difference between the
clothing, eating, drinking, lodging, and, in a word, the
whole manner of living of this servant of God, and
that of worldlings, who never think they have enough,
and are always slaves to their own corrupt inclinations.
Paul coveted nothing, and wanted nothing ; and therefore was always easy and content : they are always
coveting and wanting, and never perfectly easy. Paul
with his mean fare enjoyed long life and health, together with a good conscience and interior peace :
their intemperances and lusts, their passions, their
pride, their ambition, their avarice, their envy, their

cares and fears, and the contradictions of their will
and humor, to which they are perpetually exposed,
rob them of their health, shorten their days, and banish both grace and peace far from their souls. In
fine, Paul with all his poverty and mortifications, was
happy even here in the experience of the love of hi
God, in the sense of his divine presence, in the contemplation of his heavenly truths, in the sweets he
found in mental prayer, and an inward conversation
with our Lord ; in the consolations of the Holy Ghost,
&c., and by this means he passed his days in good
things, (truly such) till he was in an instant put in full
possession, by death, of the sovereign and infinite good
for eternity : whereas they, after their short deluding
dreams of an imaginary happiness, which is ever flying
away from them, awake in a moment, and find themselves immersed in the bottomless pit of real, endless,
and insupportable miseries.

ST. ANTONY.

From his Life, written by the great St. Athanasius

St. Antony was born in Egypt about the middle of
the third century, of parents noble and wealthy ; according to the world, but withall pious and religious.
By them he was trained up at home, in great inno-

rence, so as to be a stranger in a manner to the world ; and was by his own inclinations, entirely restrained from the company of others of his age, and even from frequenting the schools with them, for fear of his morals being corrupted by their conversation or bad example. His whole desire was bent upon God : he frequented the church in the company of his parents, assisted there with great modesty, gravity, and attention ; and endeavored to follow in his practice the instructions and rules of life which he there learnt. He was not fond, as children usually are, of dainties, or such things as are sweet and agreeable to their appetite, but always took what his parents gave him, and sought nothing more.

He was about eighteen or twenty years old, when his parents dying, left him master of all their wealth. which was considerable, with a little sister that was very young. But scarce six months were passed after their death, when one day going to church according to his custom, and thinking with himself how the Apostles had left all to follow our Lord, and the primitive Christians (Acts iv.) had sold their possessions, and laid the price at the feet of the Apostles, to be by them distributed to such as were in want, and how great would be the reward .n heaven, of them that did in this manner. At his coming into the church he heard the gospel read out of Matt. xix. where our Saviour says to the young man that was rich. v. 21

*If thou will be perfect, go sell what thou hast, and give
to the poor, and thou shalt have treasure in heaven,
and come follow me.* These words he took as addressed by our Lord to himself, and particularly designed for him : and in consequence of this divine call
he presently parted with his whole estate in lands
sold his moveables, which were of great value, and
distributed the price to the poor, only reserving a
small matter for the use of his sister. Some time
after, when he had heard in the church that part of
the gospel read (Matt. vi.) where our Lord warns his
disciples not to be careful for to-morrow, he concluded
to part with his house also, and to distribute all that
remained to the poor ; and having recommended his
young sister to the care of certain devout virgins, to be
trained up in their way of life, he quitted the world
for good and all, and entered with a strong resolution
upon the narrow and arduous path of religious perfection.

There were not very many at that time in Egypt
who professed a monastic life; and those that did retired
not into the deserts, but only lived in separate cells in
the country, at a small distance from their respective
villages. One of these, now advanced in years, who
from his youth had followed this manner of life, lived
in the neighborhood: him Antony proposed to imitate; and accordingly he began to follow the same
kind of life, but in places something more remote from

his own village. Accordingly, as often as he could
hear of any one that labored with more diligence than
ordinary in the pursuit of virtue and perfection, he
was sure to visit him, and to seek in his conversation
and method of life, some lessons for his own instruction and edification. In the mean time he labored
with his own hands for his daily food; and all that he
gained over and above what was necessary to purchase
his pittance of bread, he gave to the poor. He prayed
very much, and endeavoring quite to forget the world
and all his worldly kindred, he turned all his affections
and desires towards the purchasing the hidden treasure of true wisdom, and the precious pearl of divine
love. In order to this he gave diligent attention to
the word of God, contained in the holy Scriptures,
which he heard, and by meditating thereon, laid up
all these precepts of our Lord in such a manner in his
soul, as never to forget any of them; but to have them
always written in his memory, as in a book. He en-
vied no one, but had always a great deference for the
other servants of God; and was continually studying
to remark those virtues, in which each one of them
excelled, in order to imitate them; and thus assemble
as it were, and unite together in himself the different
perfections which he observed in the rest. Thus he
quickly outstripped them all: and yet remained al
ways most humble, meek, and full of brotherly love
and charity, so as to be ever most lear to them all.

5

The devil, who was enraged to see so much ardor
in the pursuit of virtue in a person so young, employed all his arts and stratagems to divert him from
his holy undertaking, and to bring him back again
into the world; and for this end, he strongly represented to his imagination the riches and possessions
which he had quitted, the nobility of his family, the
glory of this world, the advantages and pleasures of a
worldly life; and, on the other hand, the extreme difficulties and labors to be undergone in this way which
he had chosen; the weakness of his body, unfit for
such extraordinary fatigues; the long time he might
have to live under this insupportable burthen, &c.
suggesting withall that it was a crime in him to have
abandoned, in the manner he did, his little sister,
whom he was obliged to have taken care of.   By these
and such like representations, he strove to induce him,
after he had put his hand to the plough, to look back,
and to return again to the world.   But the Saint
overcame all his temptations, by a lively faith in
Christ crucified, and by continual and fervent prayer.
Wherefore the enemy changed his batteries, and assaulted him in a most violent manner, night and day,
sleeping and waking, with carnal suggestions and allurements to lust.   But the holy young man, armed
with divine grace, which he procured by earnest and
constant prayer, conquered also all these temptations,
by perpetually opposing to them, watchings, fastings,

and mortifications of the flesh, together with the faith
and remembrance of the judgment to come, of the
worm that never dies, and of the eternal flames of
hell. By these means he gained so complete a victory
over the enemy, that he ceased to molest him any
more in this kind. It was in consequence of this vic
tory, that the unclean spirit one day appeared to the
Saint in the shape of a most filthy, ugly, black boy;
bitterly weeping and lamenting, that after having deceived and seduced so many, he had been overcome
by him. On being asked who he was, he answered
he was the spirit of impurity, who made it his business to wage a continual war against youth, in which
he was commonly successful; and that it was he that
had so often attacked him, but had always been repulsed. Upon this the Saint, giving thanks to God,
was animated with a new courage against this detestable spirit; and began to sing aloud those words of
the Psalmist: *The Lord is my helper, and I will despise my enemies.* (Ps. cxvii. 7.) At which the filthy
phantom was put to flight.

These first victories did not render Antony negligent, as if he might now think himself secure, and on
that account might relax in his spiritual exercises; for
he very well knew that the devil never sleeps, and tha
he has a thousand ways of tricking and deceiving unwary souls, especially as he holds a close correspondence with the flesh, our domestic enemy, and with our

unhappy self-love and its passions. Wherefore the
holy young man resolved to be still more upon his
guard, and to make every day, still greater progress in
religious perfection. He chastised his body, and
brought it under subjection by extraordinary austerities; which how difficult soever in themselves, became
sweet and agreeable to him, by reason of that ardent
affection wherewith he embraced them. He frequently watched whole nights in prayer;—he eat but
once in the four and twenty hours, and that not till
after sunset. His food was nothing but bread and
salt, his drink nothing but water, which he drank in a
small quantity: he sometimes fasted two days, or
more, without taking any food whatever. His bed
was a sort of mat made of bulrushes, with a covering
of hair cloth : and sometimes only the bare ground.
His application to God in prayer was without intermission, like the Apostles (Philip iii. 13, 14,) *forgetting the things that are behind*, that is, all that he had
already done, he was continually *stretching forth himself to those that are before;* and pressing, with
all his power *towards the mark, for the prize of
the supernal vocation of God in Christ Jesus:* ever
considering himself as if he was just beginning, and
thinking of no more than of the present day.

All this not being sufficient to satisfy his hunger and
thirst after perfection, he chose for himself a dwelling
amongst the tombs or monuments of the dead. In

one of these he shut himself up, and received from
time to time his necessary sustenance from a religious
man who came to visit him. The devil, foreseeing the
consequences he had to apprehend from this new kind
of enterprise, and fearing lest by degrees this young
man should draw many by his example into the desert,
to the prejudice of his usurped empire, was resolved
not to suffer him to go on thus; and therefore (God
so permitting for the greater merit and glory of his
Saint,) Satan gathering together his infernal spirits,
attacked him one night with the utmost fury, inflict-
ing upon him many stripes and grievous wounds, till
he left him stretched out like one dead, without either
speech or motion. In this condition his friend found
him the next morning, and carried him back to the
village on his shoulders, where a great multitude of
his kindred and neighbors were assembled about him
to perform his funeral obsequies; when, behold, towards midnight, coming to himself, like one awakened
from a deep sleep, and looking about him, he perceived his friend there watching by him (for the rest were
all asleep) and he made a sign to him to carry him
back again to his monument, without waking any of
the company. He did so, and Antony being now
alone, but not as yet able to support himself on his
feet, by reason of his late treatment, performed his devotions, as well as he could, lying prostrate on the
floor. At the end of his prayer, lifting up his voice

ir defiance of the spirits of darkness, he ciied out with
a lively faith and confidence in his God, " Lo, here am
I : here is Antony, ready to encounter with you all ;
I shall not run away ; do your worst; none of you
hall be able to separate me from the love of Christ;"
'hen he began to sing with the Psalmist: *If the ar-
nies in camp should stand together against me, my
heart shall not fear.* Ps. xxvi. 3.

The enemy not enduring to be thus outbraved, re-
assembled his hellish fiends, and returned to the charge
with greater violence than before, and raising a sudden,
violent tempest, which shook the very foundations of
the place, he laid it open on all sides ; and entering in
with all his wicked ones, in the shape of wild beasts
and serpents of sundry kinds, he not only sought to
terrify the Saint with their hideous yelling, roaring,
howling, hissing, &c., but also made him feel their
fury in a most sensible manner, by the fresh wounds
they inflicted upon him. But his courage and constancy was proof against all their attempts ; so that
notwithstanding the excessive pains he felt in his
wounded body, he mocked at all their vain efforts,
reproached them with their weakness and cowardice,
and with those forms of brutes, to which they were
now reduced, who had formerly proudly aspired to be
ike unto God. At length Jesus Christ was pleased
to come in a visible manner to the assistance of his
servant in the midst of this conflict ; for lifting up his

eyes, he saw the top of the place open, and a bright
ray of divine light to enter in, which instantly dissipated those infernal spirits, and released him from all
his pains. The Saint understanding that his Lord
was present, thus addressed him : " Where wast thou
my good Jesus, all this while ? Where wast thou !
Why didst thou not come before to heal my wounds ?
The Lord answered, I was here Antony ; but I waited
to see thy combat. And now because thou hast fought
so bravely, and not yielded, I will always assist thee,
and make thy name famous over the whole earth."
Antony having heard these words, raised himself up
to pray, and found that our Lord had now given him
greater strength than he had before. At the time
when this happened to him he was about thirty-five
years old.

After this, being desirous of advancing still more in
christian perfection, he took a resolution of retiring into
the desert, and of withdrawing himself altogether from
the conversation of men. This resolution he communicated to the old monk his friend, of whom we spoke
above, proposing that he should accompany him ; but
the old man excused himself, alleging his advanced
age, and the novelty of such an enterprise. Antony,
however, no way discouraged, set out upon his journey towards the heart of the wilderness, at that time
utterly uninhabited, and lying at a very great distance
from any town or village. As he walked along, he

saw a large dish of silver with which the enemy sought
to interrupt his journey, lying on the ground ; but he
easily discovered the artifice, and cried : " This is a
trick of thine, Satan ; thou shalt not divert me from
my resolution ; keep thy silver to thyself, and let it
perish with thee." At which words the dish was immediately dissolved into smoke. Afterwards a large
lump of true gold was flung in his way ; but this was
no more capable of interrupting his journey, than the
glittering appearance of the silver dish : for as soon as
he perceived it, he flew from it with as much speed, as
if he were flying from a devouring fire ; and proceeded on his way until he came to a mountain, where he
found an old desolate castle, full of serpents and venemous creatures, which had taken up their abode therein by reason of the length of time it had remained
uninhabited. This place he made choice of for his
dwelling ; taking in with him his provisions of bread.
which with a little water, according to his scanty allowance, might suffice him for six months.

At his coming to take possession of this castle, all
its old inhabitants, the serpents and other venemous
creatures, having fled away, he shut up the entrance
with stones, and during the twenty years that he dwelt
therein, he neither went out at any time himself, nor
suffered any one to enter, not even those who brought
him, at the end of every half year, a fresh provision of
bread : which they conveyed to him by getting up to

the roof and letting it drop down. They that came thither, as many did in process of time, out of a desire of seeing him, or learning what was become of him, sometimes remained the whole night at the door ; and ere frequently surprised at hearing the noises where ith the devils sought to molest him, and the voices, as it were, of many persons contending with him and saying : " Why camest thou into our habitation ? What hast thou to do in the desert ? Depart from these coasts which belong not to thee ; never think to be able to remain here, or to resist our attacks." When those that were without heard these or such like words, they at first imagined some men had found means to get into his habitation, and were there contending with him ; but looking through the chinks, and seeing him all alone, they understood that the voices they had heard proceeded from the evil spirits, seeking to drive him thence ; and being upon this occasion very much frightened, they called to Antony, begging his assistance, whilst, he comforted and encouraged them from within, bidding them to arm themselves with the sign of the cross, and not to be alarmed at these vain terrors. At other times when they came, and scarcely expected to find him alive, they heard him cheerfully singing within, and repeating those words of the 67th Psalm : " *Let God arise, and let his enemies be scattered : and let them that hate him flee from before his face ; as smoke vanisheth,*

so let them vanish away : as wax melteth before the
fire, so let the wicked perish at the presence of God.

At the end of the twenty years he had spent with
God in this solitude, Antony, yielding to the importunity of the multitude that resorted to him, and were
even ready to force their way into his habitation, more
especially as many of them desired to learn and imitate his manner of life, came forth, as it were out of a
heavenly sanctuary, with so serene a countenance, and
such animation, strength and vigor in his whole person, as attracted the admiration of all who saw him.
And here God was pleased to work many miracles by
him, in casting out devils from such as were possessed,
and healing various diseases. The Saint took occasion, at the same time, to make powerful exhortations
to those that addressed themselves to him : he comforted the afflicted ;—instructed the ignorant ;— reconciled such as were at variance, and earnestly exhorted
all to look to the welfare of their souls, and to prefer
nothing before the love of Christ. He set before the
eyes of his auditory the greatness of the good things
to come in a happy eternity—the infinite goodness and
mercy of God—the benefits he has conferred, and the
love he bears towards mankind, particularly manifested in not sparing, but delivering up his own Son to
death for the salvation of us all. By these and such
like discourses, the Saint brought over a great number
of his hearers to a contempt of all those things that

pass away with time, and to an effectual resolution of
dedicating the short remainder of the days of their
mortality to the love and service of God, in a solitary
and religious life. Thus, by degrees, the deserts and
mountains began to be peopled with a number of holy
souls (all acknowledging Antony for their father, founder, and master,) who, by the purity and sanctity of
their lives, seemed to resemble so many angels in human bodies. They renounced all the honors, riches
and pleasures of this world: or rather, exchanged
them for others by far more great and solid even in
this life, and for such as shall never end hereafter.
They watched and prayed without ceasing ;—they meditated frequently on the word of God ;—they sung
his praises day and night ;—they kept, in a manner,
a continual fast ;—they labored with their hands for
their own support, and to have wherewith to supply
the necessities of their indigent neighbors : in fine,
they all lived in a holy union and perfect charity, without murmurs or detractions, and felt no other ambition
or strife, but who should excel his neighbor in all kind
of christian virtues : so that to behold this multitude
of holy solitaries separated at a distance, both in place
and manners, from the children of the world, in those
vast deserts, and leading there such angelical lives, was
enough to make any one cry out with Balaam, Numb.
xxiv. *How beautiful are thy tabernacles, O Jacob,
and thy tents, O Israel ! As woody vallies, as water*

*ed gardens near the rivers, as tabernac;es which the
Lord hath pitched, &c.*

St. Athanasius sets down at large an excellent discourse which Antony delivered one day, by the desire,
and for the instruction of his disciples, in which, (after
earnestly exhorting them to such an unwearied fervor
and constancy in pursuit of their holy undertaking, as
never to slacken their pace, but daily to renew their
resolutions as if they were just now beginning, and to
strive to advance by great strides towards religious
perfection,) he puts them in mind, first of the short-
ness of the time of this mortal life, of the length of
eternity, and how trivial those services are which God
requires of us for the purchasing of eternal life :—that
all the labors and sufferings of this life shall shortly
have an end, but that our reward shall continue for
ever. Secondly, he would therefore not have them
imagine they had made any great sacrifice to God in
parting with their estates, houses, or money, from
which they must, whether they will or not, be in a
short time separated by death : since what they were
to receive in exchange from our Lord, would infinitely
surpass in value the possession of the whole earth, and
be theirs for all eternity. Thirdly, he inculcates to
them, that a Christian ought never to fix his affection,
or bestow his care upon any of those things which he
cannot take along with him when he dies, but only on
such as may help him on his way to heaven, and there

remain with him during eternity: such as true wisdom—purity of soul and body—christian justice—
fortitude—charity, and tranquillity of soul, by a victory over our passions: for these are the real goods
of a christian, which are alone worthy of his love.
Fourthly, he puts them in mind, that they are strictly
obliged, in consequence of their *creation,* to dedicate
their whole lives to the service of that Lord who *made
them* for this very end, *that they should be his servants ;* and who, by all manner of titles, has an indis-
putable right to their service ; and that neither their
past, nor present labors can exempt them from continuing therein till death ; so that if they would not
lose their crown, they must resolve to labor to the end,
relying always on the assistance of their good God,
who never forsakes those who do not first forsake him.
Fifthly, he recommends to them the remembrance of
death ; the certainty thereof, as well as the uncertain-
ty of the hour in which we shall be called from hence
—of the judgment that is to follow after death, and
of the eternity to come, as so many powerful restraints
to preserve them from sin ; and as sovereign means to
cure their sloth—spur them on to the practices of virtue—wean their affections from transitory things, and
teach them to tread under their feet the riches and
pleasures of a world which we must so suddenly part
with. Sixthly, he tells them that the Greeks took
great pains, and travelled into distant countries, in or-

der to meet with masters from whom they might learn
vain and empty sciences, such as were of no service to
their souls in order to eternity : but that the christian,
in order to acquire *true wisdom* and the *science of the
saints*, which conducts to eternal life, needed to go no
farther than into his own soul : where he should, if he
sought him by a spirit of recollection and prayer, find
his true master, the kingdom of God, and with it all
good.   Seventhly, he exhorts them to fight in a particular manner against the *tyranny*, as he calls it, of
the passion of *anger*, as a mortal evil and capital enemy of the justice of God ; and therefore he would
have them to keep a constant guard upon their own
hearts : the more so, because of the enemies that are
continually waging war with Christians, but more especially against religious men and women : and who
employ a thousand tricks and artifices to deceive the
unwary.   And here, as one that had long experience
in this kind of warfare, he acquaints them with the
different stratagems and manifold temptations by which
these wicked spirits labor, without ceasing, to withdraw religious souls from the service of God, and bring
them back to the broad road of the world, and the
ways of iniquity and sin : but for their comfort and
encouragement, he assures them, that these enemies
have no power over such as heartily resist and despise
their suggestions : that Christ has triumphed over
them by his death : and that a lively faith—a purity

and sincerity in seeking him—a diligence in the spiritual exercises of watching, praying, fasting, &c. together with the virtues of meekness, voluntary poverty,
humility, contempt of vain-glory, and especially an ar
dent devotion to Christ crucified, are weapons which
all the powers of hell cannot withstand. By such les
sons as these, but more especially by the great exam
ple of their master, the disciples of Antony were en
couraged and spurred on to a daily progress in the
ways of christian perfection.

When the persecution, which had been first set on
foot by Diocletian, and carried on with great fury by
Maximinian Galerius, raged exceedingly in Egypt,
where it crowned innumerable martyrs, many were led
to Alexandria out of the country to be put to death
for Christ. On this occasion Antony quitted his cell,
to follow these that were going to become the victims
of Christ: saying to his disciples, " let us go to the glorious triumphs of our brethren, that we may either
share with them in the fight, or at least be spectators
of their conflict." He was in hopes of obtaining for
himself the crown of martyrdom; but could not deliver himself up, nor obtain permission to associate
himself with the glorious confessors that were con
demned to the mines or confined in the prisons.
However, whenever any were brought before the
iudge, he accompanied them into the court, and with
great liberty and diligence exhorted them to constancy

and perseverance; and when they were sentenced to die, he rejoiced as much in their victory as if it had been his own, and failed not to accompany them to the place of execution, to be a witness of their happy triumph. The judge seeing the courage and zeal of Antony and his companions, published an order prohibiting any of the monks to be present in court during the trials of the Christians, and enjoining them all to depart from the city. Upon these orders the others absconded for that day; but Antony, fearing nothing, washed his garments, and took the next opportunity to present himself in a more eminent place in sight of the judge, desiring nothing more than to suffer for Christ. But God was pleased to accept of his good-will, and to reserve his servant for the benefit of innumerable souls. However, he continued assisting and encouraging the confessors of Christ upon all occasions till the storm of the persecution was blown over, and then returned with new fervor to his former solitude, where he redoubled his watchings and fastings, wearing always a garment of hair-cloth next to his skin, and never washing his body; insomuch, that no one ever saw Antony naked during his life.

And now he began again to shut himself up for a time in his cell, without admitting any one to come in to him. But still he could not prevent many from resorting to his door, nor even from remaining there the whole night, in order to seek a cure for their dif-

ferent maladies, through the experience they had of
the miracles that God frequently wrought by him; so
that partly to avoid the distractions occasioned by this
concourse of people, and partly to fly the danger of
vain-glory, he took the resolution to fly as far as the
higher Thebais, where no man might know him.
Wherefore, taking some bread with him, he went to
the banks of the Nile, and there sat down, waiting for
some boat that might pass that way. And here he
heard a voice, saying to him, "Antony, whither art
thou going? and to what end?" He, as one accustomed to such colloquies, answered without fear: "Because the people will not suffer me to remain quiet,
but require things of me that are out of the reach of
my weakness, I have thought it best to go away to
the higher Thebais. "If thou goest," said the voice,
"to the place thou proposest, thou shalt endure a
greater, yea, a double labor; but if thou desirest to
be quiet indeed, go thy way now to such a place,"
naming a mountain in the heart of the wilderness.
"But who," said Antony, "shall show me the way?
for there are no tracks or paths that lead thither, and
I know nothing of the country." He that spoke with
him replied, that there were some Saracens or Arabians
at hand, who were come into Egypt to trade, and that
they would show him the way. Antony followed this
heavenly direction, and going up to the Saracens, desired they would take him along with them in their

journey through the desert: and after having travelled
with him three days and three nights, he arrived at a
very high mountain, the place appointed him by
heaven, at the foot of which there was a spring of
clear water, and in the adjacent field a few wild palm-
trees.   Here then he resolved to fix his abode, where
he might live quiet separated from the conversation
of men.   As to his food, he contented himself with a
little bread (which the Saracens, admiring his virtue,
gave him at parting, or bestowed upon him afterwards
when they passed that way,) and with the small provision of wild dates which the palms afforded him, till
his brethren, having found out the place of his retreat,
brought him necessaries from time to time.   Antony,
desirous to ease them of that trouble, having procured
by their means some wheat, and a proper instrument
for the purpose, found a little spot of ground wherein
he sowed the wheat, which brought him a crop sufficient for his use, to his great satisfaction' at being thus
enabled to live by the labor of his hands, without becoming troublesome to any one.   He also cultivated
a little garden with herbs, in order to entertain his
wearied brethren after their journey, when they came
to visit him through the burning deserts.   This spot
of ground lay exposed to the beasts which resorted
thither for the sake of the spring, who did no small
damage to Antony, by feeding upon his herbs and
corn: wherefore having caught one of them, he said

to them all : "Why do you this wrong to me, who do
none to you ?   Get ye gone : and, in the name of the
Lord, never come hither any more." From which
time they were never after seen to come near that
place.

Whilst Antony remained here entertaining himself
with God, the devils, his unwearied enemies, ceased
not to wage perpetual war against him ; but he despised all their efforts, and always triumphed over them,
by his usual arms of a lively faith and fervent prayer.
His disciples who came to visit him, and were sometimes witnesses of his conflicts relate, how they heard
the tumultuous noise and voices of a numerous people, with the rattling of arms, and had seen the whole
mountain covered by a multitude of devils, with Antony
fighting against them, and putting them all to flight
by his prayers.   "It is indeed, worthy of admiration,"
says St. Athanasius, "that in so vast a wilderness one
man alone should have stood his ground so long,
without either apprehending the daily encounters he
met with from wicked spirits, or yielding to the fury
of so many wild beasts and serpents as swarm in those
deserts.   But it was with good reason that David
sung, Psalm cxxiv.   *They that trust in the Lord shall
be as mount Sion : he shall not be moved for ever* ·
for so Antony, by keeping his mind firm, quiet, and
immovable in God, put all the devils to flight, and *the
beasts of the earth shall be at peace with thee*," (Job

v. 23.) and subject to him.   One night whilst he was
watching in prayer, the devil brought such a multitude
of wild beasts together about him, that it seemed as
if there were none left behind in the whole desert, all
of whom, encompassed him on every side, with open
jaws, threatened to tear him in pieces.   The Saint understanding the artifice of the malignant spirit, said,
unconcernedly: "If the Lord has given you any power
over me, make use of it in devouring me; but if you
are brought hither by devils, depart instantly, for I am
a servant of Christ."   No sooner had he spoke these
words but the whole multitude of wild beasts fled
away, and left him alone to continue his devotion.
One day whilst he was at work, according to his custom, making baskets, to exchange them for the provisions which the brethren brought him, a monster presented itself before him, in the shape of half a man
and half an ass; having on this occasion made the
sign of the cross, and said: "I am a servant of
Christ—if thou art sent to me, here am I;—I don't
run away."   At these words the monster instantly
fled, and falling down in the midst of its flight, burst
and was destroyed: to show all the attempts of
Satan against Antony should in the end perish, and
come to nothing.

   After some time the brethren prevailed on the man
of God to come down from his mountain, in order to
visit their monasteries.   Now in their way homeward

through those burning deserts, the provision of water quite failed them; and as none could be found, and the weather being violently hot, they were all in danger of perishing. Antony on this occasion had recourse to prayer; when, after withdrawing himself at a little distance from the company, and falling upon his knees, he had implored, with his hands stretched forth to heaven, the mercy of the Lord, behold the tears which he then shed presently brought forth a spring of water out of the earth, with which they both refreshed their own thirst, saved the life of their camel, and filled their vessels for the remainder of their journey. The Saint who was received with great joy by all the religious, as their common father, conceived no less joy within himself, to see the fervor and resolution with which they all applied themselves to their spiritual exercises. And that he might not seem to come to them from his mountain empty handed, he made them excellent exhortations in order to their spiritual progress. He had also the comfort to hear the agreeable news, that his sister, whom he had left so young in the world, was now grown old in the profession of virginity, and was become mistress and superior of other holy virgins in a religious state of life.

After some days, Antony returned again to his mountain, where he again received more frequent visits, as well from his own religious as from others, who, being possessed or obsessed by evil spirits, or afflicted

with various infirmities, had recourse to his prayers for
their delivery; on which occasion God wrought many
miracles by him; favoring him also with prophetic
light. and other extraordinary graces and gifts. He
exhorted all that came to see him to have a strong
faith in Jesus Christ:—to love him with their whole
hearts;—to keep their minds pure from all evil
thoughts, and their bodies uncontaminated from all
uncleanness;—not to suffer themselves to be imposed
upon by gluttony;—to hate vain-glory;—to pray very
often;—to sing psalms to the divine praise every
morning, noon, and night;—to meditate on the precepts of the word of God;—to have the great example of the saints always before their eyes, in order to
spur themselves on to the practice of all virtues;—*not
to let the sun go down upon your anger*, Eph. iv. 26.
which precept of the apostles he applied to all other
sins; recommending to all to call themselves to a strict
account by a daily examination of conscience, and to
repent and amend without delay whensoever they
found themselves to have failed in any thing. He
added, that if they did not discover any guilt in themselves, they must not therefore be puffed up with self-
conceit, or presume to justify themselves, and despise
others; but rather fear, least self-love should blind and
deceive them; remembering that an all-seeing God is
to be their judge;—that his judgments are very dif
ferent from those of men;—and that *there is*, accord

ing to the wise man, Prov. xiv. 12. *a way which seem-
eth just to a man : but the ends thereof lead to
death."*

One day, about the ninth hour, viz. about three of
the clock in the afternoon, when he had begun his
prayers before the taking of his meal, he was seized
with a rapt or ecstacy in which he saw himself in
spirit carried up aloft by angels, whilst the demons of
the air, opposing his passage, alledged against him the
sins of his younger days, even from his very childhood ; and when the angels replied, that these sins,
by the mercy of Christ, had been forgiven, they bid
them to charge him, if they could, with any material
sin he had committed since he had consecrated himself to God in a religious state of life. Accordingly
these lying spirits having forged many false accusations against him which they could not prove, they
were therefore forced to leave the passage free for him.
Upon this Antony returned to himself, but so greatly
affected with what he had seen, as well as with the
dreadful and dangerous conflict a poor soul has to pass
through with these princes of darkness, that he forgot
his food, and spent the remainder of the day, as well
as the whole night, in sighs and lamentations, at considering the dangers from these wicked spirits, that
threaten the souls of men both in life and death, which
thoughtless mortals nevertheless so little apprehend.
One night, whilst his disciples had been questioning

him concerning the state of souls immediately after death, he was called upon by a voice saying, "Antony arise, go out, and see." He arose, and went out, and looking up towards heaven, he saw a spectre of a monstrous height and dreadful aspect, whose head reached the clouds : he saw also persons with wings that sought to fly up to heaven, and he perceived that the monster, with outstretched hands, strove to stop them in their passage : some of whom he caught and cast down to the earth, but could not prevent the rest from flying above his reach, or of mounting up to heaven. By this vision he was given to understand, that the devil had power to stop the flight of those departing souls who were in sin, but that he had no power over pure and holy souls, nor could prevent their flying up to heaven. These visions Antony related to his disciples : not out of ostentation or vain-glory, being always averse to attributing any thing to himself, or suffering any thing to be ascribed to him, but merely for their instruction and edification.

As to the rest, no one could be more meek, patient, or humble than Antony. He entertained a particular respect and veneration for all the clergy ; giving even to the lowest clerk in minor orders, the preference before himself, and even bowing down his head before bishops and priests, to crave their benediction. Although he had so great a mastery over himself in spirituals, and was so divinely taught, yet he was never ashamed to seek instruction, not only from the clerks that came to visit him, but even from his own disciples; and whatsoever good he heard from any one, he humbly and thankfully acknowledged himself assisted thereby. Among other gifts with which he was favored by our Lord, he was particularly remarkable for an admirable grace that showed itself in his countenance, which distinguished him in such a manner from all the rest of the holy inhabitants of the deserts, that any stranger who came to visit him, though he happened to be in the company of a multitude of other monks, leaving all others would be sure to run up to him: as if the purity of his soul had shone forth from his very face, which was always modestly cheerful and amiable, and never altered either by prosperity or adversity. However, he would have no communication with schismatics or heretics; but exhorted all that came near him, to fly their dangerous conversation and impious doctrines. He had a particular horror for the blasphemies of the Arians, whom he considered as the forerunners of Antichrist. He even quitted for a while his solitude, at the desire of Athanasius and the catholic bishops, to go to Alexandria to confute their wicked assertions; where, by his doctrine and miracles, he not only effectually confuted the heretics, and confirmed the catholics in thei faith, but also brought over a great number of infidel to the christian religion. The heathen philosophers

7

also came often to dispute with him about religion, imagining they could easily entangle a man so entirely illiterate, and an utter stranger to all human sciences as Antony was known to be, with their captious reasoning and learned sophistry; but they were surprised beyond conception to find with what depth of wisdom he answered all their objections, and proved the truth of the christian religion in a manner to which they knew not what reply to make, and even confirm it with miracles wrought in their presence.

The reputation of Antony's sanctity and heavenly wisdom was not confined to Egypt: it spread itself far and near through a great part of the then known world : it even reached the imperial court, insomuch that the emperor Constantine the Great, and his sons Constan and Constantious, wrote several times to him, and begged that he would favor them with an answer. As for his part, he made very little account of this honor, and told his disciples that they were not to think it much that an emperor, who was no more than a mortal man, should write to him ; but rather ought to admire and bear always in mind, that the eternal God had been so good as not only to write his law for man, but to send down his only Son to deliver his word to them. However, at the desire of all the brethren, he returned them an answer, in which, after congratulating with them for their believing in and worshipping Christ, he gave them wholesome instruc-

tions for the welfare of their souls ; advising them not
to make any great account of their worldly grandeur
and power, nor of any of those things that pass away
with time. and never to forget that they were mortals,
who must quickly appear before another judge. He
also put them in mind of their obligation of showing
clemency to their subjects, of rendering them justice,
and of succouring the poor and distressed ; and they
must remember that the true and everlasting king of
all ages is Jesus Christ alone.

After Antony had finished the business that brought
him to Alexandria, he hastened back to his cell on the
mountain, and to his usual exercises and austerities.
For he used to say, that a religious man conversing
with seculars out of his monastery was like a fish out
of water, which is in danger of perishing, except it
quickly be restored again to its element ; and therefore, as to his part, he would never come out of his
solitude, but when some work of great charity obliged
him.   However, he willingly received those seculars
that came to him, and entertained them with heavenly
discourses ; exhorting them to look beyond this world,
and to labor for a happinees that shall have no end :
and such was the unction and efficacy which God gave
to his words, that many were moved by his exhortations to give up their honors, their riches, and all their
worldly expectations, in order to dedicate themselves
eternally to the same happy service in which they saw

him engaged. He seemed to have been given to the
land of Egypt by our Lord, as an excellent physician
to heal all their spiritual diseases: for whoever came
to him in his troubles and temptations found a sensible benefit in his conversation;—if he came with sorrow, he returned with joy;—if he came with rancour
in his heart against his neighbor, he returned with dispositions of peace and charity;—if he came oppressed
with the sense of his poverty and distress, he returned
with the contempt of this world,—a willingness to
take up the cross, and to wear the livery of Jesus
Christ. The lukewarm learnt from him to be fervent
in the service of God; nay, the very libertines returned from him with a desire of embracing a chaste and
penitential life: for such was the gift he had of dis-
cerning spirits, that he seemed to read in the faces of
all, the interior dispositions and state of their souls,
and accordingly accommodated his instructions and
prescriptions to the nature and quality of their disorders. Nor was this benefit confined to Egypt alone:
for as the fame of Antony had reached all parts of the
world, so men came from all parts to see him, and no
one visited him without fruit: no one ever complained that he had lost his labor in coming to see him,
how long or difficult soever his journey might have
been.

The multitude who went to see him did not interrupt his interior attention to God any more than his

daily labors, which he sanctified with mental prayer.
Oftentimes whilst he was walking or sitting with his
visitors, he was ravished out of himself, so as to remain for a long time insensible ; at which time many
secrets were revealed to him. Once in particular he
beheld a vision in his ecstacy, by which he was admonished two years before it happened of the cruel havoc
the Arians would make in the church of Alexandria :
which, when he returned to himself, he related with
many sighs and tears to those that were with him ;
but then added for their comfort, that this storm would
quickly blow over, and that the church should again
be restored to her former lustre. This persecution
was raised against the church of Alexandria, when the
Arians, having procured the banishment of St. Athanasius, introduced one Gregory, a man of their faction,
to be the bishop in his place : upon which occasion
Balacius, an Arian, the commander of the troops, particularly exerted himself in persecuting the faithful ;
which he did with so much rigor, that he ordered even
the sacred virgins, and the religious men to be publicly scourged, as if they had been the vilest malefactors.
St. Antony wrote a letter to him to deter him from
this cruelty, to this effect : " I see the wrath of God
coming upon thee : cease to persecute the Christians,
lest that wrath should overtake thee which already
threatens thee with approaching destruction." The
unhappy man slighted the warning of the Saint, and

spitting upon the letter, flung it down upon the ground;
then after having abused the persons that brought it,
bid them go tell Antony, that he should serve him also
in the same manner as he had done these monks for
whom he interested himself. But not many days passed
before the vengeance of God overtook the wretch, when,
as he was riding out to a place in the neighborhood,
in the company of Nestorious the governor, one of his
own horses, who was before remarkably gentle and
quiet, with a sudden bite brought him down to the
ground, and standing over him, knawed and tore his
thighs in so terrible a manner, that he died within
three days.

And now the time drew near when Antony, now
about one hundred and five years of age, should exchange his mortal pilgrimage for a happy immortality.
He went, according to his custom, to visit his brethren
that dwelt in the nearer desert, signifying to them that
his dissolution was at hand, and that this was the last
time they should see him. These words drew tears
from their eyes: they all embraced him as their parent about to depart from them into another world.
They would have detained him with them, desiring to
be present at his death. To this he would not consent; but after having given them his last instructions,
he strongly exhorted them to fervor and perseverance
in their holy institute, and to constancy in the catholic
faith; showing the utmost joy that he was now shortly

to depart from this place of banishment to his true and everlasting home; and taking his last farewell of them he hastened back to his mountain. A few months afterwards, finding his death to draw near, he called the two disciples, (who for the last fifteen years of his life had their cells in his neighborhood) and said to them: " My children, I am now going, according to the expression of the Scripture, the way of my fathers: for now the Lord calls for me : I long now to see the heavenly mansions. But as for you, my dearly beloved, I admonish you to beware lest you lose on a sudden the labor of so long a time; but every day consider yourselves if you had but that day entered upon a religious life, and the strength of your purpose shall daily increase. You know the various artifices of the devils; you have also seen their furious assaults, and how weak and cowardly they are. Retain an ardent love for Jesus, let the faith of his name be strongly fixed in your mind ; a strong faith in Jesus will put all the devils to flight. Remember also the lessons I have given you, and the uncertain condition of this mortal life, which may be cut off any day; and make no doubt but the heavenly mansions shall be your portion. Avoid the poison of schismatics and heretics, and follow my example in keeping them at a distance, because they are enemies of Christ. Make it your principal care to keep the commandments of the Lord, that so after your death the saints of God

may receive you as their friends and acquaintance into
the eternal tabernacles." He added, as his last request, that they should bury his body privately, and
let no man know the place; lest the Egyptians, according to their custom, should take it up to embalm it,
and keep it as they did their mummies. "As to my
garments, (said he) give my sheep-skin, and this old
cloak which I lie upon, to bishop Athanasius, who
brought it me new; let bishop Serapion, another generous defender of the faith, have my other sheep-skin;
and keep my garment of hair-cloth for yourselves: so
fare you well, my children, for Antony is departing,
and shall remain no longer with you in this world."

When he had made an end of speaking, as his disciples were kissing him, he drew up his feet a little,
and met death with a joyful countenance, (anno 356)
breathing out his pure soul into the hands of the angels, who were there ready to receive him, and carry
him to the happy regions of eternal bliss. His disciples buried him privately, as he had desired: "And
his legatee, says St. Athanasius, (speaking of himself)
"who had the happiness to receive by the orders of
blessed Antony, his old cloak and his sheep skin, embraces Antony, in his gifts, as if he had been enriched
by him with a large inheritance; he rejoices in the
garments, which present before the eyes of his soul
the image of his sanctity." The same holy doctor of
the Church and champion of the faith, wrote the life

of St. Antony, from his own knowledge of him, and
from the testimonies of his disciples, which we have
here abridged, and which was then and has been ever
since received, embraced, and admired in all parts of
the world, by every well-wisher to Christian piety, for
the important lessons it contains. The share it had in
bringing the conversion of the great St. Augustine to
a happy conclusion, is too remarkable to be passed
over in silence.

The Saint relates in his Confessions (lib. 8. ch. 6.)
how, whilst he was yet struggling under the load of
those wicked habits, which he could not resolve effectually to cast off, he was one day visited by Pontitianus, one that belonged to the emperor's court, but a
good Christian, who introduced a discourse " concerning Antony, a monk of Egypt, whose name, says St.
Augustine, speaking to God, was exceeding illustrious
among thy servants, but to that hour unknown to us:
which he perceiving dwelt the longer upon that subject, informing us of the life of so great a man, and
wondering that we had heard nothing of him. We
were astonished (speaking of himself and his friend
Alipius) to hear of thy miracles so very well attested,
done so lately, and almost in our days, in the true
faith, and in the catholic church: and indeed we all
wondered ;—we, that they were so great, and he, that
they were unknown to us. Thence he changed his
discourse to the societies of monasteries and to their

manner of life, yielding a sweet odor to thee, and to
the fruitful breasts of those barren deserts; of all
which we had heard nothing, although there was then
without the walls of Milan a convent full of good
brothers, under the care of Ambrose, and yet we knew
it not. He proceeded in his discourse, to which we
listened with a silent attention, and related how upon
a certain time, whilst the court was at Triers, and the
emperor was one afternoon entertained with the sports
of the circus, he and three of his companions went out
a walking among the gardens, near the walls of the
city, and there, as it happened, going two and two
together, one with him took one way, and the other
two another; and that these two, as they were wandering about, lighted upon a certain cottage, where some
servants of thine dwelt, *poor in spirit, for theirs is the
kingdom of heaven*, (Matt. v.) and there they found a
book, containing the life of Antony, which one of them
began to read, to admire, and be inflamed with : and
whilst he was reading, he began to think of embracing
the same kind of life, and of quitting his worldly office
in the emperor's court to become thy servant. Then
being suddenly filled with divine love, a wholesome
shame, and anger at himself, he cast his eyes upon his
friend, and said : Tell me, I beseech thee, with all the
pains we take in this world, whither would our ambition aspire to? what do we seek? what is it we propose to ourselves in this employment? can we ever

hope for any greater honor at court than to arrive at
the friendship and favor of the emperor? and there—
what is to be found there, that is not brittle and full
of dangers? and through how many dangers must we
ascend to this greater danger? and how long will this
continue? But the fiiend and favorite of God, I may,
if I please, become now presently, and remain so for
ever. Having said this, and laboring as it were in tra-
vail of a new life, he again cast his eyes on the book,
and continuing to read, was changed where thou saw-
est, and his mind totally stripped of the world, as soon
appeared: for whilst he was reading, the waves of his
heart, rolling to and fro, cast forth some sighs and
groans, till at length he concluded and resolved upon
better things; and being now wholly thine, he said to
his friend: Now I have entirely bid adieu to our former hope, and am fully resolved on being a servant or
God, and upon beginning to be so from this hour and
in this place. If thou be not willing to do the same,
do not at least offer to oppose my resolution. The
other replied: That he would stick by him as a companion in the service of so great a Master, and for such
immense wages. By this time Pontitianus and his
companion, who were seeking after them, came to the
same place; and having found them, reminded them
of returning home, because the day was far spent.
But they acquainting them with their determination,
as well as with the manner in which they had taken

this resolution, and were confirmed in it, requested
that if they did not choose to join with them, they
would at least give them no disturbance.   Whereupon
being nothing altered from what they were before,
they nevertheless bewailed themselves, and after
piously congratulating them, and recommending themselves to their prayers, with hearts weighed downwards towards the earth, they returned to the palace,
whilst the other two, with hearts elevated to heaven,
continued in the cottage : both of them were contracted to young ladies, who as soon as they heard
their resolution, consecrated in like manner their virginity to thee.   These things were related to us by
Pontitianus," concludes St. Augustine, who declares
in the following chapter, the wonderful effects this discourse had upon him ; and how, as soon as Pontitianus was gone, he set upon Alipius, and exclaimed :
" What is this we suffer? what is this tho.. hast been
hearing ? the unlettered rise up and seize heaven by
force : and whilst with all our learning we, remaining
without courage or heart, still wallow in the flesh and
blood.   Are we ashamed to follow them, because they
have got the start, and are gone before us?   But
ought we not to be still more ashamed, if we do not
so much as follow ?"   With these words he hurried
himself away into the garden, where, after a strong
conflict, he was at length fully converted, by taking
up, by the admonition of a voice from heaven, the

epistles of St. Paul, and reading there the sentence that first occurred, Rom. xiii. 13, 14. *Not in rioting and drunkenness, not in chambering and impurities, not in contention and envy; but put ye on the Lord Jesus Christ, and make not provision for the flesh in its concupiscences.*

ST. HILARION.

From his Life written by St. Jerome

HILARION was born at a village called Thabatha, **five** miles from the city of Gaza, in Palestine, of infidel parents, who sent him, when very young, to study at Alexandria, where he gave proofs of an excellent genius for his age, and of his good dispositions to virtue. Here he embraced the faith of Christ, and young as he was, could find no pleasure either in theatrical shows, incentives to lust, or any other worldly diversions, but delighted only in frequenting the church, and in religious exercises. Hearing of the fame of St. Antony, he went to visit him in the desert, and put off his secular habit, in order to embrace the same institute. He remained with the Saint about two months, making it his study to observe and learn perfectly the whole order and method of his life;— his

continual prayer—his humility—his charity—his mortification—and all his other virtues. Then returning
into his own country with some other religious men,
and finding that his parents were dead, he distributed
his whole substance between his brethren and the
poor, without reserving anything for himself, bearing
in mind that saying of our Lord : *He that doth not
renounce all that he possesseth, cannot be my disciple*,
Luke xiv. 33. Thus stript of the world, and armed
with Christ, being only in his sixteenth year, he took
the resolution of retiring into the wilderness (which
lies on the left of the road that leads from Gaza into
Egypt), without apprehending the dangers which his
worldy friends objected, from the robberies and murders for which that place was infamous ; but rather
despising a temporal death, that he might escape that
which is eternal ; nor regarding the tenderness of his
own constitution, which made him very sensible of
cold, heat, and other injuries of the weather, and of
the hardships and austerities that are incident to that
kind of life which he was going to undertake.

On going into the desert, he took no other clothing
with him than the frock of a peasant, a sackcloth and
hair-cloth, with a leathern habit to wear over it, which
St. Antony had given him. Here he built himself a
little hut, covered with sedges and rushes, to modify
the inclemency of the weather, which served him from
the sixteenth to the twentieth year of his age, and af

terwards in a cell, which, according to St. Jerome's account, who had seen it, was but four feet wide, five feet high, and in length but a little longer than his body, so that as he could not stand in it upright, it seemed rather a tomb for a dead corpse, than a dwelling for a living man. Here his diet was suitable to his lodging : his food for the first years being but fifteen dry figs in the day, and that not till after sunset. Afterwards, from the twenty-first to the twenty-seventh year of his age, he took only about eight or ten ounces of lentiles, steeped in cold water, or a little dry bread, with salt and water. For the space of three or four years more, he lived upon nothing but the wild herbs, or roots of the shrubs of the wilderness. From the thirty-first till the thirty-fifth year of his age he confined himself to six ounces of barley bread per day, and a few pot-herbs without oil ; which rule he continued to observe to his sixty-third year, when he began to allow himself a little oil with his herbs, but tasted nothing else, either of fruit or of pulse, or of any other kind of food. From that time, as he now supposed that by course of nature he could not have long to live, instead of relaxing in his austerities, he redoubled them ; so that from the sixty-fourth year of his age till his death, that is, till he was eighty years old, he totally abstained from bread, and eat nothing, during the forr and twenty hours, but a kind of mass composed of meal and herbs, which served him both for

meat and drink: and this in so small a quantity, that
his whole daily sustenance did not weigh above five
ounces.   Such was his austerity, with respect to his
food, that, throughout these different periods of life, he
ever observed it as a constant rule, never to eat or
drink till after sun-set, how weak soever his health
might be, not even on the greatest solemnities.

Hilarion had no sooner, in imitation of his great
model and master St. Antony, entered upon this course
of life in a vast and frightful desert, where no man
before had ventured to dwell, and, like him, applied
himself incessantly to God in prayer, than the devil,
not bearing to see himself thus trodden under foot by
a young man, began to assault him with violent temptations of the flesh, filling his mind with impure imaginations, and inciting him by sensual allurements, to
carnal pleasures, of which before he had no conception.   The chaste youth perfectly abhorred himself,
when he perceived these abominable emotions to lust
in his body and mind.   He struck his breast, as if he
meant by this exterior violence to put those lewd suggestions to flight: he condemned himself to longer,
and still more rigorous fasts and hard labor, saying
thus to himself: " thou little jack-ass, I will teach thee
to kick ; instead of corn thou shalt feed only on
straw ;—I will tame thy courage with hunger and
thirst: I will lay heavy burthens upon thee :—I will
make thee work both in summer and winter, that in

stead of wanton pleasures thou mayest think of thy meat." The Saint was steadfast in his resolution: fasting without intermission, sometimes for three or four days together, and then taking only a little juice of herbs and a few figs for his meal: incessantly pray ing, singing psalms, and working at the same time, either in digging the earth or in making baskets, till at length, by these exercises, he reduced his body to a mere skeleton. Wherefore the enemy perceiving he could not prevail this way, began to trouble him with fantastic apparitions and other temptations. One night he was on a sudden surprised with hearing the crying as it were of children, the bleating of sheep, the bellowing of oxen, the lamentations of women, the roaring of lions, and the confused noise of an army of barbarians, with strange and frightful voices. Suspecting them to be nothing but diabolical illusions, he armed himself with the sign of the cross, and with a lively faith, cast himself down upon the ground, to be the better enabled, in this humble posture, to en-counter the proud enemy. Then looking forward, it being a clear moon-light night, he perceived, as it were, a coach, drawn by furious horses, coming with a violent gallop towards him: at the sight of which he called upon the name of Jesus, when behold on a sudden the whole fantastic scene sunk down into the earth before his eyes: upon which he burst forth the praises of his Deliverer. At several other times this

indefatigable enemy sought various ways, both by **day**
and night, to molest him : either by exhibiting naked
figures to excite him to concupiscence, or by seeking
to interrupt his devotion and distract him at prayer by
a variety of either comic or tragic scenes : but none
of these, or any other of his attempts, were able to
shake the resolution of the servant of God, or prevent
his perpetual application to the love and service of his
Maker.   One day whilst he was praying with his head
fixed on the ground, it happened that his mind wan-
dered on some other thoughts, the watchful enemy,
taking advantage of this distraction, jumped upon his
back, as if to ride upon him ; and whipping and spur-
ring, cried out: " What, art thou asleep ? Thou a
saint ! come shall I give thee some provender ? "   But
this, like the rest of his vain efforts, only served to
excite the Saint to still more vigilance and fervor.

About the eighteenth year of his age, the robbers
that frequented the desert, took it in their heads to
pay him a visit; expecting either to find something
in his hut to take away, or looking upon it as a rash
attempt in a single boy to venture to dwell alone in
their dominions, and not be afraid of them.   They
therefore began their search after him in the evening,
and continued it till the sun-rising, without being able
to find his lodging : but meeting him at day-light,
they asked him as it were in jest, " what he would do
if he were visited by robbers ? "   " Oh ! " said he, " he

that has nothing to lose fears no robbers." "But," said they, "perhaps they may kill thee." "True," said he, "but I do not dread death : and therefore am not afraid of them, because I am prepared to die." Amazed at his constancy and faith, they acknowledged that having sought him during the night, they were so blinded as not to be able to find him ; and so deeply were they affected with his words, that they promised to amend their lives.

Hilarion had now spent twenty-two years in perfect solitude in the wilderness, conversing only with God and his angels, and only known to the world by the fame of his sanctity, which was spread over all Palestine, when a certain woman of the city of Eleutheropolis, who had lived fifteen years in the state of wedlock without bearing a child, finding herself despised by her husband on account of her barrenness, ventured to break in upon his solitude ; and coming unexpectedly upon him, cast herself upon her knees before him, saying : "Pardon my boldness ; pity my distress : why do you turn away your eyes from me? Why do you flee from your petitioner? Do not look at me as a woman, but as a distressed fellow-creature. Remember that a woman brought forth the Saviour of the world : those that are well stand not in need of a physician, but they that are ill." At these words he stood still ; and having learnt of her, the first woman he had seen since his retiring into the desert, the

cause of her grief, he lifted up his eyes towards heaven, bid her be of good heart, and weeping for her,
sent her away; but behold, within a twelvemonth she
returned, bringing her son with her to visit him.
This, his first miracle, was followed by a greater.
When Aristeneta, the wife of Elpidius, a christian nobleman (who was afterwards advanced to one of the
first posts in the empire), was on her return from
Egypt, where she had been, with her husband and her
three sons, to see St. Antony; she stopped at Gaza on
account of the illness of her children, who were all
seized by a semitertian fever, and brought so low that
their lives were despaired of by the physicians. The
disconsolate mother, hearing of the sanctity of Hilarion, whose wilderness was not far distant from Gaza,
went in haste to visit him, accompanied by some of
her servants, and thus addressed herself to him: "I
beg of thee for God's sake: for the sake of Jesus our
most merciful God; through his cross and his blood;
that thou wouldst vouchsafe to come and restore
health to my three sons, that the name of the Lord
our Saviour may be glorified in that pagan city: that
when his servant comes into Gaza, Marnas (the idol
which they there worship) may fall to the ground."
The man of God excused himself, alledging, that he
never went out of his cell, not so much as into any
village, much less into a populous city; but she, casting herself down upon the ground, ceased not to im

portune him with many tears; often crying out, "O
Hilarion! thou blessed servant of God, restore to me
my sons: Antony has laid his hands upon them in
Egypt, but do thou save their lives in Syria." Her
earnest entreaties at length obliged him to promise
her that he would come to Gaza after sun-set. No
sooner had he arrived at their lodgings, and seen them
confined to their beds in burning fevers, bereft of sense,
than he called upon our Lord Jesus, when immediately a copious sweat, issuing as it were from three
fountains, followed his prayer, and in the space of an
hour they took their meat, knew their mournful mother, blessed God, and kissed the hands of the Saint.

No sooner was this miracle published abroad, than
multitudes of the inhabitants of both Syria and Egypt
began to visit him. Many infidels were by his means
converted to the faith of Christ, and many also, by his
example, embraced a monastic life; for, before his
time, there were neither monks nor monasteries in
Palestine or Syria: he must therefore be considered
the father, founder, and first teacher of the monastic
institute in those provinces. And now it was that he
began to be joined by many disciples, whom he trained up to religious perfection, who were witnesses of the
wonderful miracles that God wrought by him. St
Jerome, as one perfectly well informed, has recorded
several of the most remarkable, with all their circumstances. A woman of the neighbourhood of Rhinoco-

rura (a city on the confines of Egypt,) who had been blind for ten years, was brought to the Saint to be healed: after having told him that she had expended her whole substance on physicians, " you had done better (said he) if you had given it to the poor; you would then have given it to Jesus Christ, the true physician, who would have healed you." She earnestly begged that he would have pity on her; and he, with spitting on her eyes, restored her to her sight. A charioteer of Gaza was also brought to him on his bed, struck in such a manner by the devil, that he could not stir any of the members of his body except his tongue, with which he besought the servant of God to heal him. The Saint told him, that if he desired to be healed, he must first believe in Jesus Christ, and promise to renounce a profession which exposed him to the immediate occasion of sin. To these conditions he agreed, and having received his cure, he returned home, rejoicing more for the health of his soul, than for that of his body.

Marsitas, a young man of the territory of Jerusalem, of an extraordinary bulk and strength, who had been possessed by an evil spirit, and done much mischief to many, was dragged by ropes to the cell of the servant of God, like a mad bull bound in chains. The brethren at the very sight of him were affrighted, but the saint bid the people bring him up and let him loose: which when they had done, he commanded him to

bend down his head and come to him. The poor
man trembling bent his neck, when laying aside all
his fierceness, and falling down he licked the feet of
the man of God; and after seven days' exorcisms was
entirely cured. Another man, named Orion, a principal citizen of Aila, a city near the Red Sea, who was
possessed by a whole legion of devils, was brought in
like manner loaded with chains to the Saint, who happened at that time to be walking with his disciples,
and interpreting to them some passages of the Scripture: when behold the possessed man broke loose
from those that held him, and running up to the man
of God, whose back was turned towards him, lifted him
up from the ground on high in his arms: at which all
that were present cried out, apprehending that he
would do the Saint some mischief; but Hilarion said,
smiling, "suffer me to wrestle with my antagonist."
Then putting back his hand, he laid hold on the hair
of Orion, and bringing him before his feet, kept him
down howling, and turning back his neck, so as to
touch the ground with the top of his head. Then
praying, he said: " O Lord Jesus, I am a poor wretch;
do thou release this captive; thou canst as easily overcome many as one." On this occasion they were all
astonished to hear so many different voices issuing
from the mouth of the possessed person, and a confused out-cry, as it were of a whole people: but their
wonder ceased when they saw the multitude of wicked

spirits that was expelled from him by the prayers of
the humble servant of God. Orion came shortly afterwards with his wife and children to return thanks to
the Saint, and brought him large presents out of gra
titude, which he absolutely refused to accept: but
when he besought him with tears to take at least what
he had brought, and to give it to the poor, he answered; "thou canst better distribute thyself what
thou wouldst have to be given to the poor; for thou
frequentest cities, and knowest the poor; why should
I, who have left my own, covet the goods of others?
Many have been imposed upon by avarice, under the
name of the poor. Do not make thyself uneasy; it is
for both thy sake and mine I refuse thy presents : for
if I should accept of them, I should offend God, and
the legion of devils would return to thee."

One Italicus, a Christian of Maiuma, the haven of
Gaza, who bred horses for the public races that were
to be exhibited at Gaza, came to the Saint to beg his
prayers against the enchantments wherewith his pagan
antagonist, one of the magistrates of the city, had bewitched his horses. Hilarion, who disliked all these
public games, was unwilling to employ his prayers on
so vain an occasion. But the other representing to
him that it was not by his own choice, but by his
office, he was obliged to do what he did; and that
the honor of God and religion was here at stake, because the men of Gaza, who, for the most part, were

infidels, would take occasion, from his being worsted, to insult, not so much over him as over the church of Christ: the Saint, at the request of the brethren, ordered his earthen pot, in which he used to drink, to be filled with water, and given to him. Italicus took the water, and with it sprinkled his stable, his horses, his chariot, and his drivers, in the sight of the pagans, who made a jest of it, whilst the Christians, confiding in the prayers of the Saint, made no doubt of success. Wherefore, as soon as the signal was given, the horses of Italicus sprung forth with incredible speed, whilst those of his adversary were presently distanced, and could scarce keep within sight of them that were gone before. Upon this a loud cry of all the people were immediately raised, and even the very adversaries cried out, that *Marnas, the God of Gaza, was worsted by Christ.* This miracle gave occasion to the conversion of many.

There was also in the same town of Maiuma, a virgin dedicated to God, with whom a young man in the neighborhood was vehemently in love. After having employed, without success, flattering speeches, idle jokes, and other freedoms, which too often pave the way to greater crimes, he went to Memphis in Egypt, to seek a remedy for his wound from the priests of Esculapius. They furnished him with certain magical spells and monstrous figures, graven upon a plate of copper, which he buried under the threshold of the

9

house where the maid dwelt, when behold immediately
(in punishment of her having laid herself too open to
the enemy, by not flying, as she ought, or not resist-
ing former freedoms) the maid ran mad with love,
tearing off her head clothes, whirling about her hair,
gnashing with her teeth, and calling upon the name
of the young man. Her parents, therefore, took her
to St. Hilarion, when presently it appeared how the
case stood; for the devil began to howl within her,
and to cry out: " I was forced in hither; I was brought
from Memphis against my will: where I succeeded
well, in deluding men with dreams. But, oh! what
torments dost thou make me suffer here! Thou com-
pellest me to depart, but behold I am bound fast, and
kept in by the thread and plate that lie under the
threshold. I cannot go out till the young man who
keeps me here, lets me go." " Thou art very strong
indeed!" said the Saint, "if thou art held by a thread
and a plate. But tell me, how didst thou dare to
enter into a maid dedicated to God!" " It was," said
he, " to preserve her virginity." " What! thou preserve her virginity," said the Saint, "who art the
mortal enemy of chastity. Why didst thou not rather
enter into him that sent thee?" " Oh," said the devil,
" there was no necessity for my entering into him, who
was already possessed by my comrade, the demon of
wanton love." The Saint would hear no more, nor
send for the young man, not order the things men-

tioned to be taken away, to show the little regard that is to be had to the devil's speeches or signs, but instantly delivered the maid from her wicked guest, and sent her away perfectly cured, after severely reprehending her for admitting of those liberties which had given the devil the power to possess her.

It would be endless to recount all the other miracles that God wrought by this Saint, which rendered his name illustrious, even in the most remote provinces. St. Antony himself, hearing of his life and conversation, wrote to him, and gladly received letters from him; and when any diseased came to him for their cure from any part of Syria, he blamed them for giving themselves the trouble to come so far, since you have, said he, in those parts my son Hilarion. His bright example attracted great numbers to the service of God, so that now there were innumerable monasteries, or cells of religious, throughout Palestine, who all looked upon him as their father, and resorted to him for their direction. These he exhorted to attend to their spiritual progress; ever reminding them, "that the figure of this world passeth away, and that eternal life can only be purchased by parting with the pleasures and affections of this life." He visited all their monasteries once a year for their instruction and edification: and such was his diligence and charity on these occasions, that he would not pass by the cell of the least or meanest of the brethren without calling in to instruct and console him, insomuch that he went as far as the desert of Kadesh, on purpose to visit one single monk who dwelt there. In this journey he was accompanied by a great number of his disciples into the city of Elusa, on the confines of the Saracens, on a festival day, when the people were all assembled in the temple of Venus, who was there worshipped by the Saracens on account of the star that bears her name. No sooner had they heard that Hilarion, of whose sanctity and miracles they had been previously informed by several of their nation whom he had delivered from evil spirits, was passing by, but all the men, women, and children ran out in crowds to meet him and to beg his blessing. The Saint received them all with the utmost tenderness and humility, and begged that they would henceforth worship the living God, rather than stocks and stones: shedding at the same time many tears, and looking up towards heaven, he promised, if they would believe in Christ, that he would frequently come to see them. So wonderful was the grace that accompanied the words and prayers of the man of God, that they would not suffer him to quit their city, till he had first marked out a plot of ground for the building of a church; nay, their very priest had received the sign of the cross of Christ, in order to his baptism.

Another year, when the Saint was making his visitation, a little before the time of the vintage, he came with all his companions to the monastery of one of the brethren, who was remarkable for being a niggardly miser. This man had a vineyard, and apprehending lest the multitude of the monks that accompanied the Sain' should eat up his grapes, he set several men to keep them off with stones and clods in slings, and would not so much as let them taste of them. The servant of God smiled at the treatment they had met with, but taking no notice of it to the niggard, he went on the next day to another monastery, where he and his whole company were kindly received by a monk named Sabas, who kindly invited them (it being the Lord's day,) to go and feast themselves in his vineyard. The Saint ordered that they should first take the food of their souls, by applying themselves to their religious exercises of prayer, singing psalms, and paying their duty to God: and then after giving them his blessing, he sent the whole multitude of his disciples to the vineyard to take their corporal refection. The blessing of the man of God was attended with so miraculous an effect, that whereas the vineyard of Sabas was not before thought capable of yielding more than a hundred gallons of wine, it yielded that year three hundred, whilst the vineyard of the niggard yielded much less than usual, and the little that it produced turned into vinegar, a circumstance which the man of God had foretold. Hilarion could never endure in religious men any thing that looked like

covetousness, or too great an affection to any of these
things that pass away with this transitory world : he
was moreover endowed by God with the gift of discovering who were addicted to this, that, or any other
kind of vice, by the stench that proceeded from their
bodies or garments.

And now the Saint, seeing that his hermitage was
converted into a great monastery, and that the wilder
ness about him was continually crowded with the
people who resorted thither, bringing their diseased,
or such as were possessed with unclean spirits, and that
not only the common sort of people from all the neighboring provinces, but even the gentry,—ladies of the
first rank,—clerks, monks, priests, and bishops, were
daily visiting him, and interrupting his devotions, he
bitterly regretted the loss of his former solitude, perpetually lamenting, weeping, and saying, that since he
had returned back into the world, he apprehended he
should have his reward in this life, because all Palestine and the neighboring provinces took him to be
somebody, &c., nor did he cease to mourn and bewail
his condition, till he took a fixed resolution to quit his
monastery, and retire into some place where he might
be unknown, and more freely enjoy his God without
the interruption of so many visits. In the mean time,
whilst he was meditating upon his flight, the lady
Aristeneta, whose three sons he had cured, came to
see him, acquainting him with her design of returning

into Egypt, to make a second visit to St. Antony. He replied, with tears in his eyes, that he could have wished to have taken the same journey, if he were not kept prisoner in his monastery, but that it was now too late to find Antony alive; for, said he, two days go the world was deprived of so great a father. Having believed him, she did not proceed in her journey, and, behold, after some days the news of his death was brought from Egypt. When it was known abroad that the man of God was upon the point of quitting Palestine, the whole province took the alarm, and no less than ten thousand people, of all degrees and conditions, were gathered together, in order to stop and detain him. But his resolution was not to be altered; and as he had learnt by revelation the havock that the infidels of Gaza were about to make in his monastery, and all through that neighborhood, under the reign of Julian the Apostate, he gave them broad hints of this his fore-knowledge, saying, that he could not call in question the truth of what God had said; nor could he endure to see the churches destroyed, the altars of Christ trodden under foot, and his children massacred. In short, he assured them he would neither eat nor drink till they let him go. And thus, after he had fasted seven days, they were contented at last to suffer him depart, accompanied by about forty of his monks. With these he made the best of his way to Pelusium, (now called Damietta) in

Egypt, and after visiting the holy solitaries who lived
in the neighboring deserts, he waited upon Dracontius
and Philo ; two illustrious confessors of Christ, of the
number of those catholic prelates who had been banished from their sees by the fury of the Arians, under
the emperor Constantius. After paying these visits,
he hastened to keep the anniversary day of the happy
decease of St. Antony in the place where he died :
and being conducted by the deacon Baisanes, upon
dromedaries, three days' journey through that vast and
dreary wilderness, he arrived at length at the mountain of the Saint. Here he found his two disciples,
who showed him all the places where their master had
been accustomed to sing psalms—to pray—to work—
and sit down to rest himself, after being wearied with
his labor ; as also the garden he had cultivated—the
trees he had planted—the instrument with which he
had dug the earth—the private cells to which he often
retired towards the top of the mountain, &c. and then
agreeably entertained him with divers particulars of
the acts of the latter part of St. Antony's life. Hilarion was much moved to devotion with the sight and
recital of all this ; and after watching in prayer the
whole night of the anniversary of the Saint, he return
ed the same way he came, through the dreary wilder
ness to the neighborhood of the town called Aphrodi-
ton. Here, in an adjoining desert, with two of his
disciples whom he kept with him, he led so abste-

mious, abstracted, and silent a life, that on feeling the fervor he now found within himself, he seemed never to have before begun to serve Christ in earnest.

He had not been above two years in this wilderness, when the fame of his sanctity brought all the people of the neighboring country to him, to beg his prayers for rain. For from the time of the death of St. Antony, no rain had fallen upon their land for the space of three whole years, so that being afflicted with a great famine, they resorted to him, whom they considered as the successor of St. Antony, for a redress of their misery. Moved to pity by the sight of their distress, he lifted up his hands and eyes to heaven to pray for them, and his prayer was immediately followed by plentiful rains. But the rains, whilst they fertilized the earth, having, in falling on the dry, hot sand, also produced an incredible multitude of venomous reptiles and insects, with which innumerable persons were struck, they were again forced to have recourse to the Saint, who gave them some oil which he had blessed, with which they were cured. But now finding himself after these miracles greatly honored, he would stay no longer in this place, but departed in order to go and hide himself in the desert of Oasis. In his way thither he passed through Alexandria: and as he made it a rule never to lodge in any city, he went on to a place in the neighborhood, called Bruchium, where there was a monastery of the servants of God. From hence,

when night drew on, he hastened away, telling the
brethren, who were greatly afflicted, that they should
soon know the reason of his sudden departure. Accordingly, on the next day their monastery was
searched by the Gazites, accompanied by officers sent
from the governor of Alexandria to apprehend Hilarion, of whose arrival there they had received intelligence. For the infidels of Gaza, who bore a mortal
hatred to the Saint, as soon as Julian came to the empire, destroyed his monastery, and obtained an edict
from the tyrant, that both he, and his disciple Hesychius, should be sought for and put to death wherever
they were found. Of this the Saint had a fore-knowledge by prophetic light, and thereupon withdrew
himself: so that the infidels, who had thought themselves certain of seizing their priest, finding he was
gone, departed, saying to each other, that now they
were sure he was a magician, and had a foresight of
things to come.

He had not been a year in the wilderness of Oasis,
before he found that fame had also followed him
thither; and therefore now despairing to be able to
conceal himself upon the continent, he formed a resolution of seeking out a place in some of the islands
of the Mediterranean, where he might hide himself.
In order to this he embarked, with one only disciple,
at Paretonium, a haven on the coast of Lybia, on
board a vessel bound for Sicily; hoping that hence-

forward no one should know him, or become troublesome to him in his retirement. When, behold, in the
midst of the voyage the son of the master of the ship,
or rather the devil by his mouth, cried out: "Hilarion, thou servant of God, let me alone, at least till we
come to land ; how comes it to pass, that even at sea
thou art still persecuting us." The Saint would have
disguised the grace which God had given him, fearing
lest the sailors and passengers should publish his fame
when they came to land, and therefore mildly replied :
"If my God permits thee to stay, stay if thou wilt ;
but if he cast thee out, what hast thou to do to complain of me, who am but a poor beggar and a sinful
man." However, upon the solemn promise of the
father, and of all the rest, that they would not discover
him, he cast the devil out of the boy. When they
arrived at Pachynum (now Capo Passaro), he would
have paid for the passage of himself and his companion, by giving the captain the book of the Gospels,
which was all his wealth, but he, seeing their poverty,
would not receive it. Wherefore the Saint leaving the
sea-coast, withdrew himself into a little kind of wilderness, about twenty miles within the land, and there
fixed his abode ; living upon what little he could get,
by making up faggots, which his companion carried to
a neighboring village, bringing from thence in exchange
what they stood need of for their food.

But the Saint could not long lie concealed here ; for

soon after his arrival, a man possessed with an evil spirit, being under the exorcisms of the Church at St. Peter's in Rome, the devil cried out thus by his mouth: "Hilarion, the servant of Christ, is some days since come into Sicily, where no man knows him, and he thinks himself secret: but I will go and discover him." This man therefore taking some of his servants with him, and going on board a ship sailed immediately for Sicily; and after coming to shore, being conducted by the devil, he went straight to the hut of the servant of God, and there casting himself at his feet, was perfectly cured. This being noised abroad, great multitudes, who labored under various corporeal diseases, resorted to him to obtain their cure; whilst numbers also of devout and religious people applied to him for their spiritual profit. Amongst the rest, he cured upon the spot one of the principal men of the island, who was swollen up with the dropsy, and who on the same day, returned home in perfect health. This man offered to make him considerable presents, which the Saint absolutely refused, alledging the precept of our Saviour, Matt. x. 8. *Gratis you have received, gratis give:* which rule he invariably observed in all the other innumerable miracles which he wrought, whether in Sicily or elsewhere, for, he never would receive any thing, no not so much as a morsel of bread from any one of those on whom he had wrought those miracles.

And now his beloved disciple Hesychius, after hav-

ing sought after him in vain through many different
regions came at length to Sicily, upon the report he
had heard at Modon in Greece, from a Jewish pedlar,
that a christian prophet had appeared in Sicily, who
wrought all kinds of wonderful miracles. No sooner
had he found him than the Saint gave him to understand, that he wanted to depart from Sicily into some
strange country where he might be utterly unknown.
Wherefore, in compliance with his desire, he conveyed
him away by a ship to the coast of Dalmatia, where
for a short time he led a solitary life, not far from the
city of Epidaurus, now called Ragusa. But neither
here could he remain long concealed, his miracles every
where betraying him. There was at that time, in the
neighborhood of Epidaurus, a monstrous serpent, of
that species named *boas*, which did great, mischief in
destroying both men and cattle; the Saint, to put a
stop to this calamity ordered the country, people to
heap up a pile of wood, and after addressing a prayer
to Christ he called the serpent out, of his den, and
commanded him to go on the top of the pile of wood,
and then setting fire to it, he burnt the monster in
sight of a great multitude of people. This miracle
was followed by another still greater. About this
time, viz. the second year of the reign of Valentinian
the first, there happened so remarkable an earthquake
that, according to Amianus, a cotemporary historian,
its like was never recorded, either in authentic or fab-

ulous history.   On this occasion, the swelling seas, in
several places, broke in and overflowed the land in
such a manner as to threaten the earth with a second
deluge, and in some places the waves ran so high as
to carry the ships along with them, and leave them
hanging on the cliffs.   The Epidaurians perceiving the
danger in which their city as well as many others
were in of being destroyed, had recourse to Hilarion,
and opposed him to the mountains of water that were
just upon the point of overwhelming them.   No
sooner had the Saint made three crosses on the sand,
and lifted up his arms to heaven, than the swelling
waves, though they raged, foamed, and rose up to an
incredible height, not able to advance, gradually returned back again and subsided.   This wonder, says
St. Jerome, who was then a boy in the same province,
the city of Epidaurus, as well as the whole country,
recount to this day—the mothers relate it to their
children, in order to transmit the memory of it to
posterity.

The applause that followed these miracles would
not suffer the humble servant of Christ to remain any
longer in Dalmatia; therefore taking boat privately by
night he fled away, and within two days found a ship
departing for Cyprus, on which he embarked.   In this
voyage his ship being pursued by some pirates in two
light vessels, there appeared no hopes of escaping
them.   The ship's crew being in the utmost conster-

nation, the Saint turning to his disciples said: "Why are you afraid, O ye of little faith?" And wl en the pirates were now come within a stone's cast of the ship, he stood on the fore-deck, and stretching out his hand to them, he said: "*You have come far enough;*" when behold immediately their vessels fell back, and the more they tugged and rowed, in order tó push forward towards their expected prey, the more rapidly were they carried away from it. The Saint landed at Paphos, a noted city of Cyprus, and chose himself a dwelling place about two miles from thence; being now wonderfully pleased that he had found rest, at least for a short time, in this solitude; but scarcely had twenty days elapsed when the devils in different parts of the island published his arrival by the mouths of those that were possessed; and several of these, both men and women, hastened to him and were delivered. Here he remained about two years meditating upon some private place of retirement. In the mean time he sent Hesychius into Palestine, to salute the brethren there, and to visit the ashes of his monastery; and upon his return proposed that they should sail into Egypt, and advance a great way into the country, to some place, inhabited only by pagans. But Hesychius opposed this; and after a long search, discovered a place in the island about twelve miles distant from the sea, amongst mountains and woods that were almost inaccessible, which proved quite to his

mind.   In this solitude, to which no one could arrive
in several places but by creeping on hands and knees,
they found springs of water on the sides of the hills,—
a little garden within, with several fruit trees, of which
however the Saint would never eat, and near the garden the ruins of an ancient temple, from whence, as
both he and his disciples related, were often heard, both
night and day, a great noise, like the voices of a whole
army of devils.   In this solitary abode the man of
God dwelt for the last five years of his mortal life, seldom visited by any one but Hesychius, on account of
the difficulty of coming at his dwelling, as also because
the people were persuaded that the neighborhood was
haunted with a multitude of demons.   However, there
were some that ventured to come to him for the cure
of their maladies ; their necessities overcoming all difficulties, especially after it was known, that he had
cured upon the spot, the bailiff of the place of a palsy,
which had deprived him of the use of his limbs, by
only stretching out his hand to him, and lifting him
up with these words : *In the name of the Lord Jesus
Christ, rise up and walk.*

But now the time arrived which was to put a period
to all the labors of his mortal pilgrimage, and unite
him eternally to his God, when being now eighty years
old he was seized with his last illness.   Although
Hesychius was then absent, he nevertheless bequeathed to him by will all he had, viz. his book of the gos-

pels, his sackcloth, cowl, and habit. Many religious men from Paphos came to attend him in his sickness, who had heard of his having said, " that he was now going to our Lord ;" and with them a holy woman named Constantia, whose daughter and son-in-law he had delivered from death by anointing them with oil. And now he was drawing near his end, when in the very agony of death he distinctly spoke these words : " Go forth my soul : what art thou afraid of? Go forth, why art thou at a stand ? Thou hast served Christ almost seventy years, and art thou afraid to die ?" and with these words he gave up the ghost. He was immediately buried as he had desired, in the same place : where the devout lady Constantia frequently passed whole nights in prayer at his sepulchre, speaking with him as if he were alive, and desiring the assistance of his prayers. His disciple Hesychius, after ten months, privately conveyed his body away to Palestine, where it was solemnly interred in his own monastery ; at which time it was found entirely incorrupt, and sending forth a most fragrant odor. Many great miracles were daily wrought through his intercession, even to the time when St. Jerome published his life, as well at his sepulchre in Palestine, as at the place where he was first buried in Cyprus.

ST. MALCHUS.

Abridged from St Jerome

WHILST St. Jerome in his younger days made some stay at Maronia, a village of Syria, about thirty miles distant from Antioch, he learnt that there dwelt in that neighborhood a religious man, now advanced in years, whose name was Malchus, and near him a decrepit old woman, both eminent servants of God, constant in the church, and wholly addicted to the exercises of religion : of whom the neighbors published wonderful things and extolled their sanctity to the skies, which gave occasion to St. Jerome, in order to his own justification, to visit that holy man, and to learn from his own mouth the particulars of his history; which he afterwards published to the world in a small book, of which the following is an abstract.

Malchus was a native of the territory of Nisibis, a city of Mesopotamia, upon the confines of the Roman and Persian empires. Being the only child of his parents they looked upon him as the heir and support of their family, and therefore, when he was grown up, they pressed him to marry; but declaring himself quite averse to this state of life, he made known to them his desire of entering into religion, and of wholly dedicating himself to God. But as they ceased not

ctill to importune him, both with flatteries and threats
to part with the treasure of his virginal purity, which
he valued above all the possessions of the world, in
order to rid himself of their importunities, and to secure his treasure, he took a resolution to withdraw
himself entirely from house and home, parents and
country. Accordingly, taking a trifling matter with
him for his journey, he travelled westward, till at
length he arrived at the desert of Chalcis in Syria.
Here he found some servants of God leading a monastic life, and put himself under their direction, following the same institute as they did, living by the
labor of his hands, and restraining the rebellions of
flesh by rigorous fasting. In this course of life he continued for many years, till the common enemy, envy-
ing the progress he made in virtue, suggested to him,
under specious pretexts, to leave the monastery, and
to return to his own country to see whether his mother
were yet alive (for he had heard of his father's death),
and if she were, to comfort her in her widowhood, and
after her decease to sell the estate, distribute part of
the money to the poor, employ another part in building a monastery, and to reserve what remained for his
own use; a design which he afterwards lamented, as
a grievous transgression and infidelity to his religious
engagements.

His Abbot was no sooner informed of his purposes,
than he remonstrated with him, in the strongest terms,

that the whole was a temptation of the devil, who, by such plausible pretences as these, had oftentimes imposed upon religious men, and drawn them back again into the world; alledging also several examples from Scripture, of the wiles and impostures of this wicked old serpent. When the abbot saw that his remonstrances were not hearkened to, he even cast himself down upon his knees, and earnestly entreated his disciple not to abandon him, nor fling himself away, nor to look back after setting his hand to the plough. But all in vain: Malchus imagined that his superior, in seeking to detain him, had more an eye to his own comfort and satisfaction, than to his advantage, and therefore would not be diverted from his design. When he set out upon his journey, his abbot followed him out of the monastery, bewailing him, as if he had been following his corpse to the grave; and at their last parting told him plainly, that the sheep which had left the fold must expect nothing but to fall an immediate prey to the wolves.

In his journey he was to go from Beroea to Edessa, by a road which borders upon an extensive wilderness, much infested by parties of the Saracens or Arabians, who robbed or carried off all they met with. This obliged the travellers who passed that way, to travel in large companies for their mutual defence; and it happened that there were at this time no less than about three-score and ten persons in company with

Malchus, young and old, men and women. But this
precaution could not secure the fugitive, who was running away from his Lord, from being overtaken, or
from meeting with captivity and slavery, instead of
the possessions to which he imagined himself return·
ing. For behold a party of armed Saracens, some on
horseback, others upon camels rushed suddenly upon
them, made them prisoners, and then, by lot, divided
their captives amongst them. Malchus happened to
fall into the hands of the same master with a married
woman, one of the company, whose husband fell to
the lot of another : and both he, and the rest of the
prisoners, now slaves, being set upon camels, were carried for many days through an immense wilderness,
living in the mean time upon meat half raw and camels' milk ; till having passed over a great river, they
came into the heart of the country. Here Malchus
and his fellow captive were brought in, and being presented to their master's wife, were obliged, according
to the manner of the custom of the country, to prostrate themselves and do reverence to their new mistress and her children. And now, instead of his monastic habit, or any other clothing, Malchus is obliged
to go naked, as well on account of his condition of a
s'ave, as by the violent heat reflected by the sun-beams
on those Arabian sands, which would not suffer him
to wear any other covering than what modesty indis·
pensably required. His office was to tend his mas·

ter's sheep in the wilderness; in which it was his
comfort to be generally alone, seldom seeing either
his master, or any of his fellow-servants.   He pleased
himself also with the thought, that in his way of life
he resembled some of the ancient Saints who had in
like manner fed sheep in the wilderness.   In the mean
time his whole diet was new cheese and milk, and his
whole employment continual prayer and singing of the
psalms which he had learnt by heart in the monastery.
He now became delighted with his captivity, and gave
thanks to God for the wonderful dispositions of his
merciful providence, in conducting him to find the
monk again in the land of his slavery, which he was
going to lose for ever in his own country.

The devil, who could not endure to be a witness to
the great advantages our captive made of his present
condition, by the help of his solitude, recollection, and
continual prayer, contrived a dangerous stratagem for
the robbing him at once both of his chastity and all
his other virtues, which he sought to bring about in
the following manner :   The Saracen, finding that his
flock increased under the hands of Malchus, that he
served him honestly and with fidelity, took it into his
head, doubtless by the suggestion of the enemy, to reward him, and as it were, to fix him for ever in his
service, by giving him the same married woman for a
wife who was taken captive with him :—this he proposed as an act of friendship, or a favor which he was

desirous to confer on him. But when Malchus replied that this could not be, because he was a Christian, and therefore could not, by the law of God, marry
a woman whose husband was still living, the barbarian, in a rage, drew his sword, and would have instantly killed him upon the spot, had he not hastened
to take his fellow-captive by the arm, which his master mistook for a token of his consent to the marriage.
When night arrived they went both together with a
heavy heart into a ruinous cave, which served Malchus
for his lodging, neither of them knowing the dispositions of the other. Here Malchus casting himself
upon the ground, grievously lamented his wretched
condition, that after having in his younger days forsaken all his worldly pretensions, together with his
country, parents, and estate, purely to preserve his virginity, he should now in a more advanced age, lose it
in so illegal and wicked a manner : accusing himself
withal of his sins, especially of his crime in quitting
his monastery to return to his own country, to which
he imputed his being now caught in this labyrinth,
out of which he knew not how to extricate himself
but by death : and this he was strongly inclined to
choose, as the only means remaining, as he thought,
to preserve his virtue. His fellow-captive, perceiving
the excessive trouble and agitation of mind under
which he lay, and hearing him talk of making himself
a martyr of chastity, cast herself at his feet, and beg

ged, for the sake of Jesus Christ, that he would not
think of doing himself any harm; that, for her part,
she abhorred the proposed marriage as much as himself, and would rather suffer death than consent to any
unchastity: but why may we not live together, said
she, as brother and sister, in perfect purity, whilst ou.
master and mistress take us for man and wife?   These
words calmed the soul of Malchus, and made him
esteem and admire the virtue of the woman, and love
her the more; but, according to God, with a holy
friendship, cemented by heavenly charity.

Pursuant to this proposal, they lived a long time
together, in perfect chastity of mind and body, and
were beloved by their master and mistress, who entertained not the least suspicion, either of their not being
married, nor of any danger of their making their escape: so that Malchus was accustomed to be absent
with his flock for a whole month together in the wilderness, at a great distance from his master's house.
One day, whilst he was sitting alone, he began to consider the great advantages of a spiritual life that are
found in well ordered religious communities: remembering in particular the helps and directions he had
received from the good abbot, his ghostly father, and
regretted his leaving him: when behold, in the midst
of his meditation, he perceives at a little distance a
hillock of ants (a creature proposed to us by the wise
man as a pattern of industry and wisdom), and was

pleased to see the order and harmony which they observed in their labors—that mutual help which they
gave to each other, and how they ran to the assistance
of such as fell under their burthens. This seemed to
him a lively representation of a regular community;
and joined to his foregoing considerations made him
begin to be weary of his captivity, and long to return
to his abbot and his monastery. When he came
home at night, the woman perceived him to be pen-
sive and melancholy, and having learnt the reason,
persuaded him to set off, offering at the same time to
accompany him. Having concluded upon so doing,
and watching a proper opportunity, he killed two large
goats of his flock, made vessels of their skins, and prepared part of the meat to support them during their
journey. On the next evening they set out, making
the best of their way to a river about ten miles distant, which they crossed by the help of the vessels
they had made of the skins of the goats. In crossing
the river they lost some part of the meat they had
carried with them, so that what remained was scarce
sufficient to support them for three days, and as to
drink, they took plenty of water, not knowing when
they should meet with more.

They made what haste they possibly could through
the sandy deserts, looking back from time to time,
with fear and trembling, to see if any one were in pursuit of them, travelling mostly by night, as well to

avoid the meeting with any of the Saracen rovers, as
on account of the excessive heat.   They had been now
three days upon their journey, when looking behind
them, they saw at a distance two men riding on camels, and hastening towards them, one of whom they
concluded to be their master, who had discovered the
way they had gone by their tracks in the sands, and
now they expected nothing but certain death.   There
happening to be a den or cave at hand that reached a
considerable way under ground, they ran thither for
shelter; but fearing the serpents and other venomous
creatures that usually resort to such places in order to
avoid the heat of the sun, they would not venture to
penetrate to the further end, lest in flying from death
in one shape, they should meet it in another.   Wherefore discovering within, near the entrance of the den,
a hole on their left hand, into which they had no
sooner trusted themselves, when behold their master,
with one of their fellow servants, tracing them by their
footsteps, quickly came up to the mouth of the cavern.   The master having sent his servant in to drag
them out, stood without, holding the camels, and waiting for them with his drawn sword.   The servant
passed by the hole where they lay concealed, without
being able to see them, on account of his being just
come out of the light, and advancing forward made a
great uproar, crying aloud: " Come forward, ye vil

tains and receive your wages : come out, your master calls for you : come out, and die." Malchus and his companion saw him pass by them, and looking after him, perceived a lioness, roused by the noise, flying at him, and strangling him, and then drawing his bloody body further into the den. The master, ignorant of what had happened, finding that the servant did not come out, supposed that they, being two, might make resistance against one. He came therefore in a great rage to the entrance of the cave, with his sword in his hand, and raving at the cowardice of his servant, began to enter in ; but before he had passed the lurking hole where Malchus lay, he was suddenly seized by the beast before their eyes, and served in the same manner as his servant had been. Thus by an extraordinary providence were these servants of God delivered from the hands of those that sought their life : but they remained still in dread lest they should meet with no less cruel death from the furious beast that was so near them. In this fear they remained close, without making the least motion or noise, having no other means of defence or dependence but the providence of God, and a good conscience in point of chastity, which is respected even by lions. But it was not long before the lioness, finding herself discovered, and disturbed in her den, taking up her whelp (for she had but one), carried it out with her teeth, in order to go and seek for another lodging, and thus abandoned the whole cave to themselves. The apprehension, however, of meeting with the beast, kept them close prisoners till the evening, when they ventured out, and found the two camels (who were of the kind which for their great swiftness are called diomedaries), and with them fresh provisions, of which they were in great need : and thus, after refreshing themselves with food, they mounted upon the camels, and continued their journey through the desert, and on the tenth day arrived at the Roman camp, on the confines of the empire. The commanding officer, after having heard their history, sent them to Sabinianus, the governor of Mesopotamia, who gave them the price of their camels, and so dismissed them.

And now Malchus would have returned to his good father, the abbot of his monastery, in the desert of Chalsis : but being informed that he was gone to sleep in the Lord, he turned his course towards Maronia, and there associated himself with the monks of that place : and as to his companion, he committed her to the care of the nuns that were there ; ever *loving her as if she had been his sister,* as he told St. Jerome, *yet never trusting himself to her as a sister,* or exposing himself to danger by any familiarity with her. Here, as St. Jerome concludes his narration, we cannot pretend to add any further particulars of the acts of this servant of God, only that he continued to the end

the saintly life he had begun, and crowned it with a
happy death; so that he has deserved to have his
name recorded amongst the Saints of the Roman Mar
tyrology, October 21.

SS. PACHOMIUS AND PALEMON.

Abridged from the Life of St. Pachomius, by an ancient
writer, who had his information from the companions
and disciples of the Saint

St. PACHOMIUS was born in Thebais, or the higher
Egypt, about the year 292, of infidel parents, who
carried him, when as yet a child, to the temples of
their idols, to make him a partaker of their impious
sacrifices; but as a presage of what he was one day
to be, when they gave him a little of the wine of the
devil's libations, or drink offerings, to taste, he presently cast it up again; and when upon another solemn
occasion he had accompanied them to celebrate the
festival of an idol that was worshipped upon the banks
of the Nile, the devil was restrained, by his presence,
from returning answers, and deluding the people with
his usual tricks, till by the mouth of the priest he had
ordered Pachomius to be sent away as an enemy of
the gods. Yet all this while he was totally ignorant

of the christian religion, but otherwise led a very moral life, and was always modest, temperate, and chaste.

When about twenty years old, Constantine being
then emperor, he was, with many other of his countrymen, impressed for the service, on account of a war
just then breaking out. The young recruits were put
on shipboard, in order to pass down the Nile, and so
to be carried to the army. In their way they arrived
at a certain city, where they found the inhabitants remarkably officious in administering all the comfort
and assistance in their power to some young men, who
were kept close confined by their officers, and in great
distress. Pachomius enquired who these men were
that showed so much humanity and benevolence to the
afflicted and distressed? On being told they were
Christians, a set of men who made it their business to
do good to all men, and especially to strangers in distress, he further enquired what was meant by the name
of Christians, and what were their tenets? They told
him they were godly and religious people who believed
in Jesus Christ, the only Son of God, and exercised
themselves in all the virtues and works of charity, in
expectation of an eternal reward from God in another
life. Pachomius was touched with this account, and
being visited by the divine grace, withdrew himself
into a corner, and lifting up his hands and heart to
heaven, he called upon the great God, who made
heaven and earth, to enlighten his soul with the

knowledge of the true and perfect rule of life which he would have him to follow; and promised, if he would deliver him from his present bondage, that he would yield himself up to his divine service during the remainder of his life, and quit all worldly hopes, to adhere to him alone. The emperor having shortly afterwards obtained a complete victory over his enemies, and put an end to the war, ordered the new raised troops to be discharged. Pachomius having now recovered his wished-for liberty, returned to his own country, and presently enrolled himself in the number of those that were under instructions in order to receive baptism, and being baptised shortly afterwards in the church of the town of Chinoboscium, he was on the following night favored with a heavenly vision, which strongly moved him to consecrate the residue of his life to divine love.

In obedience to this call, he repaired immediately to Palemon, a holy anchoret, who led a recluse life in a neighboring desert, with a desire of putting himself under his conduct and direction, and of spending the remainder of his life with him. This servant of God, who led a very austere life, at first refused him admittance, alledging, that several others had in like manner pretended to put themselves under his discipline, but became quickly tired of his way of life. Pachomius requested that he would at least put him to the trial, for that he trusted God would enable him to ex-

ecute all that he should require of him. ' My son,"
said Palemon, " the way of life that I follow is not the
easiest.   I eat nothing but bread and salt, and wholly
refrain from oil and wine.   I watch one half the night ;
employing that time in solemn prayer, and in meditating on the word of God ; and sometimes I pass the
whole night without sleep." Pachomius replied, that
he hoped the grace of our Lord Jesus Christ, with the
help of his prayers, would inspire him with the necessary courage to embrace, and patience to suffer all this
rigor, even to the end of his life.   Palemon perceiving
the lively faith and steadfast resolution of the young
man, was content to receive him, and clothe him with
the monastic habit ; and Pachomius, on his part, from
the very beginning, embraced the exercises of a religious life with so much ardor, and advanced with such
large steps, day by day, in the paths of virtue and perfection, as to give unspeakable satisfaction and joy to
his master, who continually returned thanks to Christ
for the wonders of his grace which he discovered in
his disciple.   In the mean time they lived together in
the same cell, performed the same practices of abstinence and prayer, and labored together in the same
manual exercises, that they might not only support
themselves without being burthensome to others, but
also to have wherewith to entertain and relieve their
indigent brethren.   After the labors of the day, they
watched and prayed together for the best part of the

night; and if, upon these occasions, Palemon observed
that Pachomius was in danger of falling asleep, he led
him out of the cell, and employed him in carrying
loads of sand from one place to another, in order to
vercome his drowsiness; telling him, that if he hoped
o persevere to the end in his holy undertaking, he
must not by any means suffer himself to relax in
watching and prayer.   Besides these exercises, Pachomius, in a more particular manner, applied himself to
the cultivating and purifying his interior.   In order to
this, whilst he was reading the holy scriptures, and
committing them to his memory, which was a part of
his daily occupation, he paused in silent and deep
meditation upon each of the heavenly precepts, suffering them to sink deep into his soul, and studying to
reduce each of them to practice; but the favorite virtues in which he particularly labored to excel were, a
profound humility, unwearied patience, and unbounded charity and love both for God and his neighbor.

When Easter arrived, Palemon ordered Pachomius
to prepare them a dinner for that great festival.   The
latter readily obeyed, and, in consideration of the solemnity of the feast, mingled a little oil and salt together to be eaten with the wild herbs which he had
gathered.   But when, after having prayed together,
Palemon came to table, and saw the sallad prepared
for him, instead of eating it, he wept bitterly, saying:
" my Lord was crucified, and shall I indulge myself

in eating oil!" Neither would he at any rate be in-duced to take any other food but his bread and salt as usual, blessing it with the sign of the cross before he eat thereof, and returning humble thanks to our Lord afterwards.

One day, whilst Palemon and Pachomius were watching together by a fire they had kindled in their cell, another religious man coming to them, desired admittance, whom they courteously received. After some discourse the stranger proposed to them, "that if they had as much faith as he had, they would show it, by standing with their bare feet over the burning coals, which himself was ready to do, whilst they re-peated at leisure the Lord's prayer. The servants of God were shocked at the arrogance of their guest; and Palemon besought him to desist from so mad an attempt. But instead of hearkening to him, being puffed up with pride and presumption, he went and stood upon the coals, and by the help of the enemy, God so permitting, in punishment of his pride, receiv-ed no injury whatsoever. The next morning at de-parting, he added to his pride the insolence of insult-ing the two saints, by reproaching them with their want of faith. But it was not long before his arro-gance was most dreadfully punished: for the devil perceiving that his self-conceit had already stripped him of divine grace, and left him in a condition to be-come an easy prey to lust, came one day to his cell,

m the shape of a most beautiful woman, pretending to
be in the utmost distress, and being admitted, enkindled in his heart the fire of concupiscence. The
unhappy man readily yielded to these wicked suggestions, and attempting to put them in execution, was
so unmercifully handled by the evil spirit, as to be left
extended upon the floor, without speech or sense.
Having however, after some time, come to himself, he,
as soon as he was able to walk, went to the cell of St.
Palemon telling what had happened, and acknowledging that he had drawn all this evil upon himself by
his pride, and begging their prayers, that the devil
might not tear him in pieces, or otherwise destroy him.
The Saints lamented his case, and wept for him; but
the enemy to whom he had made himself a slave,
would not suffer him to remain with them; for all on
a sudden he jumped out of the cell, and after running
about the wilderness like a mad man, he went to the
neighboring city of Panopolis, and there, having flung
himself into the furnace of the hot baths, he perished
in the flames—a deplorable example of the dreadful
consequences of pride and presumption.

Pachomius, from hearing the direful exit of this unhappy man, took occasion of being still more humble,
mortified, and fervent in prayer; and as he had an
extraordinary love for solitude, he often withdrew from
his cell into lonely places, spending his whole time in
prayer; earnestly begging of the divine Majesty to de-

liver him from all the deceits and snares of the wicked
one.   There was also in the neighborhood a wild
place full of thorns, to which he often went to procure
wood for their use.   Upon these occasions it was his
custom to walk bare-foot among the thorns, pleasing
himself with the pricks and wounds that he received
in his feet, by the meditation of the piercing of the
feet of our Saviour upon the cross.   One day, going
to a greater distance than ordinary from his cell, he
came to a place called Tabenna, at that time altogether uninhabited, where having, according to custom,
remained a considerable time in prayer, it was revealed to him, that he should there build a monastery, to
which many should resort, and put themselves under
his conduct; for whose instruction and direction he
should receive a rule from heaven; a sketch of which
was then presented him by an angel.   When he returned back to Palemon, he acquainted him with this
revelation, and prevailed on him to accompany him
to Tabenna, where they built a small cell, and for
some time remained together, performing their accustomed exercises, till at length Palemon, seeing the extraordinary grace that God had conferred on Pachomius, went back again, and left him sole possessor o
this new cell, upon condition, that, as long as they
lived, they should frequently visit each other for their
mutual comfort and spiritual assistance.

    And now the time drew near which was to crown

the labors of St. Palemon with an eterna. recompense
in the land of the living. Previous to his death, he
was seized with a grievous and most painful illness,
which the brethren who came to visit him, attributed
to his austere and penitential manner of life, and
therefore prevailed upon him to admit of some little
comfort, in point of eating and drinking, in consideration of his age and weakness. But he quickly returned again to his former manner of diet, alledging, that
the change had only contributed to increase his pains,
and that if the martyrs had bravely suffered so many
cruel torments for the love of Christ, and thereby purchased a happy eternity, it would be shameful in him
to forfeit the eternal reward prepared for patient suffering, by a cowardly murmuring under his light and
momentary pains. After he had continued about a
month, suffering with invincible courage and constancy, his soul, sufficiently purified in the furnace of tribulation, took her happy flight, accompanied by angels
to the heavenly mansions. His name stands recorded
amongst the Saints in the Roman Martyrology, on the
eleventh of January.

After Pachomius had buried his holy father, and
was returned to his cell at Tabenna, God was pleased
to send him his own brother for a companion, who,
having heard of his wonderful life, came to visit him,
which was the first time the Saint had seen any of his
relations since his conversion, and proposed to live with

12

him.   Pachomius having joyfully received him, found
in his brother all the dispositions that could be desired
in a perfect religious man.   The two brothers continued together, meditating incessantly on the law of
God both by day and night, with all the affection of
their souls, ever tending towards him, and totally dis-
engaged from the least affection towards the things of
the earth.   They labored with their hands for their
daily food, and never reserved any thing for to-morrow; but whatever they earned above the necessary
sustenance of the day they gave to the poor.   Pachomius to his former austerities added that of humbling
his soul and body, by wearing hair-cloth; and during
the space of fifteen years, notwithstanding his hard
labors, long watchings, and continual fastings, never
allowed himself to lie down at night to take his rest;
but whatever sleep he admitted of, he took sitting in
the midst of his cell, without having any thing at his
back to support himself, or to lean against for his
ease.

In the mean time, the Saint being a second time
admonished from heaven concerning the religious congregation he was to institute, and the rules he was to
give them, began to enlarge the place of their habitation, and to build several additional cells for the reception of those whom he expected would come in good
time to join him in the service of so great a Master
His brother, whose spirit inclined rather to the life of

an anchoret, in a more perfect solitude, after some
time blamed his proceedings, and being the elder
brother, took upon him to bid him desist from so useless a labor. The Saint, although he could not help being troubled at this opposition, yet bore it with meekness and humility, without making the least reply.
But the following night, prostrating himself alone in
prayer in the new building, he remained till morning
in this humble posture, lamenting his misery, and imploring the divine mercy for having suffered any emotions of impatience or resentment on this occasion to
take place in his soul, begging the grace of God to
guard and protect him from sin, and so powerfully to
assist him for the future, that he might acquire a perfect mastery over all his passions, and serve him with
all perfection all the days of his life. So numerous
were the tears he shed that night, so great the fervor
of his prayer, and the weather so violently hot, that
what with his weeping and sweat, the place on which
he lay prostrate became as wet as if water had been
cast upon it. At other times, during his devotions
by night, he used to excite himself to watching and
fervor in prayer, by stretching out his arms, keeping
his body as immovable as if he were fastened to the
cross, and remaining for several hours in this painful
posture. On all occasions Pachomius behaved himself with such humility, meekness, and condescension
towards his brother, that they lived together in the

most perfect harmony and peace, till God was pleased
to take the brother to himself. Pachomius took care
for his ·burial, and spent the whole night in singing
psalms and hymns over his body, and recommending
his soul to God.

And now Pachomius, as if all he had hitherto done
had been nothing, *forgetting*, with the Apostle, *the
things that were behind, stretched forth himself to the
things that were before*, by a new fervor in the study
and practice of religious perfection, having the congregation which he was to establish in that place always
before his eyes. This drew upon him the inveterate
envy and malice of the wicked enemy, by whom he
was incessantly plied with temptations of every kind,
and frequently with fantastical apparitions ; who
sought either to puff him up with pride and vain-
glory, by the honors he pretended to pay him, or to
allure him to lust, by placing the figures of impudent
women with bare bosoms before him, or by interrupting and distracting him in his devotions, by a variety
of illusions and ludicrous scenes ; sometimes also assaulting him with open violence, and even laying
many blows and stripes upon him. But the Saint,
armed with a lively faith and strong confidence in
Jesus Christ, whom he called to his assistance by fervent prayer, ever came off victorious in all these conflicts, and even with a great increase of virtue, to the
utter confusion of all the powers of hell · so that being

now enabled by the gift of God, to tread under his feet serpents and scorpions, the very crocodiles obeyed him. In the mean time he would have willingly debarred himself even of the short time he was obliged to allow to necessary sleep, which he would have gladly spent in prayer, and earnestly prayed that the Lord would enable him to live without it, that he might be wholly intent on his divine love, which, in some measure, as far as his mortal condition could bear was granted to him. Now the great subject of his prayer, both night and day, was *that the will of God might be ever accomplished in all things.*

Shortly afterwards he was again visited by an angel who told him that it was the will of God that he should not only serve him himself, with all purity and perfection, but also that he should assemble a great multitude of religious men together, and train them up, and dedicate them to his divine service, according to the method and rule which had been shown him before. So that now he began to receive all such as came to him, that were desirous to fly from the contagion of the world, and, by penance, present themselves as humble suitors to the mercy of God. After having made them pass through a long and severe noviceship, he admitted them to the monastic profession, incessantly inculcating to them the strict obligation of their institute, as well with respect to flying from all the allurements of the world, as of diligently exercising themselves in the ways of virtue and holiness : adding, that a monk, according to the directions of the gospel, ought *first,* to renounce the world in general : *second-ly,* all disorderly affections of flesh and blood to his nearest kindred and worldly friends ; and, in the *last place,* the most difficult of all, he ought to renounce and deny himself, take up his cross and follow Christ.

As the number of those that resorted to him in-creased every day, he distributed them into different classes and monasteries, appointing to each of them their regular exercises and different employments, ac-cording to their several abilities and dispositions, and making himself all to all, not only by a general solici-tude for their spiritual progress, but also by his readi-ness to serve even the least of them in the meanest offices, so as to make himself, on every occasion, their cook—their gardener—their porter—and especially their *infirmarian,* by the tender care he always show-ed to *the sick,* on whom he attended both night and day.

He delivered to all his monks the rules he had re-ceived from heaven, appointing for them a very mod-erate food, a mean habit, and no more sleep than ne-cessity required.   He labored to inspire them with a well-grounded *humility,* as the necessary foundation of all virtue, without which the spiritual edifice of a religious life is sure to fall to the ground.   To exclude all ambition, or desire of preferment and superiority,

he would not even allow his monks to be promoted to
the priestly dignity, choosing that they should rathe₁
remain in the humble condition of laics ; and therefore,
till God sent him some priests, who desired to be ad-
ꞏmitted to his congregation (for such as these he did
ot refuse, but received with great respect), he was
forced to have recourse to some neighboring clergy-
men, requesting them to come and say mass, and administer the holy communion to the religious in his
monasteries. But above all things he recommended
a ready and perfect *obedience*, as the very soul of religion, and the shortest way to religious perfection, by
divesting them of their own will, and making them
securely find, and faithfully follow, in all things, the
blessed will of God.

He had the bowels of a tender parent towards all
his children, but a more particular affection and compassion for the aged and sick, as also for young boys,
serving them, and exercising the works of mercy towards them with his own hands, and feeling a more
than ordinary solicitude for their comfort and instruction. Nothing could equal the respect he retained for
the clergy in general, more particularly the bishops of
God's church, or the zeal he had for the purity of the
catholic faith, which made him conceive a horror
against the Arians and other heretics, as enemies of
God's truth : and, as at that time the writings of Origen, who had unhappily blended the errors of the

Platonic philosophers with the Christian doctrine, were
very much handed about among the Egyptian monks,
to the great prejudice of their souls, Pachomius declared open war against them, and prohibited all his
monks the reading of them.

Being likewise animated by an extraordinary zeal
for the salvation of the souls, not only of his own religious, but also of all others whom he saw in want of
spiritual assistance, and observing in that part of the
country many of the meaner sort of people employed
in the care of the cattle, who had for want of having
a church at hand to which they might resort, lived in
great ignorance, deprived of the use of the sacraments; to remedy so great an evil, he applied to the
bishop of Tentyra, and procured that a church should
be built for them in the neighboring village; and as it
was some time before they were provided with clergy-
men, he went himself with his monks, on Sundays
and holidays, and read lessons out of the divine Scriptures, proper for their instruction, in so edifying a manner, with such a saintly air of devotion, and so serene
and heavenly a countenance, as made his auditory receive him, and attend to him, not as to a man, but as
to an angel sent them from heaven. Numbers upon
this occasion were brought over by his instructions
from the gulf of infidelity and error to the christian
faith; and the more so, because he, on his part, employed not only the words of exhortation and doctrine

in their behalf, but also the more effectual arms of fervent prayer for their conversion, accompanied with
many sighs and tears.

About this time the great St. Athanasius, bishop of
Alexandria, in visiting the churches of Egypt, which
were all under his jurisdiction, came also to Tabenna,
where our Saint had established his monasteries.
Pachomius, who had venerated this holy patriarch, as
the great pillar of the church of God, and respected
him much more for his sanctity than for his dignity,
caused all his monks to go out to meet him, singing
psalms and hymns, and to receive him with great reverence and joy; yet so that he himself would not appear at their head, nor any way distinguish himself
amongst them, but hid himself in the crowd, to avoid
being particularly taken notice of by that great prelate, who, as he feared, would promote him against his
will to the priestly dignity, at the recommendation of
the bishop of Tentyra his diocesan, who very much
desired to have him ordained priest.

Whilst Pachomius was thus happily employed in
conducting a great number of holy souls in the ways
of eternal life, and directing them to perfection, both
by word and example, his sister, hearing the fame of
his sanctity, came one day to his monastery, desiring
to see him. The Saint, who never admitted any woman into his monastery, sent her word by the porter
that he was alive and well, and requested she would

return home in peace, and not make herself uneasy on
account of her not seeing him in this transitory life;
but added, that if she desired to follow the same kind
of life as he did, in order to find mercy with God, and
secure to her soul a happy eternity, she should think
seriously of it ; and if this should be her fixed resolution, he would give orders for building a proper mansion for her at a distance from his monastery, where
she might serve the Lord, under regular discipline, in
all purity of soul and body, and in time engage many
others, by her example, to dedicate themselves in like
manner to the love and service of Christ in a religious
life : for, to expect to find, said he, any solid rest, content, or happiness, but in works of godliness, as long
as we carry this body of death about us, is a thing
utterly impossible. His sister hearing this, shed a
flood of tears ; and being at the same time touched
with a powerful grace, determined upon the spot to
choose that better part which he had so strenuously
recommended to her ; and accordingly, as soon as the
monastery which he ordered to be built for her, was
in readiness, she entered into it, and there served our
Lord with such sanctity and perfection, as to attract
many others of her sex to join in her holy undertaking, and consecrate themselves to Christ under her
direction. This was the origin of the nuns of the order of St. Pachomius, to whom the Saint gave the
same rules as to his monks : and took the strictest

care imaginable, that the one should have little or no communication with the other, so that he might cut off all occasions of temptation.

Among the disciples of St. Pachomius, the most illustrious imitator of his virtues, and his successor in sanctity, was St. Theodore, whose history is briefly as follows: He was born of noble and wealthy christian parents, according to the world. His father dying when he was very young, left him heir to a plentiful estate, under the care of a tender and affectionate mother. But he had a better Father in heaven, who showed his great care and tender love for him by an early weaning of his heart from the love of the world and its vanities; and sweetly inviting him to his divine service in a very extraordinary manner, when he was as yet scarcely twelve years old. His conversion happened upon a solemn occasion of public mirth, whilst a great feast was preparing in his house, which abounded in rich furniture and all kind of worldly wealth, when behold he was suddenly visited with a heavenly light in his interior, which clearly convinced him of the nothingness of transitory things, accompanied with a strong call to give up all to follow Christ. "Alas! what would it profit thee, O unhappy Theodore," said he to himself on this occasion, "if thou shouldest even gain the whole world, and enjoy all the temporal delights the world can give, shouldst thou lose by these means the eternal goods and immortal joys of heaven!

for there is no pretending to pass thy life here in these
vain pleasures and delights, and yet expect to merit
everlasting rewards hereafter." With these sentiments he withdrew himself into a private closet, and
there prostrating himself on the floor, with many sighs
and tears he prayed thus to our Lord : " O Almighty
God, who knowest all the secrets of hearts, thou knowest there is not any thing in this world that I prefer
before the love of thee. Wherefore I implore thy
mercy, that thou wouldst direct me to accomplish thy
holy will, enlightening my poor soul, that she may
never sleep in the darkness of sin and eternal death,
but being redeemed by thy grace, may be brought to
praise and glorify thee for ever." Whilst he was praying to this effect his mother came in, and finding him
all in tears, asked him who had given him any trouble
or offence, that he should grieve in such a manner, and
separate himself at dinner time from the company ?—
that they had been seeking him every where, and were
greatly concerned about him. He begged of her to
make herself quite easy, and to go to table, but desired withal to be excused from bearing her company.
From this time he accustomed himself, in going to
school, to fast every day till the evening, and frequently to eat nothing for two days; and for two whole
years, whilst he remained in the world, he totally refrained from all delicacies, contenting himself with the
meanest and coarsest kind of food. After some time

he quitted all that he seemed to possess in the world, and entered into a monastery : where he had not been long before he heard of St. Pachomius, and was inspired with a desire of putting himself under his discipline. Having followed the call, he went to Tabenna, was cordially received by the Saint, and, in a short time, by the great fervor with which he applied himself to watching, fasting, and prayer, and to all good works, made a very considerable progress in all virtues.

Whilst Theodore was climbing up the hill of christian perfection, by a constant attention to please God, and omit nothing which he conceived would promote his spiritual advancement, his mother having heard where he was, attempted to bring him back again into the world. Wherefore having obtained letters of recommendation from some bishops, to whom she knew Pachomius could refuse nothing, she went to the monastery of the nuns, and wrote from thence to the holy abbot, desiring that she might see her son. Pachomius called for Theodore, and told him how the case stood ; and that to satisfy his mother's desire, and in consideration of the holy prelates whose letters she had brought, he thought he might go and see her. And will you assure me, reverend father, said Theodore, that after receiving such great lights and calls from God, as I have received, and leaving both my mother and all things else in the world, for the love

of Christ, I shall have nothing to answer to our Lord,
at the last day, if I should go now and see my mother
to gratify flesh and blood, and give this disedification
to my brethren? Nay, said Pachomius, if you don't
judge it expedient for your soul, I don't wish to compel you: for it is far more becoming a true monk
whose profession it is to renounce the whole world,
and himself also, to shun all manner of unprofitable
worldly visits and vain conversation, and to admit of
no other company but of those from whose godly discourse he may be edified in the ways of God. This
refusal, however disagreeable it might be at first to
the mother of Theodore, turned to her great advantage, in order to the salvation of her soul; for in
hopes of meeting with some opportunity, sooner or
later, of seeing her son amongst the other religious,
she resolved to continue with the nuns, and to follow
the same holy way of life. And as to Theodore, his
whole life from this time was so perfect and saint-like
in every regard, that after his death he was enrolled
amongst the saints. His name occurs in the Roman
Martyrology on the twenty-eighth of December.

But to return to St. Pachomius. As he had received unspeakable joy and comfort on occasion of the
fervor of Theodore and many others of his monks,
whom he saw advancing rapidly in the way of religious perfection, so he was exceedingly afflicted when
he met any one, who, under the habit of religion, had

nothing of the spirit of religion, but lived rather according to the flesh, not having as yet put off the old
man of their former worldly·conversation. With such
as these he spared no pains, but employed every means,
such as admonitions—exhortations—corrections—fervent prayers to God, and tears poured forth in their
behalf, in order to obtain for them the grace of a perfect conversion : and did not desist till they were either
brought to a sense of their duty, and reclaimed from
their evil ways, or else, if they proved incorrigible, en·
tirely cut off from his congregation. A young man,
named Silvanus, who had been an actor upon the
stage, quitting his sinful profession, came to put himself under the discipline of the Saint, and was received
in his monastery. But whilst he was here, he led for
some time a careless life, breaking through the rules
of the congregation, and spending his time in entertaining himself and others with his former ridiculous
buffooneries, to the great scandal of his brethren, who
desired the holy abbot to dismiss him. The man of
God, who was very unwilling to send back again into
the world any of his children, employed, besides his
charitable remonstrances and exhortations, which were
without effect, his more potent arm of continual prayer, sighs and tears, for this poor soul ; and then taking
him aside, represented to him, in so strong and powerful a manner, the truths of eternity, the dreadful
judgments that threaten impenitent sinners, with the

rest of the motives that are most proper to excite in
souls both the fear and love of God: that the grace
of God entering into the heart of Silvanus, he was
immediately touched with so lively a sense of his sins,
and such deep compunction for them, as not only entirely to refrain for the time to come from his former
faults, and begin to lead a new life of great edification
to the rest of his brethren, but also in every place, and
in all his occupations to be continually weeping and
lamenting so bitterly for his past crimes, that he could
not refrain from sobbing and mourning, even whilst
he was taking his meal with the other religious.
When his brethren desired him not to afflict himself
to such an excessive degree, since it became even troublesome to them, but rather to restrain these outward
tokens of grief which were no way necessary even to
the most perfect compunction, the true seat of which
dwelt within the heart, he answered, that he would
gladly obey them, and accordingly made all the efforts
he could to refrain from them ; but he found a certain
flame burning within his breast, that would not suffer
him to be quiet. But, said they, what subject or occasion is there for all these flood of tears ? " Ah !"
said he, " how can I help weeping, when I see so
many holy brethren, the dust of whose feet I ought
to venerate, so charitable as to take notice of me ?
When I see a wretch that is come from the playhouse,
quite laden with sins, receive so many good offices !

Alas! I have reason to fear, lest the earth should open under my feet, and swallow me down, as it did Dathan and Abiron, in punishment of my having profaned all that was sacred, after so clear a knowledge and experience of divine grace, by leading so slothful and wicked a life. Wonder not at my weeping. Oh? my brethren, I have just reason to labor to expiate my innumerable sins with ever flowing fountains of tears; and if I could even pour forth this wretched soul of mine in mourning, it would be all too little to punish my crimes." With these sentiments of humility and contrition he made so rapid a progress in virtue and sanctity, as to be admired by the holy abbot himself, who proposed him to the rest of his monks, as a singular pattern of humility, and assured them that neither Theodore himself, nor any of the rest of them, whose lives had been the most innocent, and who seemed, by their good works, to have already trodden Satan under their feet, were near so much out of danger of this enemy rising up against them, and overthrowing them by pride, as Silvanus was, whose perpetual contrition and humility kept the devil at so great a distance, that he could lay no manner of hold on him. This glorious penitent, after eight years spent in thus continually offering to God the sacrifice of a contrite and humble heart, put a happy end to his penitential course of life, by dying the death of the saints: and St. Pachomius gave testimony, that at the

hour of his death a multitude of heavenly spirits conveyed his soul along with them, with great joy, and
presented it as a choice sacrifice to Christ our Lord.

There was another also of the religious whose sanctity was much esteemed by Pachomius, whom he likewise proposed as an extraordinary pattern of virtue
and perfection to the rest of his monks.   His name
was Zacheus; who, after he had for a long time
served the Lord with great diligence and fervor in a
religious state, fell ill of the jaundice, which forsook
him not till his death.   On this occasion he had a cell
appointed him, in which he lived separated from the
rest of the religious ; yet he omitted none of the regular exercises of the community, but was always with
the rest at all the hours of prayer.   He never allowed
himself in his illness any sleep in the day ; and every
night, before he laid himself down to rest, he employed himself for a considerable time in meditating on
some passages of the holy Scriptures, and then signing
his whole body with the sign of the cross, and glorifying God, he took his short repose.   About midnight
he rose again, and continued praising God till the
time of the morning prayers.   His entire food was
only bread and salt, and the whole time that was vacant from other duties, he spent in making mats, and
working with his hands.   In twisting the palm-leaves
which he made use of in his work, though his hands
became so much galled and wounded thereby as often

times to shed blood, yet he never interrupted his work,
nor betrayed the least emotion to impatience. One
of the brethren, on seeing his hands grievously wounded, and all bloody whilst at work, entreated him to
consider his illness, and to spare himself; for that God,
who knew what he suffered, and how much he was
otherwise afflicted by his disease, would not impute it
to him for sin, nor charge him with sloth, if he did
not work ; and as to the community, they expected it
not from him ; but as they willingly exercised hospitality to the greatest strangers, and to all that were in
want, they would, no doubt, take a much greater
pleasure in serving him. Zacheus answered that he
could not possibly think of living without working.
Well, said the other, if you are fixed in your resolution of continuing to work, at least anoint your hands
with oil, to prevent the loss of so much blood. Zacheus followed his advice ; but instead of finding any
ease by the application of the oil to his wounded
hands, the pain increased to such a degree as to become quite insupportable. St. Pachomius came to
visit him on this occasion, and treating him as one
that stood not in need of milk, but was capable of di-
gesting the strongest diet, reprehended him for having
sought this assuagement of his pains, which God had
sent him for his profit, and not having resigned himself wholly to him, but rather trusted in this visible
medicine than in the living God. Zacheus made no

apology for himself, but meekly answered : " Forgive
me, reverend father, and pray to the Lord for me. that
he may vouchsafe in his mercy to remit me this sin
also, together with all my other sins." My author
adds, from the testimony of many of the brethren, that
he bewailed himself for a whole twelvemonth on this
occasion, and observed during that time so strict a fast,
as to eat but once in two days, and that in a small
quantity. Pachomius used to direct such as were
afflicted, or oppressed with sadness, to this holy man,
for he had a wonderful talent of administering comfort to all that were in trouble or affliction of mind
He continued his labors and conflicts to the end;
when in a good old age he passed from temporal sorrows to eternal joys.

St. Pachomius was invited by Varus, the holy bishop
of Panopolis, to come into his diocese, in order to establish some monasteries of his institute. In this way
he visited divers religious houses included in the number of those that were under his direction. On entering into one of these houses, he met the brethren carrying out the corpse of one of the religious, accompanied by his worldly friends and relations, in order
to be buried with a solemn office in an honorable
manner. At the sight of the Saint they all stood
still, desiring him to pray both for themselves and the
deceased brother. Having finished his prayer, understanding in spirit the wretched state of his soul, (for

the man had led a very careless and indolent life), he forbid them to proceed in their psalms, and ordered them to strip off the fine garments with which they had clad him, and to bury him without any solemnity or tokens of honor, which, as the holy abbot assured them, would be rather prejudicial than beneficial to his unhappy soul; which proceeding of the Saint was designed as a warning to all his disciples not to rely so much on wearing the habit, as in leading the life of a religious. After remaining here two days, teaching and instructing his monks, and arming them against the deceits of Satan, a message was brought him from the monastery of Chenoboscium, that one of the religious there, who was near his end, desired to see him, and to have his last blessing before he died. Thither he hastened with the utmost speed : but when he came within two or three miles of the monastery, he heard a heavenly melody in the air, and looking up beheld the soul of the servant of God carried up by angels to heaven, who died at the very instant of time, as the companions of the Saint, to whom he related what he had heard and seen, found when they returned to the monastery.

Pachomius was received with great honor by the bishop, who assigned proper places to him and his monks for the building of their monasteries, which, whilst they were rising up, some wicked men, by the instigation of Satan, pulled down in the night what they had built during the day. On this occasion the Saint preached patience to his people; but God took his cause in hand for one night, whilst these wretches were intent upon their wickedness, they were suddenly consumed by fire, and seen no more. On several other occasions God was pleased to work miracles in favor of the faith and sanctity of his servant Pachomius, of which the following instances may suffice. A woman, who had labored for a long time under an issue of blood, was suddenly cured, by coming behind him, and only touching his habit whilst he was sitting in the church of Tentyra, with Denys the priest. Many others were healed of divers diseases, and delivered from the possession of wicked spirits, by his prayers. A man came to him one day, desiring him to cast the devil out of his daughter. The Saint told him that he and his religious never spoke to women, but that he should send him in any garment that belonged to his daughter, which he would bless in the name of the Lord: and that he trusted in Christ she would be rescued from the power of the enemy. The father accordingly brought him one of her garments, which when the holy abbot beheld, he presently understood in spirit the case of the young woman, viz. that she was guilty of sins of impurity, by which she had violated the vow of chastity she had made to God, and that upon this account the devil had permission to take possession of her. He returned therefore the garment to the father, telling him how the case stood, and that if he desired his daughter should be delivered from the devil, she must first repent, be converted from her sins, promise not to be guilty of them any more, and that then she should find mercy. Her father took her to task, and at length she acknowledged her guilt, with great signs of repentance, and promised, in the most solemn manner, to refrain from committing the like sins for the future. Upon which the man of God gave the father some oil which he had blessed, by the use of which she was presently cured, and never ceased to glorify God, who had delivered her at once, both from the possession of the devil, and from her sinful habit. The Saint on his part was never puffed up with pride or vain glory on account of any of the miraculous cures that God wrought by him; but continuing always in the fear of God, and in a perfect sense of his own nothingness, he kept his soul always even, so as neither to be elevated by good success, nor depressed with evil: and if at any time God did not grant the things for which he petitioned, he was perfectly resigned to the divine will, knowing that to be best, both for himself and for all others, which God ordained, and saw to be most fitting.

One of the religious, who was a diligent imitator of the virtues of the holy abbot, standing one day in prayer, was struck in the foot by a scorpion, and though the torment he suffered on that occasion was extreme, and the pain, together with the poison, had spread itself even to the heart, and threatened him with present death, yet he would by no means interrupt his devotions. nor stir from his place, till he had finished his prayer; and then Pachomius prayed to our Lord in his behalf, and he was presently healed On the other hand Theodore, being afflicted with a violent pain in the head, desired the man of God to pray for his cure: but he answered, that it was far better for him to bear the pain, which God had sent for his profit, with perfect resignation, patience, and humility, how long soever it might continue to afflict him, and to thank his divine Majesty for it, as for a great favor; saying, that a religious man might merit more, and please God better, by patience and conformity to his divine will in sufferings and sickness, than by the most rigorous abstinence, or long continual prayers in the time of health.

And now after our Saint had established his congregation upon a solid foundation, and assembled together a multitude of holy souls, serving God in great perfection, many of whom he had sent before him to heaven, he himself was seized with his last illness a little after Easter, anno 348. In his sickness he preserved always a serene and cheerful countenance: and after having called together the brethren, and made an excellent exhortation to them, begging of them to ever remember all the lessons he had given, to avoid the conversation of heretics, and to be ever vigilant in prayer and all other exercises of virtue, he recommended to them the choice of a successor : and after two days, arming himself with the sign of the cross, and looking with a cheerful aspect on an angel of light, who was sent to conduct him to heaven, he breathed out his holy soul, to take her flight to her heavenly country, upon the ninth of May. His name stands recorded among the Saints in the Roman Martyrology, on the fourteenth of May; and in the Menologies of the Greeks on the fifteenth ; where also they affirm that the number of his monks, before his death, amounted to one thousand four hundred. But Palladius, afterwards bishop of Helenopolis, who has given an abstract of the life of St. Pachomius, in his *Historia Lausiaca*, chap. 38, and who had visited in person the holy inhabitants of the deserts of Egypt, some years after the death of this Saint, affirms that the whole number of the monks, whom St. Pachomius had under his care in all his monasteries, amounted to seven thousand ; and that in his own monastery of Tabenna alone, there were no less than one thousand four hundred monks, who maintained themselves by the labor of their own hands, without being troublesome to any one, and who, at the same time, by their frugal way of living, were enabled also to exercise hospitality, and to give liberal charities to the poor.

ST. AMMON, ABBOT.

From St Athanasius, in his Life of St Antony, chap **32.** Rufinus and Palladius, in their History of the Holy Fathers of the Deserts of Egypt

St. Ammon, or Amon, the first founder of the monasteries of Nitria, and as some authors affirm, the first author of a cenobitical or conventual life, was born of noble and wealthy Egyptian parents in the third century. From his youth he embraced a saintly life, desiring to serve God in perfect purity both of soul and body; but when he arrived at the age of twenty-two, his relations compelled him to marry a christian virgin animated by the like virtuous dispositions as himself, as appeared shortly after; for as soon as they were left alone on their wedding night, Ammon represented to his spouse how much happier and more pleasing to God the state of virginity was, than that of the use of matrimony, strengthening his arguments with the authority of holy Scripture, and at the same time so powerfully exhorting her to preserve the treasure of her virginal purity, and instructing her in the manner of life she should lead to please Christ, the true spouse of virgins, that she willingly agreed that they should live like brother and sister in the same house, in perfect continence, lying in different beds, and only united with the bonds of the spirit, in charity and prayer. After this manner they lived together in the world for the space of eighteen years; Ammon dividing his time in such manner as to dedicate the best part of it to labor, by working in his garden and balm-yard, and the rest to his exercises of prayer and devotion, usually fasting till the evening. At the expiration of this time, their parents and friends, who had obliged them to marry, being now dead, they mutually agreed to live asunder, and each of them to embrace a monastic life. Ammon, therefore, left her in possession of the house, which, in process of time, she converted into a nunnery: many devout virgins resorting to her, and putting themselves under her direction, whilst he retired into the wilderness of mount Nitria, forty miles distant from Alexandria, where he built two cells, and laid the foundations of that admirable religious institute, which was afterwards followed by no less than five thousand religious, who, although dwelling in about fifty different habitations, yet all meeting to their public devotions in one large church, served by eight priests.

As to the particulars of the acts of St. Ammon, after his retiring to mount Nitria, as none of his contemporaries have given us his life at large, we must content ourselves with briefly inserting what is incidentally related of him in the life of St. Antony, chap. 32. Here we are informed by St. Athanasius, *first,*

that St. Ammon, who was united with St. Antony in
the bands of a most holy friendship, frequently visited
him;—*secondly*, that from his childhood to an advanced age, he always lived the life of a saint;—
thirdly, that he was greatly renowned for signs, won
ders, and miraculous graces;—and *fourthly*, that at
the instant of his death, his happy soul was seen by
St. Antony, then at the distance of thirteen day's journey from Nitria, taking her flight to heaven, escorted
by a multitude of celestial spirits. As an instance of
his great favor with God, and how great a lover he
was of modesty and purity, St. Athanasius relates, that
upon a certain occasion, when he was obliged, together
with his disciple Theodore, a man also of great sanctity to pass over the river Lycus, then swelled by sudden rains, he desired Theodore to retire, and keep at a
distance whilst he put off his garments, that they might
not behold each other naked; but whilst he was thinking to strip, he felt a great repugnance to divest himself, through modesty and shame of seeing his own
naked flesh, when behold, being on a sudden seized
with an extacy or trance, he found himself on the
other side of the river, without knowing how he came
thither. Theodore coming up, was surprised to find
he had been so expeditious in passing the river, and
the more so, as he could perceive no marks of moisture
either on his feet or garments, and did not cease to
importune him to let him know how it happened,

which he refused, till after he had promised to keep
the matter a secret as long as Ammon should live.
Though this Theodore be different from St. Theodore,
the disciple of St. Pachomius, yet he has deserved no
less than he, by his extraordinary virtues. a place
amongst the saints, with whom his name stands
enrolled in the Roman Martyrology on the seventh
of January.

Rufinns, in his Lives of the Fathers, chap. 30, and
Palladius, in his *Historia Lausiaca*, chap. 3, relate
several other instances of the grace, miracles, and prophetic spirit of St. Ammon. Whilst he lived retired
in the wilderness, a youth, who had been bit by a
mad dog, was brought to him bound in chains in a
frantic condition. His parents, who accompanied him,
begged that the Saint, who at this time was renowned
for miracles, would cure him. " You demand that of
me which far exceeds my merits; but thus much,"
said he, " I will tell you, if you restore the poor widow
the ox you have privately stolen, your son shall be
healed." They were frightened as well as astonished,
when they heard him speak of the theft, which they
were sensible he could not know but by revelation.
However, having made the restitution which was required, the young man, at the prayer of the servant
of God, was perfectly cured.

On another occasion, when two men, who had come
to visit him in his solitude, found that he stood in need

of a large vessel to keep water for the use of such as
resorted to him, they promised to bring him a vessel
sufficiently capacious for that purpose; the one being
master of a camel, the other of an ass.   The former,
after his return home, repented of his promise, and told
his companion that he would not risk the life of his
camel by loading him with so heavy a burthen.   Well,
said the latter, rather than be worse than my word, I
will venture to lay upon my ass the load which you
say would kill your camel; trusting that the merits of
the man of God will make that possible which appears
impossible.   Having done as he said, the ass carried
the vessel with as much ease as if he felt no burthen
whatever.   When he came to the cell, the Saint commended his faith, and told him that his neighbor had
in the mean while lost his camel by death: and accordingly, on his return home, he found that whilst he
was on his way to the Saint, the camel had been wor-
ried and killed by wolves.

As to the disciples of St. Ammon, as well as the
monks his successors in the congregation of mount
Nitria, they were for a long time after so renowned
for their regular discipline, hospitality and charity, that
Rufinus and Palladius, from their own experience, who
had been some time among them, hesitate not to bestow on them the highest encomiums.   St. Jerome
also, as we learn from his apology against Rufinus,
made a journey on purpose to visit them.   "I want,"

says he, "to Egypt to survey the monasteries of Nitria, and plainly perceived some asps lurking amongst
the choirs of the saints," alluding to the errors of
Origen, which had crept in amongst some of the religious. We also learn from the authors above-named,
that as soon as they and their companions were come
within sight of the monasteries, the religious, according to their custom, came out to meet them, bringing
loaves of bread and pitchers of water to refresh them,
after the fatigue of their journey over those burning
sands; that then they conducted them to the church,
singing psalms, where, after washing and wiping their
feet, they contended which of them should introduce
them into their cells, and there entertain them not
only with all offices of humanity and charity in their
power with regard to their corporal refreshment, but
also with excellent lessons of spirituality for the benefit of their souls; in which they particularly inculcated
the practice of their favorite virtues of humility and
meekness, in which they themselves singularly ex
celled.

For the entertainment of strangers and foreigners,
they had built a large hospital near to the church,
where all that came were welcome to stay as long as
they pleased, although it were for two or three years;
yet so, that after the first seven days they were employed in some kind of work, as all the monks were; or
at least if they were persons of note, in reading such

good books as they put in their hands. They were also to have no conversation together, but to keep silence at least till noon. As to the afternoon, about the ninth hour, "one might stand," says Palladius, chap. 7, "and hear in every one of the monasteries the religious singing hymns and psalms to Christ, and joining prayers with their hymns in so sweet and melodious a manner, that one would be apt to think himself elevated on high, and translated into a heavenly paradise."

About ten miles from Nitria, further on in the wilderness, there was a place named *Cellia*, from the multitude of *cells* that lay every where dispersed up and down. Here such of the Nitrian monks as aspired after greater solitude and perfection made themselves cells, in which they lived as anchorets, at a good distance from each other; never conversing together, or seeing one another, but when they met twice a week at church, unless the case of sickness, or some office of charity, required that any one should visit the cell of another, or break in upon his silence and solitude. In this place, charity, piety, and sanctity, were seen to reign in the utmost perfection.

St. Ammon passed to a better life on the fourth of October, on which day he is commemorated in the Menologies of the Greeks, about the middle of the fourth century.

ST. PAUL THE SIMPLE.

From Rufinus, chap. 31, and Palladius, chap. 28

PAUL, surnamed *the Simple*, from his innocent simplicity, was, by his education, a plain honest husband-
man, who had led a blameless life to the age of sixty,
in a married state, when, upon a certain occasion, having caught his wife in adultery, he resolved to forsake
both her and the world; and after travelling eight
days into the wilderness, addressed himself to St.
Antony, requesting he would receive him into the
number of his disciples, and teach him the way to
save his soul. St. Antony told him he was now too
old to think of becoming a monk, and that he could
never be able to support the difficulties and austerities
of a monastic life, especially in his eremitical way:
"but go," said he, "into the village, and there employ
yourself in working for your bread, and praising God:"
and having said this, he went in and shut his cell.
Paul nevertheless, continued fasting and praying at
the door during three days and three nights, till Antony, at length seeing his faith and perseverance, came
out and told him, that the way to salvation was obedience, and that if he would be his disciple, he must
do all that he said to him; to which Paul readily
gave his assent, and made good his word, by comply-

ing to a title with every injunction of the Saint, how
difficult or irrational soever it seemed to be. Antony,
in order to try him, imposed upon him a variety of
labors, mortifications, and humiliations, till at length
he found him to be a man entirely humble, simple,
and quite according to his own heart. He gave him
therefore a rule of life which he should follow, and
after some time appointed him a cell, at the distance
of three miles from his own, where he frequently visited him; teaching him to spend his solitary hours in
such a manner, as that whilst his hands were at work,
his heart should be in heaven: and as to his corporal
sustenance, he directed him never to eat or drink till
evening, and even then with such moderation as never
to satisfy his appetite, especially in his drink, though
his beverage was nothing but water.

By following these rules, but more particularly by a
constant and fervent application of his soul to God in
mental prayer, Paul quickly arrived at great perfection
in all virtues; amongst which his obedience, as well
as his humility, were particularly remarkable. One
day, when many religious were assembled with St.
Antony, conferring about spiritual matters, on making
frequent mention of the prophets, Paul, who was one
of the company, according to his simplicity, asked
whether the prophets lived before or since the time of
our Saviour? St. Antony, by way of reproving his
putting such an absurd question, made a nod to him,

saying: *Go, hold your peace.* Paul, who had previously resolved to obey every word that Antony said
to him, as if it had been an oracle from God himself,
immediately departed to his cell, and kept there so
trict a silence, that he would not upon any occasion
tter so much as a single word; till Antony hearing
of it, desired him to speak, and asked him the meaning of his long silence? "Why father," said he, "i'
was in obedience to you: for you bid me go and hold
my peace." St. Antony took occasion from hence to
say to the rest of his disciples: "This man condemns
us all; for whereas we are so often wanting in our
obedience to our great Master, who speaks to us from
heaven; he always scrupulously observes every single
word, of what kind soever he hears from my mouth."

By these large steps of obedience and humility,
Paul advanced rapidly towards God, and was rewarded by him with such admirable gifts and graces, as to
work even more and greater miracles than St. Antony
himself; insomuch that this holy abbot used to send
such possessed persons to Paul as he himself could
not cure. An instance of which is thus recorded by
Palladius. A young man, possessed by a most furious and obstinate devil, being brought to Antony, he
told the people, that this evil spirit was one of the
principal demons, and that the power of casting them
out was not as yet given to him, but to the humble and
simple Paul. Having therefore himself conducted

him to Paul, he said: " Here cast out the devil from
this man, that he may return home and glorify God."
" Why don't you do it yourself?" said Paul. " I
have something else to do," replied Antony, and so
hastened back to his cell. Paul fell prostrate in
prayer, and then rising up said to the devil, in his
innocent way, " Get thee gone out of the man : father
Antony says thou must go out." The devil called
him a foolish old man, and told him he would not:
and when he urged him a second time, repeating
again that Antony said he must out, he abused both
him and Antony, calling them by contemptuous
names, and still refused to depart. " If thou wilt
not go out," said Paul, "I will go and tell Jesus
Christ, and it shall be worse for thee." The devil
broke out into blasphemies against Christ, and obstinately kept his hold. The holy man therefore went
out of his cell, in the broiling heat of the sun at noon-
day (which, in Egypt, says my author, is not unlike
the Babylonian furnace), and standing upon a rock,
addressed his prayer to Jesus Christ crucified, protesting in his simplicity, that he would neither come down
from the rock, nor eat or drink, till he was pleased to
hear him, and to force the devil out of the man
when, behold, whilst he was at prayer, the devil roar
ed out, " I go, I go, I suffer violence, this is an intolerable tyranny ; I am departing from the man, never,
never more to return. It is Paul's humility and sim

plicity casts me out: I know not whither I must go."
With these words the man was presently delivered;
and as a token of the devil's departure, a serpent of
an unusual length was seen at the same time to crawl
towards the red sea.

Many other still greater miracles were wrought by
the prayers of this Saint; but what is related of him
in an ancient author, published by Rosweydus, in the
7th book of the Lives of the Fathers, c. 23. is still
more admirable; viz. that he had received the gift
from God, of reading in the countenances of the
brethren their very thoughts, and the whole state of
their souls. Thus, one day, whilst the religious were
entering into the church, he saw all of them go in
with a great serenity and brightness on their countenance, attended by their good angels full of joy, except
one who appeared black and gloomy, having on either
side of him a devil, who held him with a bridle,
whilst his good angel followed behind at a distance,
and appeared sad and sorrowful. The man of God,
on seeing this, spent the whole time they were at
church in weeping and lamenting for his soul, which
he understood to be in the deplorable state of mortal
sin; but on looking at him when they came out
again, he found him quite changed,—his countenance
now bright and beautiful,—his good angel rejoicing,
and the devils standing at a distance, grieving for
having lost their prey. At the sight of this wonder-

15

ful change, the Saint could not contain his joy, but
broke out into the praises of God, extolling aloud the
wonders of his mercy, manifested in behalf of poor
sinners.   Having related what he had seen, he earnestly entreated the converted monk, for the glory of
God, and the edification of his brethren, to declare
what change he had experienced in his interior, which
could occasion the sudden and wonderful alteration he
had remarked in his exterior.   In compliance with
the request of the Saint, he publicly confessed, that
his soul had been, through a habit of impurity, in a
most wretched condition, but that upon hearing those
words, of God, by the prophet Isaias, read in the
church, (*Be clean, take away the evil of your devices
from my eyes, cease to do perversely, learn to do well,
—and then if your sins be as red as scarlet, they shall
be made white as snow.—If you be willing, and will
hearken to me, you shall eat the good things of the
land; but if you will not, and will provoke me to
wrath, the sword shall devour you, because the mouth
of the Lord hath spoken it*), he found himself not
only strongly affected with a sense of the heinousness
of his sins, had a horror and compunction for them,
joined with a great love of the infinite goodness and
mercy of God, but had also firmly resolved on the
spot to renounce his evil ways, and dedicate himself
henceforward in good earnest to the love and service
of so good a God; and that this had been the sub-

ject of his thoughts and prayers during the whole
time he was in church. Upon this declaration of
their penitent brother, all the monks that were present magnified the mercies of God, who so readily for
gives the greatest sinners, when, like the prodigal son,
they return to him with a contrite and humble heart
Whilst this whole passage, as recorded by our author,
is an instance of the wonderful efficacy of a perfect
contrition, in the speedy reconciliation it effects between
the sinner and God, it shows at the same time the
wonderful efficacy of the prayers and tears of our
Saint, which procured for this sinner the effectual
grace of a perfect contrition.

St. Paul the Simple is registered amongst the saints
in the Roman Martyrology on the seventh of March.

ST. MACARIUS THE ELDER.

From Rufinus, chap. 28. Palladius, chap. 19, 20, and
other ancient Records

THE lustre of the sanctity and miracles of this Saint
shine forth in an extraordinary manner in the history
of the primitive religious of the deserts of Egypt.
Besides one of the same name who attended on St.
Antony the last fifteen years of his mortal life, sup

posed ᴏ be one of the two disciples that buried him, of whom we know few other particulars, there were also two others greatly celebrated by antiquity for their sanctity and miracles, each of them cotempora- ries with, if not also disciples of St. Antony, and both honored with the priestly character : the *elder*, by some authors sirnamed *the Egyptian* and the *younger*, *the Alexandrian*, from the former being a native of Egypt, and the latter of Alexandria.

Macarius *the Elder*, or *the Egyptian*, was born about the year 300. Being as yet a youth, he retired into a cell near his village, where he began to serve God with such perfection as to be held in the highest estimation by the whole neighborhood, and thought worthy to be promoted by his bishop to the minor orders. But his humility, seeking to decline the office and ministry of a clerk, induced him to retire to a dis- tant solitude, where he might be at liberty, without let or hinderance, to practice an anchoretical life ; work- ing with his hands for his subsistence, whilst his heart was in the mean time conversing with God. Here a certain secular, of a religious disposition, observing the penitential life he led, came in order to minister to him, and assist him in selling his baskets. But as great trials, in one shape or other, are commonly the attendants or forerunrers of the most eminent sancti- ty, Macarius met with a very severe one, upon the fol- lowing occasion.

A young woman in the neighboring village was un-happily seduced and corrupted by a fellow of the neigh-borhood. On being found with child by her parents and friends, and interrogated concerning the person that had corrupted her, she by the suggestion of the devil, said it was by that hermit who passed for a Saint, meaning Macarius. Upon this the whole town was in an uproar, and going out, they dragged the servant of God out of his cell into the village, where, hanging pots and pans about his neck, they led him through all the highways, crying aloud to all they met: "This hermit is the villain that has seduced our girl;" beating him at the same time in so unmerciful a manner, that it was expected he would have died under their hands; nor did they desist, till at the re-monstrances of an old man whom they met, they con-sented to let him go, provided any responsible person would become a surety for his maintaining the girl and her child. His friend who had followed him all the way, and been insulted on his account, for having given testimony before to his sanctity, undertook to be responsible for him; and having delivered him out of their hands, brought him back to his cell, where he was now obliged to redouble his labors night and day in making baskets, in order to have wherewithal not only to procure food for himself, but also to furnish a maintenance for the unhappy woman by whom he had been thus basely calumniated. He bore this heavy cross with wonderful cheerfulness till the time the young woman fell in labor, and suffered such extraordinary pains for several days, without being able to be delivered, as brought her to a sense of her crime, when she acknowledged the wrong to Macarius, and declared who was the real father of the child. This gladsome news having presently come to the ears of the good man, the friend of the Saint, he ran with great joy to announce to him the joyful tidings, adding, that all the people were coming out to beg his pardon for the wrong they had done him. Macarius, on hearing this, being more afraid of honor than of humiliations and disgrace, would not wait for their coming, but presently withdrew himself into the desert of Scete, or Scithi, being then about thirty years of age.

This desert, in which no man had dwelt before, was of a vast extent, but so destitute of all the necessaries of life, that it was hard to meet with even a drop of water among the burning sands, and the little that could be found, was of so very disagreeable a taste and smell, as to render it unfit for use. Hither Macarius went, by divine inspiration, to seek a solitude, to which no way nor path conducted; and here he began to lay the foundation of that sublime perfection to which God afterwards raised him, and to which many others were raised by his means, who, in process of time, followed him into this frightful wilderness, and put themselves under his discipline, whose number, in a short time, became very considerable, and amongst whom were several eminent saints; for such was the general character of the solitaries of Scete, for the austerity and sanctity of their lives, that they were looked upon by all the rest as models of religious perection. Macarius had been about ten years in this desert, when the number of the brethren increasing, it was thought necessary that a priest should be ordained for them, to feed them both with the word of God and the holy sacraments; on which occasion the Saint was obliged to accept of the priestly order and to execute its functions amongst his religious; being already so far favored by divine grace, as to have received from God the power of casting out evil spirits, and of working other wonderful miracles, together with the spirit of prophecy, and a foreknowledge of future events.

As an instance of his prophetic spirit, Palladius relates how he often forewarned his disciple John against the spirit of covetousness, telling him, that if he did not mortify his unhappy inclination to worldly pelf, as he labored under the vice of Giezi, so he should incur the punishment of Giezi. Which happened accordingly, when fifteen or twenty years after the Saint's death, appropriating to himself what should have been given to the poor, he was struck with the leprosy in so terrible a manner, that there was not one sound place to be discovered in his body. The same author relates also several instances of his power over evil spirits, in casting them out, and destroying their magical operations by his prayers, as in the case of a woman that was bewitched in so strange a manner as to appear to herself and friends metamorphosed into a mare, but was delivered by the Saint's pouring upon her head some holy water which he had blessed. The Saint, on sending her home, admonished her never to neglect the public worship of the church, nor the frequentation of the sacraments; for that the enemy could not have had this power over her, had she not, for five weeks, kept away from the sacred mysteries.

Many were the miracles whereby God evinced the sancity of his servant Macarius, and some of them of the first magnitude. It happened that a murder was committed in one of the places bordering upon the wilderness wherein the man of God dwelt, and that an innocent man was accused thereof, who fled for refuge to the cell of the Saint. The people having pursued him, and found him, were for binding him, and carrying him off, in order to deliver him up to justice. The man strongly pleaded his own innocence, protesting by all that was sacred, that he knew nothing of the murder; whilst they, on the contrary, insisted upon taking him away, alledging, that they should be called to an account themselves if they let him escape. Macarius having enquired where they had buried the murdered man, accompanied them to the place, when kneeling down by the grave, and invoking the name of Jesus Christ, he said to the standers by; "The Lord will now show whether this man be guilty or not." Then raising his voice, he called on the dead man by his name, and conjured him, in the name of Christ, to tell whether this was the man that had murdered him; when behold, a tremendous loud voice was heard to issue from the grave, declaring that he was not the man. Upon this all the by-standers, struck with dread and astonishment, fell prostrate on the ground, at the feet of the man of God, earnestly requesting that he would put one question more to the deceased, to learn from him by whom it was that he had been murdered. "No," replied the Saint, "it is enough for me to clear the innocent; it is not my business to detect the guilty; for who knows, if he be suffered to live longer, but he may have the grace to do penance for his crime?"

A certain heretic of the sect called *Hieracites*, a branch of the *Manichean heresy*, coming into the wilderness, endeavored not only to corrupt the brethren, with his captious arguments, but had the temerity also to attack Macarius upon the score of his faith in the presence of many of the religious, and to oppose to the solidity of the Saint's reasonings from the Scripture, delivered with his usual meekness and simplicity, a number of such frothy words and sophisms as are but too apt to impose upon the weak and ignorant. Wherefore the man of God, apprehending lest the faith of the by-standers should be endangered on this occasion, proposed instead of *contend not in words, for it is to no profit, but to the subversion of the hearers*, 2 Tim. ii. 14. that they should go out to the burying place of the religious, and put the cause upon this issue, viz. ·that he who could raise a dead man to life should be acknowledged to be the teacher of God's truth, and consequently that his faith should be followed. This proposal being universally applauded, the heretic consented, provided that Macarius should be first to make the trial. When therefore they had arrived at the cemetery the Saint prostrating himself on one of the graves, employed some time in silent prayer; and then lifting up his eyes to heaven, he said: "Be pleased, O Lord, to make it manifest to all here present, which of us two holds the right faith, by restoring this dead man to life." With this having called the brother that had been last buried by name, he presently answered; and upon opening the grave, by removing all the earth that was laid upon him, was taken out alive and presented to the man of God, to the great astonishment as well as confusion to the heretic, who immediately fled away, and never durst show his face any more in Scete.

But let us pass from the miracles of Macarius to his virtues. We find the eminent sanctity for which

he has been so justly admired by all succeeding ages,
was built upon its true foundation, *viz.* a knowledge
and contempt of himself, united with a profound hu
mility, which was always apparent by his ever joyfully embracing humiliations, and flying from honors
and applause. Those were always his most welcome
guests who abused or ridiculed him most; to such he
more freely opened himself, whereas he was ever silent
and reserved with those who came, as many did, to
hear him speak of the things of God, or showed him
any particular marks of honor or esteem : this was so
generally known and observed that at length such as
came with a desire to hear his heavenly lessons, would
on purpose, begin their conversation, by telling him
the many ridiculous or wicked things of which they
had heard him to have been guilty in his youth, and
then they were sure to please him best. The devil
himself was obliged to acknowledge that it was the
humility of the Saint, and not his extraordinary austerities, that had kept him hitherto out of his reach.
Having appeared to him one day, as he was returning
to his cell, laden with palm-leaves for his work he endeavored, but was not able, to strike him with a
sharp scythe which he held in his hand. Upon which
he cried out: " It is a hard case, O Macarius, that I
should suffer so much from thee, and yet not be able
to hurt thee : whereas in point of fasting and watching, I do a great deal more than thou dost; for

though thou fastest and watchest often, yet sometimes thou eatest and sleepest; but as to me, I never eat, nor close my eyes to sleep. Nevertheless, I acknowledge there is one thing in which thou overcomest me." "What is it?" said the Saint. "Thy humility," replied the devil: "Oh! there is nothing else conquers me." Whereupon the Saint, having stretched forth his hand to heaven in prayer, the enemy presently vanished.

The humility of the Saint was ever accompanied with an extraordinary meekness: as these two sister-virtues generally walk hand in hand. By this his extraordinary meekness he wrought greater wonders, in conducting souls to God, than by any of his other miracles. An instance hereof appears in the case of a pagan priest, who having been incited to fury, by the contemptuous treatment he had met with from one of the religious, was not only appeased, but gained over on the spot to Jesus Christ, by the mildness and sweetness wherewith he was treated by St. Macarius: insomuch, that he immediately quitted the world to become a religious man, and gave occasion, by his example, to the conversion of many other pagans.

The humility of Macarius was also accompanied with a wholesome fear of the divine justice, together with a deep sense of, and an extraordinary compunction for his sins, which continued with him even to the end of his life. In proof whereof, we read, that shortly before his death, when the monks of Nitria invited him to come over to their mountain that they might receive his blessing before he departed to the Lord, declaring, that otherwise they would all come in a body to visit him; he complied indeed with their request; but when the multitude of the brethren were assembled about him, expecting to hear the word of God from his mouth, instead of a sermon, he entertained them with a flood of tears, saying: "Let us weep, my brethren, let us weep whilst we have time. Let torrents of tears flow from our eyes to wash away the stains of our sins, before we depart hence into another world, where our tears will come too late, and only serve to nourish the flames of our torments." At these words, accompanied by the tears of the Saint, all the congregation wept, and cast themselves down on the ground, to beg the assistance of his prayers.

A certain brother desiring to know from the Saint how he might secure the salvation of his soul: "Fly," said the man of God, "from the company of men—keep close to thy cell, and there weep continually for thy sins, and as the best penance for them, be equally careful to mortify thy tongue by keeping silence, as thy belly, by fasting and abstinence." To the like effect he said one day to the brethren as they were coming out of church after mass: "Fly, my brethren.

fly." " Whither, O father," said one of them, " wouldst thou have us fly? can we go farther from the world than we are at present in this vast solitude?" The Saint put his finger to his tongue, and said, I mean that we should fly from this; and saying no more, he entered into his cell, and there remained in silence and recollection.

The prayers of St. Macarius were in a manner incessant, particularly in the mental and contemplative way. He is said to have been often almost in an ecstasy, ravished as it were out of himself, and for the greatest part of his time entertaining himself with God in so absolute a state of insensibility, as to forget every created object. That he might apply himself with more freedom to God in prayer, he had made a passage under ground from his cell, to a certain cave at about half a furlong distance, to which he frequently retired, and there kept himself concealed from all other company, to the end he might be alone with God, free from the interruption of the visits of the many strangers who resorted to him on account of the great reputation of his sanctity. He had, during five years, been pressed by frequent thoughts to proceed further into the desert to try what he should there discover; but as it was his maxim to do nothing rashly, he examined well these suggestions, lest they should prove to be temptations. The inclination, however, still continuing, he concluded it to be God's holy will, and ac-

cordingly following the call, he penetrated into the remote parts of the wilderness, where he found a lake
of water, and in it a small island, inhabited by two
solitaries, who had dwelt there for the space of forty
years, quite secluded from the conversation of mortals,
and in so great a state of perfection, that Macarius,
after having seen and conversed with them, according
to his humble way of thinking of himself, professed
to the religious of Nitria, who had some time after requested he would deliver a discourse of edification in
the monastery of Abbot Pambo, " that for his part he
was not worthy to be called a *monk*, but that he had
seen *monks* indeed : and that the lesson he had learnt
of them was, that to be a *monk indeed*, a man must
absolutely renounce every thing in this world, and
that if he thought himself too weak to practice this
renunciation, in the manner they did, he should return
back to his cell, there to sit and bewail his sins."

The zeal that Macarius had for his own spiritual
advancement, carried him also another time a fifteen
days' journey from the desert of Scete, to visit St. Antony, then residing on his mountain. When he arrived with his strength quite exhausted by the fatigue
of his long travelling through those burning sands, he
knocked at the door of the Saint's cell : Antony coming forth, asked him who he was? and upon his answering that he was Macarius, he went in again, and
shut the door ; for although he had a great desire for

a long time to see him, knowing his extraordinary
sanctity, yet he was willing to make this trial of his
patience and humility. Macarius remained at the
door till Antony, thinking he had now sufficiently put
his patience to a trial, opened it to him; and having
lovingly embraced him, entertained him with the best
that his cell could afford. In the evening, Antony
prepared a certain quantity of the leaves of palm-
trees for himself to work on at making of mats; Macarius, was ever a lover of manual labor, and hated
idleness, desired to be employed in the same manner;
and thus having sat down together, whilst they worked
with their hands, they entertained each other with
heavenly discourses and the praises of their great Master. In the morning Antony was surprised to behold
the quantity of matting that Macarius had made during the night; and taking his hands he kissed them,
affirming, that there was much virtue in them. I
know not whether it was upon this, or some other occasion, that he saw the Holy Spirit descend upon Macarius; for I find it recorded of St. Antony, that he
himself declared he had seen the Holy Ghost descend
upon three eminent servants of God, who in their lives
appeared to be in an extraordinary manner replenished
with his graces, and that these three were, St. Athanasius, St. Pachomius, and St. Macarius.

As to the penitential exercises practised by St. Macarius and his disciples the solitaries of Scete, they ap-

pear more the objects of our admiration than of our imitation, especially in the point of fasting; for we read in some ancient writers, that it was their custom to eat but once in the week; but as to St. Macarius himself, he told his disciple Evargius upon occasion of his complaining of a violent thirst which he felt in the excessive noonday heat of the Egyptian climate, that for his own part he had never for twenty years satisfied, himself either in point of eating, or drinking, or sleeping;—that he always weighed out the small quantity of bread he eat;—that he always drank his water by measure; and instead of lying down, leaned always against a wall, when he stole, as it were, the little sleep which he could not absolutely dispense with.

But if he was so perfectly mortified in his eating, drinking and sleeping, we may truly say he was as much, or more so with respect, not only to his passions, but his whole interior, and that he himself practised diligently the excellent lessons he had so often taught his disciples. He used frequently to say, that he only was a *true monk*, who overcame himself in all things : that the way to escape the death of the soul by sin, was to receive and embrace *contempt* like *praise*, *poverty* like *riches*, and *hunger* and *want*, like *plenty* and *feasting*. A young man having once addressed himself to our Saint, desiring to learn of him the practice of religious perfection, he sent him to a

place where there were a great many dead bodies, and
bid him treat them with reviling, scornful language,
and such other like affronts and injuries, and even to
pelt them with stones to try if he could provoke them
to passion.   Having done as he was ordered, when he
returned back, the Saint asked him how the dead had
received all those outrages, and what they had said?
He answered that they had said nothing.   On the
day following he sent him again, and bid him treat
them with honor, with fine speeches and commenda-
tions, and then see how they would behave ; and as
they still remained equally insensible both to his good
and mal-treatment, the Saint told him, that if he would
be a perfect religious man, he must follow their example, and neither suffer himself to be provoked to
anger or resentment by ill treatment, nor to be puffed
up with the esteem or praises of men, but always to
have his eye on Jesus Christ, and seek to please him
only.

St. Macarius had now arrived at the age of seventy-
six, when a violent persecution was raised against all
the religious by Lucius the Arian, who, after the death
of St. Athanasius, had usurped the see of Alexandria,
by the favor of the emperor Valens.   This unhappy
man, finding the monks in general averse to his wicked tenets, and the people very much influenced by
their example, to adhere to the catholic faith, led out
a multitude of soldiers into the deserts, in order to

oblige these servants of God, by all manner of cruel‧ ties, to renounce the ancient faith. A great number of the solitaries of mount Nitria were martyred on this occasion, and a vast multitude of other religious, to- gether with many bishops, priests, and deacons, were sent into banishment. Amongst these were Macarius, and his name-sake, the other St. Macarius, of Alexau- dria, St. Isidore, of Scete, and St. Pambo, the holy abbot of Nitria; who, by the orders of Lucius, were taken out of their cells privately in the night, and car- ried away into a certain island in Egypt, which was inhabited only by pagans, to the end that they might have no opportunity of exercising their priestly func- tions, nor meet with any comfort or support from any one. There was in this island an ancient temple of the devils, for which the inhabitants had so great a veneration, that it was this that kept them in their idolatry. But behold the wonders of God! as soon as the boat that brought the saints thither drew near the land, the devils who inhabited the temple were all in an uproar, and one of them presently entered into the daughter of the priest of the temple, whom the people venerated almost as much as their god, and caused in her strange and violent agitations and con- tortions, accompanied with such loud shrieks and cries as reached the very heavens, and drew all the people about her. In this condition she ran about amongst the people, falling down sometimes and rolling herself

on the ground, foaming and gnashing with her teeth,
till all of a sudden she was lifted up into the air, and
carried to the place where the saints by this time were
set on shore, the people all following to see what would
become of her. Here she fell down at the feet of
Macarius and his companions, and cried out (the
devil speaking by her mouth, as he did heretofore by
the girl at Philippi, Acts xvi.) "Ah! ye servants of
Jesus Christ, how terrible is your power! ye servants
of the great God, why do you come to drive us away
from a place of which we have so long kept possession!
Here have we hidden ourselves, after we were expelled
from the rest of the land; for you have banished us
from the towns and villages, from the mountains and
hills, and even from the places where none before you
durst inhabit. We expected to be quiet at least in
this little island, in the midst of bogs and marshes,
and now you come to deprive us of our last refuge,"
&c. Whilst the devil was uttering these and other
similar words, by the mouth of the girl, the Saints, on
their part, made use of the power their Lord had conferred on them, and commanded the devil, by the sacred and awful name of Jesus Christ, the Son of God,
to depart out from her; whilst he, unable to resist,
was immediately constrained to obey, and left the girl
stretched out on the ground as if dead. The Saints
prayed for her, and lifting her up from the ground,
presented her to her father in perfect health, both of

mind and body.   Then taking occasion from what had
passed, they began to preach Jesus Christ to the people, already disposed, by the miracle they had seen,
to hearken to their words ; and so great was the blessing God gave to their preaching, that instantly both
the priest himself, with his daughter, and all his kindred, cast themselves down at the feet of these new
apostles, desiring to learn of them what they must do
to be saved.   All the people of the island, by their
example, were immediately converted to Jesus Christ,
and embraced the faith with so much fervor, that they
presently demolished their temple which they had before so much revered—built up a church in its place,
and after proper instructions received baptism.   Thus
the expulsion of these servants of God contributed to
the propagation and illustration of the faith for which
they were banished, and to the confusion of their enemies and persecutors, who, upon receiving the news
of what had passed, gave orders to have them removed
again out of the island, and privately conveyed back
to their former solitudes.

St. Macarius outlived this persecution many years;
and after having attained the age of ninety, sixty of
which he spent in the wilderness, he passed to the enjoyment of his God about the year 390 or 391.   His
name is recorded among the Saints in the Roman Martyrology on the fifteenth of January.

There are extant in the *Bibliotheca SS. Patrum*,

fifty homilies, or discourses of piety, which St. Macarius made to his religious on several occasions, truly worthy of his spirit and sanctity.

ST. MACARIUS OF ALEXANDRIA.

From Palladius, Bishop of Helenopolis, some time disciple of the Saint, Historia Lausiaca, chap. 19, Rufinus and others

ST. MACARIUS, commonly called the Alexandrian, to distinguish him from the other St. Macarius, of whom we have been just treating, was born at Alexandria about the beginning of the fourth century. In his younger days he endeavored to obtain an honest livelihood by selling fruit, sweetmeats, and such like wares, till being called by God to greater perfection, he forsook all things to follow Christ in an anchoretical life, and put himself under the direction of St. Antony, in order to learn from so great a master the true science of the saints. The progress he made in this school of grace, was so extraordinary, that he became qualified to instruct many others in the way of perfection, as St. Antony himself saw and acknowledged, when one day Macarius being with him, and asking him for some beautiful palm-branches, which he kept for his work, he told him it was written : *Thou shalt not covet thy neighbor's goods :* at which words the palm-branches in an instant actually withered away, and grew quite as dry as if they had been touched by the fire, which St. Antony, seeing, told Macarius that he perceived the Spirit of God had taken up his abode in his soul ; and that from this time forward he should look upon him as the heir and successor of all those graces and gifts which the divine bounty had bestowed upon himself.

Shortly after the devil seeing him in his wilderness exceedingly fatigued with travelling, and quite exhausted for want of food, suggested to him, since you have received the grace of Antony, why do not you make use of his power, and ask the necessary supply of food and strength from God, that you may be enabled to pursue your journey ? The Saint replied : " The Lord is my strength—the Lord is my glory ;— but as for thee, Satan, be gone, and don't presume to tempt one that is determined to be the servant of his divine Majesty." The devil upon this assumed the shape of a camel that appeared to be wandering about the desert, laden with all kinds of necessaries for life, and coming up he stood near to the Saint, who suspecting it to be a diabolical illusion, prayed to God, and presently the phantom sunk into the earth, and disappeared.

From the desert of Thebais, where St. Antony re

sided, Macarius passed to that of Scete, and partly
there or on mount Nitria, or in the neighboring wilderness called Cellia, or the place of the cells, he
spent the greatest part of his mortal life.   In this last
place he was, on account of his eminent sanctity, ordained priest, and in that quality had the charge of
the church, and the superiority and direction of all the
saintly souls that lived dispersed in separate cells
throughout that holy solitude.   Here his virtues shin-
ed forth with such extraordinary lustre and miracles,
as to make him be looked upon, both then and ever
since, as one of the brightest lights of the Church of
God in his time, and on that account he had also a
great share in the persecution which fell in a particular manner upon the religious of these quarters, under
Valens the Arian emperor; when he was also, as we
have seen above, sent into banishment with some
other servants of God, who had miraculously converted the inhabitants of the island to which they were
banished from idolatry to the faith of Christ.

As to the employment of his time in these wildernesses, we find he distributed it in such manner, as
to spend the best part of it in prayer, in which he exercised himself a hundred times in the space of every
twenty-four hours ; another part he dedicated to manual labor, in order to obtain his livelihood : and the
remainder he gave to those that came to consult him
about the affairs of their souls, and to receive his in-

structions. In the mean time, the austerities of the penitential life to which he condemned himself were so great, that we may truly say, they were more to be admired than imitated. His fasts were long and rigorous:—for seven years he never eat anything but raw herbs or pulse, moistened with cold water, without bread, or anything whatever that had come near the fire.—For three years more he lived only upon four or five ounces of bread in the day, with water in proportion. Once, for the space of twenty days, he labored to live without any sleep whatever; and to this purpose, during all that time, he never entered under any cover, but exposed himself the whole day to the parching heat of the sun, and all the night abroad to the cold air, till unable to hold out any longer, he was at length constrained to yield to nature. At another time, to punish himself for a small fault, or as others say, no fault, but to extinguish a temptation of the flesh, he condemned himself to pass six whole months in the marshes of Scete, in the remote parts of the desert, infested, by a number of large gnats with stings like wasps; by which, during his course of penance, he was so roughly treated, and stung in so terrible a manner, that at his return home his whole body appeared like that of a leper, and he could only be known by his voice.

The reputation of the extraordinary austerities, and the excellent lives of the religious of Tabenna, under

17

their holy founder St. Pachomius, inspired Macarius
with a desire of going thither and joining their holy
company, yet so as not to be known who or what he
was. In order thereto, having changed his habit for
the dress of a common laborer, he travelled fifteen
days' journey through the deserts till at length he arrived at the monastery of Tabenna. Here calling for
the Abbot St. Pachomius, he begged to be admitted
amongst his monks. The abbot told him, that at his
time of life he could not be able to conform himself to
the austerities which were practised in his monastery,
and therefore refused to admit him. Macarius however did not desist, but continued seven days at the
gate, begging for admission, and fasting the whole
time, till his perseverance prevailed with the abbot and
community to receive him. And now the penitential
time of Lent arrived, in which the religious assigned
to themselves the particular exercises of devotion and
penance in which they designed to pass that holy
time : some of them resolving to eat but once in two
days,—others only twice in a week,—others again,
after spending the whole day in manual labor, proposing to watch and pass the night in prayer without
ever lying down to take their rest. Macarius for his
part said nothing ; but gathering together a large pro
vision of the leaves of the palm-trees for making mats,
passed the whole time standing at work in a corner by
himself, with his heart raised to God in silent prayer

without once sitting down or leaning against any thing whatever. He eat only on the Lord's day, and then nothing but some raw leaves of cabbage, without bread or any thing else, or even drinking any liquid whatsoever The rest of the religious observing him to practice these extraordinary austerities, began to murmur against their abbot for having admitted amongst them, for their condemnation, a man that seemed not to be made of flesh and blood ; whereupon St. Pachomius, who was frequently favored with divine revelations, applying himself to God in prayer, with a desire to know who this person was that had passed the Lent in so extraordinary a manner, learnt from God that it was the Abbot Macarius, of whose sanctity he had heard so much. Whereupon taking him by the hand, and leading him into the chapel before the altar of the monastery, he said : " Is it then you, venerable Father ? Are you the celebrated Macarius, and would not let me know it ! As it is a long time since I have had a desire to see you, now I must return you thanks for the stay you have made amongst us, by which you have humbled my children, and taught them not to think much of their own austerities. You have sufficiently edified us by your presence, I beg of you, therefore, to return home and pray for us." And thus dismissed the Saint, requesting him to go back to his former habitation.

But if these rigorous penances and extraordinary

austerities of St. Macarius may seem to be beyond the
reach of our imitation, we cannot say as much with
respect to the following instance of the spirit. as well
of mortification as of charity, which both himself and
his brethren showed upon a less occasion, as recorded
in the history of his life.   Some one having sent him
a fine bunch of grapes at a time when he had a longing desire after that kind of fruit, in order to exercise
himself at once both in abstinence and charity, he sent
them to another solitary, who being sick and infirm
stood more in need of them.   The good sick man, after
thankfully receiving the present, which, had he followed his own inclinations, he would gladly have eaten,
through the same spirit of mortification and charity,
refrained from eating them, and sent them to a third
who lived at some distance in the wilderness, the third
again in like manner to a fourth ; and so on till they
had passed from one to another of most of the inhabitants of the cells dispersed through the desert, without
any one ever tasting them.   At length he who received them last, not knowing from whom they first came,
and thinking they might be agreeable to their holy
father, sent them to St. Macarius.   The Saint perceiving the grapes to be the very same, and learning also
upon inquiry through how many hands they had passed, gave God thanks for that spirit of abstinence and
self-denial which his brethren had showed on this occasion ; and for his own part was animated thereby to

a greater fervor in all the exercises of a spiritual life, but nevertheless could not be induced to eat of the grapes himself.

As to the miracles of our Saint, church history assures us, that the two Saints Macarius were equally illustrious, not only for the works of faith, but also for the miraculous graces, and other supernatural gifts wherewith God favored them;—that they equally excelled in the knowledge of the secrets of God,—in the power they had to make themselves terrible to the devils,—to cure diseases, and work all kinds of wonders. It is particularly recorded of our Saint, that he had an extraordinary grace in casting out unclean spirits, and delivering numbers that were either possessed or assaulted by them. The tempter one day took occasion from thence to suggest to him thoughts of vain-glory, which tended to withdraw him from his solitude, under the specious pretext of doing good to many, and to carry him to Rome, that he might exercise his talents in casting out devils, and curing all diseases in the capital of the universe. Macarius saw through the deceit, and strongly resisted the suggestion : and as the temptation did not cease, but rather acquired additional strength, he laid himself prostrate on the threshold of his cell, and cried out to the demon of vain-glory, by whom he was tempted, that he would remain there till the evening ; and that if he would remove him from thence, it should be by main force, for that with his good will he would never go, how violently soever he might tempt him. After sun-set finding the temptation returning again with more violence than ever, he took a large basket that held two bushels, and filling it with sand, laid it on his shoulders, and being loaded in this manner, walked up and down in the desert Theosebius, surnamed Cosmetor, a native of Antioch, having met him whilst he was at this exercise, said : " What is the meaning of this, holy father ? Why do you thus torment yourself? Let me ease you of your burthen." Macarius replied : " I am plaguing one that is plaguing me : and who, seeing that I am lazy at home, will needs have me go and travel abroad :" and thus he continued carrying about his load of sand, till being quite wearied and spent, and all bruised with his burthen, he returned to his cell.

As to the particulars of the many miracles wrought by St. Macarius, we shall not pretend to recount them here : we shall only take notice of one recorded by Palladius, of which he was an eye-witness. This prelate relates, that being at that time himself a disciple of the Saint, he came one day to his cell, and found there lying before the door, a priest of a country parish, in the most wretched condition that can be imagined ; his head being eaten in such a manner by a cancer, that a great part of his skull was seen quite bare. He came hither to seek his cure from the

Saint, who would take no notice of him whatsoever. Upon which Palladius going in, began to intercede for him. The Saint answered, that he was unworthy to be delivered from this evil, which God had sent him for a punishment. "But," said he, "if you desire he should be cured, prevail on him to resolve never more to presume to approach the altar to celebrate the sacred mysteries. For this punishment has been sent him on account of being guilty of acts of impurity, and saying mass in that sinful condition." Palladius told the poor man what the Saint had said; when upon his promising with an oath never more to exercise any of the priestly functions, the Saint received him into his cell, and after he had confessed his sins, with a sincere resolution of never more returning to them, he laid his hands upon him, and in a few days sent him home perfectly cured and glorifying God.

As to the other extraordinary gifts and graces of St. Macarius, it is recorded of him that he frequently saw in spirit, not only the state of the souls of his religious at the time of their communion, but also their inward thoughts and dispositions in the time of prayer. One night the devil knocked at his cell, crying out: "Arise, abbot Macarius, that we may accompany the brethren to midnight prayers." The Saint knowing, by the light of God, that it was the enemy, replied: "And what hast thou to do, O lying spirit, thou enemy of all truth, with the assembly of the Saints, or

their night prayers?" "Assure thyself, Macarius,"
replied the devil, "that the religious never meet to
pray without us: Come along, and thou shalt see."
The Saint having previously prayed to God that he
might know whether what the devil vaunted of was
true or not, went to the place where the brethren were
assembled for the night office ; and at the time they
were reciting the psalms, saw a number of these wicked spirits in the shape of filthy blackamoors, running
about the church, and playing a variety of tricks, with
a view either to distract the religious, or overcome
them with sleep ; and when, after the twelve psalms
were ended, they prostrated themselves in silent prayer,
he perceived how busy they were about them, repre
senting to one the figure of a woman,—to another a
building or a journey,—and to others a prodigious
variety of such like phantoms and images.   Now
there were some of the brethren who seemed to drive
them away by a superior force, and to fling them
down upon their backs with so much violence that
they durst not approach them any more ; whilst
others, more indolent and negligent, suffered them to
ride upon their heads and shoulders, and to make a
mockery of them at pleasure.   The Saint being much
moved with this spectacle, addressed himself to God,
with many tears, in behalf of his religious, begging
he would deliver them from all the snares and deceits
of these spirits of darkness : using these words of the

royal prophet, Ps. lxvii. *Let God arise, and let his enemies be scattered : and let them that hate him flee from before his face.* After the prayers were ended, calling to him the brethren, he found upon enquiring of each one in particular that had been so distracted with those vain or wicked imaginations which the Saint had seen represented to them by those blacks ; hence they came to understand that those distracting thoughts, which so often interrupt the attention and devotion of the soul at the divine office or other prayers, are illusions of the wicked spirit: and that the best way to repel them and keep them at a distance, is to watch over ourselves, and to keep our souls closely united to God by a fervent application of all its powers and faculties.

It is also recorded of St. Macarius, that being one day in company with the other Saint of the same name, and obliged to pass over the Nile in a barge that served for that purpose, it happened that two tribunes or colonels were ferried over at the same time, each having a pompous equipage and great retinue to attend him. These officers beholding the two Saints in their mean garb at one end of the barge, with all that serenty, recollection, and interior peace of mind, which seemed apparent in their faces, together with a sovereign contempt of all that this world admires, could not help extolling to each other the happiness of such a kind of life as that which these servants of God led. Accordingly one of them addressing himself to the Saints, said : " You are both happy, who are thus above the world, and tread it under your feet. You speak as if it were by a prophetic light," replied our Saint, " in calling us *happy*, for the name of both of us is *Macarius*, which in the Greek signifies *happy*. But if you have great reason to say, that they who have renounced all things else to consecrate themselves entirely to the service of God are happy, inasmuch as they tread the world under their feet, we have also great reason to compassionate your happiness, in being slaves to the world, and suffering yourselves to be mocked by it." These words of the Saint made so deep an impression upon him, that on his return home he resigned his commission, —distributed his substance to the poor,—and quitting the world, embraced a solitary and religious life.

We shall conclude our account of the life of St. Macarius with a remarkable history, recorded by St. Jerome, of a certain solitary of Nitria, who by the price of his work, which was making linen-cloth, had saved so much money, that when he died there was found by him the sum of one hundred crowns. The religious assembled on this extraordinary occasion to deliberate what should be done with the money; which some thought should be given to the poor or to the church, and others to the kindred of the deceased. But Macarius, our Saint, Pambo, Isidore, and others who were called the fathers, being inspired by the Holy Ghost, ordained that they should cast the money into the grave together with the corpse, repeating those words of St. Peter to Simon Magus, *Keep thy money to thyself, to perish with thee.* And this wholesome severity spread such a terror amongst all the religious of Egypt, that they looked upon it as a crime for any one of them to leave so much as one crown behind them after death.

St. Macarius, after having served God for sixty years in a religious life, departed to our Lord about the year 395. His name is registered in the Roman Martyrology on the second of January.

SS. ISIDORE AND PAMBO.

WE join these two together, and give them a place immediately after St. Macarius, with whom, as we have seen above, they are joined by St. Jerome. as having been inspired by the Holy Ghost, and the most eminent in their days amongst the fathers of the deserts; with whom also, as well as with the other St. Macarius, they are celebrated by all our church historians, for the brave stand they made against the Arian heresy, under Valens the emperor;—the persecutions they suffered on this occasion,—the eminence of their

sanctity ;—and finally, on account of the great signs
and wonders which God wrought by them. They
were each of them, for some time, disciples of St. Antony, and afterwards on account of their extraordinary
virtues and merits, advanced to the priestly dignity
and made chief superiors ; *Isidore* of the religious of
the desert of *Scete,* and Pambo of those of mount
Nitria.

It is recorded of St. Isidore, that he received so singular a grace from God, and had so great a power and
authority over evil spirits, that whenever any possessed
persons were brought to him, they never failed to be
delivered, even before they reached the door of his
cell. The brethren having asked him one day, what
could be the reason why the devils were so much afraid
of him ; he alledged no other, than that from the time
of his entering into religion he had made it his constant endeavor not to suffer the passion of anger to
rise up so high as to reach his tongue. As a proof
of his zeal for suppressing in himself the least emotion
to this passion, we are informed by an ancient writer,
that having one day carried some little baskets to
market for sale, upon meeting there with some provo-
cation, which began to excite in his heart emotions of
anger and wrath, he immediately flung down his baskets, and ran back as fast as he could to the wilderness. By this diligence in watching against, and suppressing all the irregular motions and suggestions of

his passions, and by the aid of incessant prayer, he
attained so great a mastery over himself as to acknowledge one day, to the greater glory of God, that for
the space of forty years, though he had often experienced the motions and suggestions of sin, he was not
conscious to himself that he had ever given his voluntary consent, either to an irregular desire or the least
emotion of wrath.

From his first entering into religion, instead of setting himself a task, as many did, of reciting daily a
certain number of psalms or prayers, he chose rather
to pray, without ceasing, night and day; and yet he
was always so great a lover of manual labor, that after
he was grown very old he could not be prevailed upon
to give over working even at night; and when the
brethren, upon these occasions, would sometimes beg
that he would afford himself a little more rest, he replied, that all he could do or suffer was nothing in
comparison of what the Son of God had done and
suffered for him, and he therefore thought he could
never do nor suffer enough for the love of his Saviour.
He one day addressed himself thus to the assembly
of the Solitaries of Scete: "Have we not retired
hither, my brethren, in order to suffer many labors
and pains in the body, by the means of which we may
merit everlasting rest for our souls in heaven; and yet
how little do we suffer here at present? For my part
I think of taking my sheep-skin, and seeking some

18

other place, where I may find something more to suffer." This he said, because at this time the number
of those that resorted to this desert gave occasion to
the introducing of certain conveniences of life, and
some better accommodations than they had been accustomed to in the beginning, when they were in **a**
manner quite destitute of every thing.

"It is also recorded as a maxim of St. Isidore,
"That the whole science of the Saints consists in
knowing and following the will of God; because then
only can a man be perfect indeed, when raising himself above all other things he subjects himself to the
eternal Truth and Justice. For since man was made
after the image and likeness of God, who is that same
eternal Truth and Justice, he cannot expect to meet
with either perfection or happiness, only in a conformity with his divine original. On the other hand, he
said, that the most dangerous of all temptations was
to follow the suggestions of our own hearts and
thoughts, instead of the will of God;—that the pleasure which a man pretends to find in the gratification
of his own inclinations is quickly changed into bitterness, and leaves nothing behind but the regret of having been ignorant of the secret of true beatitude, and
of the way of the Saints. From whence he concludes,
that the true way to happiness consists in being willing to labor and take pains in the service of the Lord,
and in patiently suffering the short tribulations of this

life, in order to secure the eternal salvation of our souls."

This Saint had also a special talent from God of healing the spiritual maladies of the religious when any of them were diseased in their souls; insomuch that whenever it happened that the other superiors were for dismissing any of their subjects, on account of negligence, slothfulness, impatience, passion, or other defects, he desired they might be brought to him : when, by treating them with his usual charity, humility, and patience, he generally brought them to a right sense of their duty, and in time cured them effectually of all their vices and faults of what kind soever.

When Theophilus was made patriarch of Alexandria, anno 385, St. Isidore went thither to pay him a visit. On his return from thence to the wilderness, the brethren enquired of him, what news he brought from the city ? " I have seen nobody there," he replied, " but the patriarch." Being much surprised at his answer, they asked him, " What then was become of the inhabitants of that great city ? Surely," said they, " they are not all swallowed up by an earthquake." This obliged him to explain himself, by letting them know that he had kept so strict a guard over his eyes, as not to allow them to look upon any one.

St. Isidore departed to our Lord shortly after, in a good old age, though the particular year is not known.

and his name stands recorded in the Roman Martyrology on the fifteenth of January.

Amongst several great men of the name of Isidore,
there was another, a contemporary with our Saint,
who was abbot in Thebais, over a thousand monks in
great reputation for sanctity, and under such strict enclosure that none of them were ever allowed to go
out, nor any from abroad permitted to enter the monastery, except he came to remain during life, never
more to depart from it. They had gardens and wells
within their own enclosure; and when there was a
necessity of any thing from abroad, two of the ancients were deputed to provide such necessaries, all
the rest attending only to their regular exercises.

But to come to St. Pambo: it is recorded of him,
that being in his younger days a disciple of St. Antony, he desired his master to instruct him in the
most efficacious manner of saving his soul; St. Antony told him, that in order to do this, he must be
careful to do true penance for his sins;—that he must
never place any confidence whatsoever in his own
righteousness;—that he must always endeavor to act
in such manner, as to never after have any occasion
to repent of what he had done;—and that in particular he must labour to put a restraint as well upon
his tongue as upon his appetite.

In those days he also applied himself to another of
the religious to be instructed in some of the psalms.

This brother began with the thirty-eighth Psalm : *I said I will take heed to my ways, that I sin not with my tongue;* which words Pambo had no sooner heard, but without waiting for the second verse, he retired to his cell, saying, it was enough for one lesson, and that he would go and endeavor to learn it in practice. Six months afterwards the brother, finding that he did not apply to him for any more lessons, asked him the reason why he staid away so long from him. O brother, said he, I have not yet perfectly learnt to practice the first verse which you taught me. Many years after this, one of his friends asked, if he had not now at least learnt his lesson? To whom he replied, that it was with much difficulty he could yet reduce it to practice, notwithstanding his nineteen years application. However, by his perpetual attention not to offend in his words, he arrived at length at so great perfection in this particular, that he is thought in this to have equalled if not excelled St. Antony himself. When any one consulted him, either upon any passage of the scripture, or any other spiritual matter, he never would answer upon the spot, but desired time to consider of it. Sometimes he employed whole months on these occasions in examining before God what answer he should give ; but then, the answers he returned carried with them so much weight, and were so holy, that they were received by all like oracles dictated by heaven.

St. Pambo did not continue always with St. Antony; but leaving Thebais, he took up his abode, either in the desert of Scete, as some say, or in that of Nitria, where he had a monastery on the mountain. He was also for some time in the wilderness of the Cells, where, Rufinus says, he went to receive his benediction, anno 374. As to his exterior practices, St. Pemen used to relate, that he had remarked three things in St. Pambo, which he judged to be very extraordinary, viz. his fasting on all days till the evening, —his continual silence,—and his great diligence in manual labors. He also related that St. Antony had given testimony in favor of St. Pambo, that the fear of God which posssessed his soul, had induced the Spirit of God to take up his resting place with him. The eminent grace of his interior is said to have broke forth and discovered itself in his exterior, by a certain brilliant majesty in his countenance, like what we read of Moses, so that a person could not look steadfastly on his face. He often earnestly begged of God, during the space of three years, that he would cease to glorify him in this manner upon earth; but his divine Majesty, instead of attending to his prayers in this particular, chose rather to establish so profound a humility in his soul, as not to be altered or any ways prejudiced by this glory.

St. Athanasius once desired St. Pambo to come from his desert to Alexandria, in order that by the testimony of so holy a man to the divinity of Jesus Christ he might confound the Arians : upon which occasion it is recorded of him, that seeing an actress in that city dressed up in an extraordinary manner for he stage, he wept bitterly : and being asked the rea- on of his tears, he answered that he wept partly for the wretched condition of the soul of that unhappy woman, and partly to think that on his part he did not take so much pains to please God as she took to make herself agreeable to sinful man.

Palladius relates, in the tenth chapter of his *Historia Lausiaca*, that Melania the elder, a noble Roman lady, on coming into Egypt, and hearing of the sanctity of St. Pambo, went to visit him in his monastery on mount Nitria, taking with her three hundred pounds weight of silver, which she presented to him, desiring he would accept of some part of the store with which God had blessed her. The holy man was sitting at his work making mats when she came in, accompanied with Isidore, the administrator of the hospital of Alexandria ; and without interrupting his work, or looking at either her or her present, he con- tented himself with telling her, God would reward her charity. Then turning to his disciple, he said : "Take this, and distribute it amongst the brethren that are in Lybia and in the islands, whose monasteries are the most poor of all ; but give no part of it to the monas- teries of Egypt, because this country is more rich, and abounds more in all things." The lady stood still, expecting that he would give her his benediction, or express at least his esteem for so considerable a present, by word or other sign; but seeing that he went on with his work, without once casting so much as an eye towards the chest of money which she had given him, she said to him : " Father, I do not know whether you are aware that here is three hundred pounds weight of silver ?" " Daughter," said he, without once taking off his eye from his work, "he to whom you make this offering, knows very well how much it weighs, without your telling him. If indeed you had given it to me, you might have had some reason to inform me of its weight ; but if you designed it as an offering to God, who did not disdain, but even preferred the poor widow's two mites before the large offerings of the rich, do not say any more about it." This passage Melania herself related to Palladius.

When Theophilus was made patriarch of Alexandria, he went to visit the religious of mount Nitria, who were all assembled on this occasion to do honor to the patriarch. They desired St. Pambo, as their superior, to make some discourse to this prelate, with which he might be edified : the holy abbot, agreeably to his maxims and practice, replied, " If he is not edified by my silence, I shall never edify him by my words" The Saint did not long survive this visit: Melania was present at his death, to whom he be-

queathed, by way of legacy, a basket which he had at
that time just finished. When he was near his end,
he blessed God, that from the time of his first coming
into the wilderness of Nitria, and built himself a cell,
he had never been burthensome to any one, having
always earned his bread with the labor of his own
hands; and that he could not recollect a word he had
spoken of which he had afterwards cause to repent:
nevertheless, said he, I am now going to the Lord as
one that hath not yet begun to serve him. He expired without any sickness, pain, or the least fever or
agony. Melania took charge of his burial, and carried
away the basket he had given her, which she kept till
her death.

There was also another abbot Pambo, or rather
Pammon, whose monastery was in the neighborhood
of Antinoe, greatly esteemed by St. Athanasius, who,
together with St. Theodore, the disciple and successor
of St. Pachomius, in the monastery of Tabenna, accompanied this Saint when he fled from the persecution of Julian, and who, together with the same St.
Theodore, assured him on this occasion, by prophetic
light, that his persecutor was now actually slain in
Persia, and had for his successor in the empire one
that was a good Christian, but whose reign should be
short: all which proved to be actually true. This
holy man departed not long after to our Lord, full of
years and good works; and St. Athanasius, in a dis·

course he made in the great chuich of Alexandria, in
the presence of his own clergy, and of many bishops,
has given the most ample testimony of his extraordinary sanctity, declaring that he was indeed a great
man of God, and worthy to be compared with St. Antony himself.

ST. JULIAN SABBAS.

From Theodoret, in his Philotheus, or Religious History, chap. 2

St. Julian, surnamed *Sabbas*, or *the venerable father*,
was a native of Mesopotamia, who, following the divine
call, withdrew himself in his youth from the world,
and took up his habitation in a den or cavern, in a
vast wilderness on the borders of Osrhoena, a place, on
many accounts, inconvenient to dwell in, but preferred
by him on account of its solitude, before the most com-
modious palace in the world. Here he undertook a
life of perpetual penance and incessant prayer, eating
but once a week, and then only some coarse bread
made of millet, with a little salt, and drinking so small
a quantity of water at his meal, as was insufficient to
the quenching of his thirst,—continually nourishing
his soul with the singing of psalms, in which he took

great delight, and with an interior conversation with God in prayer, by means of which the divine love took such possession of his heart, that he had no relish for any worldly thing, passing the night and day always thinking of his Beloved, insomuch, that even in his sleep he could dream of nothing else.

The great reputation of his sanctity attracted by degrees many disciples to join him in the desert, who were desirous to learn the science of salvation. These he received into his cavern, and trained up to an imitation of the exercises which he himself followed; teaching them to discard all care and solicitude for this perishable carcase, and be content to lodge and eat like himself. However, as their number increased, and as the dampness of the cavern spoiled the little provisions of pickled herbs which they provided for the sick, he consented that a hut should be built for their better preservation. Having gone out at this time, as he frequently did for greater solitude and recollection in prayer, to a distant part of the wilderness, employing several days by himself in spiritual exercises, and at his returning home, finding they had erected a larger building than he had ordered, he told them: "I fear brethren, that whilst we are enlarging our earthly dwelling, which we can occupy but for a short time, we shall suffer detriment with respect to our heavenly mansions which are eternal."

The method of prayer and of performing the divine

office which this saint taught his disciples, was as fol·
lows : before day they all sung hymns, psalms, and
canticles to the praise of God together within the cave ;
then early in the morning they went out into the wilderness, two by two, and observed the same manner of
worship, with this difference, that one of them sung
fifteen psalms, standing upright, whilst the other lay
prostrate on the ground in silent prayer and adoration,
till the fifteen psalms being ended, he that had sung
them prostrated himself in his turn on the ground,
and adored, whilst his companion, rising up, sung
other fifteen psalms : and thus alternately singing and
adoring, they passed a considerable part of the day.
Before sunset, they betook themselves to a little rest,
and afterwards meeting all together in the cave, they
sung their evening hymns to the praises of their Creator.

As to the Saint himself, he made, as we have already
said, frequent excursions to a great distance from his
cave, and spent eight or ten days together in the remoter parts of the wilderness in his spiritual exercises.
On these occasions he often took one of the brethren
with him, particularly a holy man named James, a
native of Persia, but never without desiring his companion to keep himself at a distance, that he might
be no occasion of distraction to him in his devotions.
One time, whilst James was following him in the wilderness, he found a monstrous serpent lying dead in

the way, which the Saint had killed by the sign oι the cross, as he acknowledged upon his disciple's putting it home to him, but with a strict injunction to keep the matter a secret during his life. Another time, when Asterius, a young religious, endued with more courage than strength, had by his importunity obtain- ed leave to accompany him in one of those excursions in the heat of the summer, which in those deserts is very violent, after two or three days the young man was so parched with thirst by the sun continually beating upon him, and no water being to be found in those sands, he was just upon the point of perishing, had not the Saint by his prayers and tears obtained of the Father of mercies, that a fountain of water should spring up to save the young man's life, in the very spot which he had sprinkled with his tears; which fountain, says Theodoret, continues to flow to this day. The same Asterius was afterwards one of the most illustrious amongst the disciples of St. Julian, and propagated the holy discipline he had learnt of his master, by founding a famous monastery near Gindare, in the territory of Antioch, where he trained up many souls to religious perfection.

But these were not the only miracles wrought by the prayers of St. Julian, for he frequently cast out devils, and healed divers diseases. To avoid the con- course of people which the fame of his sanctity and miracles brought to see him, as well as the honors they showed him, which were troublesome to his humility, he withdrew himself from his Mesopotamian cavern, and taking with him some of his disciples, with necessary provisions for a long journey, he tavel led as far as mount Sinai in Arabia, taking care to avoid any town or village that lay in his way. Here he took up his habitation, being charmed with the tranquillity he enjoyed in this holy solitude; but after having built a church, or oratory, and sanctified for some time his new residence with the holy exercises of prayer and penance, it was the will of God he should return again to his disciples whom he had left behind him in his former habitation.

Here he was informed of the threats of Julian the Apostate, who was then engaged in his expedition against the Persians, and of his impious designs against the church of Christ, if he should return with victory. Whereupon, to divert this impending storm, he employed ten whole days in most fervent prayer, to implore the divine mercy and protection for the church. At the end of which time he learnt, by divine revelation, the unhappy death of that prince, and declared the same to his disciples.

Valens, an Arian, who succeeded not long after to the empire, was a great persecutor of the church and and an earnest promoter of such as were addicted to his heresy. In his time the Arians made a great havoc in the church of Antioch, where also they had the impudence to publish that St. Julian was of their sentiments. Upon this occasion the Saint, at the request of the Catholics, leaving his desert, took a journey to Antioch, to bear testimony to the faith, and to repress the insolence of the heretics. In his way thither he miraculously preserved the life of the child of a good woman who had entertained him at her house, that by accident had fallen into a deep well, and was given over for lost, but was afterwards found sitting and playing upon the water. Upon being drawn out, he declared he had seen the Saint all the while holding him up, and keeping him from sinking to the bottom. When he arrived at Antioch, great multitudes from all parts flocked about him; some to behold a man so much renowned for his sanctity, others to seek by his prayers a deliverance from the evils wherewith they were afflicted. Here it pleased God that he himself should be seized by a violent fever. But as the Catholics were apprehensive that the people would be shocked on the occasion, at their desire. he prayed to God, that if his recovery might be of any service to the church, he would be pleased to restore him to health. His prayer being immediately followed by a sweat, his fever abated, and he presently recovered. Many others were healed upon the spot by his prayers. After which he went to the place, out of town, where the faithful assembled to their devotions. In his way thither he passed by the gate of the emperor's palace, where a poor cripple, who had been deprived of the use of his legs, was instantly cured by the touch of his garment, so as to be able to rise up immediately and leap or run. The report of this miracle being noised abroad, brought an immense crowd about the Saint, to the great confusion of the Arians, whose impostures were not only clearly discovered, but confuted by the public testimony the Saint gave to the Catholic truth, and by his confirming it by evident miracles which they could not contradict, as the governor of the eastern district (who being grievously ill, had sent for the Saint), was one of the number of those who were miraculously cured by him.

On his return home from Antioch, he passed through Cyrus, a city of which Theodoret was afterwards bishop. Here the faithful represented to him the danger they were in from one Asterius, an Arian, who had been intruded upon them for a bishop, and was preparing a sermon against the faith of the Trinity, to impose upon them by his eloquent sophistry. The Saint exhorted them to fasting and prayer; and joining with them in these spiritual exercises, by the efficacy of his prayers in their favor, Asterius was suddenly seized upon with a mortal illness, which within twenty-four hours hurried him before the judgment seat of Christ, on the very eve of the festival which he designed to have preached his impious doctrine in the cathedral of that city.

The Saint after this returned to his solitude, and there continued his accustomed exercises, till having attained to a good old age, he exchanged his mortal pilgrimage for a happy immortality. He is spoken of with the greatest eulogium by St. Jerome, Epist. 13, and by St. John Chrysostom, writing upon the epistle to the Ephesians. His name is recorded in the Roman Martyrology, January 14.

ST. ABRAHAM.

From his Life by St. Ephrem

St. Abraham was born in Mesopotamia, about the year 300, of wealthy parents, by whom he was tenderly beloved, and who provided him with a worldly spouse, to whom they from his childhood had promised him in marriage, designing to procure him an advantageous settlement, and desiring nothing so much as to see him advanced to some post of honor or dignity in the world : but God, who had other designs upon him, inspired him with the love of purity, and an early affection to the practices of piety and devotion. He was remarkably diligent in frequenting the church,—in attending to the holy scriptures,—

and in carrying home the divine lessons he there
heard, in order to make them the subjects of his meditation both day and night.   When he had come to
man's estate, his parents pressed him so closely to
marry the girl to whom they had before contracted
him, and after having resisted their solicitations for
some time, he was at length constrained to acquiesce.
But after celebrating the marriage feast, when night
came on, a ray of divine light having penetrated his
heart, accompanied by so strong a call to quit all for
the love of God, that he immediately arose, and left
both his spouse untouched and his father's house, and
going to some distance off, hid himself in an empty
cell which he found fit for his purpose, and there with
great joy began to sing hymns of praise to his divine
Deliverer.

His parents and friends not knowing what became
of him, after a diligent search of seventeen days discovered him in his cell at his prayers.   But as they
found him fixed in his resolution to remain there, in
order, as he said, to bewail his sins, and dedicate the
remainder of his life to prayer and penance, they left
him to follow the call of God, and returned home.   At
parting he desired that they would not come any more
under pretence of visiting him, to interrupt his spiritual exercises ; and that he might have as little communication as possible with the world, he walled up
the door of his cell, leaving only a little window

through which he received, from time to time, the slender provisions which maintained his life. Here, free from the cares and distractions of the world, he lived in the greatest austerity, abstaining even from bread,—in watchings, penitential tears, and a continual practice of the most profound humility, wonderful charity and meekness, which he showed, without respect of persons, to every one. In this solitary state he continued for the space of many years, without ever remitting or being wearied out by his long penance, but rather finding an unspeakable sweetness therein, with which he was never satisfied. He considered every day as if it were the day of his death, and suffered not so much as one day to pass without weeping, but was never seen to laugh. Yet with all this austerity and continual mortification, he always preserved a fresh countenance, an agreeable air, and a strength and vigor of body, which must have proceeded from grace, and not from the slender nourishment he allowed himself. Nay, his very habit, which must be considered as a kind of a miracle, was not worn out during the fifty years that he remained in this penitential course of life.

The reputation of his sanctity brought many of all conditions to him, to whom he gave admirable lessons for their spiritual profit; for our Lord had rewarded his early piety with the gifts of wisdom and understanding in so eminent a degree, that his light shone

forth to all that approached him for their instruction
and edification. In the mean time his parents dying,
when he had been about ten years in this solitude,
left him their worldly substance, which was very considerable, which he desired a friend of his to charge
himself with, and to dispose of the whole in alms and
other pious uses, in order that himself might not be
distracted or interrupted in his spiritual exercises by
any temporal concerns.

There was in the neighborhood of the Saint's cell,
not far distant from the city of Edessa, a large country town, inhabited by pagans, who were not only
obstinately addicted to their idolatrous worship, and
heathenish superstitions, but also excessively barbarous
and cruel towards all such as sought to reclaim them
from their idolatry, by preaching to them the faith of
Christ, insomuch that several of the clergy and religious in those parts, who had from time to time attempted to convert them to Christianity, instead of
succeeding in their undertaking, meeting with nothing
but insults and outrages, were forced by their barbarity
to abandon their enterprise. The bishop hearing of
the heroic virtues of Abraham, cast his eyes upon him
as one whose charity, zeal, meekness, and patience,
seemed most likely to prevail over the blindness and
obstinacy of these infidels ; wherefore assembling hi
clergy, he proposed to them the advancing of the man
of God to the priestly dignity, to the end that he

might go and convert them. Having unanimously
applauded his proposition, they went in a body, with
the prelate at their head, to the cell of the holy man.
The bishop told him upon what occasion they were
come, and how great and charitable a work it would
be in him to go and endeavor to procure the salvation
of so many poor deluded souls. Abraham, at the
hearing of this proposal, being struck with surprise,
begged that the prelate would never think of sending
such a miserable wretch as he was upon so important
and arduous an enterprise, but rather suffer him to
remain in his cell to lament and to do penance for his
manifold sins. The bishop encouraged him, assuring
him that God would assist him in this great work;
that his having forsaken all things for his love, was not
sufficient to make his sacrifice complete, unless he were
also ready to renounce his own will by the virtue of
obedience, which is the true way to find out the will
of God; that whilst he stayed in his cell, he was laboring only for his own salvation; but by going where
he was about to send him, and laboring in the conversion of those infidels, the grace of God co-operating
with him, he would become the instrument of saving
the souls of many, and be entitled to a much greater
reward in eternal bliss. The man of God, on hearing
this, could resist no longer; but cried out with tears:
"The Lord's will be done! I am ready to go to whatsoever place you shall be pleased to send me." Thus

the bishop, having brought him out of his cell, ordained him priest, and sent him to preach to that
pagan people.

He began his mission by pouring out prayers and
tears before God in behalf of these poor souls, in whom
he found no manner of disposition to profit by his
words.   Then sending to his friend, whom he had
charged with the disposal of the worldly substances
left him by his parents; he procured from him a sum
of money with which he in a short time built a church,
and adorned it for divine service.   In the mean time
the people, for whose conversion he ceased not continually to sigh and pray, made no opposition, although
their curiosity brought them daily to behold the building.   But when he had finished the church, and dedicated it to the living God, with a most fervent prayer,
accompanied with many tears for the conversion of the
idolaters, his zeal carried him from the church to the
temple of the idols, where he overthrew their altars,
and broke their statues in pieces.   Hereupon their rage
knew no bounds, but falling upon him with merciless
fury, after having discharged innumerable blows and
stripes upon him, they drove him out of the town.

The next morning when they came to the church
(as they daily did, not out of devotion, but from a certain curiosity and pleasure they took in seeking its de-
corations) they were surprised beyond measure to find
him at his prayers before the altar.   But upon his be-

ginning to preach to them, and to conjure them to turn from their idols to the living God, they again fell upon him, and having beat him worse than before, they fastened a rope about his feet, and dragged him like a dead dog out of the town, where they pelted him with stones till they thought they had made an end of him. About midnight he, whom they had left for dead, came to himself, and after fervently praying, with abundance of tears to the Father of mercies, for the conversion and salvation of his persecutors, got up, and returned again into the town, and early in the morning was again found in the church singing psalms. The pagans, although astonished at the sight of him, yet were no way mollified, but rather more enraged, so that they repeated the treatment they had given him the preceding day, and dragged him again by the feet with ropes out of their town. He returned nevertheless the next day, and thus for the space of three whole years, he still persevered constant in his labors and fervent prayers for their conversion, under a perpetual succession of grievous sufferings, pains, mockeries, and outrages, without ever showing the least anger or impatience, or returning them a single angry word, or even entertaining in his soul any hatred or aversion towards them whatever, but, on the contrary, the more cruelly they treated him, the more tenderly did he love them, and the more affectionately invite them to come to Christ, *the way, the truth, and the life.*

After three years had elapsed in this manner, **the** patience and prayers of the Saint at length prevailed over the resistance he had hitherto met with from this obstinate people. Upon a certain occasion, when they were all assembled together, they began to declare to each other their great admiration at the unwearied patience and charity of the servant of God, and from thence to argue that the God whom he preached must needs be the true God, and the religion which taught him so much patience and charity the true religion. Continuing to reason after this manner with one another, they further observed how he, being but one man, had cast down and broken in pieces all their gods, without their being able to resist him, or to revenge themselves on him. These reflections, being matured by the grace of God, opening their eyes and softening their hearts, produced a general resolution upon the spot of their all going in a body to the church, to yield themselves up to the man of God, and to embrace the faith he preached, which resolution they instantly put in execution. The Saint received them with inexpressible joy, and having first instructed them in the necessary articles of the christian doctrine, he afterwards baptized them, to the number of about one thousand persons, men, women, and children. After which he continued for the space of one year, watering these young plants, till he saw them not only deeply rooted in the christian faith, but

also diligent in bringing forth the fruit of every christian virtue, some thirty, some sixty, and others an
hundred fold.

Having thus accomplished the great work for which
he was sent, and finding the affection of the people
towards him to be so great, that they would never
willingly suffer him to return to his solitude ; he, when
they least suspected it, withdrew himself from them
privately by night: having first recommended them
in the most earnest manner he could, to the divine
goodness, and making three times the sign of the
cross over their town. The affliction which these
good people suffered, when on coming to church the
next morning they could not find their pastor, and
the diligence wherewith both they and the bishop,
who was sensibly affected with their grief, made search
after him, was inexpressible, but all in vain, for he
concealed himself with so much secrecy, that they
could learn no tidings of him ; so that the good prelate, to console and assist them, went amongst them
himself, and after having greatly edified them by his
instructions, &c. he ordained priests, deacons, and sub-
deacons amongst them, for the preaching the word of
God, and administering the divine sacraments in their
infant church. When Abraham was informed how
matters stood, he gave thanks to God, and then ventured to return to his ancient cell, where he was frequently visited by his flock, in order to nourish their

20

souls with the food of the words of life, which issued
in copious streams from his sacred lips.

We pass over several other particulars of the virtues of this man of God, and the frequent assaults he
underwent from the malice of the common enemy,
who had oftentimes visibly appeared to him, but was
always so effectually vanquished by his humility, and
the confidence he placed in our Lord, as not to be able
to inspire him with the least fear. But there remains
a remarkable passage of the life of this servant of God
which must not be omitted, as it relates to the fall, the
conversion, and penance of his niece.

After the Saint had gone back to his cell, it happened that his brother, dying in the world, left an
only daughter, named Mary, an orphan of seven years
of age. This child was brought to her uncle in his
wilderness, who undertook to train her up to a religious life, and placed her, for this purpose, in a cell
adjoining to his own, with a little window between
both, through which he instructed her. Here she
made such good use of the lessons she daily received
from him, as to become a perfect model of piety and
penance, in which happy state she persevered for
twenty years, till a false religious, or rather a wolf in
sheep's clothing, under pretence of coming to be edified by the conversation of her uncle, found means to
tempt her to sin, and ceased not till she was so unhappy as to quit her cell, and yield to the temptation.

The horror and remorse that followed her crime was so excessive, that it threw her into despair; so that instead of rising after her fall, and returning to her uncle to confess and do penance for her sin, she was resolved to fly from him, and accordingly went to a distant town, where she abandoned herself to a sinful course of life.

The Saint having taken notice that for the space of two days he had not heard her sing psalms, according to her custom, called out to her to know the cause of her silence, and as no answer was returned, it presently occurred to his recollection that she was the dove he had seen in a vision swallowed up by a dragon. His grief for the loss of his dear child became inexpressible: he wept and prayed for her without ceasing, till at the end of two years, having heard where she was, and the wicked course of life to which she had abandoned herself, he took the resolution of seeking after the lost sheep, in order to bring her back to Christ's fold. In order thereto, he procured, through the means of a friend, a horse, together with a soldier's habit, and a large cap or hat, which covered a great part of his face, and taking some money with him, went to the inn in which she lived, where having ordered a splendid supper to be prepared, he told the host that he had heard much of the beauty of a young woman in his house, whose name was Mary, and desired she might sup with him. Supper being ended,

and the waiters having retired, he took off his cap,
and mingling tears with his words: "My daughter,"
said he (for so he used to call her), "don't you know
me ?—My child did not I bring you up ?—What has
befallen you ?—Who is the murderer that has killed
your soul ?   Where is that angelical habit that you
formerly wore ?—Where that admirable purity ?—
Where are those tears which you poured out in the
presence of God ?—Where those watchings employed
in singing the divine praises ?—Where that holy austerity that made you take pleasure in lying on the
bare ground ?—Why did you not, after your first fall,
come presently to acquaint me with it, since I should
certainly have done penance for you, with my friend
Ephrem (*the writer of this life*), who has been ever
since under an unspeakable affliction on your account?
—Why had you so little confidence in me ?—Alas !
who is there without sin but God alone ?"   On hearing these words she stood like one struck dumb and
motionless with confusion and horror, and it was not
without extreme difficulty, after many affecting
speeches,—lively representations of the tender mercies
of God to repenting sinners,—and even promises to
take all her sins upon himself, that she at length put
on the resolution of returning to her cell.   Then prostrating herself at his feet, she spent the remainder of
the night in prayers and tears.   At break of day he
bid her get upon his horse, and thus conducted her

back to his cell, ordering her to leave what money and goods she was possessed of behind her, as inheriting them of the devil, whom she had been serving. After her return, she gave herself up with so much ardor to the exercises of a penitential life, and bewailed her sins day and night with so deep a sense of sorrow and contrition for them, joined with so lively a confidence in the divine mercy, that God was pleased, within three years, to give her, as a token of his acceptance of her penitence, the grace of even working miracles, by restoring health to the diseased by her prayers. However, she continued her penitential course with incredible austerity during the fifteen years that she lived after her conversion, never ceasing to lament her sins, till at length God was pleased to take her to himself. At the hour of her death a certain extraordinary brightness was observed on her countenance, which gave all that were present occasion to glorify God.

As to St. Abraham, he passed to a better life five years before her, after having, as we have already seen, spent fifty years in serving God in the most consummate sanctity. No sooner was the news of his death spread abroad, than the whole city, in a manner, crowded about his cell, and as many as could procure the least scrap of his clothes, carried them home with them, as so many precious relics which would bring a blessing along with them to their

houses; and we are assured by St. Ephrem, that the
very touch of them cured all diseases upon the spot.
St. Abraham is commemorated in the Roman Martyrology, on the 16th of March, but the Greeks celebrate his festival, jointly with St. Mary, his niece, on
the 29th of October.

Theodoret, in his Philotheus, gives us the life of
another St. Abraham, a native of the city of Cyrus
who from an anchoretical life was called forth by divine inspiration to the conversion of the inhabitants
of a certain town on mount Libanus; which having
happily effected, by his zeal and charity, after three
years abode amongst them, he returned to his solitude.
The extraordinary sanctity of his life, and the general
esteem wherein his eminent virtues and great talents
for the gaining of souls to God were held, determined
his superiors to send him with the episcopal character
to the city of Carræ (or Haran) in Mesopotamia,
which as yet had not received the faith of Christ, but
was given up to the worship of devils. Here God
gave such a blessing to his labors and preaching, continual prayer, wonderful sanctity and austerity of life,
that this idolatrous people, by his means was soon
brought over to Christ. He flourished in the fourth
century.

ST. JOHN OF EGYPT.

From Rufinus's Lives of the Fathers, chap. 1   Palladius, Historia Lausiaca chap 43   and Cassian, l. 4 Institut. chap. 23 24, 25.

AMONGST all the sainsts of the Egyptian deserts, there is perhaps none, St. Antony excepted, whose name is so illustrious in church history, and the writings of the holy fathers, as that of St. John of Lycopolis (so called from the place near which he dwelt in the hither Thebais.) He was not only greatly renowned for his extraordinary sanctity and miracles, but also consulted as an oracle from all parts, on account of his eminent spirit of prophecy, not only by persons of an inferior rank, but even by the emperor Theodosius the Great himself, to whom, amongst other things, he foretold his glorious victories over the mighty armies of the two usurpers, Maximus and Eugenius. This Saint was born about the year 305, and brought up at first to the trade of a carpenter, but when grown up to manhood he withdrew himself under an ancient religious man, whom he served with so much diligence and humility, that the good old father was quite wrapt 'n admiration at his virtue. However, to put it to the trial, whether his virtue was built upon a solid foundation or not, he often enjoined him to do many things

seemingly absurd, or extremely difficult, or altogether
impossible, which the humble disciple immediately
took in hand, and endeavored to accomplish with a
wonderful faith, simplicity, and perseverance; without
so much as once allowing himself to reflect on the un-
reasonableness or impossibility of the injunction : but
believing all things possible to obedience, and looking
upon the ordinance of his superior as the commandment of God himself, an instance of which is recorded by Cassian. The old father one day fixing a *dry
stick* of wood in the ground, bid his disciple water
that tree twice a day, which task, with his usual punc-
tuality in matters of obedience, he constantly performed for the space of a whole year, whether sick or well,
or whatever other occupation required his attention,
though he was obliged to walk the distance of two
miles each time to fetch the water, till at the expiration
of the year, the old father asked him, whether the tree
had as yet taken root or not, and he simply answering
that he did not know, the father pulled the stick out
of the ground, and bid him water it no longer.

After the death of his master, having spent about
five years in different monasteries in the exercises of a
religious life, being then about forty years of age, he
retired alone to a steep mountain, about two miles distance from the city of Lycopolis, and there chose a
hollow rock of difficult access for his place of abode,
which he divided into three rooms or apartments : one

of which served him for an oratory, another for a work-room, and the third for his ordinary uses. The entrance of this cavern he closed up so effectually, that for the space of fifty years he neither went out himself nor admitted any one to enter his enclosure, conversing only on certain days through a window with such as either came to be edified by his heavenly discourses, or to seek counsel, consolation, or a remedy for their diseases ; but for the accommodation of such as came from a remote distance, he permitted a dwelling to be erected near to his grotto, where some servants of God, who had placed themselves under his direction, took care to provide them with food and lodging. But as for women, none were suffered to approach him upon any account whatsoever. He employed the whole week in conversation with God, except the Saturdays and Sundays, when he let himself be seen through his window by such as came to visit him ; and after having prayed for and with them, and entertained them with excellent lessons out of the word of God, according to their exigencies, he resolved their doubts, comforted them in their spiritual afflictions, and encouraged them to fervor and perseverance in the love and service of God. His words were seasoned with that heavenly wisdom which he acquired by a continual conversation with God ; for the more he withdrew himself from earthly things, the nearer the Spirit of God approached to him, with such heavenly light as not only to endow him with a clear understanding of things present, but also with so perfect a knowledge and foresight of things to come, that few or none of the saints since the Apostles have been found to excel, or even to equal him in the spirit of prophecy. He not only often declared the most secret thoughts of their hearts to those that came to visit him, and reproved them in private for sins of which he could have no knowledge but by revelation, but also foretold public calamities, and cautioned the people against the sins by which they were about to draw down the severe judgment of God upon their heads; and on many other occasions relating to the public welfare, he not only gave directions to those in power how to act, but punctually foretold the success. He became also illustrious for innumerable miracles: though to avoid ostentation he would never undertake to cure the diseased in his cell, but rather chose to send them some oil he had previously blessed, which never failed to heal them of all their disorders.

Palladius relates how himself had undertaken a journey of eighteen days from mount Nitria to the neighborhood of Lycopolis, on purpose to visit this saint; and that as soon as he saw him, he told him his name, and mentioned the monastery from whence he came; and that shortly after the governor of the province coming in, and the Saint having entertained him for some time in private upon the affairs of his soul, when the governor was gone he let Palladius know what had passed in the mean time in his thoughts. He told him also the temptations he lay under of quitting his solitude, and of returning to his native country, under the specious pretext of comfort‧ ing his aged father, and of inducing his brother and his sister to embrace a religious life, assuring him that such an undertaking was needless, for that they had both of them already renounced the world, and that his father would live seven years longer; and more‑ over, that he should hereafter be a bishop, and after‑ wards suffer great troubles and afflictions; all which came to pass, for when Palladius, some time after, going into Palestine for a change of air, and from thence into Bithynia, he was there made a Bishop of Helonopolis, and became a partaker in the persecution raised against St. John Chrysostome, being himself also expelled from his see on the same occasion.

Rufinus also with six others, his companions, went in like manner from Jerusalem to visit the great Saint not long before his happy death. At their first com‑ ing, when according to custom they were about to join with him in prayer, and then to receive his benedic‑ tion; he ased if there was not one amongst them in holy orders? They answered, no. But he looked on them one by one, and then pointing to the youngest of the company, he said, *this man is a deacon;* which was actually the case, though he desired to conceal it, and as only one of the company knew it, he therefore continued to deny it; upon which the saint taking hold of his hand, and kissing it, said: "My son, take care not to disown the grace you have received from God, lest that which is good should be an occasion of your falling into evil, by telling a lie under the pretext of humility. An untruth must never be told, not even under the pretence of good, nor upon any account whatever; for a lie can never proceed from God, but always from evil, as our Saviour himself teaches." The deacon received this charitable correction with respectful silence. After which, having all united in prayer, as soon as they had finished, one of the company, who was grievously tormented with a tertian ague, humbly entreated the Saint to cure him. He told him, that he desired to be delivered from what was sent him for his good, for that sicknesses, and such like chastisements, contributed to purify the soul. He however gave him some blessed oil, by the application of which he was suddenly and perfectly healed. The man of God gave orders, says Rufinus, for our entertainment, according to the strictest rules of hospitality, taking much care of us, whilst he was altogether regardless of himself; for he never eat till after vespers, and then but a very small quantity of what had never been near the fire This was his manner of fasting, in which he still persevered though he was now ninety years of age.

After refreshing their bodies by the entertainment the saint had ordered for them, they returned again to receive from him the food of their souls. Having asked them, from what place they came, and what was the motive of their journey? They answered, that they came from Jerusalem, with a desire to be edified by seeing what they had heard so much of. Upon which he told them, with a cheerful serenity of countenance, which proceeded from the inward joy and peace of his soul, that he wondered how they should take so much pains, and suffer the fatigues of so long a journey, merely to see a poor frail imperfect mortal, in whom there was nothing worthy of any one's seeking after or admiring; for even supposing they had conceived an opinion that they might be edified by what they should see in him, or hear from his mouth, yet how inconsiderable would all this be in comparison of what they might learn at any time without going abroad, from the prophets and apostles, or rather from the spirit of God in the holy Scriptures. However, seeing they came so far with a desire to hear something from him, he made them a most divine exhortation, set down at large by Rufinus; in which, after cautioning them against the danger of being puffed up by vanity, on account of their journey, or any thing they should see or hear from the servants of God, either by harboring a better opinion of themselves, or seeking to raise themselves in the esteem of

others, he proceeds to expatiate on the pernicious effects of pride and vain-glory, which not only rob us
of the fruit and reward of all our good works, but is
capable of even casting the soul, that seems to herself
to have already ascended to the top of the hill of religious perfection, headlong down the precipice that
leads to the bottomless pit, as was the case with Satan
and his angels. Of this he told them a dreadful example, which had lately happened in that very desert,
of a solitary, who dwelt in a cavern by himself, and
led an austere life, laboring with his own hands for his
subsistence, and passing both day and night in prayer;
after having attained to an eminent degree of virtue,
suffering himself to be puffed up with pride and a
conceit of his own strength, he fell an easy prey to the
enemy; who assuming the shape of a woman in distress, and being admitted by him into his cave, excited in his heart impure thoughts and criminal desires;
to which, when he had consented, and was seeking to
put them into execution, the phantom vanished away
with a most hideous noise, whilst a multitude of devils
was heard in the place, with a loud laughter mocking
and insulting him. The wretch was so much cast
down and confounded at his shameful fall, that abandoning all thoughts of endeavoring to rise again, and
repair, by penance and humility, the fault into which
his pride had betrayed him, he fell into the deep gulf
of despair, and returning into the world, he gave him

self up to all manner of impurities, industriously avoiding the meeting or conversing with any holy person, who by their wholesome admonitions might seek to reclaim and convert him.

In the sequel of his discourse the Saint also inculcates the necessity of keeping a strict guard upon our hearts and thoughts, in order to prevent any passion, or disorderly affection of the will, or the vain desire of any thing which is not according to God, from taking root in the heart; for from these roots a thousand distractions presently shoot up, to the great prejudice of our attention and devotion in prayer, as well as to the purity of the soul; "so that it is not enough," says he, " to have renounced the world, and all the works of Satan, the prince of the world, nor even to have left our goods, our lands, and all we possessed in the world, we must also renounce our imperfections, and all vain pleasures, and *unprofitable and hurtful desires*, which, as the apostle tells us, 1 Tim. vi. 9, *drown men in destruction and perdition.*—For without renouncing these things, we never effectually renounce the devil and all his works; since it is by their means the devil enters and takes possession of our heart. These disorderly affections hold a correspondence with our enemy; nay, as they proceed from him, and open to him the door of the soul. it is no wonder such souls should never enjoy rest, but rather be always agitated by troubles and commotion, since they are always encompassed by so wretched a guest to whom they have given admittance by their passions and vices. On the other hand, he that has indeed renounced the world, that is to say, retrenched all his vices and passions, and banished all disorderly affections to sin far from his soul, so as to leave no gate open by which the devil may enter;—he who represses his anger, resists and overcomes all irregular motions to evil,—avoids all lying,—abhors envy,—who not only speaks well of every one, but even denies himself the liberty of thinking evil of any one, and who always considers the good and evil of his neighbor as his own, and behaves accordingly on every occasion, such a one as this opens the gate of his soul to the Holy Spirit, who enters in and fills it with his light, and with those admirable fruits of *charity, joy, peace, patience, &c.* which are produced in the soul by this heavenly Comforter." Wherefore the Saint proceeds to recommend in a particular manner to all who are desirous of being truly religious, to labor to acquire such perfect purity, both of conscience and of heart, as may enable them to offer up to our Lord such a perfect and pure prayer as may introduce them to a certain familiarity with his divine Majesty and his holy angels, and to such a happy union of love, as to be enabled to say with St. Paul, Rom. viii. 38, 39. *That neither death, nor life, nor angels, nor principalities, nor powers, nor things present, nor things to come—nor any other creature shall be able to separate us from the love of God, which is in Christ Jesus our Lord.* He further adds, that the best means to attain this perfect purity, so pleasing to God, is to retrench by the virtue of mortification, vanities, inordinate affections, and sensual delights of every kind, even in small things, and to walk resolutely in the narrow way of self-denial and penance; with which, if we join the love of solitude, silence, and recollection of spirit, we shall easily arrive at perfection, and even begin to enjoy a kind of heaven upon earth.

With these and such like heavenly discourses the Saint entertained his guests, and after three days dismissed them, giving them his blessing, and telling them at parting, that on that very day the news was brought to Alexandria of the victory which the emperor Theodosius had obtained over the tyrant Eugenius, but, said he, that good emperor shall not long survive this happy event, but shall die a natural death. All which they soon after found to be true. The man of God himself did not survive that year. During the space of three days before his death, he let no man see him; and on the fourth day, being on his knees in prayer, he breathed out his pure soul into the hands of his Creator, whom he went to enjoy for a happy eternity.

Palladius relates, as having learnt it from the Saint himself, that during the many years he had lived in

his cavern he had never seen any woman, nor one
piece of money, nor ever beheld any man eating, nor
had any man ever seen him either eat or drink.

But we must not here omit a very remarkable history relating to this Saint, which we find not only attested by Rufinus and Palladius, but also by St. Augustine, L. *de Cura pro Mortuis*, c. 17. which he had
learnt from those who had been informed thereof by
the very parties themselves to whom it happened.   A
certain tribune or colonel came to the Saint and begged he would allow his wife to see him, as she had undertaken a long and dangerous journey out of an extreme desire she had of visiting him.   The man of
God answered, that he never saw, nor admitted of
visits from any woman.   But as the colonel still pressed him, affirming that it would cost his wife her life,
through the greatness of her affliction, if she were not
admitted to see him, the Saint bid him go, and assure
his wife she should see him without giving herself the
trouble of either coming to him, or so much as going
out of her own bed chamber.   Accordingly that very
night the man of God appeared to her in a vision in
her sleep, said to her: " O woman, great is thy faith,
which has obliged me to come hither to satisfy thy
request.   However I must warn thee against desiring
in future to see the mortal and earthly visage of the
servants of God, but rather to contemplate with the
eye of the spirit their lives and other actions : *for tha*

flesh profiteth nothing, but it is the spirit that giveth life. Know this also, that I, not in the quality of a Saint, or of a prophet, as thou imaginest, but only in consideration of thy faith, have prayed to our Lord for thee, and he has been pleased to grant to thee the cure of all the corporal diseases under which thou laborest; and henceforward both thou and thy husband shall enjoy good health, and all thy house shall be blessed. But take care that thou never forget the benefits of God ; live always in the fear of the Lord, and desire no more for thy worldly subsistence than the appointment due to thy post. Content thyself then with having seen me in thy sleep, and desire no more." When the woman awaked, she related the whole vision to her husband, describing the habit of the Saint, and all the lineaments of his face, which to his great astonishment all perfectly agreed. Upon which he went the next day to return thanks to the man of God ; who as soon as he saw him, said : " behold I have fulfilled my promise, depart then in peace, and may the blessing of God go along with you both."

St. John of Egypt is celebrated in the Roman Martyrology on the seventeenth of March.

ST. ARSENIUS.

From the third and fifth book of the Remarkable Actions and Sayings of the Ancient Fathers, published
by Rosweidus.

Sr. ARSENIUS was a nobleman in great favor with
the emperor Theodosius, who committed to him the
care of the education of his two sons, Arcadius and
Honorius, in quality both of their godfather and of
their governor. In this eminent station he lived at
court the life of a courtier, in the midst of honors,
riches, and pleasures, till he was about forty years of
age, when God was pleased to call him from a worldly life into the wilderness, there to seek, by flight,
silence, and repose, the salvation of his soul. For,
whilst he was one day at his prayers, earnestly begging of our Lord to teach him what he should do to
secure his eternal salvation, he heard a voice that
answered him, saying, "Arsenius, flee the company of
men, and thou shalt be saved." Wherefore, in compliance with this heavenly call, he instantly abandoned his secular glory for the love of Christ: and quitting all his worldly possessions, retired into the desert
of Scete, in order to dedicate the remainder of his
days to the love and service of his Maker, in solitude,
prayer, labor, and penance. Whilst he repeated the

same prayer, he heard again the same voice, saying "Arsenius, flee, be silent, and quiet, (*fuge, tace, quiesce*) these are the principles of salvation, or the first things to be done in order to salvation. *Hæc sunt principia salutis.*"

To fulfil this repeated injunction of fleeing from the company of men, he chose a cell at a great distance from the other solitaries, and very rarely admitted of any visits from them. Even when he went to church, which was thirteen leagues distant from his habitation, he used to place himself behind one of the pillars, in order to conceal himself as much as possible, so as neither to see nor be seen by others. When Theophilus, the patriarch of Alexandria, went one day to visit him with some others in his company, and desired he would make some discourse to the company for their spiritual edification; the Saint asked them whether they were all disposed to observe and put in practice what he should say to them? Yes, replied they, very willingly. Why then, said he, I beg of you, that in what place soever you may hereafter hear Arsenius to dwell, be pleased to let him be alone, and never to come near him. Another time the same patriarch being desirous to see him, sent to know if he would admit of his visit. Arsenius answered, that if he came alone he should open the door to him, but if he brought any others in his company he would seek out another place, and remain there no longer; so that

Theophilus, for fear of driving him away, refrained afterwards from visiting him. The abbot Mark having asked him one day, why he kept at such a distance from men, and shunned the conversation of all the other solitaries? He answered: "God knows how dearly I love them all; but I cannot be at the same time with his divine Majesty and with them. For whereas the angels, though their number be almost infinite, yet have all but one will; it is quite otherwise with men, whose dispositions and wills are different; therefore I cannot think of leaving God to converse with men."

As to the manner in which he spent his time in this solitude, it was divided between working and prayer, or rather his whole life in the wilderness was one continual prayer; for even whilst he was sitting at work and making baskets, which was his daily employment, his soul was ever attentive to God in prayer, and for ever bewailing his sins; insomuch that he was obliged to have always a handkerchief in his bosom, to wipe off the flood of penitential tears which continually flowed from his eyes. As for the nights, he generally spent them, as we learn from his disciple Daniel, in watching and prayer; only towards the morning, when nature could hold out no longer, he used to suffer sleep, which he called his *naughty servant*, to close his eyes; but after a very short repose, which he took sitting, he rose up again to his accustomed exercises

The same disciple relates, that on Saturday evenings the setting sun usually left him at his prayers, with his hands extended towards heaven, and that he continued praying in this same posture till the sunbeams, rising the next morning, came beating upon his eyes. In order to renew his fervor in his spiritual exercises, he would frequently say to himself: *Arsenius, Arsenius, to what end didst thou leave the world and come hither?* He used also often to say that whenever he had been talking, he had always found matter whereof to repent, but had never regretted his having kept silence. He was also a great lover of holy poverty. The other solitaries said of him, that as no one was more richly clad than Arsenius whilst he lived at court, so none of the inhabitants of the desert wore a more mean or poor habit than he, after retiring from the world. His poverty was so great, that having occasion for a trifle of money to procure some little necessaries for him in sickness, he was obliged to receive it in alms, upon which he cried out: I give thee thanks, O my God, that thou hast made me worthy to be thus reduced to the necessity of asking an alms in thy name." After he had lived for many years in the wilderness, a kinsman of his, a senator. dying, left him by his last will a considerable estate. When this will was brought to the Saint, by a proper officer, in his solitude, it displeased him so much that he would have torn it in pieces, had not the officer flung himself at

his feet, declaring that it would cost him his life if the
will were destroyed. Upon this Arsenius returned
him back the will, saying, "How is it possible this
man should by his will make me his heir, since he, as
it appears, died but a little while ago, whilst I have
been dead so many years."

As to his method of fasting, and other austerities
of this kind, it is hard to describe them in particular
on account of his keeping himself so much to himself.
His disciple Daniel only informed us, that during the
whole time he knew him, they laid him in but a very
slender provision for his whole year's sustenance; and
yet that he managed it so well, as not only to make it
suffice for himself, but also to impart some of it to his
disciples whenever they came to see him. The same
disciple also took notice, that whilst he was sitting at
his work, making baskets, according to his custom, of
the leaves of palm-trees, when the water in which he
was obliged to moisten and soften them began to corrupt, he would never change it, or fling it away, but
if there were any need of fresh water, he would pour
it in upon that which was already corrupted, that so
it might always continue to yield a disagreeable smell.
The brethren asked him one day, why he would not
suffer that corrupt water to be flung away, since it infected his whole cell with its stench? "Because," replied he, "I was used when I lived in the world to
gratify myself with the most agreeable perfumes, and

therefore it is no more than just that I should now, during the time that remains of my life, in punishment of my former sensuality, support this stench, in hopes that at the last day God will deliver me from the insupportable stench of hell, and not condemn my soul with that of the rich man who had passed his days in feasting and delights."   •

But nothing was more remarkable in this Saint than his extraordinary humility, which made him so industrious in keeping himself out of sight, and in concealing every thing that might procure him the applause or esteem of men. Although he was so learned in the human sciences before he quitted the world, as to be perfect master both of the Greek and Latin, and had, after his retiring into the wilderness, received such extraordinary lights from God for understanding spirit- ual matters, that no one had a more perfect knowledge, or could better explain the most difficult passages of the holy Scriptures than himself, yet he would never speak of these matters by his own choice, nor show at any time his knowledge of them, but rather chose to consult and hearken to the most illiterate of the breth- ren, provided he were truly humble. Being asked one day why he, being so learned a man, sought in- struction and counsel from a certain solitary, who was quite destitute of all human literature, he replied: " It is true, whilst I was in the world I acquired some knowledge in the sciences of the world, and in the

22

Greek and Latin tongues, but since I have left the world, I have not yet been able to learn even the A B, C, of the true science of the Saints, of which this ignorant rustic is master." Such were his humble sentiments of himself.

After he had spent forty years in the desert of Scete, the Mazices, a barbarous people of Lybia, made an irruption on that side, where they massacred St. Moses and other solitaries, and forced all the rest from their cells. Upon this occasion Arsenius was obliged to change his earthly residence, but not the true dwelling place where his heart was fixed. He went therefore to a place called Trohe, not far from the ancient Babylon of Egypt (now Cairo), and there he continued his usual course of life for ten years, till fresh irruptions of the barbarians forced him thence. From Trohe he went to Canopus in the lower Egypt, which is not far distant from Alexandria, where, being too much disturbed with the importunity of visits from that great metropolis, he remained no longer than three years, and then returned again to Trohe, where he spent the two last years of his mortal pilgrimage. When his end approached, he told his disciples that he desired they would bury him privately, no matter how, only taking care that he should be remembered in the offering of the holy sacrifice. They that were present at his death, seeing him, said to him: "Father, why do you weep? Are you, like the rest, afraid to die?"

" Yes," said he, " very much ; and this is no new fear, but a fear that has stuck close to me ever since I first came into the desert." He departed to our Lord in a good old age, being ninety-five years old, of which he had spent fifty-five in the desert in the exercises of a religious life St. Pemen seeing him expire, cried out: "O happy Arsenius, for having wept and mourned for yourself so much in this world! since they who do not mourn in this life, shall mourn for all eternity in the next." It is also recorded of the patriarch Theophilus, that when he was at the point of death, he said: "O how happy wast thou, O Arsenius, who hadst this last hour continually before thine eyes!"

The name of St. Arsenius is recorded in the Roman Martyrology on the nineteenth of July.

ST. NILAMMON.

From Sozomen. an ancient Church Historian, lib 8 c. 19.

NILAMMON was a holy anchoret, who had made himself a little cell near Geres, a small city of Egypt, in the neighborhood of Pelusium, where he dwelt for many years in admirable sanctity. When the bishop of that city died, the clergy and people, who had con

ceived a high opinion of the eminent virtues of this
servant of God, desired to have him for his successor.
But whatsover advances they made, Nilammon's humility repelled, by refusing to submit his shoulders to
a charge which even an angel might have reason to
dread ; but being apprehensive that they would use
violence, he closed up the door of his cell, and fenced it
with stones, that they might not be able to come at him.

In the mean time it happened that Theophilus, the
patriarch of Alexandria, coming by sea from Constantinople, where he had been too much engaged in the
unjust déposition of St, John Chrysostom, was driven
by a storm upon the coast of Geres. The people
therefore took this opportunity of the presence of the
patriarch to entreat him to oblige Nilammon to accept
of the bishopric. Whereupon Theophilus going to
his cell, used his utmost endeavors to prevail upon him
to accept of episcopal consecration, and continued to
press him so closely, that Nilammon finding the patriarch would not hear any thing that he could al-
ledge to excuse himself, desired at least one day's res-
pite to set his affairs in order, telling him, that on the
following day he might do with him as he pleased.

The patriarch failed not to return on the following
day, accompanied by all the people, and then chal-
lenging the Saint to fulfil his promise, he desired him
to open the door, that they might proceed to his consecration. Nilammon proposed that some time should

be allowed him for prayer before his consecration. Theophilus applauded the proposition, and betook himself also to prayer; but the fervor of Nilammon's prayers was so excessive, that he breathed out his soul into the hands of his Creator. In the mean time, the patriarch and people who remained without, after having allowed him, as they thought, competent time for his devotion, began to be impatient, and to call aloud on him to open his door; but finding that a great part of the day passed in this manner, and that he returned no answer, they forced their way into his cell, where, to their great surprise, they found him dead. Having buried him with great honor, they erected a church over his monument, where they celebrated his festival amongst the Saints.

He died anno 403, and his name is recorded in the Roman Martyrology on the sixth day of January.

ST. SIMON STYLITES.

From Theodoret in his Philotheus, chap 26, and Antonius, Disciple of the Saint, in his Life

ALTHOUGH there were, during the life-time of St. Simon Stylites, almost as many eye-witnesses of his extraordinary course of life, and of the innumerable pro-

digies which God wrought by him, as there were men
in all the eastern regions, not to say in the then known
world, yet the great Theodoret, who undertook, whilst
the Saint was yet living, to transmit, by writing, to
posterity a faithful account of this wonder of the
world, was afraid lest he should seem to succeeding
ages to have delivered to them a fabulous rather than
a true history.   But the divine providence which raised up this Saint in so extraordinary a manner, in order to show forth the power of his grace to the whole
world, and to rouse up by so great an example the
drooping spirits of lukewarm Christians, as well as to
enlighten the eyes and touch the hearts of thousands
of infidels and sinners, was pleased that the wonderful life of Simon should not only be perfectly well
known at the time he lived through the whole extent
of the Roman empire, and all the eastern nations bordering thereon, but that for the edification of posterity
it should also be written by cotemporary authors, and
in so public a manner, that we may safely aver, there
is no fact in history better authenticated.

Our Saint was born towards the latter end of the
fourth century, at a place called Sisan, upon the confines of Syria and Cilicia.   In his tender years he was
employed by his parents in feeding their sheep in the
country, so that he seems to have had but little opportunity of frequenting the church or hearing the
word of God.   But a great snow happening to fall

one day, obliged him to leave the sheep under shelter
at home, which afforded him leisure to go to church.
No sooner had he entered the church than he became
so extremely affected, and penetrated with the fear of
God, as to give the utmost attention to the divine lessons that were read out of the Episties of St Paul and
the gospel ; and after deeply reflecting on those words
of the sermon upon the mount, *blessed are they that
mourn :* and *blessed are the clean of heart, &c.* he
addressed himself to an old man, who was one of the
congregation, desiring to be further informed what he
should do, and what course of life he should follow,
that he might live up to these heavenly lessons and
save his soul ? The good old man recommended a
retired and solitary life as the most proper to establish
solid virtue in his soul ; and spoke to him in so moving and affecting a manner, that the holy seed immediately sunk so deep into his heart as to already begin
to produce its fruit. The first thing he afterwards
did, was to retire to a solitary place, where there was
a church of the martyrs, and there, prostrate upon the
ground with the utmost fervor of soul. he besought
him who desires that all men should be saved, to
vouchsafe to direct him in the way of perfect piety, in
order to secure his eternal salvation. Having continued a long time in prayer, he fell into a profound
sleep, in which he had the following vision. He seemed to himself, as he related to Theodoret, to be dig

ging the ground, in order to lay the foundation of a building, and that he heard a voice which bid him *dig still deeper.* He did so, and then would have rested himself, but the voice a second time bid him *go deeper still.* And the same thing having been repeated four times, one after another, at length it was said to him *that is deep enough,* and that he had now nothing more to do but to build.

Arising from the ground, he went directly to a neighboring monastery, which was governed by a holy abbot named Timothy. Here he prostrated himself before the gate, employing three whole days and nights in fasting and prayer, without ever being taken notice of. At length the abbot coming out, he cast himself at his feet, and besought him with many tears to take pity on a poor soul in danger of perishing, who was desirous to learn how to serve God. The abbot taking him by the hand, encouraged him, led him into the monastery, and recommended to the brethren to teach him the rule of the house, which he, being then only thirteen years old, quickly learnt, and practised with such perfection as to surpass all the rest in humility, as well as in the exercises of fasting and penance. Here also, in four months, he learnt the whole psalter by heart, and took great delight in meditating on, and feeding his soul with these heavenly hymns. In this monastery he remained two years, exhibiting a perfect pattern of a consummate virtue and piety in so tender an age. In the mean time his parents sought after him, and bewailed him as lost, whilst he, with greater reason, rejoiced at having now happily found both himself and his God.

For his greater improvement in the silence of the saints he went from this religious house to another monastery, founded at a place called Teleda, near Antioch, by the disciples of the Saints Ammian and Eusebius, and governed at this time by the abbot Heliodorus, where he remained for about nine or ten years. There were in this monastery about eighty monks, but Simon excelled them all in the exercises of a religious life; for, whereas all the rest were accustomed to eat once a day, or at least once in two days, he fasted the whole week with such rigor as to eat nothing, except only one meal on the Lord's day. Here, having procured a rope or cord, made of the leaves of palm-trees, so hard and rough that it could scarcely be even handled, he privately girt himself with it beneath his habit, next to his skin, so tightly, that it forced its way into the flesh, till it was almost covered, and the flesh itself became perfectly corrupted with it. He concealed what he suffered on this occasion with as much care as possible, till the religious at length found out how the case stood with him, and the abbot insisted upon his parting with the cord, which was with much difficulty, and not without putting him to great tortures, disengaged from the flesh.

After the wound occasioned by the cord was cured,
the abbot dismissed him from the monastery, fearing
lest any of the other religious might suffer prejudice,
by aiming at an imitation of his extraordinary austerities.   Simon, on this occasion, retiring into a more
remote and lonesome part of the mountain, found
there a dry well, into which he went down and there
sung the praises of God.   Here he remained for several
days without either eating or drinking, till Heliodorus,
repenting that he sent the Saint away in that manner,
desired two of the brethren to seek after him, and
bring him back again.   These by the direction of
some shepherds, who had heard him singing, found
him out in his well, and with the help of a rope
brought him up, and conducted him back to the monastery, where he continued for a short time, and then
betook himself to an abandoned hut near a village
called Telanissus, situated at the foot of that mountain on the top of which he afterwards finished his
course.

In this hut he lived shut up during three years;
and here our Lord first inspired him with a desire of
fasting the forty days of Lent, without taking any
manner of corporal nourishment during the whole
time.   Upon this he desired Bassus, who was the ecclesiastical superior in that district, to wall up the door
of his cell for that Lent, and leave him quite to himself without any thing for his food.   Bassus remon

strated to him, that this would be an undertaking beyond the strength of man, and that to destroy himself,
which would be the inevitable consequence of such a
fast, could be no act of virtue, but, on the contrary, a
grievous crime. Leave with me then, father, said the
Saint, ten loaves of bread and a pitcher of water, that
I may make use of them in case I find it necessary.
Bassus accordingly furnished the loaves and the water,
and then stopping up the door, departed, and did not
return till the forty days were ended. As soon as
Easter was come he hastened to visit the servant of
God, carrying with him the blessed sacrament; but
behold, after he had removed the stones and opened
the door, he found the Saint lying extended on the
floor like one dead, without speech or motion, with
the ten loaves and the water quite untouched. However, as he found life still remaining in him, he dipped
a sponge in the water with which he moistened his
mouth, and then gave him the holy communion.
With this heavenly food he was again raised up, and
further enabled to recover his strength, by taking in a
little nourishment from the juice of herbs and pulse.
This fast of forty days during Lent, without either eating or drinking any thing whatever, from this time
forward, he constantly observed every year throughout the remainder of his life, which time and custom
had at length made easy to him. For at the beginning, after passing the first part of Lent, standing and

praising God, he was obliged, as he grew weaker, to
sit down, and in this posture to perform the divine
office, till towards the latter end his weakness forced
him to lie down stretched out at full length, as one
half dead, and on this account, during the first years
of his living and standing upon the pillar, he was obliged, for the latter part of his forty days fast, to support himself by the help of a post fastened to his pillar for this purpose, to which he caused himself to be
tied as he became weaker. But for many years before his death God had strengthened him so far as not
to stand in need of any help, but pass the whole time
of Lent with all the cheerfulness imaginable, without
any nourishment or human support whatsoever.

From his hut near Telanissus, the Saint went up to
the top of the neighboring mountain, and there made
for himself an inclosure of stones, without any covering, in which he remained for some years, taking no
other nourishment but boiled lentiles and water, and
by the means of a chain, one end of which he fastened
to his right leg, and the other to a great stone, he confined himself to such narrow limits as not to be able
to go beyond the length of his chain. But if he was
chained in body, his soul remained at liberty, and was
continually flying up towards God, by mental prayer
and contemplation. This chain, upon the remonstrances of Melecius, a Chorepiscopus under the patriarch
of Antioch, he suffered to be taken away. At which

time, as Theodoret learnt from Melecius himself, after the smith had filed off the iron, when they came to take away the leather which the Saint had put next to his skin, to hinder the chain from entering into his flesh, as the cord had done before, they found in it about twenty large puneezes, or bugs, which this prelate thought worthy of particular notice, to show the wonderful patience of the Saint, who had quietly suffered for so long a time the troublesome bites of these insects, when he might with so much ease have rid himself of them at once by destroying them.

And now the reputation of Simon's sanctity being spread far and near, great multitudes began to resort to him on account of the many miraculous graces of every kind that were obtained through the efficacy of his prayers and benedictions, struggling with each other who should first come near him and touch his garments, believing that those coarse skins wherewith he was clad, would impart to them a blessing. This became so troublesome and insupportable to the Saint, as to first suggest to him the thought of living upon a pillar, in order to be out of the reach of the crowd; to which he was no doubt instigated by a particular inspiration from God, who designed, by the means of this extraordinary manner of living, to draw great numbers of infidels to the faith, and of Christians to a virtuous and penitential life.

He began this new way of life, which was never be-

23

fore attempted by any other, about the year of Christ,
526, and continued it till his death, which happened
about seven and thirty years afterwards. The pillar
which he caused to be made at first was but six cubits,
that is three yards high, which he afterwards exchanged
for one of twelve cubits, and again, for one of twenty-
two cubits; but that on which he finished his course
was thirty-six cubits, that is eighteen yards in height.
Its diameter, as we learn from Evagrius, was at the
most but two cubits, or one yard; so that he could
not, if he would, lie down upon it at his length. In
the mean time he had no covering or shelter to defend
himself either from the rigor of the winter, the heats
of the summer, the violence of the rain or wind, or
from other injuries of the air. His ordinary posture
was standing night and day, without any other support but the strength of faith and divine grace. In
his prayer he very frequently bowed himself down to
adore God, and that in so profound a manner as to
bring his forehead almost to his toes. His rigorous
fasts, for he never eat but once a week, and then
next to nothing, reduced his body to so low a condition as to make it easy to him. These adorations he
repeated so frequently, that we learn from Theoderet,
that whilst this holy prelate was himself present, one
of his attendants counted them to the number of 1244.
He often remained for a considerable space of time in
prayer, bowed down in this manner with his forehead

upon the pillar and this, it is probable, might also be
the posture in which he slept; for certain it is, that
he sometimes slept, though fame had published that
he lived without either sleeping or eating. Be this as
it may, he certainly slept but very little; for, as he
generally passed the greatest part of the night in
prayer, so he did the best part of the day, even till the
ninth hour, viz. three in the afternoon, when he made
his exhortations to the people. But on the eves, or
vigils of the festivals, he not only passed the whole
night in prayer, but stood all the time on his feet,
with his hands stretched forth and extended towards
heaven.

The other holy inhabitants of the oriental deserts
hearing of the new and extraordinary manner of life
which the Saint had undertaken, having consulted together, sent a deputation to him, as we learn from the
historian Evagrius, lib. 1, chap. 13, to ask him the reason of his leading so unheard of a course of life, or
of leaving the common road which had been beaten
by all the Saints and the holy fathers who were gone
before him; and to order him to come down immediately from his pillar: giving, nevertheless, instructions to their deputy, that if Simon should show himself ready to obey, he should suffer him to remain
thereon, and encourage him to proceed in his undertaking, as showing by his ready obedience that what
he did was not from caprice, but by divine inspiration·

but that if he refused to obey, he should oblige him to come down by force. The deputy had no sooner delivered his commission, than the Saint, without making the least reply or demur, presently disposed himself to obey, and to come down. Whereupon the deputy told him to continue where he was, for his undertaking was from God.

This the Almighty himself sufficiently manifested by the many miraculous gifts and graces he bestowed upon him, of which there were in his life-time millions of witnesses, as there was an incredible multitude from all parts of the world continually assembled to behold this wonder of the world, to hear his divine instructions, and seek remedies through him for all their evils. "For you shall not only see there," says Theodoret, "the inhabitants of our province, Syria, but also the Ishmaelites, Saracens of Arabia, Persians, Armenians, Iberians, Ethiopians, and other nations which are still more remote. There came also people to him from the farthest part of the west, viz. from Spain, Britain, Gaul, and other neighboring provinces; and as to Italy, it is needless to say any thing, since we are assured that his name is so illustrous in Rome, that they even set up little pictures of him in their shops and porches for a protection and defence." So far Theodoret writing, whilst the Saint was yet living, the things of which he himself had been witness. He also gives several instances of the spirit of prophecy which he had experienced in this Saint, and of great and evident miracles wrought before his own eyes, and adds, that great numbers of infidels, by occasion of this Saint, were daily brought over to the faith of Christ. "One," says he, "may see the Iberians, Armenians, and Persians coming to receive baptism. And as to the Saracens, they come to him in large companies of two or three hundreds, or even of a thousand at a time, abjuring, with a loud voice, their false religion, treading their idols under their feet, in the presence of this bright light of Christianity, embracing the divine mysteries of our holy faith, and receiving from the sacred mouth of this man of God the rules of life which they were to follow for the time to come. "I myself," says Theodoret, "have been witness of all this."

As to the rest, the same learned and holy prelate gives an ample testimony to the unparalleled modesty and humility of this great servant of God, and of his wonderful meekness and affability to persons of all conditions, how poor or mean soever they were according to the world. But nothing was so admirable in him as that invincible patience, constancy, courage, and alacrity wherewith he underwent, for so long a series of years, the voluntary austerities of so severe and rigid a course of penance, which for a great part of the time was rendered still more difficult and insupportable by a dreadful ulcer in his left foot, which

he had contracted by his continual standing, and
which sent forth corrupted blood and vermin. Nevertheless, with all his fasting, watching, prayer, and
other austerities, he ceased not to labor daily for the
salvation of the souls of his neighbors, by delivering
to them from his pillar twice a day excellent exhortations to take off their hearts from this wretched earth
—to set always before their eyes that everlasting kingdom which we hope for hereafter—to tremble at the
threats of eternal torments—to despise all that passes
with time. and ever to aspire after the good things of
the Lord, in the land of the living. He was also ever
ready to give ghostly counsel to all who came ; to
hearken to their demands, cure their diseases, accommodate their differences, &c. ; and not only to attend
to the private necessities of particulars, but much
more to every occasion by which he might promote
the common good of the church ; dictating sometimes letters, to this end, to prelates, to governors, and
even to the emperor himself. Thus he usually employed his time from the third hour after mid-day till
the sunset, and then he gave his benediction to the
people, which they received with great reverence, and
thus bid adieu to men to converse with his God
alone.

At length the time being come in which God had
decreed to crown the patience and labors of his servant
with eternal glory, upon a Friday, anno Christi, 496,

having bowed down, according to his custom in prayer, he gave up his happy soul into the hands of him whom he had so constantly and so faithfully served. His body, after his death, remained in the same posture from Friday till Sunday in the afternoon, no one in the mean time knowing that he was dead; because it was no unusual thing for the Saint to pass whole days in prayer, so as to omit his ordinary times of speaking to the people. But on Sunday in the afternoon, his disciple Antonius going up the pillar by a ladder, found that he was dead, and immediately gave private notice of it to the patriarch of Antioch, and to the governor of the province, in order to prevent any tumult that might be raised by the people contending about his body. The patriarch Martynus, accompanied with six other bishops, and escorted by the governor with 6000 soldiers, came without delay, and taking the body of the Saint down from the pillar, carried it away with great solemnity to Antioch, where it was interred. God was pleased to work many great miracles by his intercession, as well at his monument in that city, as at his pillar where he lived and died. His name is recorded in the Roman Martyrology on the third of September.

There were divers other saints of the name of Simon, who are also celebrated in church history. Amongst the rest *St. Simon the ancient,* whose life is also given by Theodoret in his Philotheus, of whom he relates that he had the very lions of the desert at his beck. *St. Simon Stylites the younger*, who also passed his life upon a pillar, and is recorded in the Roman Martyrology, September the third ; St. Simon, surnamed Salus, whose name is registered in the same Mrtyrology, July the first, with the following eulogium : " *At Emesa, St. Simon, confessor, surnamed Salus, who became a fool for Christ ; but his profound wisdom God declared by great miracles.*"

ST. EUTHYMIUS.

From his Life. by Cyrillus, a faithful cotemporary
writer

EUTHYMIUS, surnamed *the great* was born at Melitene in the lesser Armenia, of noble and virtuous parents, anno 377. He was a child of prayer, his parents having obtained him of God after a long barrenness, by the intercession of St. Polyceutus, the martyr ; and having dedicated him to God from his mother's womb. at the age of three years he was put in the hands of the holy bishop Otteus, and from that time was brought up like another Samuel, in the temple of God, in the exercises of any early piety, and in the study of the holy scriptures, on which he constantly

meditated, even in those leisure hours which others of
his age spend in their diversions. He was ordained
lector when yet a boy, and gradually promoted to the
higher orders, giving great edification through them
all, till he was thought worthy of the priestly function
and then had the conduct, by commission, from the
bishop, of all the monasteries of the diocese of Melitene. In the mean time it was his custom to retire as
often as he could, from all other business to attend to
God and himself in solitude and silence, to which he
had a great inclination from his childhood, to spend a
great part of his time in prayer in the churches of the
martyrs, and to make an annual retreat alone by himself during the whole time of Lent, in a desert mountain, at some distance from the city. His love for solitude and retirement still increasing upon him, at length
determined him to withdraw himself entirely from his
own country, his friends, and acquaintance, and to go
into the Holy Land; where, after visiting and reverencing the places consecrated by the mysteries of our
redemption, he chose for his abode a solitary place,
about six miles from Jerusalem, called Pharan, in the
neighborhood of a *Laura*, or residence of divers religious men, living in separate cells at some distance
from each other, but meeting for their devotions in
the same church, as the hermits of Camalduli do at
present.

This solitude was quite congenial with his inclina-

tions to retirement and silence, and therefore he made
himself a cell here, employing his hands in making
mats, or in other manual labors, that he might live
without being burthensome to any one, and be enabled to relieve such as were in want, having his
heart entirely fixed on God, and making it his whole
study to please him.   Here divine providence brought
him acquainted with a holy solitary, named Theocti-
tus, who had his cell not far off, and who followed the
same manner of life ; and the likeness of their dispositions united them so closely together in the bands
of a most perfect friendship and charity, that they
seemed to be animated with one and the same heart
and soul.   Amongst other exercises of piety, these
two servants of God never failed to make every year
a spiritual retreat, which they began after the Epiphany, and continued till Palm-Sunday.   At this time
they quitted their cells and retired into the wilderness
of Cutila, where being wholly separated from all conversation with mortals, they spent their whole time
with God in prayer and contemplation till Palm-Sunday, when they returned home again, laden with the
spiritual riches which they had acquired in their retreat, to offer them up to our Lord Jesus Christ, at
the festival of his passion and resurrection.

Euthymius had practised this for some years, when
he and Theoctistus, going according to their custom
into the wilderness, were conducted by providence to

the banks of a rapid torrent, where they discovered a large cavern of very difficult access, which they embraced as a place assigned by heaven for their happiness. Here they lived for some time, quite secluded from all human society, having no other food whereon to subsist but the wild herbs of the desert. But as the Almighty designed to bring about the salvation of many souls by the means of these his servants, he did not suffer the place of their abode to remain long a secret. They were at first discovered by certain shepherds, who published to the neighboring village their place of residence and manner of life. This discovery brought about visits from the inhabitants, who cheerfully furnished them with necessaries for their temporal life, and in return received from them wholesome instructions and exhortations, in order to their eternal life.

Shortly after the monks of Pharan also came to visit them, when the sanctity of their discourse and manner of life moved two of them, Marinus and Lucas, who were afterwards great Saints, and by degrees many others from other places, to put themselves under their direction, so that after some time they built a monastery in the same place, and converted their cavern into a church. Euthymius committed the direction and superintendency of this monastery to Theoctistus, whilst he himself enjoyed the sweets of his beloved silence and repose, seated with Mary at the feet of our Lord, yet so as often to interrupt his contemplation, by laboring to purify the souls of his brethren from their stains, and, like a skilful physician, to apply proper remedies for the cure of all their evils; for they came daily to discover their most secret thoughts to him, and to receive the rules and lessons of a spiritual life from his mouth, while Theoctistus for his part did nothing without his advice and concurrence.

He spoke to them all with the affection of a father, and constantly incalculated to them, " That they who by their religious profession had renounced the world, and the things of the world, should make it their principal study to exercise themselves in humility and obedience, and divest themselves of their own will; they should have always the hour of their death before their eyes—tremble at the apprehension of a miserable eternity, and continually aspire, with the most ardent desires, after the kingdom of heaven; that they should also incessently employ themselves in manual labors, more especially when of an age in which the passions of youth stand in need of being kept under, for in that case the body must be brought down by labor, that it may be obliged to submit to the spirit; and that they should ever remember both the example and the doctrine of St. Paul, who says, 2 Thess. iii. 10. *If any man will not work, neither let him eat*, &c. He also strenuously recommended silence, particularly in church and at meals, and could never endure to see any of the young religious, by a motion of their own will, affect to appear more aus tere than the rest in fasting, being desirous that, ac cording to the precept of the Gospel, they should ra ther hide their good works than make them known. He preferred that kind of abstinence, as the most com- mendable, which at every meal, and upon every occasion, restrains the appetite from taking its fill, and always retrenches, without ostentation, some part of what it craves. He added, that they should always be upon their guard to resist every irregular desire; —that they should carry their arms always about with them to defend themselves againt their invisible enemies, and meditate day and night upon the law of God.

Whilst Euthymius was in this monastery, Aspebet, governor of a canton of Saracens, brought his son Terebon, who had quite lost the use of one half of his body by a dead palsy, to be cured by the Saint. The religious seeing a multitude of these barbarians coming towards their monastery were all in a fright; but Theoctistus, as Euthymius was then employed in his spiritual exercises, encouraged them; and going forth to meet the band, he asked them what they wanted? Aspebet answered, we want to see Euthymius. He is in his retirement, said Theoctistus, and will neither see nor speak to any one till Saturday   Then Aspe

bet showed him his son, whose whole right side was
withered in such a manner as to appear quite dead,
and made a sign to the youth to tell him his case.
" The boy said he had been struck with this disorder
in Persia, where his father then resided in the service
cf king Isdegerdes ; that in order to his cure they had
not only employed all the natural remedies of physic,
but also the secrets of magic, to no effect ; and that
since he came with his father into Arabia, they had
again tried new experiments upon him, but all to no
purpose. Wherefore finding that there was no succor to be had from man, he had turned his thoughts
towards the great God that made man, and prayed to
him one night with great fervor, to restore him to
health, promising in that case, that he would dedicat·
himself to his service, and become a Christian. That
after this prayer he had fallen asleep and seen, in a
dream. a venerable monk, who said his name was
Euthymius ; that he lived upon the bank of the torrent in the wilderness, near the road that leads to
Jericho, at about ten miles distance from Jerusalem:
and that if he desired to be cured, and was disposed
to fulfil his promise, he should come to him, and that
God would restore him again to his health.

Theoctistus having heard this, went in and related
the whole to Euthymius, and both of them concluding
that the visions must certainly have come from God,
the Saint interrupted his retreat upon this occasion,

and going out prayed over the young man, and made the sign of the cross upon him, at which he was in an instant perfectly cured, to the great astonishment of the multitude of barbarians present, who were all con- verted upon the spot, and after proper instructions re- ceived baptism. Aspebet took the name of Peter, and made such progress in christian piety, as to be after wards ordained bishop of the Saracens, and Maris his brother-in-law, quitted the world entirely to become a disciple of St. Euthymius.

The fame of this great miracle being spread through- out the country, brought such numbers from all parts to visit the Saint, and seek the cure of their maladies which they usually obtained by his prayers, that partly to avoid the danger of vain-glory, and partly to enjoy his beloved solitude with more freedom, taking with him a holy man whose name was Domitian, he with- drew himself privately from his monastery into the desert of Ruban, that lies more to the south, near the lake of Sodom. Here for some time he fixed his abode in a high mountain, on the top of which he discovered a well, and some ancient ruins, with which he built a chapel and an altar, living the whole time on the wild herbs he found there. From hence he went to the desert of Ziph, where David formerly had concealed himself when he was persecuted by Saul, the recollection of which pleased him much; but it was not long before the inhabitants of a neighboring

town, called Auistobulias, found him out, by means of
a young man possessed by an evil spirit, who had frequently the name of Euthymius in his mouth, and
was wonderfully delivered as soon as he was brought
within sight of the Saint. This miracle brought him
many disciples, for whom the people of the neighborhood built a monastery, which the Saint for some
time directed in the ways of religious perfection.
But his love of solitude induced him to quit this monastery also, where he found himself much importuned
and distracted by visitors from all parts, and to seek
out with his companion Domitian a place more agreeable to his inclination for retirement, which he at
length met with in a cavern not far distant from his
former monastery. Theoctistus, whom he had left superior there, with all the rest of the brethren, besought
him to return to them again : but the most they could
obtain of him was, that he would visit them every
Sunday, and be present at their assemblies.

Aspebet, now named Peter, hearing where the
Saint was, introduced a great number of the Saracens
to him who were desirious of becoming christians,
whom Euthymius instructed and baptized. These
new converts being desirous of remaining under his
direction, he appointed them a place at a small distance for the building themselves a church and other
dwellings, where he often visited them to instruct them
in the way of eternal life, till finding them sufficiently

grounded in christian piety, he procured them a priest and some deacons for the care of their church, and the administration of the sacraments. But as by the daily arrival of many more, the number of his converts became very considerable, he proposed to Juvenal, the patriarch of Jerusalem, to give them also a bishop, who might take charge of all the Saracens of Palestine. The patriarch readily complied with the Saint's proposition, and ordained Aspebet, or Peter, to this function, by whose means God daily added others to his church.

Hitherto Euthymius, through his love of solitude, had recommended all such as resorted to him, in order to embrace a religious life, to the monastery of Theoctistus, till he was admonished in a vision to build a *laura* and church for the reception of such as desired to put themselves under his direction, which was soon filled with a multitude of religious souls. The number of the monks, joined to the barrenness of the place, made it difficult to procure sufficient provisions in that wilderness; but the providence of God never forsook his servants whose whole care was to please him. It happened one day, that four hundred Armenians, in returning from Jerusalem toward the Jordan, missed their way, and came down to the laura of Euthymius. The Saint seeing them, immediately gave orders that they should be hospitably entertained. Domitian represented to him, that the community was reduced to

so great straits that they had not bread enough for
the brethren, not even for one meal. The Saint, full
of confidence in God, bid him go to the bakehouse,
and see what he should find there. He obeyed, and
found the room covered with bread and other provisions in such abundance that he could hardly thrust
the door open.

God also favored his servant with the gifts of prophecy, of which our author mentions several remarkable instances. As to the manner of life which he
here followed, he assures us, from the testimony of
those that were the best acquainted with him, that he
was never seen to eat but on Saturdays or Sundays—
that he never wilfully broke silence nor opened his lips
but when necessity obliged him to speak,—that he
never laid himself down to repose, but slept sitting
and adds, that he was a close imitator of the great St.
Arsenius, and was highly delighted with hearing from
the religious who came from Egypt the particulars of
his life and conversation. He had always these words
of Arsenius present in his mind; *Arsenius, Arsenius,
on what account didst thou leave the world?* and strive
to copy out in his own practice all the great examples that Saint had given of humility—recollection—
poverty of spirit—love of silence and solitude—per-
etual compunction of heart—profusion of tears in the
ight of God—and continual watching, fasting and
prayer.

There happened in those days so great a drought in Palestine, that it seemed, according to the expression of the Scripture, as if the heavens were of brass, and the earth of iron. The cisterns and receptacles which they had made for water were filled with nothing but dust, and the whole country was reduced to the utmost extremity for want of rain. As the evil increased daily, an infinite multitude of the people of the towns and villages round about, carrying crosses in their hands, and singing *Kyrie eleison,* to implore the divine mercy, came to the Saint on the very day when he was going out, according to his custom, to make his retreat in the wilderness, as a preparation for Easter. The sight of their distress moved him to compassion, and he spoke to them as follows : " My children, as for my part, I am but a wretched sinner, and stand more in need than any other of the mercy of God, especially at this time in which we see his wrath thus enkindled against sinners, and therefore I am not so bold as to dare to lift up my eyes to him, as I know that he sends these afflictions when he pleases ; and that, as no one can shut when he is pleased to open, so no one can open when he is pleased to shut. Our sins have separated us from him—we have disfigured his image —we have defiled his temple—we have suffered ourselves to be carried away by our passions ;—envy and avarice reign amongst us, and our hatred against each other render us hateful to him : but as he is the foun-

tain of all goodness, and as his mercy knows no
bourds, let us all prostrate ourselves before his face,
and pray to him from the very bottom of our hearts,
and I make no doubt but that he will forgive us, and
give us a proof of his fatherly love by the seasonable
aid he will send us; for as David says, *The Lord is
near to all them that call upon him.*" After he had
thus spoken to the people, all cried out, begging that
he would pray for them; whereupon, after exhorting
them to join in prayer to the Lord with the greatest
fervor of which they were capable, he retired with his
religious into their oratory, and lying prostrate on the
ground with many tears implored the divine mercy;
when behold a sudden wind arose, the heavens were
obscured by thick clouds, and immediately such an
abundance of rain came pouring down as quite soaked
the whole earth which was followed by the most fruitful year that had ever been known in Palestine in
the memory of man.

The Saint had such an extraordinary zeal for the
maintenance of the purity of the Catholic faith, that
he, who was otherwise the meekest of men, could not
endure the obstinate abettors of condemned errors.
In his days a wicked heresy was broached by Eutyches,
a monk of Constantinople, who denied the distinction
of the divine and human nature in Christ. Though
his impious doctrine was condemned by the Council
of Chalcedon, still there were not wanting many chil

dren of iniquity, who instead of submitting to this great authority, spread abroad such infamous slanders against that council, and misrepresentations of the Catholic doctrine, as alienated the minds of many from the faith ; the principal of whom was Theodosius, a monk of Palestine, who under a religious habit cover-ed a diabolical spirit, and by his wicked insinuations and downright calumnies, prejudiced the mind of the empress Eudocia, who was at that time in Palestine, against the council, and by the means of her interest, and the great liberalities she exercised towards the re-ligious, gained the greatest part of them over to the Eutychian faction, the disciples of St. Euthymius ex-cepted. Not content with this, having intruded him-self into the patriarchal see of Jerusalem, he declared open war against all such as opposed themselves to his impiety, banished the orthodox bishops from their sees, and even imbrued his hands in the blood of some of them. In the mean time Euthymius opposed him-self as a wall for the house of Israel, and constantly refused to have any manner of communication with this false patriarch ; but as he was continually ply-ing him with messages, in order to bring him over to his side, by reason of the neighborhood of the laura of the Saint to the city of Jerusalem, he assembled his disciples, and having powerfully exhorted them to constancy in the Catholic faith, he withdrew into the desert of Ruban, where he remained till the usurper was obliged to quit Jerusalem, and the patriarch Ju venal was restored to his see.

In the mean time he brought back to the Church an excellent anchoret, whose name was Gerasimus, who had been also imposed upon, with many others, and drawn in to be an abettor of the impious Theodo- sious, till hearing of the eminent sanctity of Euthy- mius, he went to confer with him in the wilderness of Ruban, and by his heavenly discourses was fully re- claimed from his error, and conceived a deep and bit- ter regret at having suffered himself to be deceived, for which he did severe penance. His example was followed by four other anchorets, who, in like manner, renounced the communion of Theodosius. Gerasi- mus afterwards built a laura and a monastery near the Jordan, where he trained up many souls in great perfection, and closed a life of extraordinary sanctity by so happy a death as to have his name enrolled amongst the saints. See the Roman Martyrology, March the fifth.

The empress Eudocia, after having for a long time resisted the solicitations of her nearest relations, be gan at length to open her eyes to the bright rays of the catholic truth, and in order to her instruction therein she sent to St. Simon Stylites, as one to whom God imparted extraordinary lights to direct souls in the way of salvation, and opened to him, by her mes- senger, the bishop Anastasius, the whole state of her

interior. The Saint exhorted her to disengage herself effectually from the nets of Satan in which her
soul had been entangled by the means of the impious
Theodosious, and for this purpose desired she would
address herself to St. Euthymius, and to receive from
his mouth the pure words of life. Having complied
with the advice of the Saint, and being reconciled to
the Catholic Church, her example was followed by
great numbers both of the religious and laity. This
princess, after having built a great many churches,
monasteries, and hospitals, conceived a design of extending her beneficence also to the *laura* of St. Euthymius, which the Saint had founded in great poverty: but before she had declared her mind to any
one living, Euthymius, who by a divine light often
discovered the secrets of hearts, told her, " Daughter,
your departure out of this world is near at hand;
wherefore, instead of busying yourself with all these
cares, attend to your own interior, and think of preparing yourself for your journey hence, rather than
of settling revenues upon us; we want nothing else
of you, but that you would remember us in your
prayers." The empress followed his advice, and some
months after made a happy end.

Amongst other favors which our Lord did to his
servant Euthymius, our author relates, from the testimony of the anchoret Cyriacus, who learnt it from
two eye-witnesses, that one day whilst the Saint was

saying mass, a bright fire was seen to come down upon his head, which encompassed both him and his disciple Domitian, and remained from the *Sanctus* till after the communion. He was also often favored with the vision of angels at the time of his offering the holy sacrifice; and when he distributed the holy communion, he saw in spirit the different dispositions of the communicants; perceiving how the sacred host cast rays of light upon some, and darkness upon others, who, by being unworthy, received it to their own condemnation. The Saint was so affected with this vision, as to be ever after perpetually inculcating to his religious, the necessity of keeping their conscience always pure, that they may worthily approach to the divine mysteries: that *holy things were for holy persons:* and therefore when any of them found their conscience charged with the guilt, either of hatred, or the desire of revenge, upon receiving an injury; or of envy, or of wrath, or of pride, or of speaking evil of their neighbor, or of entertaining loose thoughts or criminal desires, or of any other vice, they should by no means present themselves at the divine table, till they had in a proper manner, expiated their sins by penance.

And now the man of God, after having passed about sixty-seven years in the deserts of Palestine, which by this time he had peopled with a multitude of Saints, was given to understand, by divine revelation, that the time of laying down his earthly taber

nacie was near at hand. It was his custom, after the
Epiphany, to begin his annual retreat, and to withdraw himself into the remoter parts of the wilderness,
where he continued his spiritual exercises till Holy
Week. Wherefore, his disciples Elias and Martyrius
(both of them afterwards, according to his prediction,
patriarchs of Jerusalem), who were used to accompany
him on this occasion, came on the octave of that festival to ask him if they were not to set out with him
on the day following? The saint replied, that he
would spend that week with them at home in the
laura, but that on Saturday at midnight he would
leave them. He passed the vigil of the feast of St.
Antony, Jan. 17, with them in prayer, and after the
morning lauds, told them this was the last vigil he
should keep with them. Then having ordered all his
religious to be assembled, delivered to them an excellent discourse, telling them that his hour was now at
hand, and conjuring them, if they had any regard or
affection for him, to show it, by faithfully and constantly practising the lessons he had taught them. In
particular he recommended to them *charity* and *humility* as the two principal ingredients of christian
perfection, telling them, that if all Christians were
bound to exercise themselves in these virtues, much
more they who by their religious profession had in a
particular manner consecrated themselves to Jesus
Christ, to the end, that being freed from all secular

cares and effections, they might have no other solic·
itude but to please him. " Labor then," said he, " my
brethren, with all your might to keep both your
bodies and minds ever chaste ;—continue all of you
together to praise and glorify God ;—practise with all
possible diligence the rule he has given us,—do all in
your power to comfort the afflicted, and to fortify by
your exhortations and instructions such amongst the
brethren as labor under temptations, that they may
not fall a pray to the enemy. Let your gate be
always open to hospitality ;—divide the little you
have with the poor and indigent, and the divine bounty will not fail to furnish you with all that shall be
needful for yourselves."

After having spoken to this effect, he asked them
whom they desired to have for their superior after his
death ? They all, with one voice, desired it might be
Domitian. " That cannot be," said the Saint, " for he
shall not survive me above seven days." Whereupon
they made choice of Elias, to whom the Saint earnestly recommended the care of his flock. After this they
retired, and Domitian alone remained with the Saint,
who, after three days departed to our Lord at the
precise time he had foretold, and his happy soul was
seen at that very time by St. Gerasimus carried up by
angels towards her heavenly country. His individual
companion Domitian, within seven days, took the
same happy road, being invited on the eve of his death

in a vision in his sleep, by St. Euthymius, to come with him to the regions of light and life everlasting, where they should live together for ever in the kingdom of their Father. St. Euthymius has a place in the Roman Martyrology on the twentieth of January.

ST. THEODOSIUS THE CENOBIARCH.

From a cotemporary Writer, published by Bollandus

THEODOSIUS, surnamed the Cenobiarch, from the multitude of religious whom he trained up in a conventual life, was born near Cesarea in Cappadocia, anno 423. Being educated by his parents in the fear of God, he from his tender years gave such proofs of virtue and piety as to be ordained a lector to read the holy Scriptures to the faithful in the church. What he read to others penetrated and made a deep impression on his own heart. The words of God to Abraham, Gen. xii. *Go forth out of thy country, and from thy kindred, and out of thy father's house,* &c. affected him as much as if they had been addressed to himself; as also that promise of our Lord in the Gospel of conferring everlasting life on those who should quit all things for love of him. By frequently meditating on these and such like passages of holy

writ, he was at length determined to follow the call
of God, and forsake every thing in this world, that he
might more securely find the kingdom of heaven.

In consequence of this resolution he set out to go
and visit the holy places at Jerusalem, taking Antioch
in his way, in the neighborhood of which St. Simon
Stylites was then living upon his pillar.   Theodosius
went to see the Saint, being desirous to recommend
himself to his prayers, and receive his benediction.
No sooner had he come near the pillar, than Simon
cried out, *Welcome Theodosius, servant of God*, and
presently desired he would ascend to him by a ladder.
After mutual embraces, he foretold to him all that
should afterwards befal him, and in particular that he
should have the direction of a numerous flock, and
should rescue by the aid of divine grace, many souls
from the jaws of the infernal wolf.   Theodosius being
confirmed in his good resolution by his conference
with so great a Saint, proceeded in his journey to Jerusalem, where, after reverencing the holy places, he
went and placed himself under the direction of Lon-
ginus, an eminent servant of God, who dwelt by himself in a small lodge in the tower of David, where
partly under him, partly under Marinus and Lucas,
disciples of St. Euthymius, he learnt the true science
of the saints to such perfection, as to become himself
a most excellent master and teacher, both by **word**
and example, of this heavenly discipline.

Some time after he was moved, by divine inspiration, to seek a more retired solitude, where he might lead an anchoretical life. For this purpose, withdrawing himself into the wilderness, he made choice of a cavern, which he found on the side of a mountain, for the place of his habitation during the remainder of the days of his mortality. Here he lived for the space of thirty years in a mortal body, as if he had been an immortal spirit, in the constant exercise of watching, fasting and prayer, together with such a continual recollection of thought, fervor of spirit, humility of heart, and abundance of tears, as could not fail to draw down the graces and gifts of the spirit of God, in the most abundant manner upon his soul. His only food during this long period of time, was dates or pulse, moistened in cold water, or wild herbs, without any bread whatsoever. He embraced labors with as much ardor as others do their pleasures, and avoided pleasures as much as others do labors. Although he desired nothing so much as to live concealed from the eyes of men, yet it was impossible for him to keep himself so secretly in his cavern, but that the bright light of his extraordinary sanctity should break out and cast its rays both far and near, and invite many to him, who were desirous to place themselves under his conduct, and learn the secrets of religious perfec fection. It was with difficulty he at first received any one into his company; but his charitable solicitude for the salvation of the souls of his neighbors, prevailed over his love of solitude, and the great success which attended his conduct and direction of souls, proved that it was the holy will of God he should be thus employed.

Although the number of his disciples did not at the beginning exceed six or seven, who all lived with him in his cavern, yet they gradually increased; and as they all made it their business to seek in the first place the kingdom of God with all their power, divine Providence never failed to add over and above the necessaries of this present life. One Easter-eve, when the Saint had now twelve disciples with him in his cavern, it happened that they had nothing whatever to eat: but what gave them most concern was, that they had not even bread for the divine sacrifice. This they represented to their holy superior, who being full of confidence in God, bid them nevertheless prepare the altar for the celebrating mass on Easter-day; when behold, about sun-set Providence sent a man to their cavern with two mules laden with bread and other provisions in such quantity as abundantly sufficed them until Whitsuntide. At another time, when they were reduced to the same extremity, Providence sent them a supply in a manner still more remarkable, which happened thus: As a man was leading his horse with a load of provisions to some other place, when he came into the neighborhood of the cavern where

the servants of God dwelt, he could not, with all his
might, force his horse to go forward ; so that conceiving there must be something supernatural in the case,
he gave him liberty of the bridle to go which way he
pleased.   The horse being then left to himself, immediately, as if he were guided by an invisible hand,
went straight up to the cavern, where the master perceiving the distress of this holy community, relieved
them very plentifully, and glorified God for having
thus wonderfully made him the instrument of his divine goodness, in supplying his servants with food.

But the number of the disciples of the Saint,
amongst whom were persons considerable for their
worldly birth and fortune, daily increasing, and his
cavern being too small to contain them, they with difficulty prevailed upon him to consent to the building
a spacious monastery and a church, close by, in the
very place appointed to him by heaven, by the remarkable circumstance of the coals in his censor catch-
ing fire of themselves.   Here he received all that
came to him ; and as their number became very considerable, he was afterwards obliged to add several
other buildings, as well for the relief of the spiritual as
the corporal necessities of the multitude that resorted
to him.   In no place was hospitality exercised with
greater affection, or with more cheerfulness and joy
than in this monastery ; for amongst all the virtues of
the Saint, his tender compassion and charity for his

neighbors, and diligence in relieving all their necessities, seemed to claim the first place. So great was his
solicitude for the sick and distressed, that he even built
several hospitals and infirmaries about his monastery
for their accommodation; of which extensive charity
of his servant, God was pleased to testify his approbation more than once in a miraculous manner. At the
time of a great famine, when an incredible multitude
of people flocked to the monastery upon a Palm-Sunday, and the religious not having wherewith to feed
so great a crowd, would have kept the gates shut, the
Saint, trusting in God, bid them open the gates and
give them all to eat. And though the number was
so great as to fill every part of the house, yet by a
miracle not unlike that wrought by our Lord in feeding the five thousand in the desert, they all eat and
were filled; and there still remained more bread than
they had at first. The like miracle happened also
another time, upon the feast of the Annunciation of
the Blessed Virgin.

As to the disciples of our Saint, the number who
put themselves under his conduct was so great, that,
according to our author, during the time of his superiority, he buried with his own hands no less than six
hundred and ninety-three religious men, whom he had
trained up in the way of sanctity; and that his successor, St. Sophronius, did as much for four hundred
more, who both in life and death followed the same

happy course. He also adds, that many illustrious bishops and abbots were taken out of this monastery; that many others who had been here brought up under our Saint, betook themselves afterwards to an anchoretical life, in which they became eminent for holiness;—that several who had followed the profession of arms quitted the service of Cæsar to enrol themselves amongst the soldiers of Jesus Christ, and to learn his ·heavenly discipline of Theodosius; that many who enjoyed posts of honor in the world, as well as several who were renowned for their learning, came also to our Saint, to take up, under his direction, the sweet yoke of christian simplicity and humility, and become his scholars in the study of the science of the saints. His conduct towards all who were under his care was ever regulated by so consummate a prudence as to accommodate his directions and prescriptions to the different exigencies and dispositions, as well as to the strength of his disciples. Whenever any of them were guilty of a fault, instead of penances, he only used words of admonition, correction, and exhortation, which were animated with such unction as made them penetrate into the very midst of their souls. In these corrections he had the art of associating meekness and affability with a just severity, in so engaging a manner as to make himself at once be both feared and loved. The lessons of all virtues which he gave to others, were enforced by his own practice. His

conversation was always extremely edifying and in-
structive, and his spirit ever attentive to God. Whether alone or in company, or in whatsoever manner he
was employed, his temper was ever calm and even,
always the same. His chief delight consisted in reading the holy Scriptures, which he made the subject of
his perpetual meditation both day and night, even to
the day of his death. Although our Saint had not
been educated to any degree in secular learning, nor
ever studied the rules of human eloquence, yet in the
discourses which he delivered to his disciples, he far
excelled the greatest orators in the arts of moving and
exciting the affections, and inflaming the heart ; because his words did not proceed from human wisdom,
but from divine grace and the spirit of God. He was
always so great an admirer and imitator of St. Basil,
that in his words and with his spirit he would often
address himself to his monks to the following effect :
" I beseech you, my children, by the charity of our
Lord Jesus Christ, who delivered himself up to death
for our sins, let us, once for all be quite in earnest, as
seriously to set about the business of saving our souls.
Let us conceive a lively sorrow for having passed our
time hitherto so unprofitably ; let us now at least begin to fight manfully in the service of God and of his
Son Jesus Christ, that we may be made partakers one
day in their glory. Let us shake off this sluggishness
and lassitude, which makes us still love to put off from

day to day the laboring in good earnest to advance in virtue; for if by suffering ourselves to be deceived by the enemy, we be found void of good works here, we can have no pretension hereafter to the joys of heaven, but shall hereafter lament in vain for having let slip the time and means of working out our salvation, when it shall not be in our power to recover them. The nature of this life, and of that which is to come, are quite opposite; the one is a time of penance, and the other of reward;—the one a time of labor, the other of repose;—the one a time of suffering, and the other of consolation. At present God is infinitely good to those who turn from their evil ways, and are converted to him; but then he shall be a just and inexorable judge, who will call us to a strict account for all our thoughts, words, and actions. Now he is patient, but then he shall be terrible. How long then shall we remain deaf to the voice of Jesus Christ, who invites us to the possession of an eternal inheritance? Shall we never awake out of this long and profound sleep? Shall we not, now at least, renounce our ill-spent life, to embrace evangelical perfection? Ah! why do we not tremble at the thoughts of that dreadful day of the Lord, when he shall receive those whose good works shall entitle them to a place at his right hand, into his kingdom; and shall condemn those who, being void of good works, shall be placed at his left, to eternal fire? We say indeed that we desire to

go to heaven ; but do we labor in earnest ; do we pursue the means of acquiring and securing to ourselves
that eternal kingdom ?   If we neglect to put in practice what our Lord has commanded, it is in vain that
we flatter ourselves with the expectation of receiving
from him that glorious recompense wherewith he will
reward those only who shall persevere to the end in
fighting courageously against sin."

So far the Saint in the words of St. Brasil.

St. Theodosius was also inflamed with an extraordinary zeal for maintaining the Catholic faith against
all condemned heresies ; of which he gave signal
proofs during the reign of the emperor Anastasius,
who was a great abettor of the Eutychian heresy, condemned by the general council of Chalcedon.   This
prince, in hopes of drawing our Saint over to favor his
impious tenets, sent him a very considerable sum of
money by the way of an alms, as he pretended, for the
relief of the poor, and the comfort of his religious in
their sicknesses.   The Saint thought it not prudent to
offend the emperor, by refusing his charity, though he
suspected that an ill design lay concealed under this
specious pretence.   Not long after Anastasius sent to
desire of him a confession of his faith, agreeable to
the Eutychian heresy.   Theodosius, instead of coming
into his measures, declared himself ready to suffer a
thousand deaths, rather than betray his conscience, or
consent to heresy.   The emperor, though chagrined

and disappointed, dissembled his resentment, and proceeded at that time no farther : but not long after
he furiously attacked the Catholic faith, and raised a
violent persecution against its professors. In this distressed state of the church, when the orthodox pastors
were either banished from their churches, or intimidated into a criminal silence, which is always advantageous to error,—when the heretics triumphed, and
a great part of the people either joined with them, or
were in doubt which side to take, the Saint seeing the
dreadful danger to which the sheep of Christ lay exposed in the midst of these wolves, fearless of the rage
of the emperor, or of the violence of his officers and
ministers, went boldly into the great church of Jerusalem, at the time of the divine service, and going up
to the tribune from whence the holy Scriptures used
to be read to the people, pronounced a loud anathema
against all who did not receive and revere, like the
four Gospels, the four general councils of Nice,
Constantinople, Ephesus, and Chalcedon, in which
the Incarnation of the Son of God, had been defined
and declared against the Arians, Macedonians, Nesto-
rians, and Eutychians. This courageous profession of
his faith in so public and solemn a manner, made a
wonderful impression on the minds of the people in
favor of the Catholic religion, and struck all who heard
him with such astonishment, that none of his adversaries, as he passed through the crowd to go out of

26

the church, durst so much as open their mouths to
speak one word to him, much less presume to stop
him.   After this he was seized with a long and painful illness, which he bore with extraordinary patience
and fortitude ; until it pleased his Divine Master to
call him to the enjoyment of that reward which he
has prepared for all who labor and suffer for his sake.

Theodoret, in his Philotheus, has given us the acts
of another saint, named also Theodosius, a native of
Antioch, who led a life of wonderful austerity and
sanctity in a mountain of Cilicia, ever praying and
singing psalms, without ceasing to labor with his
hands, and training up many disciples in the same exercises.   In order to accommodate the monastery he
had built for them, he miraculously caused a never-
failing stream of water to flow from the hard rock on
which it was erected.   So great and general was the
esteem in which he was held, even amongst the barbarians and infidels, on account of his sanctity and
miracles, that such as were in danger at sea, though
at ever so great a distance off from his place of residence, who called upon the God of Theodosius, saw
the tempest immediately cease by the invocation of
his name.   He flourished in the fourth century.

ST. SABAS.

From his Life by Cyrillus, a faithful cotemporary
Writer

SABAS, or Sabbas, was born at Mutalascus, a small
town in the district of Cesarea, in Cappadocia, anno
437. His father, who was an officer in the army,
being obliged to go to Alexandria, in Egypt, left his
son, who was then but five years old, together with
his estate, in the care of an uncle, whose name was
Hermias. But the evil treatment Sabas met with
from his aunt, the wife of Hermias, obliged him to
leave them, and go to another uncle, named Gregory
This produced a violent contest between the two
brothers which should have the care of his person
and of his estate, which inspired in the nephew,
young as he then was, so great a disgust for the
world, that resolving to quit it, he retired to a monastery called Flavian, at about three miles distance from
Mutalascus, where the abbot received him, though as
yet but a child, amongst his religious, and took care
to have him well instructed in the knowledge of the
holy Scriptures, and of all things necessary to acquit
himself worthily of so holy a profession. Here, as
he was working in the garden one day, he observed
an apple tree laden with fruit, which appeared so very

fair and tempting, that he plucked off one of them with
a design to eat it; but immediately suspecting it to be a
snare of the old serpent, who had heretofore driven our
first parents out of paradise, by tempting them to eat
of the forbidden fruit, and that he throws out no baits
so efficacious to ensnare youth as that of pleasure;
after reproaching himself with the fault he had committed, he flung down the apple, trod it under foot,
and made a resolution never to eat of that kind of
fruit as long as he lived. From that day forward he
led a life of the most extraordinary abstinence with
respect to eating and drinking. As to sleep, he slept
no longer than the necessity of nature absolutely required; and excepting the time whilst his hands were
lifted up to God in prayer, they were perpetually employed in some manual labor, for he dreaded nothing
more than idleness, on account of the opportunity it
affords the enemy to creep insensibly into the soul. By
this continual application of all his faculties to attain
to perfection, he made such a progress in the way of
virtue, that not one of the religious, who were to the
number of seventy in this community, equalled him
in obedience and humility, or in any of the exercises
of an evangelical life.

His uncles, being at length reconciled together, both
joined in soliciting him to come out of the monastery,
and to settle himself in the world in a married life.
But he resisted all their solicitations, and with the leave

of his superior, being now eighteen years old, went away to Jerusalem, in order to reverence the holy places, and then to visit the Saints that inhabited the neighboring deserts, that he might acquire still greater proficiency in the true science of the saints. Here after a short stay in the monastery of St. Pasarion, he went and flung himself at the feet of the great St. Euthymius, desiring to serve God under his holy discipline. Euthymius told him he was as yet too young for the solitary life of the laura, but sent him to the neighboring monastery of his friend Theoctis-tus, with a particular recommendation of him to the abbot, as one who was likely to become a most illus-trious saint. In this monastery the young Sabas con-secrated himself entirely to divine love. He spent the day in manual labors, and the night in fervent prayer, and was ever ready, young and strong as he was, to comfort and assist the brethren in their res-pective offices. He brought in water and wood for the use of the community :—regardless of his own health, he took particular care of the sick, and was ever the first and last at the divine office, which he always recited with a most edifying devotion:—in a word, the religious were so charmed with his obedience and humility, that they could not, without admiration, be-hold so great perfection in one of such tender years.

It happened about this time that one of the monks obtained leave of the abbot to go to Alexandria, in order to dispose of an inheritance that fell to him by the death of his parents. Sabas, being ordered to accompany him in this journey, unexpectedly met with his own father and mother, who lived at Alexandria. Having rejoiced excessively to see him, they endeavored, by the most pressing soliciation, to prevail on him to stay with them; but Sabas, having set his hand to the plough, absolutely refused to look back, remembering what our Lord had said, that such as love father or mother more than him, are not worthy of him. "If they, said he, who, after enrolling themselves in the service of an earthly king run away from their colors, are severely punished for their desertion, what punishment then should not I deserve, if after having engaged myself in the service of the King of heaven, I should abandon so holy a warfare? Wherefore cease, I beseech you, to persuade me to quit this way of life, which I find so advantageous to my soul, or else you will oblige me to consider you no longer as my parents and friends, but as strangers and enemies."—They told him that if he would not stay with them, he would at least accept of a considerable sum of money, which they would have given him. But this he also refused, and it was with much difficulty that they prevailed upon him to receive three pieces of silver; which as soon as he returned to the monastery he immediately gave to the abbot, fearing nothing more than the demon of the love of money.

After the death of the holy abbot Theoctistus, with the approbation of St. Euthymius, he betook himself to a cavern belonging to the monastery, where he passed five days of the week in perfect solitude; fasting, working, and praying the whole time. On the Saturday and Sunday he performed his devotions in the monastery, and then returning to his cavern, he carried with him the materials of which he made every week to the number of fifty baskets. And now St. Euthymius, who used to call him *the young old man*, by reason of his extraordinary wisdom, desired to have him nearer himself, and therefore took him along with him, when he entered upon his yearly retreat, on the 14th January, into the desert of Ruban, where he was accustomed to pass the holy time of Lent. After they had walked for a long time together over the barren sands of this vast wilderness, where nothing green could grow, nor any water be found, Sabas was so much exhausted with weariness and thirst, that he could hold out no longer, but was obliged to lay himself upon the ground like one half dead. Euthymius pitying his distress, prostrated himself in the presence of God, and cried out from the bottom of his heart: "Thou seest, O my God, the extremity to which this thy young soldier, who fights under thy standard, is now reduced, be pleased therefore to relieve and assist him by causing water to issue forth out of this dry and thirsty land." Having

finished this prayer, and thrust his staff three times
into the ground, behold there presently issued forth a
spring of clear and excellent water, from the drinking
whereof Sabas not only quenched his thirst, but found
in himself such vigor, strength, and comfort, as enabled him cheerfully to support all that he had afterwards to suffer in the desert.

After the death of St. Euthymius, Sabas retired into
the same wilderness near the river Jordan, which St.
Gerasimus at that time illustrated with the rays of his
sanctity.   Here, according to custom, passing the
night on a solitary mountain in prayer, he was directed by a heavenly vision to go and take up his abode
in a cavern to the east of the torrent of Siloe, with a
promise that God, who takes care of the meanest of
his creatures, would not fail to provide for him. Having immediately obeyed this ordinance of heaven, he
went down from the mountain, and was led, as it
were, by the hand to the cavern, which lay on the side
of a steep hill, of very difficult access.   Here he lived
for some time, without any other food for his subsistence but the herbs that grew wild about his cave,
and being obliged to go six or seven miles for water,
which, with the utmost difficulty he carried up to his
lodging by means of a rope, which he made to hang
down for that purpose from his cavern to the foot of
the hill.   But divine providence at length conducted
some of the country people to the place, who ascend-

ing by the help of the rope to the cavern, and admiring the sanctity of the servant of God, from that time forward furnished him with the little provisions he stood in need of.

After he had dwelt about five years in this solitary cavern, God inspired him with a desire of exercising his charity towards his neighbors, by receiving, instructing, and directing as many as desired to quit the world, and to put themselves under his guidance in the ways of God and religious perfection. To these he gave excellent lessons of a' spiritual life, and appointed them separated spots of ground for building their cells after the manner of a laura, which, in process of time, became the most considerable of any in all Palestine. He built them also a chapel, wherein, as often as any priest came into the wilderness, he procured that the divine mysteries should be celebrated ; for as to his own part, his humility made him decline the priestly dignity, of which he deemed himself altogether unworthy. The first disciples of the Saint were men of the most eminent virtue, so full of the Spirit of God, that they lived in the wilderness like angels in human bodies, continually employed in singing the praises of their Maker. Their number was bout three score and ten, amongst whom were several who afterwards became founders and superiors of other religious communities. Having at the beginning labored under great inconveniences, especially for want

of water, which they were forced to fetch, as was observed before, from a spring that was seven miles distant, the Saint one night in his devotions, earnestly
besought the Lord to remedy this evil, by affording
his servants a source of water nearer home ; when behold at the conclusion of his prayer he heard a noise,
and looking towards the place, he perceived by the
moonlight a wild ass making a hole in the ground
with his foot, and then bowing down his head, as if it
were to drink. The man of God conceiving by this
signal that his prayer was heard, went to the place,
and opening the hole a little wider, a stream of living
water issued forth, which from that time never ceased
to flow through the midst of the laura, in such a manner, as neither to be swelled in winter nor to be di-
minished in summer, though almost all the people of
the country resorted thither for water.

And now the number of those who came to place
themselves under his direction increased exceedingly ;
—but, alas ! they were not all led by the same spirit
as their predecessor ; on the contrary, some of them
formed a faction against the holy abbot, and went to
Salustius, who upon the death of Martyrius was lately
made patriarch of Jerusalem, to desire he would give
them another superior : for as Sabas was clownish and
simple, they wanted one who was a priest. The new
patriarch, who was no stranger to the merit of the
Saint, instead of regarding his accusers, sent for him

and ordained him priest in their presence, and confirmed him in his charge of abbot and superior; and
going with him to the laura consecrated for him a
church, and erected an altar in a spacious subterrane-
ous den, which had been shown to the man of God
by a pillar of fire which reached from heaven to earth.
Many others after this resorted to the Saint to put
themselves under his discipline, amongst whom were
several excellent men of the Armenian nation, to
whom the man of God made over his own first habitation with the neighboring oratory, in which he directed them to sing the praises of God in their native
language. About this time also the father of the
Saint having died at Alexandria, his mother Sophia
came to visit him, and having by his counsel entirely
renounced the world, passed the short time that remained of her life in preparing her soul, by spiritual
exercises, for a better, and made a most happy end
under his directions. The Saint consecrated a considerable sum of money which she bequeathed him, to
the service of God, by building two hospitals; the
one for the entertainment of passengers, the other for
the religious of other communities who came to visit
his laura.

Our Saint was united in a most holy bond of friendship with the great St. Theodosius, and always joined
him in promoting the cause of their common Lord, as
well in defending the purity of the catholic faith

against all the attacks of heresy, as in propagating religious discipline. Their union was so remarkable,
that the people of Jerusalem called them the two
apostles; and the patriarch Salustius, at the desire of
the religious of his district, put under their care all the
monasteries around Jerusalem, in such a manner that
Theodosius had the charge of all that lived in convents,
from whence he was named the Cenobiarch, and
Sabas the charge of all the anchorets and solitaries.
But Euthymius was the Saint whose life St. Sabas
particularly chose for the model of his own; after his
example he withdrew himself every year into the most
remote part of the wilderness, and there passed the
whole time of Lent, till Palm-Sunday, in perfect solitude, fasting, and prayer. In one of these excursions
he was conducted by divine providence to a steep
mountain, on the top of which he found a cavern, and
in this cavern a holy anchoret who had lived there for
eight and thirty years upon nothing but wild herbs,
without either seeing or being seen during all that
time by any one. The edification he received by the
heavenly conversation of this man of God brought
Sabas thither again another year to receive his benediction, but he found him dead in the posture of one
at his prayers, and interred him in his cavern.

In another of these excursions he came to a hill
called Castel, lying at a great distance from all communication with men. This place he pitched upon to

erect a monastery, and after the Easter holidays he led thither a colony of his disciples, who found in the neighborhood an old desolate building, which they converted into a church, and afterwards built them-selves cells around it. As the first inhabitants of this holy solitude were men of eminent virtue, wholly dis-engaged from all earthly cares and affections, our Lord was pleased in the beginning to provide for their sub-sistence in a wonderful manner, by charging Marcian, the superior of the monasteries of Bethlehem, in a vision, to furnish them with all necessaries, which he carefully executed.

In the mean time the malcontents of whom we spoke before were gathering strength, by seducing se-veral others over to their faction, so that no less than forty of the religious entered into a conspiracy against the holy abbot, resolving to use all means in their power to get rid of him. The Saint being apprised of their design chose to withdraw himself quietly from them, rather than proceed to any measures against them which might be inconsistent with that meekness, patience, and humility, which constitute the character of a disciple of Jesus Christ. Wherefore retiring into a desert, not far from the city of Scythopolis, he took up his abode in a cavern near the river of Gadar. Al-though this cavern happened to be a lion's den, yet the beast finding the Saint there, not only refrained from offering him any violence, but quietly yielded up

to him the possession of his dwelling-place.   Here the
reputation of his sanctity, which could no where lie
long concealed, brought many to visit him from the
neighboring cities of Scythopolis and Gadara; amongst
whom was a young gentleman named Basil, who by
an inspiration of heaven had entirely renounced the
world and came to dwell with Sabas in his cavern.
Some thieves who had imagined Basil to be rich, and
that he had carried off his money with him, came one
night in hopes of booty to visit the cavern: but finding nothing, not even the necessaries of life, they were
struck with astonishment, and retired, not without
deep remorse for the evil they had proposed to commit, and a dread of meeting with some rigorous punishment from the justice of God.   This apprehension
was greatly increased, when a little after they had left
the cavern they saw some lions approaching, whose
terrible looks seemed to threaten them with immediate
death and destruction.   In this extremity they be-
thought themselves of the sanctity of Sabas, and commanded the lions in the name, and by virtue of the
prayers of that venerable servant of God, to be gone;
when behold they had no sooner pronounced the name
of Sabas, but these furious beasts turned their backs
upon them and ran away.   This miracle not only
wrought the total conversion of the thieves, but being
rumored abroad, brought such multitudes to visit the
Saint as determined him, after having recommended

his disciples to God and leaving to them the cell he had lately built, to seek some other solitude, where he might attend to his God with less distraction.

After some time he returned again to his laura, where to his excessive grief he found no amendment in the disposition of the malcontents, since whatsoever he could either say or do to bring them to a righ sense of their duty made them rather worse than bet ter. Upon this he retired towards Nicopolis, and fixed his abode for some time under a tree in an open field, till the master of the field, admiring his sanctity, built him a cell, which in a short time was converted into a monastery. In the mean time the malcontents applied to Elias the patriarch of Jerusalem for another superior, pretending that Sabas was devoured by a lion. The patriarch gave no credit to the fable; and not long after Sabas himself coming to Jerusalem to celebrate the feast of the dedication of the Church, he obliged him to return to his laura, with an order to the rebels either to submit to him or depart. They chose the latter, and retired towards the torrent of Theon, and repaired some old cells which they found there, and called this place the *new laura*. But as they were destitute of all things, and no one was willing to assist them, the Saint in his great charity, not only labored to procure them all necessary provisions, but went himself in person to carry them to them; nor did he cease to ply them with benefits, both for their temporal and spiritual well-being, till overcoming evil with good, he at length brought them over to dispositions more suitable to the sanctity of their profession, and established them in regular discipline under a holy superior whom he appointed for them.

It would be endless to descend to all the particulars of the great things which St. Sabas did, during the many years that remained of his life, for the glory of God,—for the sanctification of souls,—and the propagation of the kingdom of Christ,—the spirit of prophecy which he manifested on many occasions,—the great miracles God wrought by him,—his labors for the public good of the Church, and maintaining the purity of faith, as well during the reign of Anastasius, the Eutychian, as during that of his successors Justin and Justinian, since these would suffice to fill a volume, they are therefore omitted as exceeding the bounds of our intended brevity. Wherefore we shall only add, that as he always lived the life of a Saint, so he died the death of a Saint, on the fifth of December, (on which day he is honored by the church) anno 532, at the age of 94; and that after his death many miracles were wrought through his intercession.

ST. JOHN THE SILENT.

From his disciple Cyrillus, the same who wrote the
Lives of SS. Euthymius and Sabas

JOHN, surnamed *Silentiarius,* or the *Silent,* from
his great affection to silence, was born in the lesser
Armenia, of illustrious and wealthy parents, anno 453,
who being themselves good Christians, gave him a
christian education. At the age of eighteen he abandoned the world, and employed that part of the estate which fell to him by the death of his father and
mother, in building a church in honor of the blessed
Virgin, together with a monastery into which he retired with ten other persons, who like himself were
desirous to think of nothing else but the salvation of
their souls. Here he led a life of the most perfect
purity of soul and body, joined with a most profound
humility. The heavenly prudence with which he conducted the religious committed to his charge recommended him first to the priestly character, and shortly after, upon the death of the bishop of Colonia, determined the metropolitan, the archbishop of Sebaste,
to consecrate no other than him to fill up this vacancy.
In order thereto he sent for John, as if it were upon
some other business, and when he came, in spite of
his remonstrances to the contrary, he ordained him

bishop. Being then about thirty-eight years of
age, he for ten years discharged himself in a most
edifying manner, of all the duties of the episcopal
ministry, continuing to practise the same religious
exercises as he had been accustomed to in his monastery.

Towards the latter end of this time, finding his
church and his clergy grievously oppressed by his
brother-in-law, the governor of the province, and that
all his remonstrances only served to make him still
worse, he took a journey to Constantinople, to seek a
remedy for these evils.   Here having, with the assistance of the patriarch Euphymius, settled the affairs of
his diocese in the best manner he could, and following a
divine inspiration, having resolved totally to withdraw
himself from the world, without acquainting any one
with his design, he privately got on board a ship, and
went to Jerusalem, where he took up his lodgings in
an hospital, to which was annexed a chapel of St.
George the Martyr ; and during the time he remained
there, continued to pray with many tears, that God
would direct him to a proper place where he might
attend to nothing else but the working out his own
salvation.   Whilst he was praying one night to this
effect, having lifted up his eyes to heaven, he perceived a light in form of a cross coming towards him, and
heard a voice that said to him: "If thou desirest to
save thy soul, follow this light." He immediately

obeyed, and following this heavenly light, he was conducted to the great laura of St. Sabas, were he found
one hundred and fifty solitaries, living in extreme
want of all temporal things, but rich in the treasures
of divine grace.

The holy abbot having received this new comer
without knowing who he was, recommended him to
the procurator of the community, who employed him
for some time in various offices for the service of the
other religious, such as fetching them water,—preparing their victuals,—carrying stones for the building which they had at that time in hand,—dressing
and carrying the workmen their dinners, at the distance of about a mile from his lodgings,—entertaining such strangers as came,—and, in a word, doing
all that any of the monks desired, with such humility,
readiness, and cheerfulness as made him both admired
and loved by them all. After this St. Sabas appointed him a little cell, in which for the space of three
years, he lived in silence, taking no manner of nourishment during five days of the week, and only coming out to the church on Saturdays and Sundays,
where he was always the first and the last, and there
sung the psalms of the divine office with such respectful awe, modest gravity, and fervent piety, as edified
all who saw him ; and assisted also at the unbloody
sacrifice and sacrament of the altar, with such deep
compunction and devotion, that he could not refrain

from shedding floods of tears during the time of the celebrating those divine mysteries.

After these three years of silence, St. Sabas appointed him to the office of procurator of the laura, to the great advantage of the whole community, God giving his blessing to his servant, and assisting him in all things. The time of exercising this office being expired, and the holy abbot seeing him so accomplished in all virtue, took him to Jerusalem, and desired the patriarch St. Elias, the successor of Salustius, and formerly disciple of St Euthymius, to impose his hands upon him, and to ordain him priest. The servant of God, on this occasion, desired he might be first allowed to speak to the patriarch in private; and having obtained of him a promise of secrecy, told him, that he had been a bishop, but that the multitude of his sins had determined him to quit his see, and to fly into the desert in order to bewail his offences and obtain the divine mercy; and in the mean time, as long as he was strong and robust to labor, all he could to assist and comfort those good religious to whom God had associated him. The patriarch was astonished at the hearing of this, and calling for St. Sabas, said to him: "This monk has discovered to me in private some particulars, which will not allow me to ordain him priest. Take him therefore back with you, and let him live in silence, and suffer no one to disturb him." St. Sabas being thus not only disappointed, but also very much concerned, through the apprehension lest some great evil might have been discovered by the patriarch which had prevented him from admitting his disciple to holy orders, betook himself to his prayers, and ceased not to importune our Lord to let him know whether John was indeed, as he had thought, a vessel of sanctification, and worthy of the priestly function or not. At length an angel, after he had spent the whole night in prayer appearing to him, told him, 'that John was indeed *a vessel of election*, but being already a bishop could not be ordained priest. St. Sabas, who was often favored with such visions, went immediately to St. John's cell, and embracing him, said. "I find, father, that you have hidden from me the grace you have received from God, but he has been pleased to reveal it to me." "You mortify me exceedingly, said John, by speaking to me thus. I was in hopes this secret would not have been known to any one, but now I perceive I must quit this country." Sabas desired him to be at rest, and made him a solemn promise that he would keep his episcopal character a secret. Upon which he was content to continue with him; yet so as to remain close in his cell, where he spent four years more in perfect solitude and silence. When the insolence of the monks drove St. Sabas away from the laura, John would remain there no longer, nor hold any communication with the rebels, but retired to the desert of

Ruban, where he found a cavern in which he passed
nine years, conversing with God alone, and living
upon what wild herbs or roots he could find in the
wilderness.

Whilst he dwelt in this solitude one of the religious
came to visit him, and staid a short time with him;
but being quickly wearied with so austere a kind of
life, and such close retirement, he proposed that they
should return together to the laura, in order to celebrate the approaching feast of Easter with the brethren,
and not to starve in that barren desert.—The Saint,
who could not think of returning to the laura as long
as Sabas was absent from thence, exhorted the brother
to a confidence in divine providence, which, as it had
heretofore fed six hundred thousand men for the space
of forty years in the wilderness, could with as much
ease abundantly provide for them both. But this exhortation having made no impression on the mind of
his companion, he presently took his leave of him and
departed. He was scarcely gone when an unknown
person came to the cavern of the Saint, driving an ass
laden with all sorts of provisions, which he bestowed
upon the servant of God; whose faith his divine Majesty was pleased to reward in this wonderful manner:
whilst the other, instead of going back to the laura,
lost his way in the wilderness; but after wandering
about for the space of three days, being now quite exhausted and famished, returned to the Saint, and see-

ing all the good things that God had sent him, acknowledged his own error, and asked pardon for it.

Whilst St. John dwelt in this desert, the Saracens made an inroad upon the borders of the empire on the side of Palestine, and committed great outrages. On this occasion the Saint was pressed by the monks of the laura to come and take shelter amongst them, where he would be more remote from the danger of the enemy's parties, and protected by the Roman soldiers; but he, who had found by experience how sweet it was to converse alone with his God, chose rather to remain where he was putting his whole trust in him, who has given his angels charge over his servants to guard them in all their ways; and his divine goodness was pleased to show his approbation of this entire confidence which his servant placed in him, by sending him as our author learnt from the Saint's own mouth, a great lion to be his visible guardian. At the first sight of the beast, the man of God was struck with some fear, but he quickly recovered himself, and found that the creature, instead of meaning him harm, carefully attended him by day and night, and suffered no enemy to approach near his cavern.

At the expiration of the nine years, St. Sabas visited him, and brought him back to the laura, where he lived for many years shut up in his cell, no one, except the holy abbot, knowing all the while of his being a bishop, till God was pleased it should be made known

to the whole community, by the means of Atherius,
an Asiatic prelate, who having made a pilgrimage of
devotion to Jerusalem, was directed from heaven to go
and visit our Saint in the laura of St. Sabas, and there
acquainted the religious with the treasure they possessed, as well as with all the particulars of this former
course of life.   When John was now seventy years of
age, it pleased God to take St. Sabas to himself.   Our
Saint was sensibly touched with the loss of his holy
father, and the more because, being shut up in his
cell, he had not been present at his death.   But behold St. Sabas appeared to him in a dream, desiring
that he would not be afflicted at his death; for that
though they were now separated in body, they were
still united in spirit.   John desired he would pray to
God for him, that he would be pleased to take him
also out of this miserable world; but Sabas told him
that could not be as yet, because his longer stay in the
world was necessary to support the brethren under the
grievous conflicts and temptations to which they were
like to be exposed from the enemies of the faith.

Twenty years afterwards, when the saint was now
fourscore and ten years old, my author, who had been
received whilst a child by St. Sabas into the number
of his disciples, was directed by his pious mother to
St. John, in order to be guided in all things by his
counsels for the welfare of his soul.   The Saint told
him, if he desired to save his soul, he would advise

him to enter into the monastery of St. Euthymius. But being then young and giddy, he neglected the advice, and chose rather to go towards the Jordan, to dwell in some of the religious houses in that part of the country. Having fixed on the laura called the Reedfield, he was there taken violently ill, being unaccustomed to the yoke of religious discipline, and suffered at the same time a great anguish of mind, as well as bodily pain, when behold the Saint appeared to him in a dream, saying: "Behold, how thou art now chastised, because thou wouldst not be advised by me. But rise up, and go to Jericho, and there thou shalt find in the hospital of the abbot Euthymius, a very ancient religious man, follow him into the monastery into which he shall conduct thee, and there thou shalt find the salvation of thy soul." Upon this he awoke, and found himself instantly cured; and presently after getting up, receiving the blessed sacrament, and taking some nourishment, he walked the same day to Jericho. From hence he went to the monastery of St. Euthymius, and from that time always applied to our Saint for his spiritual direction.

This afforded him an opportunity of being an eye-witness of the wonders which God wrought by our Saint. As when in his presence one, whose name was George, brought his son who was grievously tormented by an evil spirit, and left him before the window of his cell, (as no one ever came within the door)

who was immediately delivered, upon the Saint's praying for him, and anointing him with the oil of the
cross. But the miracles wrought by him for the cure
of souls were the most remarkable. The abbot Eustatius applied one day to the Saint upon occasion of a
most violent and obstinate temptation of blashphemous
thoughts, desiring him to pray for him. The servant
of God did so; and then turning to him he said:
"God be praised, my son, you will never more be
troubled with the like thoughts," as was actually the
case: this our author learnt from Eustatius himself.

A lady, named Basilissa, who was deaconness of the
great church of Constantinople, having taken a journey
to the Holy Land, in the company of a kinsman, who
though otherwise virtuous and religious, was nevertheless infected with the errors of Eutyches, hearing of
the wonderful graces bestowed upon our Saint, conceived a great desire to see and speak to him. But
being informed that no woman was allowed to come
within the enclosure of the laura, she sent to Theodore
his disciple, and begged of him to take her cousin
along with him to the Saint, in hopes that by his
blessing and prayers he might be converted and reclaimed from his errors. Theodore took the young
man with him, and knocked at the Saint's window,
according to custom, which when he had opened, they
both knelt down and craved his blessing. The man
of God told his disciple, that as for his part he gave

him his benediction, but that he could not do as much for his companion, because by schism and heresy he was an alien from the Catholic Church. The young man, astonished to hear him describe in this manner the state of his soul, which he could not know but by divine revelation, was by an evident miracle of divine grace, perfectly converted upon the spot, and renouncing his heresy, after a competent preparation, was admitted by the Saint to the holy communion. The lady, overjoyed at his conversion, conceived a still greater desire of seeing the Saint, and of treating with him about the state of her soul, insomuch that she had formed a design of putting on man's clothes, that so she might have access to him; but the Saint, knowing by revelation her design, sent to her to lay aside so useless a scheme, for that he would not be seen by her in that manner; but if she would stay where she was, she should see him in her sleep and then might put what questions she pleased to him. The following night, or shortly after, the Saint appeared to her in a dream, and said to her: " God hath sent me to you, you may now propose to me all that you want to know." She then declared to him all that she had in her mind, and received from him full satisfaction in every particular, for which she returned great thanks to God. All this, says our author, I can aver for truth, having heard it from her own mouth.

And here our author concludes his account of ou

Saint, who was, at the time of his writing, actually
living, doubting not, as he says, but that others would
deliver in a more ample manner to posterity the great
things that God had wrought by him, as well as his
many labors and sufferings in defence of the faith of
the church.   The Saint was at that time one hundred
and four years old, and though weak in body, yet perfect in all the faculties of his soul, and by a cheerful
countenance ever showed forth the joy of his heart,
and the purity of his conscience.   How long he lived
afterwards, or in what year he departed to our Lord,
we have not found ; but his name stands recorded
among the Saints in the Roman Martyrology on the
thirteenth of May.

ST. JOHN CLIMACUS.

From Daniel, Monk of Raithu, his Cotemporary, and
from his own Writings.

JOHN, surnamed *Climacus*, from his celebrated book
entitled *Climax*, or the *scale* or *ladder* of christian and
religious perfection, was born, as it is thought, in some
part of Palestine, about the year 525.   After an innocent education at home in the exercises of Christian
piety, joined with the study of the human sciences,

when he had attained to the age of sixteen, he formed
the happy resolution of quitting the world and all terrestrial things, in order to discover the treasure of
evangelical perfection in the field of religious discipline. The place he pitched upon for his retirement,
in which he might spend the remaining days of his
mortality, was mount Sinai, where the Lord heretofore
gave his law to Moses, and which from the time that
St. Antony and St. Hilarion began to propagate the
monastic institute, had always been peopled with holy
solitaries. Some of these lived as hermits in lonesome
cells, others in the vast monastery on the top of the
mountain, which was at this time one of the most celebrated in the church of God ; but John chose a middle
way, declining the multitude of the convent, as exposing him to more distractions, and yet not venturing,
because he was young and unexperienced, to live quite
by himself as an anchoret, he put himself under the
discipline of a holy man, who dwelt in a cell on the
side of the mountain, whose name was Martyrius, and
lived with him for nineteen years, in the exercises of so
humble and faithful an obedience, as that he seemed,
from his very first entering upon this course of life, to
have left his own will behind him : and notwithstanding his great wit and learning, which is so apt to puff
men up, to judge of nothing by his own choice, but to
regulate himself in all things, by a humble dependence
on the conduct and direction of his superior, as the

surest way to be conducted and directed by God him·
self.

After a trial of four years he made his solemn profession, by which he eternally dedicated himself to God
At which time a holy abbot, who was present, foretold
that this young religious man would be one day one
of the greatest lights of the Church of God. From
the time of his profession, John continued still to live
with the same simplicity and humility under the direction of Martyrius, making a continual progress both in
virtue and the knowledge of the holy Scriptures, on
which he meditated day and night Martyrius sometimes took him to visit the saints who dwelt in that
neighborhood. One day he brought him to a servant
of God whose name was Anastasius, who fixing his
eyes upon him, told Martyrius that his disciple would
be one day abbot of Mount Sinai, which situation was
looked upon in those days as one of the highest pro-
motions in the whole monastic order, and a dignity to
which none were raised but such as were most emi
nent in sanctity, no others being thought proper to be
the fathers and superiors of so many saints as then inhabited that holy mountain. At another time, when
they went together to visit John, surnamed the Saba·
ite, because he had been a disciple of St. Sabas, this
holy man, according to the custom of the solitaries,
washed the feet of his guests, beginning with the dis
ciple, and on being asked the reason, he said he did

not know who that young man was, but he believed he saw in him an abbot of mount Sinai.

At the end of nineteen years our Lord took Marty rius to himself, and then our Saint, by the counsel of George the Arsilaite, an eminent servant of God, undertook an anchoretical life in a cell by himself, at the foot of the mountain, at the distance of five miles from the church, to which nevertheless he repaired on all Saturdays and Sundays to join the rest of the religious in the divine office, to assist at the sacred mysteries, and receive the blessed sacrament. In this hermitage he continued forty years, practising in the highest degree of perfection the three principal virtues of a solitary life, which he has so much recommended in his writings, viz. a total disengagement of his thoughts and heart from temporal things, an incessant watchfulness and continual prayer, which consisted, as we learn from his own doctrine (Grad. 27.) in having God always for his object, and his divine will for his rule in all his exercises, words, thoughts, and in every motion and step that he took, and in doing nothing but in the presence of God, with an internal fervor of spirit. This gift of continual prayer was accompanied by the gift of tears, which he frequently poured forth in private before our Lord, bewailing his sins with the deepest compunction of heart. Nor did his frequent application to the reading of the Scriptures and writings of the Saints, interrupt his prayers or tears but rather served as a fuel to that inward fire of divine love, which produced both the one and the other Nor was the knowledge he here acquired, nor the particular lights which the spirit of God imparted to him for the instruction and conduct of others, in the least prejudicial to his humility, or make him think he was left upon earth for any thing else, but to bewail his sins in solitude, and do penance for them.

Many persons, as well religious as seculars, came from time to time to consult him about the concerns of their souls, to whom, with great candor and simplicity, he communicated the lights which God gave him. A solitary, whose name was Moses, not content with only coming to consult him, prevailed on him by the intercession of the ancients of mount Sinai, to receive him in quality of his disciple. This Moses being sent one day by the Saint to fetch earth from a place at some distance for the use of their little garden, the fatigue of the work and the heat of the sun, obliged him, towards noonday, to go and rest himself on the side of a bank, under the shadow of a rock, or great stone, that hung over his head. Here laying himself down he fell fast asleep. In the mean time the Saint, who had been praying in his cell, happened also to fall into a slumber, in which there appeared to him a venerable person, that said: "Dost thou sleep, John, without any concern? get up, for Moses is upon the brink of danger." Having immediately awoke upon this admonition, he betook him-self to his prayers, to beg deliverance for his disciple. But whilst he was praying for him, the divine good-ness was pleased that Moses also should hear, as he thought, in his sleep, the voice of his master calling upon him to get up with all speed; upon which he presently started up in a fright, and ran away fiom the bank, and within less than a minute the great stone under which he had been sleeping fell down, so that had he remained there but one minute longer, he must have been inevitably crushed to death.

The common enemy of the good of souls behold-ing with an envious eye the great advantage that many reaped from the instructions and spiritual dis-courses which the Saint made to those who visited him, stirred up the jealousy of certain persons who pretended to be scandalized at his speaking too much, saying that he was a vain babbler, who only loved to hear himself talk. The Saint, who sought not to pro-mote his own fame, but the glory of God; who had no vain opinion of his own talents, but had only yield-ed to speak through the importunity of his brethren, and from an impulse of fraternal charity, far from justifying or excusing himself, or even being offended at what they said of him (believing they had only meant to give him a charitable admonition and frater-nal correction), was resolved to comply therewith, and of consequence condemned himself to an inviolable silence, which he kept for a whole year, till at length those very men, overcome with his wonderful humility and modesty, and sensible of the detriment they had done the public, by depriving them of his wholesome instructions and directions, joined with all the rest of the brethren in begging of the man of God to resume his former practice.

The Saint had now led the life of an anchoret for the space of forty years in his cell, when all the religious of mount Sinai, with one accord, chose him for their abbot; and notwithstanding all his resistance, obliged him to quit his hermitage to come and be their director and general superior. Thus was this great light set in the candlestick, from thence to cast his bright rays on every side, to enlighten the whole world. The lustre of his sanctity reached even as far as Rome, from whence our most holy Pontiff, St. Gregory the Great, wrote to him, testifying the great esteem he had of his eminent virtue. It was about this time that John, the abbot of Raithu, a famous monastery on the confines of Egypt, obtained permission of our Saint to commit to writing the great lights he had received from God for directing and conducting souls to the very top of the mountain of religious perfection. This he has happily executed in his excellent book, entitled *Climax*, or the *Ladder* of thirty steps or degrees of christian virtues, by which the soul ascends to the heavenly paradise. It appears that the Saint, before the composing of this work, had made a visit to a famous monastery in Egypt, supposed to have been of the order or congregation of St. Pachomius, of which he makes frequent mention, bestowing the highest encomiums as well on the holy abbot, as on several of the monks by name. Here he continued a considerable time, and, with the leave of the superior, went also to see the monastery, or rather prison of the penitents, which was distant about a mile off from the abbey, and remained therein thirty days. The wonders of divine grace, which he there discovered in the whole demeanor of these happy penitents, are inserted at large in his fifth step of his Ladder, viz. *penitence :* of which, as it may serve as a stimulus to penitent sinners, we shall here give an abstract.

"Being come," says he, "into this monastery of the penitents, I beheld things which the eye of the slothful has never seen, the ear of the negligent has never heard, and which have never entered into the heart of the sluggard,—things and words capable of doing violence, if I may use the expression, to the Almighty. I saw some of these penitents standing whole nights upright, without allowing themselves any sleep or rest whatsoever ;—others, in a pitiful manner, looking up towards heaven, and calling for help from thence with groans, sighs, and prayers ;—others, who whilst at prayer, had their hands bound behind them like criminals, bowing down their pale countenances towards the ground, declaring aloud that they were unworthy to lift up their eyes to heaven, and that they durst not presume to speak to God, &c.—I saw some, (says he,) sitting on the floor covered with hair-cloth and ashes, hiding their faces between their knees, and striking their foreheads against the earth ;—others beating their breasts with inexpressible contrition of heart, some of whom watered the ground about them with their tears,—others grievously lamenting that they could not weep,—several mourning with a loud cry over their own souls, as we mourn over the dead corpse of a dear friend,—others ready to roar out for grief, eagerly struggling to stifle the noise of their complaints, till being no longer able to repress them, they were forced to let them break forth with greater violence ;—others appeared so astonished, that one would have supposed them to be statues of brass, so insensible of all things had the excess of their sorrow rendered them. Their heart was plunged in an abyss of humility, and their scorching grief had dried up all their tears, &c. There might you have seen the words of David fulfilled in these holy penitents, *I am become miserable, and am bowed down even to the end : I walked sorrowful all the day long. I am afflicted and humbled exceedingly.* And again, *I am smitten us grass and my heart is withered, because I forgot to eat my bread.—For I did eat ashes like bread, and mingled my drink with weeping.* No other words could be heard amongst them, but such as these : woe, woe to me, a miserable sinner ; 'tis with justice, O Lord, 'tis with justice ; spare us, O Lord, spare us ; have mercy on us.—Some of them afflicted themselves by standing parching in the most violent heat of the sun ; others, on the contrary, exposed themselves to suffer no less from extremity of the cold.—Some, in the violence of their thirst, taking a small quantity of water, contented themselves with only tasting of it, whilst others, after eating a morsel of bread, cast the rest away, saying : they were not worthy to eat the food of men, who had acted more like irrational creatures : there was no room for laughter ;—none for idle talk ;—none for resentment, anger or contradiction ;—none for mirth, the care of the body, good cheer, or the pleasures of eating or drinking ;—none for the least spark of vain-glory. No earthly cares distracted them, nor did they know what it was to judge or condemn any man but themselves   Their whole employment, day and night, was to cry to our Lord, and no voice was heard amongst them but that of prayer. Some there were who, beating their breasts with all their might, as if they were knocking for admittance at the gate of heaven, said to the Lord : O open to us through thy mercy, the gate which we have shut against ourselves by our sins.—Another, *show us only thy face, O Lord, and we shall be saved.*—Another said., show thyself, O Lord, to thy poor supplicants, that sit in darkness and in the shadow of death, &c Having always the hour of death before their eyes, they would say, O what shall our end be?—What sentence shall then be pronounced upon us?—Will God revoke the judgment we have deserved?—Has our prayer been able to force its way to the presence of the Lord?—Has it been regarded, coming from such unclean hearts and lips as ours?—Has some part at least of our sins been blotted out? for as they are very great, they stand in need of many penitential labors and sorrows to be wholly effaced.—Who can tell whether even our good angels are near us, to present our prayers, or whether the stench of our sins has not driven them away? &c. To these interrogations some replied : who knows, brethren, as the Ninevites said heretofore, but that our Lord may grant us pardon, and deliver us from that dreadful penance of the world to come? Let us neglect nothing that depends on us; let us continue to knock at the door of his mercy, even till the end of our lives : perhaps he will yield to our importunity and perseverance ; for he is good and merciful. Let us run, brethren, let us run, for we have need to run, and to run with all our speed, that we may recover what we have lost. Let us run, and not spare this filthy flesh ; let us make it suffer in time, because it has exposed us to the danger of suffering for eternity. Thus said these holy crimi nals, and they were as good as their words. Their knees were hardened by incessant kneeling;—their eyes appeared sunk into their sockets;—the hair of their eye-lids was fallen off by their continual weeping;—their cheeks were rivelled, and, as it were, parched with the scalding brine of their tears;—their breasts bruised with blows," &c.

The Saint having·added a great deal more, with regard to the sentiments and dispositions of these holy penitents, and all that he saw and heard during his stay amongst them, concludes his narration in the following manner: "After I had remained thirty days in this prison, I returned to the great monastery, the holy abbot, seeing me quite altered, like a man utterly astonished, and comprehending the cause of my amazement, said: Well, how fares it, father John? Have you seen the labors and conflicts of our penitents? Yes replied I;—father, I have both seen and admired them, and cannot but esteem them more happy who mourn in this manner, after falling into sin, than those who have not fallen, and therefore bewail not themselves; because it seems to me that their fall has been to them an occasion of a most happy and secure resurrection."

Our Saint, after publishing this book, did not continue long in his station of abbot, but exchanged it for beloved solitude, returning into the desert to prepare himself for eternity. He departed to our Lord, in an

advanced age, about the year 605, and his name is en-
registered amongst the Saints, in the Roman Martyrology on the thirtieth of March.

ST. JOHN THE ALMONER.

**From his Life written by Leontius, his Cotemporary,
Bishop of Neapolis, in Cyprus**

THIS Saint, whose life has been commonly published
with those of the fathers of the desert, though it does
not appear that he ever lived in the desert, was born
at Cyprus, about the year 552, his father, Epiphanius,
being at that time governor of the island. He was
brought up from his childhood in christian piety, and
amongst other virtues, he was always in a particular
manner addicted to alms-deeds, and to the works of
mercy and charity to the poor; from whence he has
ever since been distinguished by the surname of *the
Almoner*, or *Alms-giver*. He was confirmed in the
love and practice of this heavenly virtue, by a vision
he had in his youth, which himself afterwards related
in the following manner: " When I lived in the island
of Cyprus, being then no more than fifteen years old,
I saw one night in a dream a young virgin crowned
with olive, of an incomparable beauty, and more

bright than the sun, who, standing by my bed, struck me on the side, and awaked me. Being at length awake, I still perceived her standing in the same spot, and supposed her to be a woman ; wherefore, making the sign of the cross, I asked who she was, and how she could have the boldness to come to my bed side whilst I was asleep ? She answered, with a sweet and smiling countenance; I am the eldest daughter of the great celestial King: take me for thy friend, and I will conduct thee into his presence; for no one has so much power and interest with him as I have, since it was I that even brought him down from heaven to earth, and made him become man, in order to save man. Having said these words, she instantly disappeared. As soon as I recovered from my surprise, I began to think that this heavenly beauty represented alms-deeds, and mercy and compassion for the afflicted; because it was indeed the mercy, compassion, and goodness of God towards mankind, that made him come down from heaven, to clothe himself with our humanity. Having arisen, I immediately dressed myself and without awaking any of the family, went at the first dawning of the day to the church. In my way I met a poor man trembling with cold, and in order to make, as it were, an experiment of the truth of the vision, I pulled off my cloak and gave it him. Presently after, before I had reached the church door, a stranger, clothed in white, came up, and put a purse

into my hands, containing a hundred pieces of money,
saying: Take this, my brother, and distribute it as
you think fit. The joy, together with the surprise in
which I then found myself, induced me to receive the
purse without demur; but when, upon reflection, I
turned back to follow the person, and to return him
his money, as having no want or occasion for it, he
vanished out of my sight. From that day I often
gave alms to my brethren the poor, saying within myself: *now I shall see whether Jesus Christ, acrording
to his promise, will return me a hundred fold;* by
which I became guilty of a great sin in tempting God,
and afterwards conceived a great remorse of conscience
for it, yet I still received from him, at sundry times,
and in divers manners, all the satisfaction I could desire." So far the Saint, speaking of his younger days.

St. John had given the most brilliant examples of
all virtues, more especially of an unbounded charity
in a secular life, till about the fifty-fourth year of his
age, when the great reputation of his sanctity, which
now spread itself far and near, recommended him so
strongly to the church of Alexandria, that upon the
death of Theodore its patriarch, he was chosen his
successor; the emperor Heraclius, in the mean time,
using his utmost influence to overcome the repugnance
the Saint had to this promotion, of which he thought
himself infinitely unworthy. As soon as he arrived
at Alexandria, he sent for the archdeacon and officers

of the church, and said to them; "It would be unjust,
O, my brethren, if we should begin with any other
care or concern, before that which we owe to Jesus
Christ; wherefore be pleased to go through the city,
and let me have an exact list of all my masters." As
they seemed not to understand his meaning, he explained himself, saying, that he considered the poor
not only as his lords and masters, but his coadjutors
also, who, by their prayers, were to help him to heaven. The list of the poor which they brought in was
found to amount, in that great and populous city, to
upwards of seven thousand five hundred; yet notwithstanding their being so numerous, the Saint gave
orders that a daily allowance of necessaries should be
given to every one of them out of his revenue.

After his consecration, he immediately applied himself, with all diligence and fervor, to execute every
branch of his pastoral charge with the utmost perfection; and, as a true father of his people, to procure
them whatever, was either for their spiritual or corporal welfare. He began, by putting an effectual stop
to the frauds and injustices committed in trade, particularly by false weights and measures, a practice
which, said he, God, as we learn from his divine word,
utterly abhors; and, as he was informed, that they
who had the administration of the temporalities of
his church, were often biassed by presents which were
made them so as to be partial in the discharge of their

office, he sent for them, and after appointing them a larger salary, strictly forbid them to receive any presents from any person whatsoever; because said he, a fire shall consume the houses of those that take bribes. Being also informed that many who labored under injuries and oppressions, were intimidated by his secretaries, and other officers, from laying their complaints before him; as a remedy to so great an evil, he ordered a chair to be placed before the great church, with a bench on each side, where he attended for several hours, on every Wednesday and Saturday, to give audience, and redress the grievances of all that pleased to come for that purpose, and would charge the proper officer to see that what he ordered should be presently executed. Upon which occasion he used to say: "If we poor mortals are allowed at every hour to enter the house of God, in order to address our supplications to him, and lay all our wants before him, though his Majesty be incomprehensible, and infinitely elevated above all created beings, if we," continues he, "are so anxious that he would hear our prayers, and make haste to help us, how ready ought we to be to hear the petitions, and grant the just demands of our fellow-servants, remembering that saying of our Lord Jesus, *with what measure you have measured, it shall be measured to you again.*" Matt vii. 2.

On these occasions, it was the custom of our Saint

who hated idleness, either to employ his time in reading the holy Scriptures, whilst he, was waiting in or
der to give audience to such as should apply to him,
or in spiritual conferences with some servants of God:
but one day having remained there till noon, without
being applied to by any one, he withdrew, with tears
in his eyes, saying: that none of his people had favored him that day, or afforded him any opportunity of
offering something to Jesus Christ, in order to cancel
his own innumerable sins. Sophronius, a great servant of God, who sat by him, replied, that he ought
rather rejoice to find that God had made him his instrument in establishing so good a harmony and per
fect a peace amongst the sheep committed to his
charge, that there was not even one to be found
amongst them that had any difference or misunder
standing with his neighbor; for this indeed, said he,
is converting men into angels.

This Sophronius, with John his companion, men
equally eminent both for their wisdom and their sanctity, were sent by divine providence to the assistance
of our Saint. He made use of them, upon all occasions, as his counsellors and directors, and obeyed
them with as much submission as if they had been his
fathers; and his esteem, as well as his love for them
were the more increased by the success that attended
the exertion of their eminent talents in bringing back
to God innumerable souls who had been unhappily

seduced by the Eutychian heresy, which then greatly prevailed all over Egypt, even amongst many of the religious. By means of these holy men, the Saint had the comfort of beholding in his days, not only many private houses and families, but also several churches and monasteries, delivered out of the jaws of the infernal wolf, and again restored to the true fold of Christ, the Catholic Church. As to our Saint, he incessantly warned his flock to avoid all communion in spirituals with any who were separated by heresy from the communion of the church, and not so much as to enter into their churches or meeting houses, much less to join with them in prayer, even though any one should be so unhappily circumstanced as to be confined during his whole life to a place where he could never see a catholic priest, or receive any of the holy sacraments; for, said he, as the laws of God and man forbid any one, who has a wife living, to cohabit with another woman, how distant or for how long a time soever his lawful wife may be separated from him, so he who has been espoused to Christ in the Catholic Church, cannot without the crime of *spiritual adultery*, upon any pretext whatsoever, engage himself in the communion of heretics.

Exclusive of the assistance that our Saint received in the discharge of his pastoral office from those two great men, he was also desirous of participating in the prayers and merits of the holy solitaries, for whose

manner of life, though he had never been a solitary
himself, he conceived the utmost esteem.   To this end,
having assembled together a number of saint-like anchorets out of the deserts, he distributed them into
two bands, and built cells for them in two chapels
erected at his own charges ; the one dedicated to the
blessed Virgin, the other to St. John ; furnishing them
with all necessaries out of his own farms, in order, as
he told them, that whilst he, under God, took upon
himself the care of providing for their corporal sustenance, they, on their part, should provide for the spiritual necessities of his soul, especially by offering up
to God in his behalf their evening and midnight devotions.   These foundations of our Saint were of great
edification to the faithful of Alexandria, many of
whom, in different parts of the city, were excited by
the example of these holy men, to pass whole nights
in singing the praises of God.

It would be an endless task to relate the particulars
of all the great things done by our Saint during the
ten years of his episcopal administration, as well fo.
the promoting of the glory of God, as for the sanctification and salvation of the souls committed to his
charge, together with the many wonderful examples
he gave of humility,—meekness,—patience,—charity
for all, even his enemies,—and the rest of the evangelical virtues; but as the most distinctive traits in
his character were the most tender compassion for the

poor and distressed, and an unbounded liberality in
point of alms-deeds, we cannot refrain from adducing
the following extraordinary instances. In his time
Chosroes, king of Persia, having laid waste Syria, and
other parts of the eastern empire, and carried off a
great number of Christians into captivity and slavery
such as could escape his hands made the best of their
way to Alexandria, and presented themselves in great
multitudes to the man of God, as the known refuge of
all the distressed. The Saint received them all with
open arms, and as many of them were sick and wounded, he placed in hospitals or other lodgings, where
they were all entertained at his charges, and as long
as they themselves chose to remain, the most tender
care was taken of them ; and as to the rest, who were
innumerable, he ordered his almoners to give a piece
of silver to every man that applied to them for charity,
and two to every woman or girl, in consideration of
the weakness of their sex. His almoners perceiving
amongst the great numbers of those that applied for
relief, some to be richly clad, made a scruple of giving
them any money, and came to consult the Saint on
the subject ; but he being highly displeased at their not
having complied to the letter, with those words of our
Lord : Luke vi. 30. *Give to every one that asketh
thee*, desired they would not in future be so inquisitive
into the circumstances of those who came to crave
alms, but rather distribute that which belonged to

God with a bountiful hand, according to the will and commandment of Christ. " But if your *little faith*," said he, " makes you apprehend lest my income should not be sufficient to furnish wherewith to relieve such great numbers, I will by no means become a partaker in your *unbelief;* for since it has pleased God to make me, though most unworthy, the dispenser of his goods, if all the men in the world were to come to Alexandria to crave alms I would relieve them, under an entire confidence that they would never be able to exhaust his immense stores, nor those of the church."

Whilst this great multitude of strangers remained at Alexandria, one of them, in order to put the Saint's extreme charity and compassion for the distressed to a trial, presented himself in a ragged garment one day when the man of God was going to the hospital to visit the sick, which he constantly did twice or thrice in a week, and begged he would have pity on a poor captive, and order him some relief. The Saint immediately ordered his almoner to give him *six pieces of silver*. No sooner had he received this alms but he departed, and having changed his dress, and met the Saint again in another street, he cast himself at his feet, saying, he was a poor man in the utmost distress, and begged his assistance. The holy prelate then told his almoner to give him *six pieces of gold*, although this officer had just whispered in his ear, and told him

30

it was the very same person whom he had relieved a little before. Again he came a third time, still imploring the charity of the man of God, and when the almoner signified that it was the same identical person, the Saint answered, give him *twelve pieces of gold;* for possibly, said he, this may be *Jesus Christ,* my Saviour, who is come on purpose *to try me;* alluding, in all probability, to what had happened not long before to St. Gregory the Great.

In the mean time the Persians continuing their devastations in the eastern provinces, drove still greater numbers of people to Alexandria, to shelter themselves there under the charitable wings of our Saint, who not content with relieving all that came, sent also considerable alms to Modestus, the patriarch of Jerusalem, at this time reduced to the greatest extremity with all his people by the Persians, who had taken that city and burnt the churches. With this alms he sent also a letter to the patriarch, apologizing for not sending something more worthy of the temple of God, and declaring how glad he should be, if circumstances would permit him to come himself in person, and labor with his own hands in rebuilding the holy church of the sepulchre and resurrection of our Lord, requesting also that he would excuse his want of the means, and obtain for him, by his prayers, that his name might be written in the book of life.

At this time the innumerable multitude of persons

that came from all parts to Alexandria, made all sorts of provisions exceedingly dear, more especially as the harvest had failed in Egypt, the Nile not having overflowed that year as usual. The Saint, who could not endure to see distress laid out all the money he had or could any way procure, either by begging or borrowing of good people, till at length, all being spent, no one could be found that would lend him any more, every body apprehending, lest by the continuance of the famine, they should come themselves to want; when behold, amidst these extremities, as if God had a mind to try the fidelity of his servants, a rich citizen, who was desirous of being promoted to holy orders, but was prevented by the canons of the Church, on account of his having been twice married, made him an offer of two hundred thousand bushels of wheat which he had stored up, together with a very large sum of money to be disposed of in charities, upon condition he would dispense with the irregularity he had incurred by his bigamy, and ordain him deacon. The Saint told him, that although the offering which he proposed could never come at a time in which it was more wanted, he nevertheless could not accept it, as it was defective and tainted by the condition to which it was annexed, because the law of God required that the sacrifice offered to him should be clean and without blemish: and as to the present necessities of his brethren, the poor, as well as those of the Church, he

was confident that the same divine goodness which
had hitherto taken care of them, would still continue
to feed and support them, provided, said he, we invio-
lably observe what he commands us.   No sooner had
he returned this answer, and dismissed the ambitious
aspirer to a spiritual promotion, but his people brought
him the gladsome tidings that the two great ships belonging to the Church, which he had sent to Sicily,
were just arrived in the port laden with corn ; upon
which the man of God prostrated himself on the
ground, and returned hearty thanks to our Lord, who
had not only preserved him from sin under that trial,
but had immediately sent him such a seasonable and
abundant provision.

It was wonderful to relate the many other occasions
wherein it pleased God to furnish his servant with extraordinary supplies in order to support his boundless
charities, so that, generally speaking, the more he gave
away, the more he received from the divine bounty
through the hands of charitable Christians, and sometimes not without an evident miracle.   A citizen, who
after living in opulent circumstances had been suddenly reduced to extreme poverty, applied to the Saint
in the church for an alms ; he recollecting him to have
been not long before a wealthy man, had great compassion on him, and whispered to his almoner to give
him fifteen pounds of gold ; which when the almoner
was going to execute, he was persuaded by the secre-

tary and the steward to give him only five pounds.
The Saint returning home from the church, was met
by a rich widow, who put a promissory note in his
hands, in which she obliged herself to give him five
hundred pieces of gold for the poor. Having received
the note, and knowing in spirit that it was sent to recompense the charity given to the abovementioned
citizen, he required and found out that his officers had
only given him five pounds instead of fifteen, whereupon he told them they would be answerable to God
for the other thousand pieces of gold which the good
lady that had given the note for the five hundred had
designed for the poor, if they had not abridged her
charity by not complying with his. In order to convince them thereof, having sent for the lady, he asked
her in their presence, if the sum mentioned in the
note was what she originally intended to give to Jesus
Christ, or whether she had proposed to give him a •
larger sum? She suspecting by this question that
what had passed had been revealed from heaven, she
was struck with fear and astonishment, and assured
him in the most solemn manner, that she had actually
written *fifteen hundred pieces of gold*, but that looking at the note just before she had presented it to him
at church, she found to her great astonishment, the
fifteen hundred changed into five hundred, but knew
not by what means nor by whom, as the paper had
never been in any other person's hands but her own,

and therefore concluded it to be the will of God that she should give no more than five hundred.

A captain of a ship, a stranger, having suffered great losses at sea, besought our Saint, with many tears, that he would have the same compassion for him as he had on all others in distress; he ordered his almoner to give him the weight of five pounds in gold; which sum enabled him to repair his vessel and put to sea again. But scarcely had he sailed out of port, when a storm arose which obliged him to fling all his goods overboard, and it was with the utmost difficulty he saved his ship. Again he applied to the Saint, begging he would have compassion on him for the sake of him who had shown pity to the whole world. The holy prelate having told him, that this misfortune had befallen him in consequence of his having mingled the charity money which he received of the church with what remained of his own former illgotten wealth, and that therefore he had lost both, gave him now the weight of ten pounds in gold, bidding him take care not to mix it with any other money. Thus being enabled to repair and load his vessel with a fresh cargo, he tried his fortune a second time, but with worse success than ever, for being cast away upon the coast he lost both ship and cargo, and hardly escaped with his life. This latter misfortune drove him into so violent a fit of despair, that he was almost tempted to make away with himself, if the holy patriarch, who had

.earnt by revelation all that had happened, had not
sent for him to comfort him, with the assurance that
'he like misfortune should never again befall him, and
.hat this was permitted in consequence of his having
obtained by unjust means possession of his ship.
Then in order to set him up in the world again, the
Saint appointed him captain of the large vessel belonging to the church of Alexandria and sent him out
laden with twenty thousand bushels of wheat. What
follows is an abstract of the account given by the captain himself, with the most solemn asseveration of its
veracity:—" We sailed," said he " during the space
of twenty days and twenty nights with so violent a
wind that not being able, either by the stars or the
sight of any land, to know in what part of the world
we were, we should have given ourselves up for lost,
had not the pilot assured us that he saw the holy patriarch by his side at the helm, bidding him not to
fear, for that we were in the right road. On the
twentieth day we came within sight of England,
where, when we put to land, we found a great famine.
Upon our making it known that we were laden with
corn, the principal magistrate of the place told us God
had sent us to assist them in their extremity; and
having given us our choice either to receive money or
the weight of our corn in British tin, we chose one
half in coin, the other in tin. But behold a still
greater wonder wrought by our Lord, as a recompense

for the charity of our Saint: as soon as the ship re turned safe back to the coast of Egypt, some of the British tin being sold by the captain to a dealer in pewter, who on melting it down, found it pure silver; upon which, when he went to reproach the captain, as if he had suspected his honesty, and meant by a strat- agem to put it to a trial, the whole was carefully ex- amined, and all found to be excellent silver.

But as our Saint had, on so many occasions, received these miraculous supplies, in order to enable him to continue his extraordinary charities, so was he also sometimes tried, like Job, with great losses, which were shortly after repaid to him with interest. Nice- tas, the governor, urged on by some evil counsellors, under the pretence of the pressing necessities of the state, on account of relieving of the Persian war, de- manded and carried off, in the name of the emperor, all the money that had been brought to our Saint for charitable uses, leaving him master of only one hun- dred crowns; but on the same day, a stranger, from the coast of Barbary, brought him large sums of mo- ney, sent by charitable christians; and the governor himself, before it was night, (upon reading a paper sent on this occasion by the man of God, in which he had written these words, " Our Lord, who has said, *I will not leave thee, neither will I forsake thee,* cannot tell a lie, because he is the truth; and therefore a wretched man, who must shortly be the food of worms, ɪannot tie up the hands of God, who furnishes all his creatures with both food and life,") returned all the money he had taken fɪom him, adding thereto three hundred crowns of his own, and offering to undergo what penance the patriarch should be ᵖpleased to im· pose on him for hiɓ crime.

At another time the Saint sustained a very great loss, when all the vessels belonging to the church of Alexandria, to the number of thirteen, meeting with a ᴠiolent storm in the Adriatic sea, were constrained to fling their wholo freight, consisting of corn and other goods, overboard. On this occasion the holy patriarch said with Job, i. *the Lord gave and the Lord hath taken away, as it hath pleased the Lord, so it is done, blessed be the name of the Lord :* and told his friends who came to condole with him on his misfor- tune, that with respect to himself he rather consider- ed it more to his advantage than his loss, imputing it entirely to his having taken too much complacency in his alms, without sufficiently guarding against the danger of being infected by ᴠainglory ;—that he was very sensible of what service afflictions and humilia- tions are to purify the soul from the dross of pride and vanity, being conᴠinced as well as the psalmist, *It is good for me that thou humbled me, that I may learn thy justifications,* Ps. 118 ;—that however severely, as to his own paɪt, he deserᴠed to be punished on ac- counᵗ of his haᴠing given occasion, by his vanity, tɤ

so many innocent persons being thus reduced, yet as
God was still the same as he was in the days of Job,
he trusted, that notwithstanding his own unworthiness,
he would help them out of their distress.   This confidence of our·Saint was amply recompensed, for not
long after our Lord restored him by one means or
other, twice as much as he had lost, the whole of
which he employed in comforting and assisting more
abundantly than ever the poor and distressed.

The Saint being informed that one of his servants
had labored under a pressing necessity, gave him privately with his own hand the weight of two pounds
in gold; and when the man, confounded at the excess
of his goodness towards him, told him he did not
know he should be able to look him any more in the
face : " Brother," replied the Saint, " I have not yet
shed my blood for you, as Christ our common Master
and God has done for us all, and has commanded us
to do for our brethren."

One of the citizens being closely pressed to pay a
debt, which he had not at that time the means to discharge, addressed himself to a rich nobleman, begging
he would lend him fifty pounds of gold upon proper
security.   He assured him he would, but delayed to
put his promise in execution, whilst the other, still
closely watched by his creditor, apprehending he
would proceed to extremities, had recourse to the
holy patriarch whose heart and hand were ever open

tc relieve the necessities of all. No sooner had he told him his case, but the Saint replied: "My son, if your necessity required it, I would even give you the clothes off my back," and without further hesitation he lent him the whole sum. The following night the nobleman saw in a dream a person standing upon an altar, to whom many others approached to make their offerings, and for every offering they laid upon the altar they received a hundred fold in return. He seemed also to observe the holy patriarch come in immediately after him, and that there lay a sum of money upon a bench before him, which one of the bystanders bid him take up and offer upon the altar, that he might receive a hundred fold; but as he hesitated and was dilatory in doing as he was desired, the patriarch, who stood behind him, stept forward, took up the offering, and putting it upon the altar, presently afterwards received a hundred fold. The next morning the nobleman having sent for the man, offered to let him have the money he wanted; but he replied, that his lordship's delays to fulfil his promise had obliged him to have recourse to the holy patriarch, by whom he was immediately relieved; upon which the other related the vision he had seen, and severely condemned himself for having lost, by his want of diligence in doing good, that great reward wherewith God recompenses those works which are done for his sake

Amongst the many others who, on seeing the boundless charities of the Saint, brought their money to him to be disposed of at his discretion for the relief of the poor. a man who had an only son aged fifteen years, came one day and presented him the weight of seven pounds and a half of gold, assuring him it was all he had, and only besought him to pray for his son, whom he had sent in a ship to the coast of Africa, that God would protect him and conduct him back in safety with his vessel to the haven. The Saint did not only pray himself, but also earnestly recommended the welfare of the youth and the vessel to the prayers of his clergy, as the man had desired ; when behold, before the expiration of thirty days, the boy being taken ill died, and shortly after the ship, in which was also the uncle of the youth, on returning home, was cast away near the port of Alexandria, and nothing whatever saved but the lives of the persons on board, and the boat which conveyed them on shore. The melancholy news of the loss of his son and his ship arriving so rapidly one after the other, caused the most inexpressible affliction to the poor man. The holy patriarch was also exceedingly affected with it, more especially on account of the death of his only son ; wherefore, not knowing what else to do, he besought the *Father of mercies, and God of all consolation,* to comfort the afflicted parent. Then sending a messenger to the man, as he had not the courage to see or speak to himself in person, he desired him not to lose his confidence in God, whose judgments, though inscrutable, are nevertheless just, and according to what he knows is best for us, though we do not; and therefore cautioned him against any want of resignation on this occasion, lest he should bereave himself of the immense reward which God had prepared to recompense his faith and charity, manifested in the offering he had made to God. This message was followed by a dream or vision the ensuing night, in which the man of God appeared to the afflicted parent while asleep, and said to him, "Why do you afflict yourself, dear brother, and suffer yourself to be thus oppressed with grief? Did not you desire me to pray to God to save your son, and behold he has saved him. For I can assure you, that had he lived he would have become a very lewd man; and as for your ship, had not God been moved to mercy, by the good work you did in addressing your charity to me, it would have been utterly lost, together with every person on board, so that you would have lost your brother also. Arise, then, and return thanks to God not only for preserving the life of your brother, but also for having saved your son, by taking him to himself before he became corrupted by the wicked maxims and vanities of the world." Having awoke and found himself wonderfully comforted, he went early in the morning to the patriarch, to return thanks to God and to him, and related to him the vision he had seen. The holy man having

glorified God, for his infinite goodness, desired **the**
other not to attribute any thing of what happened to
his prayers, but to God alone, and the faith he had
placed in God ; for the blessed prelate had always the
meanest opinion of himself, as was ever apparent from
all his words and whole comportment, as he would
never suffer any thing of good to be ascribed to him.

One of the principal men of the city, observing that
the Saint, who was so liberal to others, allowed himself only a poor little bed on the floor, with an old tat-
tered blanket for a covering for his lodging, sent him
in one day a rich coverlet that cost six and thirty
pieces of silver, conjuring him to make use of it for his
sake.   The servant of God, yielding to his importunity, used it for one night ; but as they that lay in the
same chamber observed, that instead of sleeping he
spent the whole night in reproaching himself in the
following manner with lying beneath such a rich covering, whilst the brethren of Jesus Christ, as he called
the poor, lay starving with hunger and cold, and destitute of all the commodities of life : " and thou who
aspirest after the joys of a happy eternity," he said to
himself, " thou who drinkest wine, eatest good fish,
art well lodged, and, like one of the children of this
wicked world, art also warmly covered, and liest at thy
ease under a coverlet that cost six-and-thirty pieces of
silver ; surely living in so unmortified a manner, instead of expecting the joys of heaven hereafter, thou

hast rather cause to apprehend that sentence pronounced on the rich man will fall to thy lot, to whom it was said, Luke xvi. *Thou didst receive good things in thy life time, and likewise Lazarus evil things : but now he is comforted, and thou art tormented."* The result of these reflections was, that he resolved to get rid of this rich piece of furniture the next morning, and sell it for the benefit of the poor, which he did without any delay. When the gentleman saw his present exposed for sale, he purchased it, and sent it to him again, entreating him to make use of it : he sold it a second time, and again in like manner a third time, giving the price of it to the poor, and telling his friends, with a pleasant countenance, " we shall now see which of us shall be first wearied out." This gentleman being very rich, and one from whom the Saint received many things, which he gave to the poor, upon these and similar occasions the Saint used to say, it was no harm to get all he could from the rich for the service of the poor, since by so doing he served both the one and the other; the poor, by relieving their wants, and the rich, by affording them the occasion to purchase heaven by their alms.

Amongst other exercises and lessons of charity which the Saint inculcated to his people, we must not pass over his sentiments with regard to the manner in which masters ought to treat their servants. Attend to the manner in which he expressed himself one day

on this subject, to one who was cruel and inhuman to
his slaves : " My son," said he, with the utmost meekness, " I understand that by the temptation of the enemy, you are apt to treat your servants ill ; let me en·
treat of you, for the time to come, to stop till your
passion is passed over before you offer to correct them.
For God has given them to us in order that they may
serve us, but not that we should beat and abuse them ;
nay, perhaps he may have given them more with a
view of exercising our patience, in supporting their
faults and defects, than for any other service they can
do. But tell me, Sir, with what price could you buy
any one of these who has the honor to have been
created. no less than yourself, after the image and likeness of God ; for, though you are his master, what
have you either in body or soul that he has not ?
Give ear to St. Paul, Gal. iii. *For as many of you
that have been baptized in Christ, have put on Christ ;
there is neither Jew nor Greek : there is neither bond
nor free : there is neither male nor female. For you
are all one in Christ Jesus.* Jesus Christ then, by
taking upon himself the form of a servant, has taught
us that we ought not to lift ourselves by pride over
those whom he had made our servants : for as the
prophet teaches us, Ps. 112, there is but one great
Master and Lord of the universe, *who is as the Lord
our God, who dwelleth on high, and looketh down
on the low things, in heaven and in earth ;* he does

not say *on the high things*, but *on the low things.*
How then can we pretend to domineer over those
who have been redeemed, no less than ourselves, with
the blood of our God and Master, for whose service he
has made the heavens, the sun, the stars, the earth
the sea, and all the things therein ;—for whose pro
tection he employs his angels, and for whom the Son
of God has subjected himself to all the humiliations
and torments of his passion ?—Can you, I say, Sir,
treat with contempt this man whom God treats with
honor ? Shall you strike him as you would a beast,
or as if he were not of the same nature as yourself ?
Tell me whether you be willing that every time you
offend God he should punish you the same moment ?
I am certain you would not. How then can you say
daily to God, *forgive us our trespasses, as we forgive
them that trespass against us ?* Do you do as you
would be done by ? "

This charity which the Saint inculcated to others he
ever practised himself, without excepting his very enemies. Instead of being offended against those who
had injured or wronged him, he, on the contrary, conferred on them greater favors, that he might overcome
evil with good ; nay, he even humbled himself sometimes to impenitent sinners, by casting himself at their
feet, and begging their pardon, although the fault was
wholly on their side, that by these means he might
bring them to a reconciliation with God and his Church.

One day a beggar having asked an alms of the holy
patriarch, he ordered them that accompanied him to
give him ten pieces of brass. The man, who expected more, instead of thanks returned him very abusive
language, and treated him in a most insolent manner. Those that were present, being moved to indignation, would have punished the wretch upon the
spot, had not the Saint severely reproved them, saying, " Let him finish what he has a mind to say ;
for why should not I, my brethren, suffer this small
injury from a poor man, I who, for these sixty years,
have been continually offending and injuring my God
by my sins ? "

Amongst other charities, the Saint also founded
several hospitals ; and whilst a great mortality raged
at Alexandria, he was very assiduous in attending such
as were at the point of death, and in assisting them in
their agony. He was also very diligent, not only in
providing himself, but in ordering prayers to be offered in behalf of the souls of the faithful departed. In
recommendation of this charity, and as a proof of the
efficacy of such prayers, he related what had happened not long before to one of his countrymen, who had
been carried away captive by the Persians, and cast
into a prison called Lethe, or Oblivion. His friends
having heard that he was dead, procured prayers to
be said three several times every year, for the repose
of his soul; at each of which (as he assures them,

when after four years he made his escape out of prison, and returned home) he was always visited and
comforted by a person shining like the sun, and was
delivered on those occasions from his chains for the
whole day.

The Saint recommended very much to his people
the remembrance of death, as a most wholesome
meditation for all men; and having been told, that
on the day of the coronation of the emperor, several
pieces of different sorts of marble were presented to
him, in order that he might choose the kind of which
he would have his tomb made, that being ever mind-
ful of his mortality and speedy return to dust, he
might not suffer himself to be puffed up with pride,
but take care to live and govern in such a manner, as
to be always prepared for his last end; he also, with
the same intention, gave orders to have a sepulchre
prepared for himself amongst the tombs of the patriarchs his predecessors, but that it should not be finished till his death; in the mean time he desired that
the workmen, upon certain solemn days, should come
and tell him, in presence of all his clergy: " My lord,
your tomb remains unfinished, give orders, if you
please, that it may be completed, since you know not
the hour, as the scripture says, when the thief shall
come." He also often entertained his friends that
came to visit him with this same subject, of the continual thought we ought to have of death, and of that

separation which shall then take place between **the** soul and body. " I am of opinion," said he, " that **the** means to work out our salvation is, to be always thinking with sorrow on the hour of our death, and **to** consider well that we shall have no one to share with us the pains and conflicts we must then go through— that at that hour the whole world shall forsake us, our good works excepted, which will never abandon us: —to think how great our astonishment and affliction must be, if at our departure hence we are not prepared for our trial:—to reflect that it will be in vain then to ask for a little more time wherein to do penance when we shall be reproached for having had so much, and made such ill use of it. " And how," said he, " shall poor John, (for so he commonly called himself) escape the claws of those cruel beasts that shall watch to catch him at his departure hence ? What can he do when he shall see before him those bands of evil spirits, who shall strictly examine him, and charge home upon him all the evil he had done ?" Which, he said, alluding to a vision in which St. Simon Styiites had seen in spirit, how, at the time of the separation of the soul from the body, when she would willingly fly up towards heaven, she meets with devils in her way, divided into different companies, according to the different vices which they usually suggest ; and that the demons of pride examine the soul upon the sins committed in that kind :—those of impurity ex

amine her upon all her carnal sins and impure delec-
tations :—those of detraction, upon every word that
has proceeded out of her mouth against her neighbor :
and so of all her other sins. Our Saint had this vision
often in mind ; as also that passage of the life of St.
Hilarion, of the fear and apprehension he had, and
the words he spoke to his soul, when he was upon the
point of death ; and therefore he would often be saying to himself : " If so great a Saint, who had served
our Lord for such a number of years, who had wrought
so many miracles, and even raised the dead to life, yet
apprehended so much that dreadful hour, what shalt
thou be able to say or do, when thou shalt find thyself encompassed by those cruel and unmerciful exam-
iners of all thy actions?   What shalt thou be able to
answer to such of these unhappy spirits as shall examine thee with regard to thy lies, thy detraction, thy
hardheartedness, thy avarice, thy remembrance of injuries, or thy ill-will, &c. O merciful God, may thy
almighty hand defend me at that hour from all the
efforts of these enemies of my salvation ! May thy
goodness send thy angels to guide and conduct me
safe in this last great and dangerous journey from time
to eternity ! " Such were the sentiments of our Saint,
in his entertainments upon this most interesting subject, of the soul's passage out of this world into the
other.

St. John had now illustrated the church of Alexandria for ten years as *a burning and a shining light*, when the time drawing near in which our Lord designed to take him to himself, he resigned his patriarchal see, and retired into his native country, Cyprus, in order to prepare himself for eternity. As soon as he arrived at Amathus, the place of his nativity, having a foreknowledge, by revelation, of his approaching death, he made his last will and testament in words to this effect: " I John, who was born a slave to sin, but have been made a free man by the grace of God, who, without any deserts of mine, has raised me to the priestly dignity, return thee most humble thanks, O Lord, that thou hast vouchsafed to hear the prayer I have made to thee, that I should not possess at my death any more than one small piece of money; and that whereas when I was made bishop I had great treasures at my disposal, and have received since immense sums from thy servants, thou hast always made me sensible that all this store was thine, and hast done me the favor ever to give back to thee without delay what belonged to thee; therefore, as this piece of money which remains belongs also to thee no less than all the rest, I desire it may be likewise returned to thee, by putting it into the hands of the poor."

St. John the Almoner departed to our Lord in the sixty fourth year of his age, anno 616. His body was interred in the church of Amathus, in the chapel of St. Tychon, formerly bishop of that see, where many

miracles were afterwards wrought through his inteices
sion. His name is recorded in the Roman Martyr
ology on the twenty-third of January.

———•◦•———

ST. SYNCLETICA.

From her ancient Life, by a Writer of the same Age
believed by many to have been St Athanasius.

ST. SYNCLETICA was born at Alexandria, about the
latter part of the third century, of noble and wealthy
christian parents, whom God had blessed with four
children, two sons and two daughters. One of the
sons died very young, the other, having attained to the
age of twenty-five, when, at the desire of his parents,
he was contracted to a young lady, and when all things
were prepared for solemnizing the marriage, he was
suddenly carried off by death into another region,
where *they neither marry nor are given in marriage.*
Synclctica, the eldest of the two daughters, from her
tender years consecrated her heart to the love of Christ,
and accustomed herself to the exercises of christian
piety and solid devotion, taking always far more care
of the soul than of the body. As she advanced in
age she increased in virtue and in the love of purity,
which determined her to choose no other spouse but

Jesus Christ. For the love of him she rejected the most advantageous worldly offers that could be made her; and instead of the outward ornaments of the body, which those of her age and quality are usually so fond of, she diligently procured the better ornaments of the interior house of her soul, where she desired to entertain the King of kings, who is beautiful above the sons of men. Hence she carefully shunned all dangerous worldly diversions and unprofitable recreations, seeking always the conversation of such as entertained her with godly discourses and exhortations to piety, to whom she hearkened with the most diligent attention, laying up their words in her memory, and meditating frequently upon them. In the mean time she was exceeding temperate, and mortified in her eating and drinking, looking upon this virtue as the best preservative of purity; and though by her fasting and other austerities, her countenance became both pale and meagre, yet she regarded it not, being not so desirous to please the eyes of men as those of God; and finding by experience that what weakened the body served to invigorate the soul. However, she was always discreet in these corporal mortifications, and took all possible care to conceal them, from being either seen or observed by others.

Her parents dying, left her mistress of all their worldly substance; so that now finding herself at full liberty to follow the call of God, and to retire alto

gether from the world, after having made a sufficient
trial of herself, by way of preparation for those austerities she designed to embrace, she disposed of all
her wealth in favor of the poor; and cutting off her
hair, in token of her renouncing the world and all its
superfluities, she withdrew herself from the town, and
chose a sepulchre, or monument, in the neighborhood,
for her dwelling place, during the remainder of the
days of her mortality, taking also along with her her
youngest sister, who was also desirous of following the
same kind of life. Here she lived separated in a manner from the conversation either of men or women, in
the exercises of mortification, penance, and continual
prayer.—Her food was coarse bread made of bran;—
her ordinary drink was water, and her bed the bare
ground; and as the watchful enemy plied her with
frequent and troublesome temptations, she opposed to
all his assaults the buckler of faith, with the helmet
of hope and confidence in our Lord, to whom she had
continual recourse; and on these occasions she redoubled her austerities in order to keep the flesh in
subjection, yet so as still to have an eye upon the *salt*
of prudence and discretion, wherewith our Lord wills
hat all the *sacrifices* we offer to him should be *seasoned*, Levit. ii. 13. Far from conceiving a good opinion of herself for having quitted her worldly goods,
she kept herself always humble; by thinking she was
still at a very great distance from what she ought to

be, and instead of contenting herself with that voluntary poverty which she had embraced when she renounced all exterior possessions, she made it her chiefest labor to purify her soul, as well from all desires and affections to any thing created, as from all those spiritual vices that are apt to lurk secretly in the interior.

Notwithstanding her utmost endeavors to hide her eminent virtues from the eyes of others, and to avoid, as much as possible, all commerce with the world, yet, as the almighty had so ordered it for his own greater glory, and the good of a great number of souls, she could not keep herself so closely concealed as to prevent the sweet odour of her sanctity from breaking forth from her sepulchre, and spreading herself, by degrees over the whole neighborhood. Hence many devout virgins came to visit her, desiring to profit by her heavenly conversation, and to learn from her lips the lessons of religious perfection and of a truly christian life. At first humility would not suffer her to converse with them, or give them the instructions they desired ; but when they pressed her to speak on divine matters, she contented herself with edifying them by her silence, sighs and tears, till at length charity prevailing over humility, she yielded to their importunity, and gave them many excellent lessons for the regulating of their lives, set down at large by our author in her life, as a rule for such holy virgins as asꝑꞇe after religious perfection, of whom she is generally considered the mother and foundress.

She begins by inculcating to them as her principal lesson, to have always before their eyes, and to imprint deeply in their hearts the two principal com mandments: *thou shalt love the Lord thy God with thy whole heart, &c. and thy neighbor as thyself:* which she tells them are an abridgment of the whole divine law, and comprise all the perfection God desires from us.—That in the exercise of this divine love, those who desire to dedicate themselves to God, must fix no bounds to themselves, but endeavor always to advance:—that they must not content themselves with being the land that bringeth forth only *thirty fold*, but must labor to bring forth *sixty*, and a *hundred fold :*—that as it would be infinitely dangerous to fall from a higher to a lower degree of virtue, from bringing forth sixty, to bring forth only thirty fold, it being so natural when we once begin to sink downwards, to fall lower and lower, till we fall headlong down the precipice, so we must never think of standing still in the way of God, which would in effect be going backwards; but as the apostle admonishes, Philip. iii. 13, 14, *forgetting the things that are behind, and stretching forth myself to those that are before, I pursue towards the mark, for the prize of the supernal vocation of God in Christ Jesus.*

In the next place she tells them, that in order to

preserve and maintain the purity of their souls and
bodies, they must exercise themselves in the mortification of their sensual appetite, not only with regard to
eating and drinking, but also with respect to the
guard they ought to keep upon their eyes, their ears,
their tongue, &c., lest the angels of darkness, who are
the robbers and murderers that are always endeavoring to do us as much mischief as they can, should
steal into our soul by any avenue that should be left
unguarded : therefore she recommends a spirit of recollection and retirement, and to have as little communication as possible with the world ; for how, says she,
can a house surrounded on all sides by smoke, escape
being sullied and made black within, if the doors and
windows are always open ?   She adds, that they must,
according to our Lord's prescription, be ever *wise as
serpents, and innocent as doves,* wisely watching against
all the deceits and assaults of the wicked one, who is
ever besieging them within and without; and in all
their actions keep close to God, by purity and simplicity, both in their intention and affection ; and that
the arms they must continually make use of in this
warfare, are the exercises of a spiritual life, more especially fasting and fervent prayer.

She proceeds in the next place to treat of the advantages of voluntary poverty, and of quitting all
things for Christ, by showing that nothing can be of
greater service to a soul that has, by the exercise of

other virtues, and the custom of mortifying herself in eating, drinking, hard lodging, &c. first to learn to be content with little, and cheerfully sacrifice her own will, inclinations, and pleasures to God; for no sooner do we renounce the perishable goods of the earth, than we easily learn to turn our eyes towards heaven, to seek that hidden treasure which alone is able to make us rich for eternity, in the happy possession of God himself. Oh! what a shame, would she say, that we should not be ready to undergo all kinds of labors and sufferings for acquiring so invaluable a treasure, when we daily behold the children of this world expose themselves to far greater labors, sufferings, and dangers, for the sake of a little worldly dirt.

She also warns them against making a parade of their virtues, or publishing their good actions, by making them the subject of their conversation with others; for as a treasure that lies exposed to the public is quickly taken away and lost to its owner, so virtue presently fades and evaporates, when we make a show of it, or publish it to the world. Praise and applause are ever apt to weaken the vigor of the soul; whilst on the other hand, it commonly receives an additional increase of strength from affronts, reproaches and injuries. She therefore exhorted them to rejoice under sufferings, and endeavor, by prayer and spiritual canticles, to banish sadness in general away from them as an enemy, that wholesome sorrow only excepted, *which is according to God*, by which we grieve for having offended him.

She goes on by strenuously recommending a constant watchfulness over their hearts, that they be ever careful and diffident of their own strength, and neve think themselves secure in this life. Upon which occasion she treats at large on the excellence and necessity of self-knowledge and humility, and warns them against the pernicious consequences of pride, self-conceit, and presumption, which she tells them are the most heinous of all sins, as well as against the passions of anger, resentment, remembrance of injuries, envy, and detraction, the daughters of pride, which being spiritual sins, frequently overlooked and neglected, are apt to leave mortal wounds behind them in the most noble parts of the soul;—wounds the more hard to be cured, as they are generally less apprehended.

The Saint also gave her spiritual daughters many other excellent lessons, inserted by the author of her life at large, who assures us, that what she taught them by words, she continually enforced by her example; and that no tongue was capable of expressing the spiritual advantages, that those who were so happy as to hear her, received from her heavenly conversation, and the incredible fruits which her instructions produced in many souls.

Syncletica continued her regular exercises of devo-

⸻n and penance, advancing daily more and more in ⸱
the love of God, till she arrived at the age of fourscore
years ; at which time our Lord was pleased to permit
her to be afflicted by the most violent interior pains
and diseases, joined with as horrible temptations as if
Satan had obtained permission from God to put her
patience to as severe a trial, and torment her as much
as he did Job, with a complication of the most severe
sufferings. She passed through this course of penance
for the space of three years and a half, with an incredible patience and courage, to the great edification of
all that approached her, to whom she ceased not to
preach both by word and example. Towards the
latter part of this time, a cancer in her mouth was
added to the rest of her sufferings, which spread itself
so far as to consume a great part of her face, and
which, besides the pain and the insupportable stench
it caused, prevented her from being able either to eat
or to speak. In this condition she remained suffering,
like a martyr, for the space of three months, supported only by divine grace, till the end of her life approaching, she was favored with a rapt, or ecstacy, in
which she beheld the glory and light of the heavenly
mansions that were prepared for her, with troops of
angels and holy virgins, who invited her to come and
join their happy company. Returning to herself, she
found herself able to give her last instructions to the
virgins that surrounded her ; exhorting them particu-

larly to constancy, courage, and perseverance in their holy undertaking, and telling them, that within three days, at an hour which she named, she should be taken away from them. Accordingly when that hour arrived, her pure soul took its flight from this vale of tears, and went to take possession of the kingdom of her heavenly Bridegroom. Her name stands recorded in the Roman Martyrology on the fifth of January.

ST. THAIS THE PENITENT.

From an ancient Greek Writer.

THAIS was a native of Egypt, who being exceedingly beautiful, was so unhappy as to be betrayed and prostituted by her own mother to infamy and sin. Having followed a most wicked course of life for a long time, she, on account of her extraordinary beauty, became the ruin of many, who spent their fortunes on her, and frequently quarrelled so much about her, that murders were sometimes committed on her account. There happened to live at this time in a neighboring desert a holy abbot, called Paphnucius, who, on hearing of the wretched life she led, and of the havoc wl.ich Satan by her means had made amongst the youth of that part of Egypt, became inspired with a desire to attempt her conversion. For this purpose, procuring a secular habit, and taking some money with him, he went to the place where she lived, and desiring to speak to her in private, was introduced by her into a chamber richly furnished. Having asked her if she had not some more retired apartment? she replied she had : but added, what can you be afraid of? for as for men, I assure you, no mortal can see us, or dare to come into the room where we are; and as for God, he would equally see us wherever we went. "Oh!" said he, "dost thou then believe there is a God, whose all-seeing eye is always upon us." "Yes, Sir," replied she, "I do believe there is an all-seeing God ; and what is more, I do believe there is a heaven, where the good shall be rewarded with never-ending bliss ; and also a hell, where the wicked shall be tormented for all eternity."

Paphnucius rejoicing interiorly to hear her make this profession of her faith began to represent to her the dismal state of her soul, and the dreadful account she must one day give for the souls of so many others whom she had seduced into sin, in so pathetic a manner. and with such powerful unction of divine grace. that perceiving him to be a man of God, she cast herself at his feet, and poured forth torrents of tears, gave herself up to be directed by him, offering without a

moment's delay, to undergo whatsoever penance he
should think proper to appoint, and in what place he
pleased; hoping, as she said, that through his prayers
God would show her mercy.   Paphnucius having men
tioned the place where she should come to him, depart
ed, whilst she immediately prepared herself to follow
him.   But first gathering what she had acquired by
sin, viz. all the rich presents of her lovers, together in
one heap, she made a bonfire of them in the midst of
the street, in the sight of all the people, and of those
who had been accomplices in her crimes, declaring
publicly an abhorrence of every thing that contributed
to detain her in that way of life.   Having made this
first sacrifice, she repaired to the place appointed by
Paphnucius, who conducted her from thence to a monastery of nuns, where he shut her up in a cell by herself,
and stopped up the door, leaving only a small aperture,
or window, to which he desired the sisters to convey
to her a little bread and water every day, which was to
be her whole allowance for the remainder of her life.

   Before he departed from her, she asked him what
prayers he would recommend to her, and in what
manner he would have her address herself to God in
prayer?   "Thou art not worthy," said he, "either to
invoke the sacred name of God with thy polluted lips
nor to stretch forth thy hands, or lift up thy eyes towards heaven, after so many abominations; let it suf
fice then for thee to sit turned towards the East, and

frequently to repeat these words: *Thou that hast made me, have mercy on me.*"

She continued this course of penance, in her solitary enclosure, for the space of three years, till at length Paphnucius, having compassion on her, went to con-sult the great St. Antony, at that time the oracle of Egypt, to learn whether God had accepted her penance and pardoned her sins. St. Antony having assembled his disciples together, and exhorted them to pray that God would be pleased to let them know what Paph-nucius so earnestly required. St. Paul the Simple saw that very night in a vision, a glorious throne, or bed of state, in heaven, surrounded by three virgins, glit-tering with beams of heavenly light; and whilst he was thinking within himself that this throne could be designed for no other than St. Antony, he was an-swered by a voice: "It is not for thy father Antony, but for Thais the harlot." This vision being notified to Paphnucius, he concluded it was the will of God that Thais should be released from her confinement, and therefore let her out, whilst she, on her part de-sired to remain where she was, but at length humbly submitted to the will of her holy director. Having told her that God had forgiven her sins, she assured him, that from the time she first entered into her cell, she had collected them together as it were into one heap, and placing them before her eyes, never ceased to think on and bewail them.

"It is on beholding your contrition," said Paphnu-cius, "that God has shown you mercy, and not on account of the rigor of your penance." She lived no longer than fifteen days after she had been released from her penitential enclosure, when she was called to see *the good things of our Lord in the land of the living.*

ST. PELAGIA THE PENITENT.

From her Life by James the Deacon, her Cotem-porary

PELAGIA was a famous actress in the city of Antioch, at that time the capital of Syria, and of the whole East. Her extraordinary beauty drew many lovers after her, and so unhappy was she as to yield herself up to a very sinful course of life, without the least re-straint, although she professed herself a Christian, and had been formerly admitted into the number of Cate-chumens who were under instruction for baptism, but had now left off her attendance at church for that purpose. It happened at this time, viz. about the be ginning of the fifth century, that several bishops, and others of the clergy, were assembled at Antioch upon some ecclesiastical affairs; amongst whom was the holy prelate Nonnus, who, from a monk of the monastery of Tabenna, was, on account of his admirable virtue and wisdom, raised to the see of Heliopolis. These prelates were .odged in the neighborhood of the church of St. Julian the martyr, where they met together to treat upon the business that had called them to Antioch. One day, whilst they were sitting before the church with St. Nonnus, who was then en tertaining them with a spiritual conference, to their great edification, Pelagia passed before them in great pomp, decked with gold, pearls, and precious stones, accompanied by a numerous train of young men and women. Her beauty with the lustre of her jewels, and her rich attire, drew the eyes of all the fond ad- mirers of these empty toys upon her; but whilst the prelates turned away their faces aside, because having no veil over her head, and her very shoulders being uncovered, they were offended at the immodesty of her dress, Nonnus only seemed to take notice of her, and to consider her with great attention. After she had passed by, turning to his fellow-bishops, he said to them, with many sighs and tears: "I fear God will one day bring this woman to confront us before the throne of his justice, in order to condemn our negli- gence and tepidity in his service, and in the discharge of our duty to the flock he has committed to our care. For how many hours do you think she has em ployed this very day in her chamber in washing and cleaning herself, in dressing, adorning, and embellishing her whole person to the best advantage, with a view to exhibit her beauty to please the eyes of the world, and particularly her* unhappy lovers, who, though alive to-day, may possibly be dead to-mor-row? Whereas we, who have an Almighty Father, an immortal Spouse, in heaven, to whose love and ser-vice we have consecrated ourselves ;—we,—to whom the immense and eternal treasures of heaven are promised as the reward of our short labors upon earth, are far from taking as much pains to wash and purify our souls from their stains, and procure for them those bright ornaments of virtue and sanctity, which alone can render them truly agreeable in the eyes of God." Having spoken to this effect, he rose up and returned home, where, prostrating himself on the floor, he bitterly lamented his misery, in having suffered himself to be thus outdone by a sinful woman, and implored the divine mercy for the forgiveness of his negligence and tepidity.

The next day being Sunday, all the bishops assem-bled in the great church where the patriarch of Anti-och celebrated mass. After the gospel was read, he presented the book to St. Nonnus, and desired him to make an exhortation to the people. The holy prelate obeyed, and made a most pathetic discourse, full of the unction of the spirit of God, on the subject of the ast judgment, and of the world to come, which drew tears from the eyes of the whole auditory, amongst

whom was Pelagia, who had not been within a church
for a long time before, and h's se mon made so deep
an impression on her soul, that she could not refrain
the whole time from sighing, and sobbing, and pouring out floods of tears, through the deep sense she conceived of her sins. As soon as the divine service was
over, she sent a letter to the holy prelate to this effect.

*To the holy disciple of Jesus Christ, from a sinful
wretch, a scholar of the devil.*

I have learnt that the God whom you worship came
down from heaven to the earth, not for the sake of the
just, but to save poor sinners, and that he humbled
himself so far as to suffer publicans to come to him,
and did not disdain to speak with the sinful Samaritan
woman at the well; wherefore, as I understand, that
though you never have seen him with your mortal
eyes, you are nevertheless a follower of his, and have
served him faithfully for many years, I conjure you,
for his sake, to show yourself to be his true disciple,
by suffering a poor sinner to come to you, and not
despise the extreme desire I have to approach to him
through your assistance." The Saint sent her word,
that if she was sincere in her desires of instruction and
conversion, she might come to him to the church o.
Julian, where he would speak to her in the presence
of the other bishops, not thinking it proper to converse
with her in private.

No sooner had Pelagia received this permission **than** she ran with all possible speed to the church, and cast herself at the feet of the holy prelate, earnestly beseeching him through the example of his great Master, to receive the worst of sinners, and cleanse her from the filth and abomination of her crimes, in the founta n of baptism. The Saint told her, that by the discipline of the Church, persons who like her had been a long time engaged in criminal habits, could not be admitted to baptism without first producing proper sureties who should answer for her returning no more to their sinful ways; but she not being able to bear the enormous weight of her sins, or to continue any longer contaminated by their filth, would hear of no delay, wherefore embracing the feet of the servant of God, and washing them with floods of tears, she conjured them to baptize her upon the spot, in order to a new life, that she might instantly be presented without spot or blemish to Jesus Christ: this petition she urged with so much fervor, such demonstrations of a lively faith, and so ardent a desire of saving her soul, that the prelates were unanimously of opinion, that as the hand of God manifested itself in her favor in so extraordinary a manner, her request ought to be admitted. They therefore sent to acquaint the patriarch with all that had passed, who approving of her being baptized, sent the lady Romana, the chief of the widows that were in the service of the great church, to attend her as godmother on the occasion. This good lady found her still bewailing her sins at the feet of the Saint, from which she could not be prevailed to remove, till he commanded her to rise, in order to proceed to the exorcisms and prayers as used by the Church before baptism. After making a public confession and detestation of all her crimes, he baptized her; and then, according to the custom of the Church in those days, administered to her the sacraments of confirmation and of the body of our Lord.

The same day, as our author relates, who being deacon to St. Nonnus was himself present, whilst the holy bishop and he sat at table together, rejoicing with the angels upon the conversion of so great a sinner, they heard distinctly before the door a voice as of one bitterly complaining in these or the like words: "Alas! alas! must I be continually tormented by thee in this manner? Not satisfied with having robbed me heretofore of no less than thirty thousand souls of the nation of the Saracens, which thou hast presented to thy God; not content to have also snatched the city of Heliopolis out of my hands, where all the people worshipped me, must thou also bereave me of the greatest hope I had left? or dost thou think I can any longer bear with thee, or support the persesecutions thou makest me suffer?" In this manner did Satan express his grief at the loss of his prey, and his rage against the holy prelate, who took no notice of him, but armed his convert against all the efforts and temptations of this enemy, and taught her to drive him away by a confidence in her Saviour, and the sign of his cross.

The third day after baptism, Pelagia having taken an inventory of all her plate, jewels, rich clothes, and other goods, put it into the hands of St. Nonnus, saying: "My Lord, here is the whole of the goods I have acquired fiom the devil; I give them all up to your disposal; give such orders concerning them as you judge to be for the best. As to my part, I desire no riches for the time to come but those of my Saviour Jesus Christ." The holy prelate sent immediately for the treasurer of the church, and delivering the inventory into his hands, charged him, as he would answer for it before God, not to apply any part of her goods either to the service of the bishop or the church, but to distribute the whole to poor widows and orphans, and such like objects;—that as they had been ill gotten, they might now at least be well applied. On the same day Pelagia set all her slaves, both men and women at liberty, earnestly exhorting them, at the same time, to shake off that yoke of servitude by which they had, as well as herself, been slaves to a corrupt and sinful world; that passing over with her to the true liberty of the children of God, they might one day arrive with her at the enjoyment of that true and eternal life which knows neither sin nor sorrow.

On the eighth day, when those that had been baptized, according to the ancient custom of the Church, put off the white garment they received at their baptism, Pelagia rising privately in the night, exchanged her baptismal robe for a habit of haircloth, and an old mantle which she had received from St. Nonnus, and without communicating her design to any one but him, she withdrew from Antioch, and going into the Holy Land, took up her habitation for life in a narrow cell upon mount Olivet, where she lived as an anchoret, shut up in such a manner as to have only a small window through which she might receive the necessaries of life, and spending her whole time with our Lord in fasting and prayer. The other religious inhabitants of this holy mountain were so perfectly ignorant who she was, as not even to know whether she was a woman, so effectually had she concealed her sex, calling herself by the name of *Pelagius;* but they all admired the great abstraction, austerity, and sanctity of her life.

Some years after this, our author, James the deacon, made a pilgrimage of devotion to visit the sepulchre of our Lord at Jerusalem. Upon this occasion his holy bishop recommended to him to inquire after a servant of God named Pelagius, that led an anchoretical life upon mount Olivet. He executed his commission, little thinking that this anchoret was the famous Pelagia whom he had seen baptized, and who

presently after disappeared and was no more heard of.
But though he readily found out the cell, by inquir-
ing of the religious who dwelt in the neighborhood,
and went and spoke to her through the window, yet
being much altered by her austerities, he knew her
not. He told her he came by the desire of Bishop
Nonnus to inquire after her. Nonnus, said she, is a
great Saint, and I beg that he will pray for me
With that she shut the window and began to sing
Tierce, or the third hour of the divine office, whilst
the deacon was praying without, much comforted with
having seen so holy a person. Afterwards visiting the
monasteries round about, and finding that all the servants of God, wherever he came, conspired in giving
testimony to the wonderful sanctity of Pelagius, he
resolved to return and visit this holy anchoret once
more before he left the country, in order to receive
some wholesome instruction from him. When he
came to her cell and knocked at the window, no one
opened it to him, and when he called no one answered ;—so that having continued for some time knocking and calling aloud, he began to think the anchoret
was gone away. At length having forced open the
window, he looked in and perceived the Saint to be
dead. Having conveyed the news of her death to the
neighboring religious, they immediately came, and
opening the cell took out the body, in order to its being interred with all the honor due to so great a ser

vant of God. The secret of her sex being now discovered and noised abroad, all the holy virgins that
dwelt in the monasteries of Jericho and on the banks
of the Jordan, in the place where our Lord was baptized, came out with lighted tapers in their hands, sing-
ng hymns and psalms, to meet the corpse of the
Saint, which they conducted to their church, and there
deposited it as a rich treasure.

Her name is recorded in the Roman Martyrology
on the eighth of October, and the name of St. Nonnus on the second of December.

ST. MARY OF EGYPT.

**From her Life, written by St Sophronius, Patriarch
of Jerusalem.**

THERE was in a monastery of Palestine, a holy priest
named Zosimus, who had from his childhood dedicated himself to the love of God, and spent fifty-three
years in that community in the exercises of a monastic
life, with such perfection as to be respected and admired by all who knew him. This good father being
one day tempted with a thought that nothing more
was now wanting in him, and that he had already arrived, as he imagined, at the top of the hill of relig

ious perfection, was admonished by one appearing to
him in the shape of a man, of his error, and directed
by this messenger of heaven to another monastery
more remote from all conversation with the world,
situated in a solitary place on the banks of the river
Jordan, in order to learn still higher lessons in the
school of religion. In this place he found a company
of angels rather than men, so great was their fervor in
all that related to the service of God. They sang his
divine praises every hour of the night; and in the day,
whilst their hands were employed in manual labor, the
psalms were always in their mouths and hearts. Here
was no room for any unprofitable conversation, having
made it their whole business not only absolutely to
forget the world, but even every thing in the world,
and to live as men quite dead to all things but the
one thing necessary. Their thoughts were continually
occupied on heavenly truths;—the emptiness and vanity of all such things as pass away with time, and the
greatness of things eternal, were the subjects of their
constant meditation. Their greatest dainties for their
corporal sustenance were bread and water, whilst their
souls continually feasted on the word of God and
prayer.

It was the custom of these religious every year on
the first Sunday of Lent, after assisting at the divine
mysteries, and receiving the precious body and blood
of our Lord, to go forth into the vast wilderness be-

yond the river, there to spend that holy season in perfect solitude. They eat but very seldom, and then
only a few figs or dates, which they carried, or such
herbs as grew wild in the desert, frequently singing
psalms, and praying without ceasing. After spending
the greatest part of Lent in this manner, they all returned back again to the monastery, to celebrate the
passion and resurrection of our Lord, contriving always
to meet there against Palm-Sunday. The holy man,
Zosimus, according to the custom of the others, when
Lent came, crossed the river, designing to penetrate as
far as he could into the heart of the desert, in hopes,
as he afterwards said, of meeting with some Saint from
whom he might receive instruction and edification.
He took with him but slender provisions, and never
eat but when necessity compelled him. When night
found him. there he lay down on the ground to take
a little rest; and as soon as the daylight permitted,
he hastened forward, as if he had been making the
best of his way towards some person of his acquaintance, halting only at certain times of the day, to sing
some psalms standing, and to spend some time in
prayer on his knees.

He continued his journey after this manner till
about mid-lent, when one day stopping at the sixth
hour, and performing his usual prayers, turned towards the East, he perceived on his right the shadow,
as it were, of a human body; but when he had fin

ished his devotion, turning his eyes that way he plain
ly saw a person walking hastily towards the West,
whose naked body had grown quite black with the
heat of the sun, and whose hair was turned white as
wool.   Upon this sight Zosimus was overjoyed, hoping
he had now found what he sought, and therefore he
began to run with all his strength, in order to overtake the person whom he perceived to fly from him,
and through his earnest desire of coming up to her,
he continually gained ground of her, till coming within hearing, he cried out, " Servant of God, why dost
thou fly from a sinner, and a poor old man ?   Whoever thou art, I conjure thee, by that God, for whose
sake thou spendest thy days in this frightful desert, to
let me come near thee.   I beg of thee to stop a little,
and not to refuse thy blessing and prayers to one who
entreats thee in the name of that God who has never
cast off any man that desired to come to him."
Whilst he was thus calling after her, she arrived at a
place that had been made hollow by the water of a
torrent, but which was now dried up; and when she
had passed over to the other side, whither he not
being able to follow her, she cried, "Father Zosimus,
I beseech you, for God's sake, excuse my turning
about to speak to you, because I am a woman and
quite naked; but if you are willing to favor a poor
sinner with your blessing, fling over your mantle that

I may cover myself with it, and then turn towards you and receive your benediction."

The holy man, struck with astonishment to hear her call him by his name, which he was convinced she could not know but by revelation, readily complied with her desire, and threw his mantle over, turning his back towards her till she had covered herself therewith; which when she had done, she asked him, what had brought him so far to see such a wretched sinner as she was? or what could he expect to know or learn from her? Having already conceived a high opinion of her sanctity, he instead of answering her, prostrated himself upon the ground, and according to the custom of the religious when they visited one another, craved her blessing. No, father, said she, falling down upon her face, it is your part to bless and to pray for me, since you are a priest, and having for so many years served the altar, are admitted to a greater grace and light of God, and to the sacred mysteries of Jesus Christ. The amazement of Zosimus was inconceivable when he heard her speak of his being a priest, and therefore venerating the spirit of God within her, insisted the more upon her giving him her blessing first; nor would he rise from the ground till she had so far condescended as to bless him in the following manner: "*Blessed be the Lord, that worketh the salvatian of souls;*" to which he answered, *Amen.* When they both rose up, she began to inquire concern-

ing the state of christendom;—whether the Church
enjoyed peace;—and how the faithful behaved in
their respective stations? Zosimus answered, that
God had doubtless heard her prayers and granted
peace to the Church ; but, added he, I beseech you,
in his name, not to refuse a poor unworthy monk the
comfort he asks for the love of Jesus Christ ; which is,
that you would offer up your prayers to him for the
world in general, and for me, a poor sinner, in particu-
ular, that the long and painful journey I have taken
through this vast wilderness may not prove uprofita-
ble to me. She replied, that it belonged rather to his
function to pray both for her and the world ; however,
as obedience was a duty incumbent on her, should
comply with his command.

Then turning towards the East, with hands and
eyes lifted up to heaven, she prayed for a long time
in silence, whilst Zosimus stood without saying a word
with his eyes cast down on the ground. But finding
that she continued very long in her prayer, he looked
up a little, and saw that she was raised a cubit from
the earth, and prayed in that manner suspended in the
air, for the truth of which he afterwards called God to
witness. This sight filled his soul with so much surprise and apprehension, that he cast himself upon the
ground bathed in a sweat, crying out, *Lord have mercy
upon me.* His amazement was succeeded by a thought,
that perhaps all he had seen might be an illusion, and

that this appearance of a woman might be some evil spirit that only pretended to pray. In the mean time she turned towards him, and answering this thought which he had conceived of her, she assured him she was no spirit, but a poor sinful woman, composed of flesh and blood, dirt and corruption, adding that she had been baptized and was a Christian; in testimony whereof, making the sign of the cross upon her forehead, her eyes, her lips, and her stomach, she said, "God deliver us, father, from the evil spirit, and from all his snares and suggestions; for we know that he bears us an implacable hatred."

Hereupon Zosimus entreated her to tell him who she was,—whence she came,—when, and why she retired into this desert;—and, in a word, all that concerned her life since she came thither, as well for the glory of God as for his instruction and edification, not doubting, as he told her, but that God had brought him into that desert, and enabled him, notwithstanding his great age and weakness, to make so long a journey in so short a space of time, with no other design than that the wonders which his divine grace had wrought in her might be made manifest to the greater glory of his name. He added, that she need not apprehend any vain-glory in the recital of her life, since her motive would be no other than the glory of God and the comfort and instruction of a poor sinner She answered, that with respect to her life, there was

indeed no room for her taking any vanity in the relating the history of it, since she had been a vessel of
election, not of God, but of the devil; that she was
even ready to die with shame and confusion to think
of declaring all her infamous crimes, and that she apprehended he would fly from her as from a serpent
when he began to hear her history. However, she
was resolved to be quite sincere with him, and to
declare the particulars of her infamous life, in hopes
that he wo·ld never cease to pray to God that she
might find mercy at the last day.

Here she began to relate the history of her life, saying, that she was a native of Egypt, and had run away
from her parents when she was but twelve years old,
and went to Alexandria, where, falling into bad com·
pany, she quickly lost her honor, and afterwards abandoned herself to all kinds of lewdness, as a public
prostitute, for the space of seventeen years. That at
the end of this time, seeing a great many persons flock
towards the sea-shore in order to embark for the Holy
Land, to celebrate the feast of the Exaltation of the
Cross in Jerusalem, she had impudently thrust herself
into their company; and both during the voyage and
after her arrival at Jerusalem had made herself the
devil's instrument, introducing many into a partner-
ship in her abominations. That when the day of the
feast was come, she attempted to enter with the rest
of the faithful into the church of the Holy Cross, but

was repulsed by an invisible power; and though she saw all the people about her go in with ease, and had striven on her part with all her might to enter in along with them, yet she could never advance further than the threshold, but always found herself still thrust back again into the portico. "This happening to me," said she, "three or four times, I began to consider what might be the reason that I was thus debarred the sight of the life-giving wood of the holy cross. when a salutary thought striking my mind, and opening the eyes of my soul, I concluded that it was the filthiness of my life that prevented me from entering the temple of God. Then bathed in tears and in the utmost consternation of mind, I knocked my breast, and sighing ready to break my heart, I cried, lamented and mourned at my wretched condition, till at length perceiving over my head in the place where I stood the image of the holy mother of God, I immediately addressed myself to her, and with my eyes steadfastly fixed on her picture, I said, O sacred virgin, who hast brought forth God according to the flesh, I acknowledge myself unworthy to venerate or even to look at thy image with eyes so much defiled by uncleanness as mine have been. As thou art a pure unspotted virgin both in soul and body, it is but just that thy incomparable beauty should abominate, and drive away from thee so filthy a creature as I am: nevertheless, having been taught that the God whom thou

wast worthy to bring forth was made man, in order to
call sinners to repentance, I beseech thee to assist me,
who am here left alone destitute of all assistance.   O
receive the confession I here make of my sins, and permit me to enter into the church, that I may not be so
unhappy as to be deprived of the sight of that precious wood to which that God-man was fastened, who   •
was born of thee, without any prejudice to thy virginity, and on which he spilt his blood for my redemption.
Ordain, O blessed Lady, that the door may be open
unto me, though most unworthy, that I may salute
that divine cross ; and be thou responsible to Christ
thy Son, that I shall never more defile myself with any
of my former detestable uncleannesses, whilst I, for my
part, as soon as I shall have seen the tree on which
thy son vouchsafed to die, promise absolutely to renounce the world with all its wicked ways, and to depart immediately to the place to which thou, my surety and my guide, shall be pleased to conduct me."
So far her prayer to the blessed Virgin.

Then proceeding to her narrative, she declared that
after having made this prayer and promise, on attempting again to enter into the church she found no manner of obstacle, but went in with the utmost ease, and
penetrated, notwithstanding the great crowd, as far as
the sanctuary, and there had the happiness not only
to see and venerate the precious and life-giving wood,
consecrated with the blood of our Redeemer, but also

to be sensibly affected with the experience she now felt of the inconceivable excess of God's mercy in his readiness to forgive penitent sinners. Full of these sentiments she prostrated herself upon the ground, and having kissed the sacred pavement of the sanctuary, she then ran out to the place where she had made her solemn promise to the blessed Virgin, where kneeling down before her image, after giving thanks for the goodness and charity she had already experienced, she offered herself ready to fulfill the promise she had made, and begged of our blessed Lady to direct her now to the place to which she would have her to go to do penance for her sins. Upon which she heard a voice as of one crying out at a distance: *Go beyond the Jordan, and there thou shalt find rest.* Conceiving these words addressed to herself, and begging of our blessed Lady not to forsake her, she arose in haste to follow this call. As she was going she met with a stranger, who gave her three pieces of money, with which she immediately went and bought three loaves; and having inquired of the baker the way that led to the river Jordan, she set forward immediately without stopping, till she arrived at the church of St. John the Baptist upon the banks of the river. Here she performed her devotions, and received the blessed sacrament; eating during her short stay there the half of one of her loaves, drinking of the water of the river, and using no other bed but the bare ground. On the morning after her communion she passed over to the other side of the river: "and then," continued she, "having again prayed to the blessed Virgin, my guide, to conduct me to whatever place she pleased, I came into this desert, and from that time to this day, which I compute to be seven and forty years, I have, according to the psalmist, *gone far off flying away* from all company, *and I abode in the wilderness*, Ps. 54, looking for the mercy of my God, who saves both little and great who are converted to him."

Zosimus then inquired what she had lived upon all that time? She answered, that the two loaves and a half which she had brought with her were for a long time her only food, though they soon grew as hard as stones, so that she could eat but very little of them at a time, and that after they were consumed she lived upon what few herbs she could find in the desert. That as for clothes, those which she had brought over with her being quite worn out, she had been without any for the greatest part of the time, and had labored under inexpressible difficulties for the want of them, being broiled with excessive heat in the summer, and suffering the extremity of cold in the winter; but that under all these hardships and necessities, together with a multitude and variety of temptations which she had to struggle with, she continued to experience to that very day the power and the goodness of God in the various ways whereby he had still preserved her poor soul and

body. So that when she called to mind from how many evils the Lord had delivered her, she felt herself nourished and supported with a never-failing food, and found a banquet which satisfied her whole appetite in the hopes she entertained of her eternal salvation.

Zosimus desiring also to learn more particulars from her with relation to the conflicts she must have sustained, more especially upon her first entering on this new kind of life, she acknowledged that for the first seventeen years she was in a manner under perpetual temptations;—that she suffered much from hunger and thirst, and was frequently attacked with vehement desires of returning to partake of the flesh-pots of Egypt;—that she longed for wine which she formerly loved and drank to excess, whereas now she could not even come at a drop of water;—that the lascivious songs she had formerly been accustomed to sing were often recurring to her mind, and other impure suggestions disturbing her soul and violently moving her to lust; but that upon perceiving any of these assaults, it was her custom to strike her breast, shed many tears, and remembering the solemn engagement she had made before she came into the wilderness, to place herself in spirit before the image of the blessed Virgin, hom she had desired to be her surety, and ceased not to weep and lament, and to beg of her protectress to drive away from her those wicked thoughts which troubled her poor soul, till after long and earnest

prayer, accompanied with floods of tears, and with the
bruising of her body with blows, she used to perceive
a light to shine round about her, and a heavenly calm
restored to her soul. "Thus," continued she, "I had
always the eyes of my heart lifted up without ceasing
to her that was my surety, beseeching her to stand by
me in my solitude and penance; and I always experienced the help and assistance of her who brought
forth the Author of all purity, and so I passed safely
through the many conflicts and dangers of those seventeen years; and from that time till now, the blessed
mother of God has never forsaken me, but always,
and in all things, has assisted and directed me."

Zosimus hearkened with great attention to all that
she said, and taking notice that she had in her relation
of her life made use of passages taken out of the psalms
and other parts of the scripture, he asked her if she had
ever learnt the psalms, or read any part of the holy
scripture? She told him she could not read, nor had
even so much as ever heard any person read or sing the
psalms, or ever seen either man or beast from her coming into the desert till that day. "But," said she, "the
Word of God, which is living and effectual, interiorly
teaches the understanding of man; wherefore, as you
have now heard all that relates to me, I conjure you
by the incarnation of the Eternal Word, to pray for
me, who, as you see, have been so vile a sinner."

When she had finished her narrative, Zosimus cast

himself on his knees, and with a loud voice magnified the Lord for the wonders of his goodness and mercy to those who fear and seek him; whilst she, on her part, begged of him, for the sake of our Lord and Saviour Jesus Christ, not to speak of the things she had related to him to any one living, till God should deliver her out of the prison of the body: and, said she, " about this time twelvemonth, by God's grace, you shall again see me; I beg of you therefore, for our Lord's sake, that when the holy time of Lent shall return next year, you would not come over the Jordan, according to the custom of your monastery, but remain at home during that time (but indeed you shall not be able to go out, if you would) and on the most sacred evening of our Lord's last supper, bring out for me, in a holy vessel worthy of so great a mystery, the divine body and life-giving blood of our Saviour, and wait for me on that side of the river which you inhabit, and I shall come and receive those precious gifts that are the life of the soul, at the very hour in which our Lord imparted that divine supper to his disciples." Having said this, and once more begged the holy father to pray for her, she hastened away into the remoter parts of the wilderness: whilst Zosimus, after casting himself down upon the ground, and kissing the earth upon which she had stood, returned through the desert the same way he came, and arrived in due time at the monastery.

During the following year he kept all that he had
seen and heard a secret to himself, longing for the return of Lent, that, he might be once more blessed
with the sight and conversation of one whom he justly held in the highest veneration. But when the
holy fast of Lent was come, he was visited with a
fever, which as the Saint had foretold, was attended
by no other consequence than that of preventing him
from going abroad into the desert with the rest of the
brethren ; wherefore, on Maunday-Thursday evening
in compliance with her desire, he carried out the body
and blood of our Lord Jesus Christ in a small pix or
chalice, to the bank of the river, and there waited,
looking attentively towards the desert, in expectation
of what he had so great a desire of seeing, but not
without some apprehension, as it was a long time before she came, that she might have been there already,
and not finding him had returned back again. Another
perplexing thought also occurred to his mind, viz.
how in case of her coming, she should be able to pass
over the river to him, as there was neither bridge nor
boat near that place. Whilst the holy old man was
revolving these difficulties in his mind, he discovered
the Saint on the opposite bank of the Jordan, by the
light of the moon, which was then at the full, and
saw her making the sign of the cross upor the river,
and presently after walking towards him upon the
water, as if it had been firm ground, with which sight

he was so much astonished, that he was going to cast himself upon his knees, had she not stopped him by crying out—" Father, what are you about ?   Recollect you are a priest of God, and that you carry with you the divine mysteries."

Having now passed over the river, she craved his blessing, and after desiring him to recite the creed and the Lord's prayer, she received the blessed sacrament from his hands; after which, lifting up her hands to heaven, sighing and weeping, she cried out: *Now dost thou dismiss thy servant, O Lord, according to thy word, in peace ; because my eyes have seen thy salvation.*   Then turning to Zosimus, she begged pardon for the trouble she had given him, and requested he would for the present return to the monastery, but on the following Lent he would not fail to come to the place where she had first spoken to him, and that there he should see her again in the manner God should be pleased to ordain.   The good old man desired her to eat something, having brought a basket of figs and dates, with some lentiles steeped in water, with him for that purpose.   She took a few grains of the lentiles, saying she had no occasion for any more ; for that the grace of the spirit was sufficient to preserve the soul in its purity.   Then begging of him again for God's sake to pray for her, and never to forget her miseries, whilst he, on his part, recommended himself and the whole church to her prayers, she took

35

leave of him, and making the sign of the cross upon the river, crossed it again in the same manner as she came to him, walking upon the waters.

The next year Zosimus going out in Lent, according to the custom of the monastery, into the desert, made the best of his way towards the place where he had first seen the Saint, in hopes of being still more edified by her sight and heavenly conversation, and of learning also her name, which he regretted not having inquired after when he last saw her. After a long and painful journey, when he arrived at the dry torrent, he found in the higher part of that concavity the dead body of the Saint extended decently on the ground, with her hands crossed, and her face turned towards the east. Hereupon he fell down at the feet of the holy corpse, which he washed with his tears, and then began to sing the psalms and recite the prayers for the burial of the dead, when behold he perceived on the ground these words written in the sand : " Father Zosimus, bury the body of poor Mary; render to the earth what belongs to the earth ; and in the name of God pray for me on the *ninth day of April*, the day of the passion of our Lord, after the communion of the divine supper." *   The old man, reading these words, could not conceive by whom they were wrote, as the

* The anniversary of her happy death, viz. the day immediately following that on which Zosimus had, the year before administered to her the blessed eucharist.

Saint had assured him she could neither read nor write. He was however not only pleased to have found out her name, but also astonished to think how quickly she had been brought back in the space o one night after receiving the holy communion, over as large a tract of ground as had taken him twenty days travelling without ceasing. Hence it appears that after her return her blessed soul had left her body, and taken its flight to heaven.

But now his greatest solicitude was how he should contrive to bury her body, as he had no proper instrument to open the earth, or dig a grave. But he was not long under this perplexity before he perceived a great lion standing by the body of the Saint, and licking her feet. To recover himself from the terror excited by the sight of so tremendous an animal, he made the sign of the cross, trusting that God and her holy body would protect him from all dangers, when behold he found the lion began to fawn upon him, as if he proffered him his service! So that being convinced that God had sent the beast to make a grave for his servant, he commanded him in the name of God to set about that work with his claws. The lion obeyed, and presently made a sufficient grave, in which Zosimus interred the body of the Saint, covering it only with the mantle she had received of him, and with many tears, having recommended both himself and the whole world to her prayers, he departed prais-

ing God. whilst the lion, like a tame lamb, went his
way into the remoter parts of the desert. Zosimus,
at his return home, related to his brethren the whole
history of the life of the Saint from the beginning, to
their great edification, concealing no part of what he
had seen or heard. After which he still continued
serving and glorifying God in that monastery, till he
was a hundred years old, with such perfection as to be
enrolled after his death amongst the Saints. His
name occurs in the Roman Martyrology on the fourth
of April, and that of St. Mary of Egypt on the second
of the same month.

ST. JEROME.

WE are about to record the monastic life of St.
Jerome without entering into the detail of his other
works, which might be foreign to our subject. Notwithstanding that he is one of the greatest doctors of
the Church, we shall here consider him only as a Solitary. He was born at Stridon, in Dalmatia, about
the year 329, but he made his principal studies in
Rome, under the famous Donatus, the grammarian.
After having been baptized, he travelled into France,
stopped some time at Trèves, and came to Aquilea in

Gaul, where he made the acquaintance of St. Valerian, bishop of that city, together with many other excellent persons.

His extreme love for study had been strikingly manifested in Rome by the progress he made, and it was with a view to perfect himself still more that he journied into Gaul. His great application had not only served to enrich his mind with an extensive knowledge of literature, but it had also been the means of keeping him aloof from those occasions of sin, wherein young persons are so often ruined. Thus, since he had received baptism, God had given him the grace to lead a life of great abstinence, and to sanctify his studies by virtue. One of his usual practices of piety was to go every Sunday, while in Rome, with his young companions, to visit the relics of the saints in the catacombs of that city.

Before he left Aquilea, he had been some time deliberating as to what place he should select for his future abode, in order to retire from the world, and apply himself peacefully to study. There was no such resting-place for him in his own country, for there he would be incessantly importuned by friends and acquaintances who were of a different way of thinking. In Rome he was too well known, so he resolved to make a journey to the East, and there establish himself. Evagrius, Innocent, and Heliodorus followed him thither, and he took nothing with him except his

books, of which he had already chosen a large number. After journeying through Thrace, Pontus, Bithynia, Galatia, Cappadocia, and Cilicia, remaining some
.ime at Tarsus, the birth-place of St. Paul, he came to
Antioch, and retired to the desert of Chalcis, on the
confines of Syria and Arabia, where he embraced the
monastic life.

He had there for companions Innocent, Heliodorus
and Hylas. The priest Evagrus had remained at
Antioch, whence he transmitted to Jerome the letters
which arrived there for him. In order that he might
succeed in his new mode of life, he commended himself to the prayers of St. Theodosia and some other
solitary saints of Syria, whom he had seen in passing,
while meditating his retreat. "I should like," said
he, "to be now with you, and, however unworthy I
may be of seeing you, I should be rejoiced to embrace
all your holy community. I should see a solitude
more agreeable than all the cities of the world, and
deserts inhabited, like the terrestrial paradise, by a
multitude of saints. But since such a sinner as myself is unworthy to live in your company, I conjure
you, at least (and I am sure you can obtain that favor
for me), to beg of God that I may be delivered from
the darkness of this world. I have already told you
by word of mouth, and I now tell you again, that
there is nothing which I so ardently desire as to be
freed from the slavery of the world . . . It seems to

me as though I were surrounded by a vast ocean, so that I am unable either to advance or recede. It is, therefore, from your prayers that I expect the favoring breeze of the Holy Spirit, whereby I may continue my course and happily arrive at my destination."

The desert of Chalcis was, then, the port whither he retired; but after having enjoyed there for some time the calm repose of solitude, the Lord, who wished to prove and to sanctify him by tribulation, began to tincture with bitterness the sweets of his repose. Death deprived him of Innocent and Hylas, and his beloved Heliodorus left him to return to Italy. These painful separations, which grievously afflicted his heart, were followed by various maladies, and finally, in the intervals of his sufferings, he was tormented by violent temptations, arising from the remembrance of the pleasures of Rome, and these kept recurring to his mind in their most vivid coloring. This he explains to the virgin Eustoquia, in his excellent letter to her on virginity, which made no small noise in Rome on its first appearance there.

"During the time," says he, "that I remained in the desert and dwelt in that immense solitude, which, scorched by the fervid heat of the sun, offers nought but a dreary waste to the solitaries who make it their bode, how often have I fancied myself in the midst of the delights of Rome. Seated as I was, alone in the depth of my cave, plunged in an ocean of bitter-

ness, clothed in a coarse linen garment, the very sight
of which was revolting to nature, with my body all disfigured and my skin blackened, till it resembled that
of an Ethiopian, my only occupation was to pass whole
days and nights in tears and lamentations. Was I
overpowered by sleep and forced, whether I would or
not, to yield, I flung on the naked ground a body
which was no more than a living skeleton. I say nothing
of my nourishment, for, in the desert, even the sick
drink only water, and it is there considered delicacy
and sensuality to eat anything cooked. Shut up there
in this species of prison, to which I had voluntarily
condemned myself in order to escape the fire of hell,
and having no other company than scorpions and fe-
rocious animals, I nevertheless failed not to imagine
myself at times amongst the Roman ladies : beneath
an exterior spoiled and defaced by a continual fast, I
carried a heart torn and tormented by evil desires ;
within a body of icy coldness and flesh already dead,
in anticipation of its final destruction, concupiscence
kept up an inextinguishable fire.

"Seeing myself, therefore, without support and
without resource, I cast myself at the feet of Jesus
Christ, watering them with my tears, and drying them
with my hair ; passing entire weeks without eating, in
order to subdue my rebellious flesh and make it obedient to the spirit. I have often passed whole days
and nights in crying and striking my breast, till the

Lord, dispelling the storm, restored peace to my heart.
I feared to enter my cell because it had seen so many
wicked thoughts spring up. Animated with just
anger against myself, and treating my body with the
utmost severity, I plunged alone into the desert; and
if I found a deep valley, a lofty mountain, or a steep
rock, I instantly made it a place of prayer, and, as it
were, a prison wherein I chained my miserable flesh.
There, bathed in my tears, and with my eyes incessantly raised to heaven, I sometimes fancied myself in
the company of angels, and sang in the transports of
my joy: *We will run after thee to the odor of thy
ointments*," Cant. 1.

With a view to get rid of these harassing thoughts,
he added to his labors the study of the Hebrew language. Accustomed, however, to the reading of Cicero and the best Latin authors, he could not, without
repugnance apply himself to the study of alphabets
and grammatical trifles; so that, tired of the undertaking, he left it off and resumed it at intervals, refreshing himself in the meantime with that polite literature
which he had never given up, notwithstanding the
rigor of his penance. But God, who intended him
for one of the most profound interpreters of Scripture
for the use of his Church, sent him a violent fever,
in the course of which he had a vision which made
known to him how displeasing to Him was that taste
for profane authors, and the rigorous account which he

should one day have to render if he continued to
pursue it with an ardor so unsuited to his solitary life.
He thus relates it in the letter to Eustoquia before-
mentioned : So great was my misery and the excess of
my passion, that after having quitted all to serve God
and gain the way to heaven, I brought with me the
books which I had collected at Rome with much care
and trouble, and which I could not bring myself to
resign. I fasted, yet I read Cicero ; and after long and
frequent vigils, after shedding torrents of tears, which
gushed from the depth of my heart at the remembrance of my past sins,—I set myself to read Plato ;
and when, entering into myself, I set about reading
the prophets, I was at once repelled by their harsh,
unpolished style. Blind as I was, and unable to see
the light, I betook myself to the sun instead of acknowledging my blindness.

"Thus seduced and deceived by the artifices of the
old serpent, I had, about the middle of Lent, a fever,
which, penetrating to the marrow of my body, already worn out by continual austerities, withered me
away until I was literally skin and bone. As my
body was already cold, and I had but a feeble spark
of life which the natural warmth still kept up, prepa-
rations for my burial were already going on, when all
ot a sudden, in an ecstasy of the mind, I felt myself
dragged before a tribunal. Dazzled by the splendor

of all around, I cast myself prostrate on the ground, not daring to raise my eyes.

"Being asked by the judge what was my profession, I replied that I was a Christian. 'It is false,' said he, 'thou art not a Christian, but a Ciceronian; for where thy treasure is, there also is thy heart.' I answered never a word, and, feeling myself more tormented by the remorse of my conscience than by the blows which they gave me, (for He had condemned me to the lash) I thought of that saying of the Psalmist: *Who, O Lord, will give thee thanks in hell?* Psalm 6. I groaned and cried aloud: *Have mercy on me,* O Lord, have mercy on me, Psalm 56. This prayer and the voice of my lamentation were incessantly heard amid the whizzing of the lash. At last, some who were present threw themselves at the feet of the judge, entreating him to take pity on my youth and to give me time to do penance for my fault, on condition that I was to be still more rigorously punished in future, if I ever again should read profane authors.

"As for myself, who, at such a crisis, would have willingly promised an hundred times more, I began to assure him with the most solemn oaths, and taking himself to witness: Lord, if I ever again read, or look at, profane books, I consent to be considered as having denied thee." Upon this, they let me go; I returned to the world, and to the great surprise of those who stood around my bed, I suddenly opened my eyes, shedding such a torrent of tears, that even the most incredulous were convinced of the pain I suffered; for this was not merely a vision, or a dream, but a dread reality; bear witness the terrible tribunal before which I had been prostrated, and the rigorous judgment which had struck terror to my soul.   Even after I awoke, I continued to feel the pain of the blows I had received, and my shoulders were all covered with bruises.   The consequence was that, ever after, I was as passionately fond of the study of sacred books as I had before been of profane authors.

Much might be said on this subject; for, while the study of Cicero is preferred to that of the Gospel, it shows that there is less love for God's truth than for the frivolous words of man.   This instance is not the only one whereby we learn that a taste for reading profane authors is very reprehensible in those who make profession of a religious life.   Many others of the Holy Fathers have condemned it as well as St. Jerome; and if some of the saints have made a practice of it, it was not from any preference for such reading, but solely for the interest of religion, as David employed the sword of Goliath to cut off his head.

St. Jerome remained but four years in the desert of Chalcis.   The schism which had broken out at Antioch in the affair of St. Paulinus and St. Mele, together with the persecution of some envious persons who went so far as to accuse him of error in the doctrine of the Trinity, forced him to retire to the neighborhood of Jerusalem, and to fly from one solitude to another. He then stopped at Bethlehem, which place he found more to his liking, so that he finally took up his abode there. He was, however, obliged to return once more to Antioch, where he was ordained priest by St. Paulinus; this dignity he only accepted on condition that he was not to be appointed to any church, nor compelled to abandon his profession of monk. He afterwards went to Constantinople, to see St. Gregory Nazianzen, under whom, as he himself testifies, he studied the Holy Scriptures and learned the best method of explaining them. St. Gregory having quitted the imperial city, our saint returned to Jerusalem; he then proceeded to Rome in company with St. Paulinus and St. Epiphanius, Pope Damasus having convoked a council. That holy pontiff kept St. Jerome at Rome after St. Paulinus and St. Epiphanius had returned home, for the purpose of having him at hand to write letters, and reply to the different consultations of the churches.

In the midst of these important affairs St. Jerome continued to lead the life of a perfect monk, so that he gained the admiration of all persons distinguished by their rank or piety. His reputation had arrived long before himself in that capital of the christian world, and his presence more than justified the praises lavished upon him. The sanctity of his morals, his profound humilty, his austere life, all these, taken conjointly with his resistless eloquence and his intimate knowledge of the Sacred Scriptures, won for him the esteem and the veneration of all who could appreciate real merit. He availed himself of this ascendency, in order to induce several persons of distinction to embrace a religious life. He had also for pupils, in sacred literature, St. Paula and many other Roman ladies, who became, under his direction, models of sanctity.

But whilst his name was in such high repute, that he was never mentioned in Rome, or even in the provinces, without respect and veneration, there arose against him, little by little, a persecution which proceeded from the envy of certain ecclesiastics, whose disorderly lives were condemned by the purity and regularity of his. This, coupled with his love of solitude, induced him, after the death of St. Damasus, to return to Palestine with his brother Paulinian, (his junior by thirty years) and they arrived there in the depth of winter. St. Jerome set out once more, in the Spring, to visit the holy solitaries of Egypt. In Alexandria he saw, amongst others, the famous Didymus. Returning. at length, to Palestine, he fixed himself permanently at Bethlehem. St. Paula, accompanied by her daughter Eustoquia, had already taken up her abode there. She built two large monasteries, one for men (whither St. Jerome retired), and the other for persons of her own sex. Our saint had the sole direction of both. We shall not here enter upon the detail of his occupations; it is sufficient to say in general that his time was divided between acts of charity and the works which he composed for the service of the Church; these last may be truly styled immense labors, whether considered as commentaries on the Sacred Scriptures, as controversial works, written in refutation of the various heresies of the time, or as apologies for himself in the persecutions raised up against him on different occasions by the heretics. Yet through all his arduous labors he never relaxed ought in his austerities. He lived always in monastic penance, and the vigor of his mind, which he preserved unimpaired, made up for the weakness of his body, exhausted by mortification, and advancing age.

Piety attracted from all parts of the world a vast number of pilgrims to the Holy Land, and these were chiefly monks. This was particularly the case after the capture of Rome by the Goths, as many persons then fled to Palestine for safety. This unusual concourse of strangers obliged St. Jerome to enlarge his monastery, so as to receive a greater number of people. He sent his brother Paulinian with a friend to sell what remained to him of his patrimonial inheritance, in order to raise funds for the purpose. He thus added hospitality to his other works, and, the duties of charity engrossing the greater portion of his time, he had only

the night for his studies; which gave him another
opportunity of doing penance   To this may be added
the functions wherewith he was charged for the service
of the Church in Bethlehem for Posthumian, who came
from Gaul to visit the Holy Land, and who remained
six months with him, says that he governed the church
of Bethlehem, which shows that he must have exercised ecclesiastical authority.

At length St. Jerome, the illustrious doctor of the
church, as he is justly styled in the prayer of his office
—the glory and ornament of the monastic state, died
at Bethlehem, worn out, as much by the rigor of his
penance and his many labors, as by the number of his
years.   His death threw the entire church into mourning, and her sorrow was only assuaged by the possession
of the invaluable works he had bequeathed to her.
Authors are divided on the duration of his life : St.
Prosper gives him ninety-one years, others still more,
and others less.   This diversity of opinion leaves it
difficult to decide.

Besides what this holy doctor has written for the
Church in general, he also labored in private with
uncommon zeal for persons engaged in the monastic
state and for Christian virgins.   In his lives of St.
Paul, the first hermit, St. Hilarion, and several holy
persons of the other sex, he has left us perfect models
of religious perfection.   The history of St. Malchus
also contains much valuable instruction.   He trans-

lated into Latin the rules of St. Pacome, of St. Theodore and of Orsise, for the use of those Latin monks who dwelt in the Theban deserts, in Egypt, and especially in the monastery of Metanea, who knew neither the Greek nor Egyptian language. This translation, which the priest Leontius with some others of the brethren had come to ask for, in the name of their community, served also for the monks of Syria, and the nuns of St. Paula's monastery. St. Paula had died before the translation was undertaken, but St. Eustoquia was still living.

Heliodorus had, as we have said, accompanied our saint from Rome to Palestine, but he having returned home, St. Jerome addressed him in a letter, showing with much force and eloquence the advantages of a solitary life, and the fidelity with which it should be always followed, when once embraced. He commences with reproaches, springing from friendship rather than from zeal ; and then he goes on entreating him to give up his native land and return to his desert: "Effeminate soldier! what dost thou in the house of thy father? What defences art thou casting up against the attack of the enemy? What winters dost thou pass there under tents?—Remember the day when thou wert enrolled by Baptism in the army of Jesus Christ; thou didst then swear to be faithful to him, and to give up even thy father or thy mother when his service requires it.

"The devil is already at work, trying to stifle Jesus
Christ in thy heart, and the enemies of thy salvation
are grieved to see thee in possession of the pledge
which was given thee when thou didst enter into his
service. Let friends and relatives do their utmost to
retain thee, fix thine eye on the standard of the cross,
and follow it steadily. . . . . I am not unfeeling; I
have not a heart incapable of being touched; I have
passed, like thyself, through all these trials.—But
when we truly love God and fear the pains of hell,
we have no hesitation in breaking these chains. Thou
wilt perhaps tell me :—'Is it then impossible to remain
in a city without ceasing to be a Christian?' You,
my brother, stand not on the same footing as others.
Hear what the Son of God says: *If thou wouldst be*
perfect, go sell what you possess, and give it to the
poor, then come and follow me, Matt. xix. You have
made a vow to seek perfection, for, when you abandoned the world you engaged yourself, at the same
time, to a perfect life. Then a true servant of Christ
ought to have no other possession than Jesus Christ
himself, for, if he possess aught besides, he ceases to
be perfect. . . . .

"You will not fail to answer me that you no longer
possess anything; but if that be so, why not fight,
since that universal detachment fits you so well for the
combat? Perhaps you imagine that you can acquit
yourself of all these duties in your own country

But do you not know that the Saviour of the world performed no miracles at home: Thence you must conclude that the solitary who never leaves his native land cannot attain perfection in his state.

"When I have driven you from this entrenchment, you will, I know, bring forward against me the example of the ecclesiastics; and, as they dwell in cities, you should like to know whether I would condemn them for so doing: God forbid that I should speak ill of those who hold in the Church the place of the Apostles. . . . . If your brethren urge you to take priestly orders, I shall rejoice at your elevation, but I shall also fear lest you fall . . . . Put yourself, therefore, my dear brother, in the lowest place, to the end that you may not be removed to a lower seat when any more distinguished guest arrives, Luke xiv. If an anchoret fall, the priest will pray for him; but who will pray for the priest if he himself chance to fall?

"O desert ever enamelled with the flowers of Jesus Christ! O solitude whence are taken the stones to build the city of the Great King, mentioned by St. John in his Apocalypse! O desert where men are enabled to converse more familiarly with God! What dost thou, then, in the world, my brother, seeing that thou art greater than the world? How long wilt thou remain under the shade of houses? How long wilt thou shut thyself up in cities which are ever cov-

ered by a black cloud of smoke? Believe me, that
here it seems like a new day. Freed as I am from
the overwhelming care of my body, I take delight in
soaring higher and higher into a purer and more serene atmosphere.

"What is it that you fear in solitude :—is it poverty? Jesus Christ says that the poor are blessed :—is
it labor? The athletes are only crowned when they
have fought and conquered. Is it anxiety about your
food ?—Faith dreads not hunger. Do you shrink
from sleeping on the bare ground and thus macerating
your body, already enfeebled by long fasts? The
Lord will repose there with you. Could you not
endure to have your hair shaggy and your face neglected? The Apostle St. Paul tells us that Jesus
Christ is the head of man. 1 Cor. xi. Do you dread
the vast extent of a boundless solitude? You can
imagine yourself in paradise, and your thoughts once
raised to Heaven, the desert will be nothing to you.
Are you afraid lest, for want of the bath, your skin
may wrinkle and become rough? When once you
have been washed in Jesus Christ, you have no further need of washing. In a word, hearken to what
St. Paul says of all these objections: *The sufferings
of the present life bear no proportion to the glory
which shall one day be revealed to us.* Rom. viii.

St. Paulinus, having given his immense wealth to
the poor, and embraced voluntary poverty, applied to

St. Jerome for rules whereby to regulate his new state. The saint, who had exhorted him, in another letter, to break away entirely from the world and devote himself wholly to God, now told him at once that no man merits praise for having been to Jerusalem, where he desired to go and wished to remain, but only for having lived well there; that each of the faithful is to be judged, not by the place of his abode, but by the value of his faith; that Heaven is equally open to the citizens of Jerusalem and the inhabitants of Great Britain, because that *the kingdom of God*, as Jesus Christ says, *is within us*, Luke, xvii; that St. Anthony and a multitude of the solitaries of Egypt, of Mesopotamia, of Pontus, of Cappadocia, and of Armenia, had gone to heaven without ever having seen Jerusalem; and that St. Hilarion, born in Palestine, went there but once, and then remained but a single day. "You may, therefore," continues he, "without hurting your faith, dispense with seeing the city of Jerusalem. . . . But, after having withdrawn yourself, by the state that you have chosen, from the crowds and tumult of the city, your study should be to live in the country, to seek Jesus Christ in retreat, to pray with him on the mountain and to seek no other neighborhood than that of the holy places, so as to give up cities altogether, and remain constantly attached to your state. . . . Let us imitate the masters of the solitary life which we profess, that is to say, the

Pauls, the Anthonies, Macarius and Hilarion ; and, if we come to the authority of the Sacred Scriptures, le' us take for our models Elias, Eliseus, and the children of the prophets, who always retired in the country and living in solitude, built themselves cabins on the banks of the Jordan.

"Shun company—avoid banquets, and all the vain observances and affected politeness of worldlings, as so many chains which serve but to make us the slaves of luxury. Eat in the evening a little herbs and vegetables, with a few little fish now and then by way of dainty. When one nourishes himself with Jesus Christ, and fixes upon him all the desires of the heart, he is very little troubled about the quality of the food wherewith he regales his body. . . . . . Be always assiduous in the reading of the Sacred Scripture ; apply yourself often to the exercise of prayer, prostrated before God ; raise your every thought to Him ; pray often during the night, and go sometimes to bed without having broken your fast. . . . . Be not vain of your mean apparel ; have no connection with people of the world, especially the great. What necessity is there that you should frequently see what you have resigned for love of the monastic state."

St. Jerome, after having exhorted Heliodorus to return into solitude, and drawn up for St. Paulinus (afterwards Bishop of Nole) the rules of a true anchoret, writes to the monk Rustique, who was a

Gaul—a native of Marseilles. He speaks to him of the cenobitic life, and the conduct which he ought to observe. He shows him at first, in the following terms, the general duties of the monastic life : " If you would, therefore," says he, " become a true solitary, and not content yourself with the bare appearance thereof, you should attend solely to the affairs of your salvation, and disturb yourself no more about the welfare of your family, seeing that renouncing it was the first step towards making you what you are. Ever manifest in your neglect of external appearance, the beauty of a pure and guileless heart; and show by the poverty of your garments how much you despise what the world esteems, always provided that vanity have no part in the display, and that your words correspond with your habit.

" Practice fasting, and never flatter the body by the use of the bath. Be moderate, however, in your fasting, and use it with discretion, lest you weaken your stomach so much that you might require to eat more than usual, in order to restore its strength. A little nourishment taken with moderation, is profitable both to soul and body. . . . Whilst you remain in your own country, regard your cell as a terrestrial paradise. Go cull from the Holy Scriptures the various fruits there abounding; make them your chief pleasure, and be always assiduous in the reading of these divine books. Apply yourself solely to the care

of your soul, and let all the rest give you little concern.

" As the object now is to form and instruct, in you,
a young solitary who has taken upon him the yoke
of Jesus Christ after having been trained from his
youth up in the study of polite literature, it becomes
necessary to ascertain whether it is more advantageous
for you to live in solitude by yourself, than to make
one in a community. For myself, I advise you to
place yourself in the company of the saints, never to
trust to your own suggestions, or enter upon unknown
regions without a safe guide. . . . . I do not pretend
to condemn the solitary life, I who have so often
recommended it ; but I would have no one retire to
the desert without having first passed through the
spiritual combats of the monastery. I would have
them first give proofs of virtue and purity of heart ;
that they should only rise above others, in the excellence of the solitary state, after having made themselves the lowest of all in the society of brethren ; in
short, I would that they should never suffer themselves
to be overcome by hunger, nor yet by intemperance ;
that they should delight in poverty, and that they
should present in their air, in their words, and in their
walk, an image of every virtue. . . .

" Have always some book in your hands ; learn the
Psalter by heart ; pray without ceasing ; watch carefully over your senses ; busy not yourself with vain

thoughts; let all that is within you tend to God; overcome by patience, the motions of anger: love the study of the Holy Scripture ; banish from your mind whatever might disturb its repose ; be always busy, so that the devil may never find you idle. If the Apostles applied themselves to manual labor, to the end that they might not be burthensome to others, why should not you do the same? Apply yourself, therefore, to making baskets or mats, or weeding the ground, or cultivating a garden, or making fishing-nets, or transcribing books, to the end that you may at the same time support your body by the labor of your hands, and nourish your soul by the reading of good books. Men who live in idleness are usually subject to a multitude of desires. It is an established custom in the monasteries of Egypt to receive none who are not able to do manual labor, and this not so much to cater for the wants of the body as to provide for those of the soul, and prevent the solitary from giving way to vain and hurtful thoughts.

"Speaking of this, I will tell you what I myself witnessed when in Egypt. There was in a certain monastery a young monk, of Grecian origin, who was so grievously tempted, that the most rigorous fasts and the most painful labors could not overcome the temptation. His superior, beginning to fear that he might, at last, yield, conceived the following plan for effecting his release:

"He ordered one of the seniors to treat him very harshly, and, after loading him with all manner of abuse, to be always the first to complain of him. Then witnesses were brought forward who were always sure to be on the side of the old monk, so that the poor brother was much grieved by the calumny heaped upon him, and because there was none to tell the truth. It was only the superior who seemed to have any compassion for him, and that was for fear he might sink under the intolerable load of his affliction. This sham persecution went on for a whole year, at the end of which time he was asked whether he was still tormented by the fierce temptations which had formerly left him no peace. "Alas!" he replied, "how could I think evil, when I have not even a moment to breathe?" Had this young man been alone, who, think you, would have helped him to overcome his enemy?

"I will not tire you with a longer detail," continues St. Jerome, "I merely propose to show you by this, that you ought not to be master of your own actions, but to live in a monastery under the guidance of a superior and in company with many others, to the end that you may learn of the one to live in humility, of the other to practice patience, of this to keep silence, of the other to be mild and docile. You will not then be at liberty to do as you please, but will be obliged to eat as others choose, to have nought but what is given you, to wear such habits as are selected for you, to do every day what work is required of you, to obey persons who may be far from agreeable to you, to lie down at night overwhelmed with fatigue, to sleep as you walk, and to be obliged to quit your bed long before you have slept enough.

You shall also sing psalms in your place; and then you must not seek to gratify the ear, but to inflame the heart. . . . . . These different occupations will shelter you from temptation, and making one labor succeed another, you will be entirely engrossed with what you have to do."

St. Jerome has written letters to persons of various conditions, giving them admirable rules for sanctifying themselves in their respective states. Bishops, ecclesiastics of every grade, married people, widows, all find in his writings instruction and advice which, if carried out, will enable them to attain perfection. For instance, writing to Heliodorus, bishop of Altino, to console him on the death of his nephew Nepotian, he makes use of these beautiful words :—" All the faithful have their eyes on the bishop. His household, and his conduct are observed by all. He ought to serve as an example to his whole church, and there is no one who will not try to do a portion of what he does." To Nepotian, when living, he had also written this advice to ecclesiastics :—" The Greek word *cleros* signifies lot and share. The name of *clerks* is there fore given to ecclesiastics, either because they are devoted to the Lord, or because the Lord is their portion. Now he who belongs to the Lord, or who has the Lord for his portion, ought to live as one who possesses the Lord, and in whom the Lord abides." We also have his epistle to the widow Furia, of the ancient and illustrious house of the Camillas, regarding the duties of a Christian widow ; and to Leta, how she ought to preserve her daughter, the young Paula, in innocence, to consecrate her to the Lord. Nothing can be wiser or more salutary than the advice which he gives her on that subject.

Finally, St. Jerome seems to have surpassed himself, when he wrote in favor of virginity and gave precepts to Christian virgins. We should exceed our limits were we to repeat all he has said on that angelic state and its incumbent duties. Those who wish to be instructed on the subject, may read his letters to Eustochia and to Demetriades. It will suffice for us to remark in general that he elevates the state of virginity to the same rank as that of apostles and martyrs ; that the life of a virgin is more conformable to that of Jesus Christ, in as much as he is their chief and the author of virginity. He advises them, above all, to renounce the vanities of the world, to shun the company of worldly-minded young women, to live in retirement, to go out but seldom and when occasion required it, to read good books, to mortify their senses,

to love labor and shun idleness, and all useless conversation ; to live, in short, so discreetly, as to inspire
others, by their virtue, with a love and esteem for
chastity. Lastly, he adds these few words which
epitomise all the sanctity of a Christian virgin :—" A
spouse of Jesus Christ must be like the ark of the
Covenant, all covered with gold within and without.
and be the depository of the law of God. As the ark
contained only the tables of the Testament, so ought
she to banish from her mind the idea of all exterior
and sensible things. It is on this propitiatory, as of
old on the wings of the cherubim, that the Lord will
sit."

ST. BASIL THE GREAT,

AND

ST. GREGORY OF NAZIANZEN.

THESE two illustrious saints have done so much
honor to the monastic order, that we cannot dispense
with their lives in this collection. We will not separate them here, since their connection was so close and
that they acted in such perfect harmony, giving each
in his own province such singular lustre to the monastic state in Syria, in Palestine, and in Egypt.

The city of Cesarea in Cappadocia, was the birth-place of St. Basil.   His birth is generally placed some-where about the year 328.   In his own family he found nobility, riches and sanctity.   He was brought up by his maternal grandmother, St. Macrina, and received from his father the first rudiments of polite literature, and apparently, of rhetoric.   He afterwards went successively to Cesarea of Palestine, to Constan-tinople and to Athens, to prosecute his other studies. It was in the last named city that he contracted an intimate friendship with St. Gregory of Nazianzen, who was nearly of his own age, and had the same virtuous inclinations.

His conduct in all these different cities was worthy of the excellent training he had received, and he every where manifested extraordinary talents in mastering the higher branches of learning.   In all the various departments of science he equalled his masters, and outstripped all his competitors.   In a short time he acquired a high reputation amongst all classes of people, and was everywhere distinguished for his pro-found erudition and vast attainments, which were far in advance of his age.   But he was even more admir-ed for the gravity of his manners and the staid decorum of his life.   The study of eloquence was but a secon-dary object with him, as he sought it only to make it subservient to Christian philosophy, which requires its assistance.   His chief study was to learn the art of detaching himself from the world to become united with God; to gain immutable and eternal treasures by the use of those which are frail and fleeting, and to purchase heaven at the expense of all terrestrial things. He continued this same mode of life in Constantinople, where he studied under the famous Libanius, who respected him then, young as he was, for the purity of his morals, and was charmed with his wondrous eloquence. Divine Providence and his laudable thirst for the sciences afterwards conducted him to Athens.

St. Gregory of Nazianzen, whom he had known at Cesarea, had arrived there before him. This saint was born about the year 329, in the town of Arianzen, in the territory of Nazianzen, from which cause it is that that city is regarded as his birth-place. His father was Gregory, subsequently bishop of the same city, and his mother was the blessed Nonna, both recognized as saints, together with St. Cesaire his brother, and his sister St. Gorgonia. His mother obtained this favor from God by the fervor of her prayers, and his childhood passed away in that happy innocence, which was nourished and preserved by the piety of his parents. From his earliest years he gave tokens of a maturity of thought far beyond his age, and giving a fair promise for the future. His love for virtue increased with his age; he loved to read pious books, and took the greatest pleasure in the conversation of devout persons. He once had a dream, in which chastity presented herself to his sight, arrayed in all her celestial charms, whereupon his heart was inflamed with an inextinguishable love of that divine virtue. In consequence thereof he renounced all the amusements of youth, and all that might induce him to love the world, and made it his chief pleasure to devote himself to the service of Christ. After receiving from his father the groundwork of an excellent education, he went to Cesarea of Cappadocia, and thence to Cesarea of Palestine, where he took lessons of Thespeces, a celebrated orator. But while cultivating profane literature he always gave the preference to sacred letters, which he considered as the only study worthy of a Christian. He also remained some time in Alexandria, and then proceeded to Athens in order to perfect himself in eloquence His voyage thither was marked by the peculiar protection of God, who destined him for the support of his church and the salvation of many. The vessel in which he sailed, was beaten about for twenty days by a violent storm, during which time those on board were exposed to the most imminent peril. Nearly all that time our saint ay prostrate on the deck, imploring the mercy of God, and renewing the oblation of himself which his holy mother had made at his birth. His father and mother had, it seems, a presentiment of the danger in which he was, and they joined their prayers to his. God heard them favorably : the sea became calm, and all those who were in the vessel were so persuaded that they owed their safety to his prayers, that they with one accord embraced the faith of Jesus Christ. He at length landed at Egina, whence he repaired to Athens; this was about the year 350, so that he might then have been twenty-one or twenty-two years of age.

St. Basil, whose history we now resume, arrived there about the year 351. It was, doubtless, a great consolation to him to meet St. Gregory; but being somewhat disappointed in his expectations with regard to Athens, he began to repent of having come. Gregory revived his drooping spirits, and restored tranquillity to his mind by representing that as the morals of men are only known by long experience, time was also necessary in order to form a correct judgment regarding their doctrine.

Their friendship, which was at first but a natural one, became closer and more solid when they began to confide so far in each other, as to interchange the mutual sentiments of their hearts; and knowing that they had no other design than that of consecrating themselves wholly to God, they had thenceforward but one home and one table, even as they had but one will to serve God as perfectly as they could. "Alas!" says St. Gregory, speaking of that blessed union, "how can I describe it here without shedding tears? Science, so very subject to envy, was the object of our pursuit, yet neither had one feeling of rivalry ; on the contrary, emulation only excited us to study well, and we strove, not for who should prevail, but for who should yield to his friend. Each of us regarded the other's glory as his own. Our sole ambition and our sole endeavor was to acquire virtue ; we lived but to render ourselves worthy of the world to come ; we labored to detach ourselves from this life before death should call us hence, and to this end all our efforts were directed. The law of God was our guide, and we urged each other on to the practice of virtue ; we had no connection with libertine scholars, but sought the company of those who were wise and virtuous ; we avoided those young men who were of a turbulent disposition, and associated only with the mild and peaceful, because it is much easier to contract vice than to communicate virtue ; we took more pleasure in the useful sciences than in those which are merely amusing ; we knew but two ways, that which led to the church, and it we loved dearly, and that which led to the school, and which we trod with less pleasure ; to others we left the road to profane banquets, to plays, balls and assemblies, for nothing should interest us that does not tend to regulate our lives. Some there are who take names, either from their parents, or according to their inclinations ; but we gloried in being called Christians, and deserving the name."

Thus spoke St. Gregory, and we have thought it expedient to record this most edifying passage, in order to present a model to students, and to deprive them of the pretext of youth, or of bad example, since these saints were then at the age when the passions are the most violent, and that they dwelt in a city, surrounded, of course, by young profligates, who, while cultivating their minds, by the pursuit of science, abandoned their hearts to their own perverse inclinations.

Julian, subsequently the Emperor and the Apostate, came to Athens while our two friends were studying there. They very soon discovered his evil propensities, although he dared not then manifest them Hence it was that St. Gregory said with deep sorrow. "Oh ! what a canker does the Roman empire foster, in the person of this young man ! God grant that I may in this matter be a false prophet!" They remained but a short time in Athens after the arrival of the prince, and Basil first left it, about the year 355, notwithstanding all the efforts that were made to induce him to remain. St. Gregory soon after followed his example. They both repaired to Constantinople and were at length re-united in Cappadocia.

St. Basil had lost his father; and having reached Cesarea, his native place, he complied somewhat with the world and the aspect of the times, according to the expression of St. Gregory Nazianzen, which may

signify that he taught rhetoric, not through ostentation, but to gratify the wishes of his fellow-citizens.
But his sister, St. Macrina, adding her entreaties to
the interior promptings of his own soul, he at length
determined to renounce the world.   "He began, therefore," says St. Gregory Nazianzen, "to live for himself, to change from a child to a man, and to make
more generous efforts to arrive at divine philosophy."
"He despised," says also St. Gregory of Nyssa, "all
the vain glory of profane learning, and chose rather
to embrace an humble life, even as Moses preferred
the Hebrews to the treasures of the Egyptians."

But let St. Basil himself describe the state in which
he then was. "After having," says he "given much
time to vanity, and spent nearly all the years of my
youth in acquiring by long and useless toil that worldly
wisdom which is condemned by God, I awoke, at
length, as from a profound sleep. In that state I
longed for a guide to conduct me into the way of true
piety. My greatest care was to reform my morals.
I, therefore, applied myself to study the Gospel, and I
there found that there is no better means of attaining
perfection than to sell all worldly goods, and divide
the amount thereof with those who are in need, to get
rid of all the cares of this life, so that the soul may
not be disturbed by any attachment to sublunary
things."

St. Gregory, who had postponed his baptism till he

should have returned to his own country, undertook, as soon as he had received it, the same perfection which he had recommended to his friend. Thenceforward, he gave himself so entirely to God that he wished for nothing but him alone. He had an absolute contempt for riches, rank, fame, power, and all the worthless luxuries of this world. "I have given all," says he in one place "to Him who has received and preserved me for his portion. To Him have I consecrated my wealth, my glory, my health, and whatever eloquence I may have; all the profit which I have derived from these advantages is a contempt for them, and the pleasure of having something that I might, if I would, prefer to Jesus Christ." Thenceforward, he regarded as valueless all the grandeur and pleasure of the world. His sole nourishment was coarse bread with a little salt and water, and he delighted more in that humble, mortified life, than worldlings do amid all the enjoyments of sense.

By this we learn that he, as well as St. Basil, then embraced the ascetic life; but they did not remain long together, however they might have wished it, as St. Gregory was obliged to stay with his father and mother, in compliance with the duty imposed upon him by nature. Hence St. Basil made alone some voyages which he judged conformable to his cherished purpose of consecrating himself to God without reserve, and he traveled through Mesopotamia, Celesyria, Palestine and Egypt. He visited the holy solitaries in those regions, and admired their austere and laborious life, with their extraordinary fervor and assiduity in prayer. He was astonished to perceive that although invincible to sleep and the other necessities of nature, in hunger, thirst, cold, and nakedness, without a wish for any species of relief, as though their body were a stranger to them; yet they always had their minds free and fixed on God showing by their conduct how men on earth may regard themselves as citizens of heaven.

It would seem that St. Basil chanced to be in Alexandria at the time when the impious George, that furious Arian, raised such a violent persecution against the Catholics and St. Athanasius. It was also in the course of these travels, and about the year 357 or 358, that he had everywhere the great affliction of seeing the most virtuous and the most distinguished amongst the bishops and clergy, banished and maltreated by the Arians, who had filled the church with schisms and dissensions. His heart was torn with sorrow, considering that, whilst men agreed together in all the different states of life of which they made profession, it was seen, on the contrary, that in the church of God for which Christ died and on which he poured down the plenitude of grace, most of its members were opposed to each other and to the rules of Scripture. But what appeared to him still more fearful was to

see priests divided in sentiments and in belief, and so
opposite in their conduct to the precepts of Jesus
Christ, ruthlessly tearing the church of God asunder,
disturbing his flock without respect for those who belonged to Him, and verifying the saying of St. Paul,
that some amongst them should teach a corrupt doctrine for the sake of gaining disciples for themselves.
He began to examine within himself what might be
the cause of these disorders, and discovered, with the
help of the holy books, that these divisions, and the
temerity of those who took the liberty of inventing
new dogmas, and of making a party for themselves in
opposition to that of Jesus Christ, rather than submit
to him, that all this proceeded solely from the fact
that these men had abandoned God and would no
longer recognize him as their King.

Dianeus was bishop of Cesarea for several years before St. Basil returned from his travels, and the prelate (who had baptized our saint) fearing lest some
other church might take him from him, gave him at
once the order of reader; but that did not prevent him
from imitating the lives of those solitaries whom he
had seen. With that intent he joined Eustachus and
his disciples who there professed the monastic life
Eustachus was a countryman of his and also one of
his earliest friends. He had built a monastery where
in he assembled several disciples, who observed a very
exact discipline; and St. Basil considered them worthy

of his esteem, seeing that their exterior was so regular
and their mode of living so nearly approaching that
of the solitaries whom he had seen in the other provinces.

Nevertheless, there were many persons who tried to
dissuade him from having any intercourse with them,
on the grounds that they were far from being orthodox in their belief with regard to the divinity of Christ.
But the saint rejected this advice, being unable to
persuade himself that these men were interiorly so
very different from their modest and penitent exterior.
He very soon found that he had erred in forming such
a favorable estimate of them, and we have only to read
ecclesiastical history to recognize in Eustachus a pupil
of Arius, a Proteus who had no other faith than that
which might best promote his own interest, and finally
the greatest persecutor that St. Basil himself ever had.

The saint was not long in Cesarea; he merely
waited there for St. Gregory Nazianzen to retire with
him into Pontus; but St. Gregory was prevented from
coming, and our saint resolved to pay a visit to his
mother, who resided with her daughter, St. Macrina,
where they had established a monastery of virgins.
There St. Basil found a solitude such as he desired.
His mother's monastery was situated near the river
Iris, at a short distance from Ibora, a small episcopal
town of Pontus, and within seven or eight stadas of
the church of the Forty Martyrs.   The solitude chosen

Ly St. Basil was on the opposite bank of the river, and he wrote a tempting description of it to St. Gregory, with the hope of inducing him to go there; but the time was not yet come.

This first retreat may be placed about the year 358. The life on which he then entered was very poor and very austere: bread, salt, and water were his only nourishment (as we have already said of St. Gregory); when he added to this a few herbs or vegetables it was on some high festival. It was then that he wrote to St. Gregory Nazianzen that excellent letter which has been placed at the head of all the others, treating at length of the conduct of solitaries, and containing much useful instruction. He there enters into a detail which may serve to direct religious persons in every action of their lives, and to make them perfect models of sanctity in their state. In the rules there laid down he does but embody his own conduct.

In order to be convinced of this, it is only necessary to read what his brother, St. Gregory of Nyssa, and St. Gregory of Nazianzen have written of him. They say that having determined to embrace evangelical poverty, that resolution was as firm in his soul as a rock amid the waves; that his delight was to have nothing and to follow in holy poverty his Saviour's cross; that he possessed nothing but his own body, devoting all that remained of his wealth to the relief of the poor. In fine, his abstinence was so great, that those

who wrote his eulogium after his death, as having
been the witnesses of his austerity during life, have
said that he gave to his body, not what nature demanded for its support, but what the law of his absti-
ence had prescribed for it.

St. Gregory Nazianzen at length yielded to his entreaties, and went to join him in his solitude. We
have a letter written by him some time after, wherein,
recalling the memory of the happy days they had
spent together in the exercises of the solitary life, he
makes known to us their manner of living. "Who,"
says he, "could be sufficiently grateful for having
passed a single month as happily as I did with you,
when our pleasure was hard work and voluntary privations : So true it is that things even the most painful become agreeable to us when they are done of our
own free will, whereas those which are in themselves
pleasing, become irksome and painful when done by
constraint. Who will restore to me those Canticles,
those vigils, those prayers which transported us from
earth to heaven ; that life which was almost disengaged from matter ; that emulation which we had for
the practice of virtue, or that zeal which we displayed
in making our actions conform to the rules of solid
piety ? What satisfaction did I not then enjoy in
applying myself to the study of the Sacred Scriptures !
And, to descend to more trivial matters, shall I see no
more those days when we labored with our hands, in

tarrying wood, hewing stones, planting trees, or digging channels to carry off the water?"

It is thus that St. Gregory reminds St. Basil of the innocent pleasures of their retreat; and it appears that they consisted solely in a taste for prayer, in the exercise of the virtues, in penitential labors, in holy meditation on the sacred writings, to which they added the study of the Fathers who had previously explained them, so as to gather from their interpretations their true signification and the tradition of the church.

About this time it was that the inhabitants of Neocesarea sent a deputation of their chief men to St. Basil, praying him to go to their city for the instruction of youth; but the love of solitude prevailed in his heart over their solicitations, earnest as they were, for he loved better to enjoy his God in silence, than to teach others the art of speaking eloquently. But although he had retired to Pontus in order to devote himself to God and his own soul, far away from the tumult of the city, he could not prevent people from coming to him, in crowds, for rules of conduct; especially as, besides the rare talent which he had for expounding the sacred maxims of religion, and his profound knowledge thereof, he exemplified what he taught by his own life.

This was what caused the establishment of a grand monastery, and in course of time, several others, whereof his charity induced him to take the utmost

care, moved thereto by his fervent zeal for the glory
of God and the salvation of souls. We learn from
St. Gregory Nazianzen, who was an eye-witness of the
fact, that the monks lived there, under the guidance
of the saint, in a marvellous union and an extraordinary ardor for the practice of virtue, animating each
other thereto, so that it might be said of them that,
by their fervor, they rendered men superior to their
own nature, and in some degree, celestial. The saint
wished them to live in common, so as to join society
with retreat, for which reason he usually calls them
communities of brethren, and, brotherhoods. The
better to establish amongst them an exact and uniform
observance, he instructed them with maxims from the
Fathers, and the earliest masters of the religious life,
and also gave them rules for conducting and sanctifying themselves in their state. Hence, we have the
precious treasure of these rules in his works, namely,
the greater rules, which contain thirty-five questions
and their answers ; and the minor rules which are to
the number of three hundred and thirteen, wherein
the subjects are not so copiously enlarged upon. He
also wrote in his solitude various letters, to monks,
virgins, and other persons. But, whilst he labored to
inspire men with the love of retirement, by the experience which he had of the advantages that it procures
for the soul, he manifested fully as much zeal to fill
the monastery of his sister, St. Macrina, with chaste

doves, whose principal exercise was to sigh incessantly
after heaven. This he expressly indicates to a lady
named Julita, who was a widow and related to him,
when he assures her that if he should one day have
he happiness of seeing her embrace that holy and
ublime state, he would need the assistance of many
other persons to give adequate thanks to God.

His zeal did not confine itself to these first foundations, for he went about through all the cities and
towns of Pontus, urging the inhabitants of that province to shake off their natural indolence, and begin
to serve God in earnest. He prevailed upon very
many persons to renounce the world for the welfare
of their souls, and to unite in a holy society for the
service of God. He taught them to build monasteries,
to establish communities, to take care of each other,
to the end that none might want the necessaries of
life; to occupy themselves with prayer, to sing hymns
and psalms, to have care of the poor, to provide them
with decent lodgings, and to furnish them with the
means of living. He also looked after the interest of
women as well as men, and instructed those people to .
bring up virgins fit for becoming the spouses of Christ
Jesus. Thus it was that he speedily changed the aspect of that province, so that almost every one began
to lead a chaste and holy life, and many persons laid
their treasures at his feet to be distributed amongst
the poor.

St. Gregory Nazianzen labored, on his side, for the glory of God; and these two great men, whom the Lord had given to his church to sustain her during the perilous times of Arianism, exerted themselves with extraordinary success, throwing in the whole weight of their genius and the product of their studies, for the confounding of sinners, the preservation and encouragement of the just, and for the defense of the true faith against the assaults of error. Basil, full of tenderness and compassion for sinners, mildly encouraged them to arise after their fall, while Gregory exerted himself to prevent them in the first place from falling into sin : the one was pure and untainted in his own faith, the other boldly announced it to others ; the one was humble before God, the other was so before men ; the one soared above the proud, looking down contemptuously upon them, the other overcame them by the force of his reasoning. It was thus that by various ways they both attained the same perfection, and were destined by God for the government of his people.

St. Gregory was not long permitted to share the solitude of St. Basil. He was called home by his father, who was bishop of Nazianzen, and had great need of his son's assistance, more especially since he had allowed himself to be so far duped by the Arians as to sign the captious formulary of Rimini, which gave rise to so many disorders in the church. From that time the monks of his diocese had separated from him, and it was for the purpose of effecting a recon ciliation, and doing away with the effects of his fath· er's fall, that St. Gregory was summoned home.

On the other hand, Dianeus, bishop of Cesarca, had, as we have already mentioned, fallen into the same error as the father of St. Gregory ; and St. Basil, although he tenderly loved him as his spiritual father (having received baptism from him), was, nevertheless, obliged to separate himself from his communion, his faith being dearer to him than any thing of this world. The simplicity of St. Gregory's father, his own natural integrity and sincerity, together with his great age, had prevented him from distrusting the specious pre· tensions of the Arians, or suspecting the venom concealed in the formulary of Rimini. So, too, the extreme mildness of Dianeus, and his total want of firmness, had led him into a similar fault.

St. Gregory, having reached Nazianzen, labored with all his might to reconcile his father with those who had separated from his communion, and he had, at length, the consolation of gaining his end. The monks, who had been the last to secede, being more grieved than exasperated by the fall of their bishop, were the first to give the example of returning. This took place about the year 364, and it was the general wish that St. Gregory should celebrate the re-union by a public discourse ; this he did, for he had pre viously received Holy Orders from the hands of his father, who had ordained him contrary to his own wishes, and he had joined St. Basil in his retreat chiefly to console himself for this elevation, from which his modesty made him shrink.

St. Basil was also ordained priest in Cesarea a short time after St. Gregory, and about the year 362. He had been summoned to that city by the Bishop, Dia- neus, who, being on his death-bed, wished to be rec- onciled with him, and protested to him that, although he had signed the formulary of Rimini, not being aware of its real character, he had never in reality meant to do any thing contrary to the faith of Nice. With this assurance the saint thought himself obliged to be satisfied. Dianeus being dead, Eusebius was elected in his place, who hastened, after his consecra- tion, to raise St. Basil to the priesthood, in order to secure him for his own diocese, and St. Basil was quite as much afflicted by his ordination as St. Gre- gory had before been. He was, therefore, obliged to remain in Cesarea, notwithstanding his ardent wish to return to his dear solitude in Pontus; and he com- plained of it in a letter to St. Gregory, who, endeav- oring to console him, answered as follows :—" You have, therefore, been caught as well as we, and we have both fallen into the same snare. They have made us priests, though neither of us had any such intention, for we can bear witness of each other that each has ever loved the humblest and most obscure life, and it might still have been the most advantageous to both. I, at least, would not venture to say otherwise, until I am convinced what was or is the will of God with regard to us. But since the deed is done, I am of opinion that we must submit, chiefly because of the times in which we live, when heretics attack us on every side, and let it be our study not to disappoint the hopes which are entertained of us, or to do any thing unworthy of the life we have hitherto been leading."

Although these two saints were grieved because of their ordination, being penetrated with a sense of their own nothingness and the great dignity of the priesthood, the Church had cause to felicitate herself on acquiring such a treasure at a time when the faithful had need of powerful succor, to bear up against the violent persecutions of Julian the Apostate, and that of the Arians. They, indeed, resisted Julian with heroic firmness, in 362, in which year the persecution of that prince was at its height in Cappadocia. The account of those troubles may be seen at length in ecclesiastical history, but here it suffices to say that, notwithstanding all the threats and all the promises of that wicked monarch, they scorned both his favor and his indignation. Julian, therefore, dreading their eloquence and their erudition as the greatest obstacles to his design of establishing idolatry on the ruins of

Christianity, proposed at length to immolate them the first to the pagan gods on his return from the Persian war, as the noblest victims he could offer. But God had decreed that he was never to return, and he died, as every one knows, in the course of the following year.

This death was a sort of triumph for St. Basil, to whom God was pleased to reveal it at the very moment when it occurred, the saint being then at prayer. But at the same time God permitted his patience to be tried by another species of persecution, which was the less expected, as it came from Eusebius, his new bishop—for who could have appeared more closely united with him than that prelate ? But, as we learn from St. Gregory Nazianzen, he was moved against him by human weakness, and it is conjectured that the glory which St. Basil had acquired through the lustre of his talents and virtues, and the unqualified admiration wherewith he was regarded by the entire city of Cesarea, made him obnoxious to the bishop, whose self-love was hurt, and his envy excited.

He manifested this unworthy sentiment by treating St. Basil with the utmost rudeness on several occasions, and he thereby gave offence to all the holiest and wisest of his church, the monks in particular, who could not tamely endure to see insult offered to a man who did such honor to their profession. Finally, the matter went so far, that the saint, fearing some dissension between the pastor and his flock, took occasion to quit the city by stealth and return to his beloved retreat in Pontus, where he was followed by St. Gregory, and resumed the government of the monasteries he had there established. The people of Cesarea seeing that he did not return, sent to assure him how much they regretted his absence, and reminding him, with the hope of inducing him to return, that Cesarea was his native city and had, therefore, a strong claim upon his affection. He, however, modestly requested them (at the same time explaining the cause of his withdrawing from the city,) to grant him yet a little time to enjoy the pleasure which he derived from the company of the saints, meaning St. Gregory and the monks of his monasteries. He manifested at the same time his zeal for their welfare, by admonishing them to beware lest the Arians, whom he calls the Philistines, might disturb the serenity or tarnish the purity of their faith by their blasphemings, · of which he makes an abridgement, and their calumnies, which he refutes.

There is nothing particular known of his occupations during this second retreat. It is believed that he then assisted St. Gregory to prepare the two discourses against Julian published by the latter about that time. It is not very likely, however, that St. Gregory then remained for any length of time with St. Basil, seeing that his father had so great need of his assistance in the government of his diocese. Eusebius showed him great respect, and invited him to attend he assemblies ; but Gregory merely thanked him by letter, and added that he must make free to tell him— supposing that a lover of truth like Eusebius could not take offence thereat—that the wrong he had done and was still doing to Basil touched him most sensibly ; that, as he had chosen him for a companion, to honor the one and abuse the other, was neither more nor less than caressing a person with one hand and giving him a blow with the other,—conjuring him, in fine, to repair the injury he had done to Basil, and assuring him that he would find it no difficult task to conciliate his friend. He, at length, succeeded in bringing about this reconciliation between Eusebius and St. Basil, and made them once more good friends to the great joy of the whole city.

And there never was a time when unanimity was more necessary amongst the pastors of the church ; for Jovian having lived but a short time, and Valens, the grand abettor of the Arians, having succeeded to him, the heretics waxed bolder under the protection of that prince, and they crowded into Cesarea with their errors and confusion. But St. Basil opposed them with so much courage, strength, and wisdom, that Valens and the Arian bishops who had accompanied him to Cesarea, were obliged to retire without having gained anything for their sect, and having nothing for their pains but the disgrace of being overthrown by Basil.

This took place about the year 366, after our saint had remained three years in his retreat in Pontus. It would be impossible to give an idea of all the good which he effected in Cesarea after the defeat of the heretics and their subsequent flight. His first care was to manage the mind of Eusebius so prudently as to banish therefrom every trace of suspicion and distrust. He was continually near him; instructing, warning, and obeying him; rendering him, in fine, all the services of an excellent counsellor, an assistant ever ready at need, and an interpreter of the divine oracles; so that it might be said, that of all the ministers whom the bishop employed, Basil was the most faithful and the most efficient. This will suffice for us to say of his conduct in Cesarea, as a more detailed account of this portion of his life would lead us away from our principal object, which is the connection of this great saint with monastic history.

Eusebius died about the middle of the year 370, and it was a great consolation for him to breathe his last in the arms of St. Basil, who succeeded him in the government of his church, notwithstanding the exertions made by many ambitious and evil-minded persons, even amongst the bishops, to prevent him from being elected. The church of Cesarea was at that time one of the most considerable, and St. Gregory speaks of it as the mother of all the churches. It was the metropolis of Cappadocia, and there are many of the learned who hold that it was the capital of all that country which the Romans called Pontus, that is to say, Cappadocia, Galatia, lesser Armenia, all the coast of Pontus, Paphlagonia, and Bithynia; which from the time of Theodoret comprised eleven provinces and more than the half of Asia Minor. It is not surprising, therefore, that this bishoprick was an object of ambition to many; but no one was so fit to govern it as the great St. Basil, whether we consider his personal merit, or the critical circumstances of the time, when it required a man of eminent sanctity, learning and ability to sustain the faith 'against the attacks of heresy.

He fully justified the hopes of those who placed him there, the principal of whom were the elder Gregory, father of St. Gregory Nazianzen, and St. Eusebius of Samosata, whom the old bishop called in to support him in his choice by the weight of his reputation and his eminent merit. "Basil," says Gregory, "began now to surpass himself, as he had before surpassed others, and there were many occasions which called forth and displayed all the solidity of his faith, the fervor of his zeal and the extent of his devotion. The history of his episcopate would furnish matter for more than one volume; it may be seen, at length, in M. Hermant and M. de Tillemont, who have collected the most authentic monuments of ecclesiastical history

We shall only give here that portion of it which relates to our particular subject.

His conduct in the episcopate may be considered either in relation to the government of his own people, what he did for the adjacent provinces, or in his labors or the universal church, whether to maintain the purity of the faith, to reform the morals of the people, or to inspire, encourage, and perfect piety. He never dreamed that his own personal affairs ought to have a share in his pastoral solicitude; he thought of nothing but promoting the glory of God and the salvation of souls. The revenues of his church did not prevent him from being poor, and he loved to feel the inconveniences of poverty in wanting what might be considered as the very necessaries of life to a prelate charged as he was, with much care and business. He all his life observed a rigorous fast, and it is impossible to describe the many diseases which he endured, the weakness to which he reduced his body by mortification, and at the same time, the labors which he underwent in the worthy discharge of his duty, without recognizing the mighty hand of the Lord who strengthened him by his grace and preserved his life, as it were by a miracle, for the good of his church. We can see no difference between St. Basil in his retreat and St. Basil in his episcopate, except that of rank and of ecclesiastical affairs: otherwise we find in him the same austerities, and the same virtues.

We know the care which he took of his people by the frequent instructions which he gave them. Not content with preaching on Sundays and festivals, he sometimes gave instructions on week-days, either in the morning or evening, and it was quite a common occurrence to see even tradesmen thronging on those days to hear him. He had established various practices to maintain the piety of the people. "They come to the house of prayer," says he in one of his epistles, "before the dawn of day; they make their confession with lively sorrow, great compunction, and torrents of tears. From prayer they pass to psalmody, and form themselves into two choirs, for the purpose of singing alternately : by this means they fortify themselves in meditation on the word of God, and prepare their souls in due recollection. One of themselves is appointed to commence what is to be sung, the others continue, and answer, &c. When the daylight is come, all join in offering to God the psalm of confession as it were with one heart and one mouth, and each testifies his contrition in words proper to himself."

He remarks, in another place, that his people were gone to pray in a church of the Martyrs from midnight till noon-day, occupied in adoring God and singing his praise, and that he himself, having gone to a more distant church to perform the liturgy, came there about noon, and explained to them the 114th Psalm. He tells us, in one of his letters, that frequent

communion was common in his church. "It is good,"
says he, "and useful, to communicate every day, since
Jesus Christ has expressly said that he who eateth his
flesh and drinketh his blood, shall have eternal life.
Who can doubt, therefore, that the more we partici-
pate in this bread of life, the more share we shall have
in his life? Hence it is that people here communicate four times in the week, on Sunday, Wednesday,
Friday and Saturday, and also on other days when
we are celebrating the feast of a Martyr."

To these special affairs of his episcopal city, St.
Basil added the visits which he made to the country
parishes, and this notwithstanding his extreme debility
and failing health. But God indemnified him for his
sufferings and privations by the blessings which he
poured upon his labors. Not the least of these was
the many letters he had to write, now consoling some
in their afflictions, now exhorting others to persevere
in piety, and to others on various subjects connected
with their spiritual interest. He also advised his
people in their temporal affairs, according as charity
required. Being their bishop, he looked upon himself as their father and their pastor, and fulfilled with
all possible tenderness, the duties of those characters.

It appeared with lustre in the magnificent asylum
which he founded for the poor, the sick, and princi-
pally for lepers. It was a building, or rather a group
of buildings, which St. Gregory mentions as a new

town. He describes it as being a little out from the city, and says that it was a common treasury whereto the exhortations of St. Basil had gathered in not only from the superfluity of the rich, but also from the moderate means of the poorer classes. "It is there," adds the saint, "where sickness is even joyfully borne, where misery itself appears happy, and where charity is proved and tested." The fact is, that according to the plan marked out by St. Basil, this was to be an asylum for all those whose infirmities or poverty made them require assistance, and even for the reception of strangers. There were means of accommodation for all those persons who were necessary for the comfort and relief of the sick; physicians, nurses, people for carrying burdens, others to wait upon the infirm, craftsmen of all the different trades, and workshops for each particular craft. Theodoret remarks that the saint, who often visited the institution, took special care of the lepers, and that his charity for them went so far as to make him embrace them as his dear brothers, unmindful of his birth and station. This hospital was famous for long after, and was called the *Basiliad*, from the name of its founder. It must have been commenced about the year 371 or 372. Besides this one, there were several smaller asylums scattered over the country for the sick and infirm or the towns and villages, and these were subject to the inspection of the vicars.

His attention was no less directed to the providing of good pastors for the church, and to preserve the clergy in edifying regularity. He had several vicars to govern under him in the various districts of his diocese, and he sometimes brought them together at the feast of St. Eupsyquis. He renewed the canons of the Fathers, whereby the vicars were to apprise the bishop of those whom they wished to place in the rank of ecclesiastics, a rule which had been for some time neglected: and he ordered his vicars to send him the names of all the ecclesiastics, the village to which they belonged, by whom they had been admitted, what was their profession, and he decreed that those who should have been only admitted by priests since the first indiction, that is to say since 358, were to be excluded from the clergy by the vicars, who had, nevertheless, the power of retaining them if they were found worthy, after a careful examination. We may judge, by this exactness in the choice of the inferior ministers, with what extreme caution he acted, in the ordination of deacons and priests.

It was this attention which filled his church with excellent priests, and obtained for his clergy a reputation worthy of their bishop. This was manifested on a certain occasion when Innocent, bishop of a large city whose name is not given, being a considerable distance from Cesarea, though still in the east, wishing to have his successor appointed before his death

for he was very old, wrote to ask the saint for an
ecclesiastic whom he named, in order to make him
his successor.   St. Basil, who knew the importance of
a suitable choice, wrote in reply that the person mentioned had indeed many good qualities, but not so
many as to qualify him for filling his seat.   He then
cast his eyes over the priests of his city, and selected
one who was advanced in years, and whom he styles
a precious vessel and a child of the blessed Hermo-
genes ; a man capable of sustaining the weight of the
episcopacy, of a venerable aspect, fit to instruct with
becoming mildness those who opposed the truth,
grave in his manners, learned in the canons, pure in
his faith, strict in observing the rules of chastity and
the practices of religious exercises, and totally detached
from the things of this world.   This man he offered
to the bishop at what time soever he might require
him.   Whereupon it has been judiciously remarked,
that he would never have done so had he not had
other priests of similar virtue and similar merit.   He
had, in fact, amongst his clergy, Meleces, whom he
calls his co-operator in the duties of his office ; Pe-
menes, his own kinsman, of whom he makes honorable
mention in one of his letters ; Philosomus, spoken of
by Paladius in his Lausiac, as having generously confessed his faith before Julian the Apostate.

We shall not attempt to follow St. Basil in all that
he effected during his episcopate : it may be seen in

detail in the writings of St. Gregory Nazianzen, St,
Gregory of Nyssa, the historians of the church, and
lastly in the works of Hermant and de Tillemont.
Finally, after a long series of cares, episcopal solicitude,
instructions, dogmatic writings, contests with the heretics, toils and persecutions endured with heroic, fortitude; after a life ever pure, yet ever penitential, ever
crossed with contradiction and opposition and ever
adorned with resplendent virtue, the frequent maladies which he had suffered brought on that hour which
was to terminate this glorious career of sanctity.

In the year 377, the Goths, whom the emperor
Valens had received as friends in Thrace, and who
from Catholics had, consequently, become Arians,
took up arms against him, God having disposed it so
that they whose faith he had corrupted should be
made the instruments of his punishment. They defeated him near Adrianople, on the 9th of August in
the following year, and burned him in a cabin where
he had taken shelter. His death caused a great
change in the affairs of the church. Gratian, the
nephew of Valens, a prince full of zeal for the catholic
faith, and being already emperor of the West, now
succeeded to the throne of the East. He recalled all
the orthodox bishops who had been banished by his
uncle, and put a stop, as far as he could, to the dis-
turbances caused by the Arians. St. Basil thus saw
his desires accomplished, and, like the holy old man

Simeon, it seemed that he could ask of God to let
him depart in peace, since he had had the consolation
of seeing the commencement of that of the churcl.
That final favor was at length vouchsafed to him on
the first day of the year 379, and it was accompanied
by a new miracle equal to any yet performed by him;
though being scarcely half alive, he would go to the
church to take his leave of it, and to lend his assistance in the consecration of some of his most faithful
disciples, " to the end," says St. Gregory Nazianzen,
" that the altar might have those whom he had himself prepared for its ministry, and who had been the as-
sistants and co-operators of his priesthood.   The infer-
ence is that he ordained several of his ecclesiastics, and
appointed them to bishopricks within his jurisdiction,
profiting by the liberty which the death of Valens gave
to the church to fill with Catholic bishops those sees
which had none.

At length his final hour arrived, and multitudes of
the citizens thronged around his house, overwhelmed
with grief, each one feeling for his own loss.   It would
seem as though they sought by their tears and lamentations to retain the soul of their bishop within its
mortal tenement ; but choirs of angels were already
waiting for him who had so long sighed for their
company.   So, having given some last instructions to
those about him, he finished his mortal course with
hose words of our blessed Lord to his eternal Father

"Into thy hands I commend my spirit," joyfully
giving up his soul, in or about the fiftieth year of his
age.

One of the finest eulogiums that could be composed
for St. Basil, is given by St. Gregory in a few words:
it is that when he died he carried with him all that
he possessed of earthly things, for he left not even as
much wealth as would provide a decent monument to
cover his remains. But that did not prevent his
obsequies from being of the most magnificent kind.
The multitude of people who followed him to the
grave was prodigious: every one hastened to touch
his body or to secure a shred of the hem of his garment; the streets, the squares, the galleries, the
houses, to the second and third stories were filled with
spectators. Tears and lamentations mingled with the
sound of psalmody. The whole city was in mourning;
pagans, Jews, and foreigners mingled with the Catholics and citizens, even vieing with them in showing
honor to the departed prelate; finally, after a difficult
passage through the dense multitudes, the body of the
saint was deposited in the tomb of the bishops, his
predecessors.

. We must now return to St. Gregory Nazianzen,
from whom we have digressed in order to follow the
brilliant career of St. Basil. We left him in the solitude of Pontus with Cesarius. He was not permitted
to remain long there, being recalled by his father, and

he, too, had his full share of cares and tribulations.
On the one side, he was obliged to assist his father in
the government of his church, he being now very old,
and on the other hand, he had to advise and direct
his mother in certain domestic affairs, particularly the
succession of his brother Cesarius, who died in the
end of the year 368, or the beginning of 369. His
health was likewise very indifferent, and he was subject to severe fits of sickness, so that he was not without his crosses ; but then they are the appendages of
the friends of God.   St. Gregory bore them as became
his piety, till there suddenly came one which was the
less expected as St. Basil himself was the innocent
cause thereof, he having still but the glory of God in
view.   Cappadocia which, down to the year 370 had
formed but one province ecclesiastical and civil, was
then divided into two in the latter department.   Cesarea remained the metropolis of the first, and the city
of Tyanes became the capital of the second.   Anthymus, who was bishop of Tyanes, pretended that the
province was divided ecclesiastically as well as civilly,
and took unto himself the rights of a metropolitan
over the churches contained in what was called the
second Cappadocia.

St. Basil opposed him, and, in order to preserve his
diocese as it had been transmitted to him, he erected
some new sees, amongst others that of Sasimes, a
small town situated on one of the main roads of Cap

padocia, and there he wished to place St. Gregory
Nazianzen to defend it against Anthymus, who had a
design upon it. *St. Gregory, who loved peace and
tranquillity, and sighed only for retirement, was very
much grieved by this appointment, and only yielded
to St. Basil with a very bad grace, and at the special
bidding of his father; this was towards the middle of
the year 372. Going to take possession of his new
church, he found it in the hands of Anthymus, and
having no mind to wrest it from him by force, he
quietly retired to a mountain hard by.

He was not long to enjoy repose; his father conjured him to return, and he only obeyed on condition
that he was not to go to Sasimes, but merely to govern the church of Nazianzen under his father, without
any engagement for the future. He acquitted himself
of that duty with the zeal which might be expected
of him, until the year 374, when he lost his father,
who was nearly an hundred years old, and almost at
the same time, St. Nonna his mother, who was nearly
as old as her husband. Although he had intended to
return to his solitude immediately after their death,
he was prevailed on by the importunities of many
persons, and especially of Bosphorus, bishop of Colonia, to change his resolution. Still he would only
consent to govern the church of Nazianzen provision-
ally, and not as titular, (a measure which was not
without precedent,) until such time as the bishops

could select a fitting pastor for the flock, which he earnestly entreated them to do.

Finally, when he had been petitioning them for upwards of three years, alleging as a reason his broken health, which unfitted him to fulfill the duties of his office (and this he really believed for he had been even dangerously ill) ; seeing that his solicitations were ineffectual, he secretly retired to Seleucia, and it does not appear that Nazianzen had a bishop again till 381, when our saint himself returned, after the council of Constantinople, as we shall soon relate. Seleucia was the metropolis of Isauria ; the relics of the illustrious saint Thecla were religiously preserved there in a church bearing her name, whence it is that St. Gregory calls it *Seleucia of St. Thecla.* He made a long stay there, most probably till 379. It was there that, having renounced glory, riches, worldly expectations, and even science, taking no other nour- ishment than a little bread, he sought to rise above visible things in order to occupy himself solely with things celestial, and he tasted the innocent delights of a life remote from the troubles of the world. Still he found his cross even there, as well in the attacks of the heretics, as in the heavy sorrow which rent his heart to see the misfortunes brought by the Arians in 376 on the church of Cappadocia ; whereupon he wrote several letters to St. Gregory of Nyssa, predict- ing, however, the end of the persecution, which soon after took place, in consequence of the death of Valens. Gratian, who succeeded him, having commenced, as we have said, to give peace to the Church, our saint began to breathe more freely ; but the death of St. Basil, which soon after occurred, plunged him again into sorrow, all the greater because he could not even have the consolation of beholding his precious remains, not being yet quite recovered from his recent illness.

Gratian, having thus given peace to the Church, on 'he 19th of January, 379, he resigned the empire of the East to Theodosius the Great, a truly Catholic prince, and full of zeal for the promotion of religion. The point now was to re-establish the faith of Nice in Constantinople, where the Arians had so long made fearful havoc. Being absolute masters there, they had exercised their power to the full extent of their hatred, against the orthodox. There was no disgrace or no opprobrium too heavy to cast upon them. They were loaded with contumely and threats of every kind ; their wealth was taken from them, and their property confiscated ; they were sent into exile, and many of them, too, were publicly massacred, even bishops and aged men. It was only the Catholics who were bereft of liberty, and they found themselves exposed to all imaginable evils. St. Gregory also says that the church of St. Sophia, which was the principal church, might be called the devil's c tadel, seeing that he had

retired thither, and made it a garrison for his soldiers
There assembled the whole army of falsehood and the
legions of impure spirits, and the cohorts of the furies;
for this latter name might be well applied to the
Arian women, who were so carried away by fanaticism
that they became, as it were, so many Jezabels.

Nor was this the only evil which weighed down the
Imperial city. The Novations had several churches
there ; the heresy of the Macedonians, who denied the
divinity of the Holy Ghost, was making rapid progress ; the Apollonarists began to assume a formida-
ble aspect, and the Eunomians had a bishop there ; but
still the Arians were the most powerful. Thus the
true faith was almost buried beneath the fetid mass of
infidelity and heresy ; still it lived and flourished in
the hearts of a small number of the faithful, who
formed, as it were, a little flock without order, without
a pastor, without fence or inclosure to protect them.
The reputation of Gregory's learning and piety, which
had crossed the seas of Asia, and heightened by the
praise of St. Eusebius of Samosata, induced the Catholics of Constantinople to call him thither, their prayer
being seconded by the bishops of the adjacent districts,
and by those of Thrace, together with St. Meleces,
Bosphorus of Colonia, another bishop of Cappadocia,
named Theodore, and finally St. Basil had himself requested him to go there.   He was even blamed for so
long postponing his departure, as we see by the rea

sons which he gives in some of his letters for not having gone sooner to Constantinople.

He arrived there in 379, and the gift of miracles
followed him there, but his chief support was the
assistance of Jesus Christ, for whose glory he was to
contend. The manner of his entrance into that second
Rome proves this, as well as his humility. He says
that his purpose must have appeared no less extraordinary than that of David when he opposed Goliath ;
that there could be no man more contemptible in the
eyes of the world than he ; that he was not only a
stranger, but a native of a paltry hamlet ; that he was
bent with sickness and old age; his head bald, and
always bowed down ; his face unprepossessing, being
furrowed with the channels of his tears, emaciated by
his continued austerities, and withered with fear of the
judgments of God ; that his speech was rude and
unpolished, his garments of the humblest kind, and
that he had no more money than he had wings."

He was received, on his arrival, in the house of some
of his kindred, who were no less akin to him in the
spirit of piety. The Catholics, having no place wherein to assemble, a chapel was fitted up in the house
already mentioned, which in process of time became a
church of great grandeur and magnificence, through
the additions made to it by the Emperors. It was
called *Anastasia* or the *Resurrection*, because the true
faith, which had been all but extinct in Constantinople,

began there to revive. There it was that this great doctor vigorously opposed the heretics, preserved Catholics from the contagion of their errors, explained the doctrine of the church, and directed the people according to the laws of the Gospel.

He particularly warned the faithful against a snare laid for them by the heretics, which was the desire to penetrate with their own mind the sublimity of our mysteries, and to judge of their truth by human reason. Thence they piqued themselves on speaking in a captious and sophistical manner, by way of passing it off for elevation of mind, and seeking to dazzle the weak, they entangled them in their errors. They also spoke of religion in private and social meetings, at table during meals, and on all similar occasions. Nothing was more indecorous or more unseasonable; and it was also exceedingly dangerous, because the heretics were everywhere, and everywhere tried to insinuate their venom.

The saint thereupon set the faithful right, advising them not to enter into any disputes on the subject of religion, showing them that every one is not called upon to speak on such subjects, and that it should not be done at all times, in all places, nor before all sorts of persons, nor should any one seek to penetrate what is beyond the reach of human reason. He thereupon gave them this fair maxim :—" There are." says he, " occasions when we may listen ; there are others when we may speak ; but there are others when fear should hold us in suspense and prevent us from either speaking or listening. It is true that it is less dangerous to hear than to speak ; but it is far safer to withdraw altogether from the contest than to stay and listen." This was an excellent preservative against the conversation of the heretics ; but, lest it might be thought that he was unable to defend the truths of faith which he wished others to believe, he made four excellent discourses, explanatory of the doctrine of the church with regard to the Trinity, and completely annihilating the false reasoning of the heretics. It was these discourses which obtained for him the surname of the Theologian.

The principal object of his preaching was the defence of the faith, and the refutation of heresy. The state of the city required this ; but still he did not so entirely devote himself to it, as to neglect the morals of his own people. He gave them for a rule, that true piety did not consist in talking incessantly, and without proper judgment of the things of religion, but in observing the commandments of God, giving alms, practising hospitality, visiting the sick, praying, sorrowing for sin, mortifying the senses, repressing anger, moderating mirth, keeping guard on the tongue, subduing the body and the mind, &c. If the eloquence which he employed in his discourses were the fruit of his study of profane authors, he had ennobled it by

the reading of the sacred books, and, as he said him
self, by *the vivifying word* , which is that of the
cross.

People ran in crowds to listen, and they sometimes
even forced the balustrade of the choir in order to
hear him more distinctly. There were no heretics of
any sect whatsoever, nor even pagans, who did not list-
en to him with pleasure, some to imbibe his doctrine,
others attracted by his eloquence, and by all he was
heard with unqualified admiration.

But the most efficient preaching was that of his
example. He was rarely seen in public places ; he
stopped not to discourse on indifferent topics with
all sorts of people, and his conversation was always
grave and serious. Although he did not wish to refuse the invitations of those who asked him to their
houses, he would prefer at any time to displease them
by refusing, rather than avail himself too often of
their hospitality. He retrenched all useless visiting,
and usually remained at home, having no other conversation than his own. It was there that he passed the
nights, either in communing alone with Jesus Christ,
or singing psalms and hymns alternately with others.
He took great delight in prostrating himself before
God, and in his presence shedding torrents of tears
for his sins. He macerated his body by his austerities
and in the oblation of the august sacrifice of our altars,
he offered himself to God in union with Jesus Christ

What tended very much to gain for him the affection of the people of Constantinople was, that they saw in him neither precipitation, nor importunity, nor violence, nor ostentation, nor vanity; whereas they saw him, on the other hand, modest, humble, retired in his habits, and like a hermit in the midst of men, leading the life of a philosopher, but of a truly Christian one. Then the example of such eminent piety, together with his powerful eloquence, reduced the heretics to silence, and did much to promote the interests of religion. These effects were so much the more important there, because Constantinople was regarded as the link between the East and West, and as the source whence the faith spread abroad on every side.

It must not, however, be imagined that this favorable result was the effect of the plaudits which he received. They were the fruits of his patience and of his labors; and it was the will of God that such should be the crown of the persecutions he had to bear from the heretics. In fact, he had no sooner appeared in the city than all the sects, who had before been bickering amongst themselves, formed a grand junction to oppose him. They tore him in pieces in their sermons and in their speeches; and after having attacked him personally by calumny, they fell on his flock like raging wolves. Fanaticism even excited apostate monks, profligate women, imprudent damsels, and beggars whom their fury rendered truly pitiable; all these allies flocked to the *Anastasia*, at the time when baptism was being administered, which might be on the evening of Easter day—which in that year, 379, fell on the 21st of April—and penetrating even to the sanctuary, they profaned the altar by their sacrileges, dashed down the sacred vessels, and placed in the pulpit their own idol; that is to say, their bishop, Demophilus.   To these excesses succeeded wine, dancing, and works of darkness unfit to be named They directed all their insults against the saint himself and the ministers of the Church.   They threw stones at them, wounded some, and killed others; and one zealous Catholic was beaten to death with clubs in the midst of the city.   Nor did the persecution end there; every imaginable outrage was inflicted on the faithful, who were driven from their houses, and even from the solitudes wherein they had taken shelter. St. Gregory was apprehended as a malefactor, and brought before the prefects, who conspired with the people against him, and treated him very hardly, although without the consent of, and even contrary to the intentions of the emperors: but Jesus Christ protected him, and brought him forth gloriously from this severe trial.

The emperor Theodosius having at length arrived in Constantinople from Macedonia, on the 24th November, 380, greeted St. Gregory with the warmest tokens of esteem, and welcomed him to the Imperial city. In that first interview the saint solicited per-mission to retire from Constantinople; but the em-peror told him: "God makes use of my agency to grant you this church. The whole city demands it, and could not, it seems to me, be persuaded to any-thing else: the people are even disposed to compel me to this step, in case I refused; but they know very well that there is no compulsion necessary — they know that I desire it as ardently as they do them-selves."

The emperor sent a message on the same day to Demophilus, Bishop of the Arians, to know whether he would embrace the faith of Nice, and thus re-unite the people in the same belief; and upon his re-fusing to do so, he commanded him to give up all the churches, which were at once restored to the Catholics. The Arians had taken possession of them forty years before, when Eusebius usurped the see of the bishop, St. Paul, in 339. The faithful were loud in their applause for this act of Theodosius, and they thought they might safely venture to ask him for St. Gregory as their bishop, protesting that it was the greatest favor he could confer upon them. The saint, overwhelmed with fear, could hardly speak, so great was his terror lest the public clamor should succeed. He sent to beg the people to desist, repre-senting to them that the only thing then needful was to return thanks to God, and that every other matter could be postponed. The people admired his modesty, as did Theodosius himself, who at once gave him possession of the Episcopal house, the ecclesiastical revenues, and all the churches of the city. Gregory refused, on the first day, to ascend the Episcopal throne, but it seems that he was forcibly placed thereon some days after. The heretics were so exasperated against him that they sought to take his life. One young man did actually attempt to assassinate him, but God did not permit him to succeed: on the contrary, he became his own accuser, and threw himself at the feet of the saint, confessing the atrocious design which he had entertained. St. Gregory forgave him, and admitted him to his friendship—a fact which tended no little to increase the esteem and veneration in which he was held. Although he might have prosecuted the heretics, and brought them to condign punishment through the favor of Theodosius, he only made use of the mildest means to win them over, hoping that his moderation would mollify them, and render them more open to conviction. Such was the course pursued by him on an occasion so auspicious for the Catholics, and so mortifying to the Arians.

His conduct during the short time that he governed the Church of Constantinople, might well be proposed as a model to form the greatest prelates.

His disinterestedness in the administration of the revenues of his church was such, that he would never profit by them, although they were very great. He took particular care of the poor, of monks, virgins, strangers, prisoners, citizens, and of all persons who made a particular profession of piety. He commissioned certain persons to watch over the wants of these respective classes. He encouraged the singing of psalms, and of vigils spent in prayers and tears. Finally, by his cares, his exhortations, his discourses so full of apostolic force, his vigilance, his vows and lamentation before God, he drew down so many blessings on his people, that true faith and solid piety became triumphant in every state of life. Services so essential deserved to have been more fully recognized than they were by the bishops who met in the second œcumenic council; but God reserved the full reward of his servant's works for heaven.

The emperor Theodosius having put the Catholics in possesion of the churches of Constantinople, decreed by letter that all the bishops of his dominions should assemble in that city to confirm the faith of Nice, to establish a bishop in the Imperial city, and to secure that peace which it was beginning to enjoy.

One hundred and fifty bishops assembled there at that time, including those from Egypt and from Macedonia, who were not in time for the opening. St. Gregory was then formally established as Bishop

of Constantinople, to the great satisfaction of the emperor, of the holiest bishops of the council, and of
others also, at least in appearance. It was only he
himself who dissented; but he was placed on the
Episcopal throne, notwithstanding his earnest and
even tearful remonstrances. Nevertheless, there soon
after turned up some affairs amongst the bishops
which so disgusted the saint with his new dignity,
that he absolutely demanded permission to resign it
and withdraw from the city. We may see in the ecclesiastical writers his reasons for this step, but here a
detail of them would be a useless digression. Nec-
tairus was, therefore, installed in his place; and as a
deer escapes from the toils, so did Gregory escape
from Constantinople to refresh himself in retirement
after the labors he had endured, and the many trials
to which the envy of certain bishops had subjected
him. He went then to Nazianzen; but even there
repose was not all at once to be had. On the
contrary, he had the affliction of seeing that church in
the position of a ship tossed about at sea, without a
pilot—having no bishop, and being almost subjugated
by the Apollonarists, who were seeking to secure it
for themselves. He tried in vain to place a bishop
there, and being unable to take charge of it himself,
because of his bad health, he retired to the estate of
Arianzen, which he had inherited from his father, for
the purpose of restoring his health. This was about

the year 381 or 382 ; but even there he did not remain altogether idle, for he wrote several letters, especially for the support of the faith in Nazianzen, where the Apolonarists had gone so far as to establish a bishop of their own sect. St. Gregory was, therefore, forced by the chief men of that city and by the bulk of the people to go there himself, their love for him being now seconded by their fear of those heretics.

His humility, which never forsook him, joined to his many infirmities, made him regard the weight of that church as far beyond his strength; and he finally succeeded in obtaining the appointment of a bishop, Eulalius, his cousin and his disciple. Thus, seeing himself at last free to think only of God and his own salvation, he retired to the country for the remainder of his life. He there led a monastic life, with some other solitaries. " I live," said he, " amongst the rocks and surrounded by wild beasts ; my dwelling is a cavern where I live all alone ; I have but one habit, and I have neither shoes nor fire ; I live only on hope; I am the scorn and opprobrium of men ; I sleep only on straw ; I am clad in linen ; my floor is moistened with the tears I continually shed." All this did not prevent some persons, of the stamp of Maximus the Cynic (who had a philosophical exterior, and mocked he austerities of the true religious) from reproaching him for this mode of living, as though it had been too luxurious and too effeminate : to these he replied in a little poem which he composed on the occasion.

He indeed wrote several poems, for he excelled in poetry, and his verse is as much admired for its eloquence as his prose; but he employed this double gift only for the glory of God, to whom he had consecrated his affections and his works. Much more might be said of the deeds and writings of this great saint; but we refer our readers to those who have treated of his life at full length, and to the ecclesiastical historians, and pass on to his happy death. God had insensibly prepared him for his end by frequent ailments of various kinds, and he awaited it in his solitude calmly and hopefully. We know not the particular circumstances of his death. St. Jerome says that he was nearly three years dead when he made his catalogue of ecclesiastical authors, in 392; so he must have died in 389 or at the beginning of 390, in the sixtieth or sixty-first year of his age, if he were born. as it is thought, in 329.

The Latin Church celebrates his festival on the 9th of May. The Greeks honor him on the 30th of January, with St. Basil and St. John Chrysostom, and by himself on the 25th of the same month. His body was tranferred from Nazianzen to Constantiople by order of Constantine Porphyrogenetus, and deposited in the church of the Apostles, near the altar and the body of St. John Chrysostom,

It was conveyed thence to Rome, and placed beneath the altar of the church of the Virgin, on the *Campus Martius*, in 1505, whence Pope Gregory XIII. had it solemnly taken, on the 11th of June, 1582, to a large chapel which he had placed under the invocation of that saint, in the church of St. Peter, and the next day had it inclosed under the altar. The feast of this translation is marked in the Roman Martyrology on the 11th of June.

ST. JOHN CHRYSOSTOM,

ARCHBISHOP OF CONSTANTINOPLE, AND DOCTOR OF THE CHURCH.

From Socrates, Theodoret, and other historians.

THIS incomparable doctor, on account of the fluency and sweetness of his eloquence, obtained soon after his death the surname of Chrysostom, or Golden Mouth, which we find given him by St. Ephrem of Antioch, Theodoret, and Cassiodorus. But his tender piety, and his undaunted courage and zeal in the cause of virtue, are titles far more glorious, by which he holds an eminent place among the greatest pastors and saints of the church. About the year 344, according to F Stilting, Antioch the capital city of the

East, was ennobled by his illustrious birth. He had
one elder sister, and was the only son and heir of
Secundus, master of the horse, that is, chief com·
mander of the imperial troops in Syria. His mother,
Anthusa, left a widow at twenty years of age, contin·
ued such the remainder of her life, dividing her time
between the care of her family and the exercises of
devotion. Her example in this respect made such an
impression on our saint's master, a celebrated pagan
sophist, that he could not forbear crying out, "What
wonderful women have the Christians!" She managed the estate of her children with great prudence
and frugality, knowing this to be part of her duty to
God, but she was sensible that their spiritual instruction in virtue was of infinitely greater importance.
From their cradle she instilled into them the most
perfect maxims of piety, and contempt of the world.
The ancient Romans dreaded nothing more in the
education of youth, than their being ill taught the
first principles of the sciences; it being more difficult
to unlearn the errors then imbibed, than to begin on a
mere tabula rasa, or blank paper. Wherefore Anthusa
provided her son the ablest masters in every branch
of literature, which the empire at that time afforded.
Eloquence was esteemed the highest accomplishment,
especially among the nobility, and was the surest
means of raising men to the first dignities in the state.
John studied that art under Libanius, the most famous

orator of that age; and such was his proficiency, that even in his youth he excelled his masters. Libanius being asked by his pagan friends on his death-bed, about the year 390, who should succeed him in his school: "John," said he, "had not the Christians stolen him from us." Our saint was then priest. While he was only a scholar, that sophist one day read to an assembly of orators a declamation composed by him, and it was received with unusual tokens of admiration and applause. Libanius pronounced the young orator happy, " as were also the emperors," he said, "who reigned at a time when the world was possessed of so great a treasure." The progress of the young scholar in philosophy, under Andragatius, was no less rapid and surprising; his genius shone in every disputation. All this time his principal care was to study Christ, and to learn his spirit. He laid a solid foundation of virtue, by a perfect humility, self-denial, and a complete victory over himself. Though naturally hot and inclined to anger, he had extinguished all emotions of passion in his breast. His modesty, meekness, tender charity, and singular discretion, rendered him the delight of all he conversed with.

The first dignities of the empire were open to John. But his principal desire was to dedicate himself to God, without reserve, in holy solitude. However, not being yet twenty years of age, he for some time pleaded at the bar. In that employment he was drawn by company into the diversions of the world, and sometimes assisted at the entertainments of the stage. His virtue was in imminent danger of splitting against that fatal rock, when God opened his eyes. He was struck with horror at the sight of the preci- pice upon the brink of which he stood; and not con- tent to flee from it himself, he never ceased to bewail his blindness, and took every occasion to caution the faithful against that lurking place of hellish sirens, but more particularly in his vehement sermons against the stage. Alarmed at the danger he had narrowly es- caped, full of gratitude to God his deliverer, and to prevent the like danger for the time to come, he was determined to carry his resolution of renouncing the world into immediate execution. He began by the change of his garb, to rid himself the more easily of the importunities of friends: for a penitential habit is not only a means for preserving a spirit of mortification and humility, but is also a public sign and declaration to the world, that a person has turned his back on its vanities, and is engaged in an irreconcilable war against them. His clothing was a coarse gray coat; he watched much, fasted every day, and spent the greater part of his time in prayer and meditation on the holy scriptures: his bed was no other than the hard floor. In subduing his passions, he found none of so difficult a conquest as vain-glory; this enemy he disarmed by embracing every kind of public humiliation. The clamors of his old friends and admirers, who were incensed at his leaving them, and pursued him with their invectives and censures, were as arrows shot at random. John took no manner of notice of them: he rejoiced in contempt, and despised the frowns of a world whose flatteries he dreaded: Christ crucified was the only object of his heart, and nothing could make him look back after he had put his hand to the plough. And his progress in virtue was answerable to his zealous endeavors.

St. Meletius, bishop of Antioch, called the young ascetic to the service of the church, gave him suitable instructions, during three years, in his own palace, and ordained him Reader. John had learned the art of silence, in his retirement, with far greater application than he had before studied that of speaking. This he discovered when he appeared again in the world, though no man ever possessed a greater fluency of speech, or a more ready and enchanting eloquence, joined with the most solid judgment and a rich fund of knowledge and good sense; yet in company he observed a modest silence, and regarded talkativeness as an enemy to the interior recollection of the heart, as a source of many sins and indiscretions, and as a mark of vanity and self-conceit. He heard the words of the wise with the humble docility of a scholar, and he bore the impertinence, trifles, and blunders of fools in discourse, not to interrupt the attention of his soul

to God, or to make an ostentatious show of his eloquence or science : yet with spiritual persons he conversed freely on heavenly things, especially with a
pious friend named Basil, one of the same age and
inclinations with himself, who had been his most beloved school-fellow, and who forsook the world to embrace a monastic life, a little before our saint. After
three years, he left the bishop's house to satisfy the
importunities of his mother, but continued the same
manner of life in her ho.se, during the space of two
years. He still saw frequently his friend Basil, and
he prevailed on two of his school-fellows under Libanius to embrace an ascetic life ; Theodorus, afterwards
bishop of Mopsuestia, and Maximus, bishop of Seleucia.
The former returned in a short time to the bar, and
fell in love with a young lady called Hermione. John
lamented his fall with bitter tears before God, and
brought him back to his holy institute by two tender
and pathetic exhortations to penance, "which breathe
an eloquence above the power of what seems merely
human," says Sozomen. Not long after, hearing that
the bishops of the province were assembled at Antioch, and deliberated to raise him and Basil to the
episcopal dignity, he privately withdrew, and lay hid
till the vacant sees were filled. Basil was made bishop
of Raphanæa near Antioch ; and had no other resource in his grief for his promotion, but in tears and
complaints against h. friend who had betrayed him

into so perilous a charge. John, being then twenty-six years old, wrote to him in his own justification six incomparable books, Of the Priesthood.

Four years after, in 374, he retired into the moun-tains near Antioch, among certain holy anchorets who peopled them, and whose manner of life is thus described by our saint: They devoted all the morn-ing to prayer, pious reading, and meditating on the holy scriptures. Their food was bread, with a little salt; some added oil, and those who were very weak, a few herbs or pulse; no one ever ate before sunset. After the refection it was allowed to converse with one another, but only on heavenly things. They always closed their night-prayers with the remem-brance of the last judgment, to excite themselves to a constant watchfulness and preparation; which prac-tice St. Chrysostom earnestly recommends to all Christians with the evening examination. These monks had no other bed than a mat spread on the bare ground. Their garments were made of the rough hair of goats or camels, or of old skins, and such as the poorest beggars would not wear, though some of them were of the richest families, and had been tenderly brought up. They wore no shoes; no one possessed any thing as his own; even their poor necessaries were all in common. They inherited their estates only to distribute them among the poor; and on them, and in hospitality to strangers, they be-

stowed all the spare profits of their work. They all
used the same food, wore a uniform habit, and by
charity were all one heart. The cold words mine
and thine, the baneful source of lawsuits and animos-
ities among men, were banished from their ce.ls.
They rose at the first crowing of the cock, that is, at
midnight, being called up by the superior; and, after
the morning hymns and psalms, that is, matins and
lauds, all remained in their private cells, where they
read the holy scriptures, and some copied books.
All met in the church at the canonical hours of
tierce, sext, none, and vespers, but returned to their
cells, none being allowed to speak, to jest, or to be
one moment idle. The time which others spend at
table, or in diversions, they employed in honoring
God; even their meal took up very little time, and
after a short sleep, (according to the custom of hot
countries,) they resumed their exercises, conversing
not with men but with God, with the prophets and
apostles in their writings and pious meditation; and
spiritual things were the only subject of their entertainment. For corporal exercise they employed
themselves in some mean manual labor, such as
entertained them in humility, and could not inspire
vanity or pride: they made baskets, tilled and
watered the earth, hewed wood, attended the kitchen,
washed the feet of all strangers, and waited on them
without distinction, whether they were rich or poor

The saint adds, that anger, jealousy, envy, grief, and anxiety for worldly goods and concerns, were unknown in these poor cells ; and he assures us, that the constant peace, joy, and pleasure which reigned in them, were as different from the bitterness and tumultuous scenes of the most brilliant worldly felicity, as the security and calmness of the most agreeable harbor are, from the dangers and agitation of the most tempestuous ocean. Such was the rule of these cenobites, or monks who lived in community. There were also hermits on the same mountains who lay on ashes, wore sackcloth, and shut themselves up in frightful caverns, practising more extraordinary austerities. Our saint was at first apprehensive that he should find it an insupportable difficulty to live without fresh bread, use the same stinking oil for his food and for his lamp, and inure his body to hard labor under so great austerities. But by courageously despising this apprehension, in consequence of a resolution to spare nothing by which he might learn perfectly to die to himself, he found the difficulty entirely to vanish in the execution. Experience shows that in such undertakings, the imagination is alarmed not so much by realities as phantoms, which vanish before a courageous heart which can look them in the face with contempt. Abbot Rancé, the reformer of La Trappe, found more difficulty in the thought of rising without a fire in winter, in the beginning of his conversion, than he did in the greatest severities which he afterwards practised. St. Chrysostom passed four years under the conduct of a veteran Syrian monk, and afterwards two years in a cave as a hermit. The dampness of this abode brought on him a dangerous distemper, and for the recovery of his health he was obliged to return into the city. By this means he was restored to the service of the church in 381, for the benefit of innumerable souls. He was ordained deacon by St. Meletius that very year, and priest by Flavian in 386, who at the same time constituted him his vicar and preacher, our saint being then in the forty-third year of his age. He discharged all the duties of that arduous station during twelve years, being the hand and the eye of his bishop, and his mouth to his flock. The instruction and care of the poor he regarded as his first obligation; this he always made his favorite employment and his delight. He never ceased in his sermons to recommend their cause and the precept of alms-deeds to the people. Antioch, he supposed, contained at that time one hundred thousand Christian souls: all these he fed with the word of God, preaching several days in the week, and frequently several times on the same day. He confounded the Jews and Pagans, also the Anomæans, and other heretics. He abolished the most inveterate ab.ses, repressed vice, and changed the whole face of that great city. It seemed as if nothing could withstand the united power of his eloquence, zeal, and piety.

Theodosius I., finding himself obliged to levy a new tax on his subjects, on occasion of his war with Maximus, who had usurped the Western empire in 387, the populace of Antioch, provoked at the demand, mutinied, and discharged their rage on the emperor's statue, those of his father, his two sons, and his late consort, Flavilla, dragged them with ropes through the streets, and then broke them to pieces. The magistrates durst not oppose the rabble in their excesses. But as soon as their fury was over, and that they began to reflect on what they had been guilty of, and the natural consequences of their extravagances, they were all seized with such terror and consternation, that many abandoned the city, others absconded, and scarce any durst appear publicly in the streets. The magistrates in the mean time were filling the prisons with citizens, in order to their trials, on account of their respective share in the combustion. Their fears were heightened on the arrival of two officers dispatched from Constantinople to execute the emperor's orders with regard to the punishment of the rioters. The reports which were spread abroad on this occasion imported, that the emperor would cause the guilty to be burned alive, would confiscate their estates, and level the city with the ground. The consternation alone was a greater torment than the execution itself could have been. Flavian, notwithstanding his very advanced age, and though his sister was dying when he left her, set out without delay in a very severe season of the year, to implore the emperor's clemency in favor of his flock. Being come to the palace, and admitted into the emperor's presence, he no sooner perceived that prince but he stopped at a distance, holding down his head, covering his face, and speaking only by his tears, as though himself had been guilty. Thus he remained for some time. The emperor seeing him in this condition, carrying, as it were, the weight of the public guilt in his breast, instead of employing harsh reproaches, as Flavian might naturally have expected, summed up the many favors he had conferred on that city, and said at the conclusion of each article : " Is this the acknowledgement I had reason to expect ? Is this their return for my love ? What cause of complaint had they against me ? Had I ever injured them ? But granting that I had, what can they allege for extending their insolence even to the dead. Had they received any wrong from them ? Why were they to be insulted too ? What tenderness have I not shown on all occasions for their city ? Is it not notorious that I have given it the preference in my love and esteem to all others, even to that which gave me birth ? Did not I always express a longing

desire to see it, and that it gave me the highest satisfaction to think I should soon be in a condition of
taking a journey for this purpose ?"

Then the holy bishop, being unable to bear such
stinging reproaches, or vindicate their conduct, made
answer : "We acknowledge, Sir, that you have on
all occasions favored us with the greatest demonstrations of your singular affection ; and this it is that
enhances both our crime and our grief, that we should
have carried our ingratitude to such a pitch as to
have offended our best friend and greatest benefactor :
hence, whatever punishment you may inflict upon us,
it will still fall short of what we deserve. But alas !
the evil we have done ourselves is worse than innumerable deaths : for what can be more afflicting than
to live, in the judgment of all mankind, guilty of the
blackest ingratitude, and to see ourselves deprived of
your sweet and gracious protection, which was our
bulwark. We dare not look any man in the face ;
no, not the sun itself. But as great as our misery is,
it is not irremediable ; for it is in your power to
remove it. Great affronts among private men have
often been the occasion of great charity. When the
devil's envy had destroyed man, God's mercy restored
him. That wicked spirit, jealous of our city's happiness, has plunged her into this abyss of evils, out
of which you alone can rescue her. It is your affection, I dare say it, which has wrought them upon us,

by exciting the jealousy of the wicked spirits against us. But, like God himself, you may draw infinite good out of the evil which they intended us. If you spare us, you are revenged on them.

"Your clemency on this occasion will be more honorable to you than your most celebrated victories. It will adorn your head with a far brighter diadem than that which you wear, as it will be the fruit only of your own virtue. Your statues have been thrown down : if you pardon this insult, you will raise yourself others, not of marble or brass, which time destroys, but such as will exist eternally in the hearts of all those who will hear of this action. Your predecessor, Constantine the Great, when importuned by his courtiers to exert his vengeance on some seditious people that had disfigured his statues by throwing stones at them, did nothing more than stroke his face with his hand, and told them, smiling, that he did not feel himself hurt. This his saying is yet in the mouths of all men, and a more illustrious trophy to his memory than all the cities which he built, than all the barbarous nations which he subdued. Remember your own memorable saying, when you ordered the prisons to be opened, and the criminals to be pardoned at the feast of Easter : 'Would to God I were able in the same manner to open the graves, and restore the dead to life!' That time is now come. Here is a city whose inhabitants are already dead; and is, as it were, at the gates of its sepulchre. Raise it then, as it is in your power to do, without cost or labor. A word will suffice. Suffer it by your clemency to be still named among the living cities. It will then owe more to you than to its very founder. He built it small, you will raise it great and populous. To have preserved it from being destroyed by barbarians would not have been so great an exploit, as to spare it on such an occasion as now offers.

"Neither is the preservation of an illustrious city the only thing to be considered; your own glory, and, above all, the honor of the Christian religion, are highly interested in this affair. The Jews and Pagans, all barbarous nations, nay, the whole world, have their eyes fixed on you at this critical juncture; all are waiting for the judgment you will pronounce. If it be favorable, they will be filled with admiration, and will agree to praise and worship that God, who checks the anger of those who acknowledge no master upon earth, and who can transform men into angels; they will embrace that religion which teaches such sublime morality. Listen not to those who will object that your clemency on this occasion may be attended with, and give encouragement to he like disorders in other cities. That could only happen, if you spared for want of a power to chastise: but whereas you do not divest yourself, by such

an act of clemency, of this power, and as by it you
endear and rivet yourself the more in the affections
of your subjects, this, instead of encouraging such
insults and disorders, will rather the more effectually
prevent them. Neither immense sums of money, nor
innumerable armies, could ever have gained you so
much the hearts of your subjects and their prayers for
your person and empire, as will this single action.
And if you stand fair for being such a gainer from
men, what rewards may you not reasonably expect
from God? It is easy for a master to punish, but
rare and difficult to pardon.

"It will be extremely glorious to you to have
granted this pardon at the request of a minister of
the Lord, and it will convince the world of your piety,
in that you overlooked the unworthiness of his person, and respected only the power and authority of
that Master who sent him. For though deputed immediately by the inhabitants of Antioch to deprecate
your just displeasure on this occasion, it is not only
in their name that I appear in this place, for I am
come from the sovereign Lord of men and angels to
declare to you in his name, that, if you pardon men
their faults, he will forgive you your sins. Call to
mind then that dreadful day on which we shall all be
summoned to give in an account of all our actions.
Reflect on your having it now in your power, without
pain or labor, to efface your sins, and to find mercy at

that terrible tribunal. You are about to pronounce your own sentence. Other ambassadors bring gold, silver, and other like presents, but as for me, I offer nothing but the law of God, and entreat you to imitate his example on the cross." He concluded his harangue by assuring the emperor that if he refused to pardon the city, he would never more return to it, nor look upon that city as his country, which a prince of his humane disposition could not prevail upon himself to pardon.

This discourse had its desired effect on the emperor, who with much difficulty suppressed his tears while the bishop spoke, whom he answered in these few words: "If Jesus Christ, the Lord of all things, vouchsafed to pardon and pray for those very men that crucified him, ought I to hesitate to pardon them who have offended me? I, who am but a mortal man like them, and a servant of the same Master." The patriarch, overjoyed at his success, prostrated himself at the emperor's feet, wishing him a reward for such an action suitable to its merit. And whereas the prelate made an offer of passing the feast of Easter with the Emperor at Constantinople, he, to testify how sincerely he was reconciled to the city of Antioch, urged his immediate return, saying: "Go, Father, delay not a moment the consolation your people will receive at your return, by communicating to them the assurances of the pardon I grant them; I know they

must be in great affliction." The bishop set out accordingly; but, to delay as little as possible the joy
of the citizens, he dispatched a courier before him
with the emperor's letter of pardon, which produced
a comfortable change in the face of affairs. The
bishop himself arrived time enough before Easter to
keep that solemnity with his people. The joy and
triumph of that city could not be greater; it is ele-
gantly described by St. Chrysostom, extolling above
all things the humility and modesty of Flavian, who
attributed the whole change of Theodosius's mind,
and all the glory of the action, to God alone. The
discourse which Flavian addressed to the emperor,
except the introduction, had been composed by St.
Chrysostom, who recited it to the people to comfort
them, and ceased not strongly to exhort them to penance, and the fervent exercise of good works, during
the whole time of their bishop's absence. After this
storm our saint continued his labors with unwearied
zeal, and was the honor, the delight, and the darling
not of Antioch only, but of all the East, and his reputation spread itself over the whole empire. But God
was pleased to call him to glorify his name on a new
theatre, where he prepared for his virtue other trials,
and other crowns.

St. Chrysostom had been five years deacon, and
twelve years priest, when Nectarius, bishop of Constantinople, dying in 397, the emperor Arcadius, at

the suggestion of Eutropius the eunuch, his chamber-
lain, resolved to procure the election of our saint to
the patriarchate of that city. He therefore dispatched
a secret order to the count of the East, enjoining him
to send John to Constantinople, but by some stratagem; lest his intended removal, if known at Antioch,
should cause a sedition, and be rendered impractica-
ble. The count repaired to Antioch, and desiring the
saint to accompany him out of the city to the tombs
of the martyrs, on the pretence of devotion, he there
delivered him into the hands of an officer sent on
purpose, who, taking him into his chariot, conveyed
him with all possible speed to the imperial city.
Theophilus, patriarch of Alexandria, a man of a proud
and turbulent spirit, was come thither to recommend
a creature of his own to that dignity. He endeavored
by illegal practices secretly to traverse the canonical
promotion of our saint; but was detected, and threatened to be accused in a synod. Whereupon he was
glad to desist from his intrigues, and thus John was
consecrated by him on the 26th of February, in 398.
In regulating his own conduct and his domestic concerns, he retrenched all the great expenses which his
predecessors had entailed on their dignity, which he
looked upon as superfluous, and an excessive prodigal-
ity, and these sums he applied to the relief of the
poor, especially of the sick. For this purpose he
erected and maintained several numerous hospitals

under the government of holy and charitable priests,
and was very careful that all the servants and attendants were persons of great virtue, tenderness, compassion, and prudence. His own family being settled in
good order, the next thing he took in hand after his
promotion was the reformation of his clergy. This
he forwarded by zealous exhortations and proper rules
for their conduct, tending both to their sanctification
and exemplarity. And to give these his endeavors
their due force, he lived an exact model of what he
inculcated to others: but his zeal exasperated the
tepid part of that order, and raised a storm against
himself. The immodesty of women in their dress in
that gay capital excited in him sentiments of the most
just abhorrence and indignation. Some young ladies
seemed to have forgot that clothing is the covering of
the ignominy of sin, and ought to be an instrument
of penance, and a motive of confusion and tears, not
of vanity. But the exhortations of St. Chrysostom
moved many to despise and lay aside the use of purple, silks, and jewels. It was a far more intolerable
scandal that some neglected to cover their necks, or
used such thin veils as served only to invite the eyes
of others more boldly. Our saint represented to such
persons that they were in some respects worse than
public prostitutes: for these hide their baits at home
only for the wicked: "but you," said he, "carry your
snare everywhere, and spread your nets publicly in all

places. You allege, that you never invited others to sin. You did not by your tongue, but you have done it by your dress and deportment more effectually than you could by your voice: when you have made another to sin in his heart, how can you be innocent? You sharpened and drew the sword: you gave the thrust by which the soul is wounded. Tell me, whom does the world condemn? whom do judges punish? Those who drink the poison, or those who prepare and give the fatal draught? You have mingled the execrable cup; you have administered the potion of death: you are so much more criminal than poisoners, as the death which you cause is the more terrible; for you murder not the body, but the soul. Nor do you do this to enemies; nor compelled by necessity, nor provoked by any injury; but out of a foolish vanity and pride. You sport yourselves in the ruin of the souls of others, and make their spiritual death your pastime." Hence he infers, how false and absurd their excuse is in saying, they mean no harm. These and many other scandals he abolished. He suppressed the wicked custom of swearing, first at Antioch, then at Constantinople. By the invincible power of his eloquence and zeal he tamed the fiercest sinners, and changed them into meek lambs: he converted an incredible number of idolaters and heretics His mildness towards sinners was censured by the Novatians; he invited them to repentance with the

compassion of the most tender father, and was accustomed to cry out: "If you are fallen a second time,
or even a thousand times into sin, come to me, and
you shall be healed." But he was firm and severe
in maintaining discipline, though without harshness;
to impenitent sinners he was inflexible. To mention
one instance of the success of his holy zeal out of the
many which his sermons furnish; in the year 399, the
second of his episcopacy, on Wednesday in Holy
Week, so violent a rain fell as to endanger the corn,   •
and threaten the whole produce of the country.
Hereupon public processions were made to the church
of the apostles by the bishop and people, to avert the
scourge by imploring the intercession chiefly of St
Peter, St. Andrew, (who is regarded as the founder
of the church of Byzantium,) St. Paul, and St.
Timothy. The rain ceased, but not their fears. Therefore they all crossed the Bosphorus to the church of
SS. Peter and Paul, on the opposite side of the water.
This danger was scarce over, when on the Friday following many ran to see certain horse-races, and on
Holy Saturday to games exhibited at the theatre.
The good bishop was pierced to the quick with grief,
and on the next day, Easter-Sunday, preached a most
zealous and eloquent sermon, Against the Games and
Shows of the Theatre and Circus. Indignation made
him not so much as mention the paschal solemnity;
but by an abrupt exordium he burst into the most

vehement pathos, as follows: "Are these things to be borne? Can they be tolerated? I appeal to yourselves, be you your own judges. Thus did God expostulate with the Jews." This exclamation he often repeated to assuage his grief. He put the people in mind of the sanctity of our faith; of the rigorous account we must give to God of all our moments, and the obligation of serving him incumbent on us from his benefits, who has made for us the heaven and earth, the sun, light, rivers, &c. The saint grieved the more, because, after all, they said they had done no harm, though they had murdered not only their own souls, but also those of their children. "And how will you," said he, "after this approach the holy place? How will you touch the heavenly food? Even now ao ⊥ see you overwhelmed with grief, and covered with confusion. I see some striking their foreheads, perhaps those who have not sinned, but are moved with compassion for their brethren. On this account do I grieve and suffer, that the devil should make such a havoc in such a flock. But if you join with me, we will shut him out. By what means? If we seek out the wounded, and snatch them out of his jaws. Do not tell me their number is but small: though they are but ten, this is a great loss: though but five, but two, or only one. The shepherd leaving ninety-nine, did not return till he had completed his number by recovering that sheep which was lost. Do

not say, it is only one; but remember that it is a soul
for which all things visible were made; for which
laws were given, miracles wrought, and mysteries
effected: for which God spared not his only Son.
Think how great a price hath been paid for this one
sheep, and bring him back to the fold. If he neither
hears your persuasions nor my exhortations, I will
employ the authority with which God hath invested
me." He proceeds to declare such excommunicated.
The consternation and penance of the city made the
holy pastor forbear any further censure, and to commend their conversion. Palladius writes that he had
the satisfaction to see those who had been the most
passionately fond of the entertainments of the stage
and circus, moved by his sermons on that subject, entirely renounce those schools of the devil. God is
more glorified by one perfect soul than by many who
serve him with tepidity. Therefore, though every
individual of his large flock was an object of his most
tender affection and pastoral concern, those were particularly so, who had secluded themselves from the
world by embracing a religious state of life, the holy
virgins and nuns. Describing their method of life,
he says: Their clothing was sackcloth, and their beds
only mats spread on the floor; that they watched part
of the night in prayer, walked barefoot, never ate
before evening, and never touched so much as bread,
using no other food than pulse and herbs, and that

they were always occupied in prayer, manual labor,
or serving the sick of their own sex. The spiritual
mother, and the sun of this holy company, St. Nica-
reta, is honoied December the 27th. Among the holy
widows who dedicated themselves to God under the
direction of this great master of saints, the most illus-
tiious were the truly noble ladies St. Olympias, Sal-
vina, Procula, and Pantadia. This last (who was the
widow of Timasus, formerly the first minister to the
emperor) was constituted by him deaconess of the
church of Constantinople. Widows he considered as
by their state called to a life of penance, retirement,
and devotion; and he spared no exhortations or endeavors to engage them faithfully to correspond to
the divine grace, according to the advice which St.
Paul gives them. St. Olympias claimed the privilege
of furnishing the expenses of the saint's frugal table.
He usually ate alone; few would have been willing to
dine so late, or so coarsely and sparingly as he did;
and he chose this to save both time and expenses:
but he kept another table in a house near his palace,
for the entertainment of strangers, which he took care
should be decently supplied. He inveighed exceedingly against sumptuous banquets. All his revenues
he laid out on the poor; for whose relief he sold the
rich furniture which Nectarius had left; and once, in
a great dearth, he caused some of the sacred vessels
to be melted down for that purpose. This action was

condemned by Theophilus, but is justly regarded by St. Austin as a high commendation of our holy prelate. Besides the public hospital near his cathedral, and several others which he founded and maintained, he erected two for strangers. His own patrimony he had given to the poor long before, at Antioch. His extraordinary charities obtained him the name of John of almsdeeds. The spiritual necessities of his neighbor were objects of far greater compassion to his tender charity. His diocese, nay, the whole world, he considered as a great hospital of souls, spiritually blind, deaf, sick, and in danger of perishing eternally; many standing on the brink, many daily falling from the frightful precipice into the unquenchable lake. Not content with tears and supplications to the Father of mercies for their salvation, he was indefatigable in labors and in every endeavor to open their eyes; feared no dangers, no not death itself in its most frightful shapes, to succor them in their spiritual necessities, and prevent their fall. Neither was this pastoral care confined to his own flock or nation: he extended it to the remotest countries He sent a bishop to instruct the Nomades or wandering Scythians: another, an admirable man, to the Goths. Palestine, Persia, and many other distant provinces felt the most beneficent influence of his zeal. He was himself endued with an eminent spirit of prayer: this he knew to be the great channel of heavenly graces, the cleanser

of the affections of the soul from earthly dross, and
the means which renders them spiritual and heavenly,
and makes men angels, even in their mortal body.
He was therefore particularly earnest in inculcating
this duty, and in instructing others in the manner of
performing it. He warmly exhorted the laity to rise
to the midnight office of matins together with the
clergy: "Many artizans," said he, "watch to labor,
and soldiers watch as sentries; and cannot you do as
much to praise God?" He observes, that the silence
of the night is peculiarly adapted to devout prayer,
and the sighs of compunction: which exercise we
ought never to interrupt too long; and by watching,
prayer becomes more earnest and powerful. Women
he will not have to go easily abroad to church in the
night-time: but advises that even children rise in the
night to say a short prayer, and as they cannot watch
long be put to bed again: for thus they will contract
from their infancy a habit of watching, and a Christian's whole house will be converted into a church.
The advantages and necessity of assiduous prayer he
often recommends with singular energy; but he expresses himself on no subject with greater tenderness
and force than on the excess of the divine love, which
is displayed in the holy Eucharist, and in exhorting
the faithful to the frequent use of that heavenly sacrament. St. Proclus says, that he abridged the liturgy
of his church. St. Nilus assures us that he was often

favored with visions of angels in the church during the canonical hours, surrounding the altars in troops during the celebration of the divine mysteries, and at the communion of the people. The saint himself confidently avers, that this happens at those times, which he confirms by the visions of several hermits.

The public concerns of the state often called on the saint to afford the spiritual succors of his zeal and charity. Eutropius was then at the head of affairs. He was a eunuch, and originally a slave, but had worked himself into favor with the emperor Arcadius. In 395 he was instrumental in cutting off Rufinus, the chief minister, who had broke out into an open rebellion, and he succeeded the traitor in all his honors : golden statues were erected to him in several parts of the city, and what Claudian, Marcellinus in his chronicle, Suidas, and others, represent as the most monstrous event that occurs in the Roman Fasti, was declared consul, though a eunuch. Being placed on so high a pinnacle, a situation but too apt to turn the strongest head, forgetful of himself and the indispensable rules of decency and prudence, it was not long before he surpassed his predecessor in insolence, ambition, and covetousness. Wholesome advice, even from a Chrysostom, served only to exasperate a heart devoted to the world, and open to flatterers, who added continually new flames to its passions. In the mean time, the murmurs and indig

nat.. of the whole empire at the pride and avarice
of Eutropius were a secret to him, till the pit was
prepared for his fall. Gainas, general of the auxiliary
Goths in the imperial army. was stirred up to revenge
an affront which his cousin Trigibildus, a tribune, had
received from the haughty minister. At the same
time the empress Eudoxia, having been insulted by
him, ran to the emperor, carrying her two little
babes in her arms, and cried out for justice against
the insolent servant. Arcadius, who was as weak
in abandoning, as he was imprudent in choosing
favorites, gave orders that the minister should be
driven out of the court, and his estates confiscated.
Eutropius found himself in a moment forsaken by
all the herds of his admirers and flatterers, without
ore single friend, and fled for protection to the
church, and to those very altars whose immunities
he had infringed and violated. The whole city was
in an uproar against him; the army called aloud for
his death, and a troop of soldiers surrounded the
church with naked swords in their hands, and fire
in their eyes. St. Chrysostom went to the emperor,
and easily obtained of him that the unhappy criminal
might be allowed to enjoy the benefit of sanctuary;
and the soldiers were prevailed upon, by the cars
of the emperor and the remonstrances of the bishop,
to withdraw. The next day the people flocked to
behold a man whose frown two days before made

44

the whole world to tremble, now laying hold of the
altar, gnashing his teeth, trembling and shuddering.
having nothing before his eyes but drawn swords,
dungeons, and executioners. St. Chrysostom on this
occasion, made a pathetic discourse on the vanity
and treachery of human things, the emptiness and
falsehood of which he could not find a word emphati-
cal enough to express. The poor Eutropius could
not relish such truths a few days ago, but now found
his very riches destructive. The saint entreated the
people to forgive him whom the emperor, the chief
person injured, was desirous to forgive : he asked
them how they could beg of God the pardon of their
own sins if they did not pardon a man who then, by
repentance, was perhaps a saint in the eyes of God.
At this discourse not a single person in the church
was able to refrain from tears, and all things seemed
in a state of tranquillity. Some days after, Eutropius
left the church, hoping to escape privately out of the
city, but was seized, and banished into Cyprus. He
was recalled a few months after, and being impeached
of high-treason was condemned and beheaded, chiefly
at the instigation of Gainas ; in compliance with
whose unjust demands the weak emperor consented
to the death of Aurelianus and Saturninus, two principal lords of his court. But St. Chrysostom, by
several journeys, prevailed with the barbarian to
content himself with their banishment, which they

underwe..t, but were soon after recalled. As unjust
concessions usually make rebels the more insolent,
Gainas heieupon obliged the emperor to declare him
commander-in-chief of all his troops. Yet even when
his piide and power were at the highest, St. Chrysostom iefused him the use of any Catholic church
in Constantinople for the Arian worship. And when,
some time after, he laid siege to that capital, the
saint went out to him, and by kind expostulations
prevailed on him to withhold his design and draw
off his army. He was afterwards defeated in passing
the Hellespont; and fleeing through the country of
the Huns, was overthrown, and slain by them in 400.

This same year, 400, St. Chrysostom held a council
of bishops in Constantinople; one of whom had
preferred a complaint against his metropolitan Anto-
ninus, the archbishop of Ephesus, which consisted of
several heads, but that chiefly insisted on was simony.
All our saint's endeavors to discuss this affair being
frustrated by the distance of places, he found it
necessary, at the solicitation of the clergy and people
of Ephesus, to go in person to that city, though the
severity of the winter season, and the ill state of health
he was then in, might be sufficient motives for retard-
ing this journey. In this and the neighboring cities
several councils were held. in which the archbishop
of Ephesus and several other bishops in Asia, Lycia,
and Phrygia, were deposed for simony. Upon his

return after Easter, in 401, having been absent a
hundred days, he preached the next morning, calling
his people, in the transports of tender joy, his crown,
his glory, his paradise planted with flourishing trees;
but if any bad shrubs should be found in it, he
promised that no pains should be spared to change
them into good. He bid them consider if they
rejoiced so much as they testified, to see him again
who was only one, how great his joy must be which
was multiplied in every one of them: he calls himself
their bond-slave, chained to their service, but says,
that slavery was his delight, and that during his
absence he ever had them present to his mind, offering up his prayers for their temporal and spiritual
welfare.

It remained that our saint should glorify God by
his sufferings, as he had already done by his labors:
and if we contemplate the mystery of the cross with
the eyes of faith, we shall find him greater in the
persecutions he sustained than in all the other occur-
rences of his life. At the same time we cannot
sufficiently deplore the blindness of envy and pride
in his enemies, as in the Pharisees against Christ
himself. We ought to tremble for ourselves: if that
passion does not make us persecute a Chrysostom,
it may often betray us into rash judgments, aversions,
and other sins, even under a cloak of virtue. The
first open adversary of our saint was Severianus.

bishop of Gabaïa, in Syria, to whom the saint had
left the care of his church during his absence. This
man had acquired the reputation of a preacher, was
a favorite of the empress Eudoxia, and had employed
all his talents and dexterity to establish himself in
the good opinion of the court and people, to the
prejudice of the saint, against whom he had preached
in his own city. Severianus being obliged to leave
Constantinople at the saint's return, he made an
excellent discourse to his flock on the peace Christ
came to establish on earth, and begged they would
receive again Severianus, whom they had expelled
the city. Another enemy of the saint was Theophilus, patriarch of Alexandria, whom Sozomen, Socrates,
Palladius, St. Isidore of Pelusium, and Synesius, accuse of avarice and oppressions to gratify his vanity
in building stately churches; of pride, envy, revenge,
dissimulation, and an uncontrollable love of power
and rule, by which he treated other bishops as his
slaves, and made his will the rule of justice. His
three paschal letters, which have reached us, show that
he wrote without method, and that his reflections and
reasonings were neither just nor apposite: whence the
loss of his other writings is not much to be regretted.
These spiritual vices sullied his zeal against the An-
thropomorphites, and his other virtues. He died in
412, wishing that he had lived always in a desert,
honoring the name of the holy Chrysostom, whose

picture he caused to be brought to his bedside, and
by reverencing it, showed his desire to make atone-
ment for his past ill conduct towards our saint. This
turbulent man had driven from their retreat fou.
abbots of Nitria, called the tall brothers, on a ground
ess suspicion of Origenism, as appears from Palladius,
though it was believed by St. Jerom, which is maintained by Baronius. St. Chrysostom admitted them
to communion, but not till they had juridically cleared
themselves of it in an ample manner. This however
was grievously resented by Theophilus : but the empress Eudoxia, who, after the disgrace of Eutropius,
governed her husband and the empire, was the main
spring which moved the whole conspiracy against the
saint. Zozimus, a heathen historian, says, that her
flagrant avarice, her extortions and injustices, knew no
bounds, and that the court was filled with informers,
calumniators, and harpies, who, being always on the
watch for prey, found means to seize the estates of
such as died rich, and to disinherit their children or
other heirs. No wonder that a saint should displease
such a court while he discharged his duty to God.
He had preached a sermon against the extravagance
and vanity of women in dress and pomp. This was
pretended by some to have been levelled at the empress ; and Severianus was not wanting to blow the
coals. Knowing Theophilus was no friend to the
saint, the empress, to be revenged of the supposed

affront, sent to desire his presence at Constantinople, in order to depose him. He obeyed the summons with pleasure, and landed at Constantinople in June, 403, with several Egyptian bishops his creatures, refused to see or lodge with John, and got together a packed cabal of thirty-six bishops, the saint's enemies, in a church at Chalcedon, calling themselves the synod at the Oak, from a great tree which gave name to that quarter of the town. The heads of the impeachment drawn up against the holy bishop were: that he had deposed a deacon for beating a servant; that he had called several of his clergy base men; had deposed bishops out of his province; had ordained priests in his domestic chapel, instead of the cathedral; had sold things belonging to the church; that nobody knew what became of his revenues; that he ate alone; and that he gave the holy communion to persons who were not fasting: all which were false or frivolous. The saint held a legal council of forty bishops in the city at the same time; and refused to appear before that at the Oak, alleging most notorious infractions of the canons in their pretended council. The cabal proceeded to a sentence of deposition, which they sent to the city and to the emperor, to whom they also accused him of treason, for having called the empress Jezabel, a false assertion, as Palladius testifies. The emperor hereupon issued out an order for his banishment, but the execution of it was

opposed by the people, who assembled about the
great church to guard their pastor. He made them a
farewell sermon, in which he spoke as follows: "Violent storms encompass me on all sides; yet I am
without fear, because I stand upon a rock. Though
the sea roar, and the waves rise high, they cannot
sink the vessel of Jesus. I fear not death, which is
my gain: nor banishment, for the whole earth is the
Lord's: nor the loss of goods; for I came naked into
the world, and must leave it in the same condition.
I despise all the terrors of the world, and trample
upon its smiles and favor. Nor do I desire to live
unless for your service. Christ is with me: whom
shall I fear? Though waves rise against me: though
the sea, though the fury of princes threaten me, all
these are to me more contemptible than a spider's
web. I always say: O Lord, may thy will be done:
not what this or that creature wills, but what it shall
please thee to appoint, that shall I do and suffer with
joy. This is my strong tower: this is my unshaken
rock: this is my staff that can never fail. If God be
pleased that it be done, let it be so. Wheresoever
his will is that I be, I return him thanks." He declared that he was ready to lay down a thousand
lives for them, if at his disposal, and that he suffered
only because he had neglected nothing to save their
souls. On the third day after the unjust sentence
given against him, having received repeated orders

from the emperor to go into banishment, and taking all possible care to prevent a sedition, he surrendered himself, unknown to the people, to the count, who conducted him to Prænetum in Bithynia. After his departure his enemies entered the city with guards, and Severianus mounted the pulpit, and began to preach, pretending to show the deposition of the saint to have been legal and just. But the people would not suffer him to proceed, and ran about as if distracted, loudly demanding in a body the restoration of their holy pastor. The next night the city was shook with an earthquake. This brought the empress to reflect with remorse on what she had done against the holy bishop. She applied immediately to the emperor, under the greatest consternation, for his being recalled; crying out: " Unless John be recalled, our empire is undone :" and with his consent she dispatched letters the same night, inviting him home with tender expressions of affection and esteem, and protesting her ignorance of his banishment. Almost all the city went out to meet him, and great numbers of lighted torches were carried before him. He stopped in the suburbs, refusing to enter the city till he had been declared innocent by a more numerous assembly of bishops. But the people would suffer no delay: the enemies of the saint fled, and he resumed his functions, and preached to his flock. He pressed the emperor to call Theophilus to a legal synod: but that obstinate persecutor alleged that he could not return without danger of his life. However, Sozomen relates that threescore bishops ratified his return: but the fair weather did not last long. A silver statue of the empress having been erected on a pillar before the great church of St. Sophia, the dedication of it was celebrated with public games, which, besides disturbing the divine service, engaged the spectators in extravagances and superstition. St. Chrysostom had often preached against licentious shows; and the very place rendered these the more criminal. On this occasion, fearing lest his silence should be construed as an approbation of the thing, he, with his usual freedom and courage, spoke loudly against it. Though this could only affect the Manichæan overseer of those games, the vanity of the empress made her take the affront to herself, and her desires of revenge were implacable. His enemies were invited back: Theophilus durst not come, but sent three deputies. Though St. John had forty-two bishops with him, this second cabal urged to the emperor certain canons of an Arian council of Antioch, made only to exclude St. Athanasius, by which it was ordained that no bishop who had been deposed by a synod, should return to his see till he was restored by another synod. This false plea overruled the justice of the saint's cause, and Arcadius sent him an order to withdraw. He refused to forsake a church

committed to him by God, unless forcibly compelled
to leave it. The emperor sent troops to drive the
people out of the churches on Holy-Saturday, and
the holy places were polluted with blood and all
manner of outrages. The saint wrote to pope Innocent, begging him to declare void all that had been
done ; for no injustice could be more notorious. He
also wrote to beg the concurrence of certain other
holy bishops of the West. The pope having received
from Theophilus the acts of the false council at the
Oak, even by them saw the glaring injustice of its
proceedings, and wrote to him, exhorting him to appear in another council, where sentence should be
given according to the canons of Nice, meaning by
those words to condemn the Arian canons of Antioch.
He also wrote to St. Chrysostom, to his flock, and several of his friends : and endeavored to redress these
evils by a new council : as did also the emperor Honorius. But Arcadius and Eudoxia found means to prevent its assembling, the very dread of which made
Theophilus, Severianus, and other ringleaders of the
faction to tremble.

St. Chrysostom was suffered to remain at Constantinople two months after Easter. On Thursday, in
Whitsun-week, the emperor sent him an order for his
banishment. The holy man, who received it in the
church, said to those about him, "Come, let us pray,
and take leave of the angel of the church." He took

leave of the bishops, and, stepping into the baptistery,
also of St. Olympias and the other deaconesses, who
were overwhelmed with grief and bathed in tears.
He then retired privately out of the church, to prevent a sedition, and was conducted by Lucius, a brutish
captain, into Bithynia, and arrived at Nice on the
20th of June, 404. After his departure, a fire breaking out, burnt down the great church and the senate-
house, two buildings which were the glory of the city:
but the baptistery was spared by the flames, as it were
to justify the saint against his calumniators; for not
one of the rich vessels was found wanting. In this
senate-house perished the incomparable statues of the
muses from Helicon, and other like ornaments, the
most valuable then known: so that Zozimus looks
upon this conflagration as the greatest misfortune that
had ever befallen that city. Palladius ascribes the
fire to the anger of heaven. Many of the saint's
friends were put to the most exquisite tortures on this
account, but no discovery could be made. The Isaurians plundered Asia, and the Huns several other provinces. Eudoxia ended her life and crimes in childbed
on the 6th of October following, five days after a
furious hail-storm had made a dreadful havoc in the
city. The emperor wrote to St. Nilus, to recommend
himself and his empire to his prayers. The hermit
answered him with a liberty of speech which became
one who neither hoped nor feared any thing from the

world. "How do you hope," said he, "to see Constantinople delivered from the destroying angel of God, after such enormities authorized by laws? after having banished the most blessed John, the pillar of the church, the lamp of truth, the trumpet of Jesus Christ!" And again: "You have banished John, the greatest light of the earth:—At least, do not persevere in your crime." His brother, the emperor Honorius, wrote still in stronger terms, and several others. But in vain; for certain implacable court ladies and sycophants, hardened against all admonitions and remorse, had much too powerful an ascendant over the unhappy emperor, for these efforts of the saint's friends to meet with success. Arsacius, his enemy and persecutor, though naturally a soft and weak man, was by the emperor's authority intruded into his see. The saint enjoyed himself comfortably at Nice: but Cucusus was pitched upon by Eudoxia for the place of his banishment. He set out from Nice in July, 404, and suffered incredible hardships from heats, fatigues, severity of guards, almost perpetual watchings, and a fever which soon seized him with pains in his breast. He was forced to travel almost all night, deprived of every necessary of life, and was wonderfully refreshed if he got a little clear water to drink, fresh bread to eat, or a bed to take a little rest upon. All he lamented was the impenitence of his enemies, for their own sake: calling impunity in sin, and honor

45

conferred by men on that account, the most dreadful of all judgments. About the end of August, after a seventy days' journey, he arrived at Cucusus, a poor town in Armenia, in the deserts of Mount Taurus. The good bishop of the place vied with his people in showing the man of God the greatest marks of veneration and civility, and many friends met him there, both from Constantinople and Antioch. In this place, by sending missionaries and succors, he promoted the conversion of many heathen countries, especially among the Goths, in Persia and Phœnicia. He appointed Constantius, his friend, a priest of Antioch, superior of the apostolic missions in Phœnicia and Arabia. The letters of Constantius are added to those of St. Chrysostom. The seventeen letters of our saint to St. Olympias might be styled treatises. He tells her, "I daily exult and am transported with joy in my heart under my sufferings, in which I find a hidden treasure : and I beg that you rejoice on the same account, and that you bless and praise God, by whose mercy we obtain to such a degree the grace of suffering." He often enlarges on the great evils and most pernicious consequences of sadness and dejection of spirit, which he calls "the worst of human evils, a perpetual domestic rack, a darkness and tempest of the mind, an interior war, a distemper which consumes the vigor of the soul, and impairs all her faculties." He shows that sickness is 'he greatest of trials, a time

not of inaction, but of the greatest merit, the school
of all virtues, and a true martyrdom. He advises her
to use physic, and says it would be a criminal impatience to wish for death to be freed from sufferings.
He laments the fall of Pelagius, whose heresies he
abhorred. He wrote to this lady his excellent treatise,
That no one can hurt him who does not hurt himself.
Arsacius dying in 405, many ambitiously aspired to
that dignity, whose very seeking it was sufficient to
prove them unworthy. Atticus, one of this number,
a violent enemy to St. Chrysostom, was preferred by
the court, and placed in his chair. The pope refused
to hold communion with Theophilus or any of the
abettors of the persecution of our saint. He and
the emperor Honorius sent five bishops to Constantinople to insist on a council, and that, in the mean
time, St. Chrysostom should be restored to his see, his
deposition having been notoriously unjust. But the
deputies were cast into prison in Thrace, because they
refused to communicate with Atticus. The persecutors saw that, if the council was held, they would
be inevitably condemned and deposed by it, therefore
they stuck at nothing to prevent its meeting. The
incursions of the Isaurian plunderers obliged St. Chrysostom to take shelter in the castle of Arabissus, on
Mount Taurus. He enjoyed a tolerable state of health
during the year 406 and the winter following, though
it was extremely cold in those mountains, so that the

Armenians were surprised to see how his thin, weak body was able to support it. When the Isaurians had quitted the neighborhood, he returned to Cucusus But his impious enemies, seeing the whole Christian world both honor and defend him, resolved to rid the world of him. With this view they procured an order from the emperor that he should be removed to Ara- bissus, and thence to Pytius, a town situated on the Euxine sea, near Colchis, at the extremity of the empire, on the frontiers of the Sarmatians, the most barbarous of the Scythians. Two officers were ordered to convey him thither in a limited number of days, through very rough roads, with a promise of promo- tion. if, by hard usage, he should die in their hands. One of these was not altogether destitute of humanity, but the other could not bear to hear a mild word spoken to him. They often travelled amidst scorch- ing heats, from which his head, that was bald, suffered exceedingly. In the most violent rains they forced him out of doors, obliging him to travel till the water ran in streams down his back and bosom. When they arrived at Comana Pontica, to Cappadocia, he was very sick; yet was hurried five or six miles to the martyrium or chapel in which lay the relics of the martyr St. Basiliscus. The saint was lodged in the oratory of the priest. In the night, that holy martyr appearing to him, said, "Be of good courage, brother John; to-morrow we shall be together." The con fessor was filled with joy at this news, and begged that he might stay there till eleven o'clock. This made the guards drag him out the more violently; but when they had travelled four miles, perceiving him in a dying condition, they brought him back to the oratory. He there changed all his clothes to his very shoes, putting on his best attire, which was all white, as if he meant it for his heavenly nuptials. He was yet fasting, and having received the holy sacrament, poured forth his last prayer, which he closed with his usual doxology: Glory be to God for all things. Having said Amen, and signed himself with the sign of the cross, he sweetly gave up his soul to God on the feast of the exaltation of the holy cross, the fourteenth of September, as appears from the Menæa, in 407, having been bishop nine years and almost seven months.

His remains were interred by the body of St. Basiliscus, a great concourse of holy virgins, monks, and persons of all ranks from a great distance flocking to his funeral. The pope refused all communion with those who would not allow his name a place in the Dyptics or registers of Catholic bishops deceased. It was inserted at Constantinople by Atticus, in 417, nd at Alexandria, by St. Cyril, in 419; for Nestorius tells him that he then venerated the ashes of John against his well. His body was translated to Constantinople in 434, by St. Proclus, with the utmost pomp,

the emperor Theodosius and nis sister Pulcheria accom-
panying St. Proclus in the procession, and begging
pardon for the sins of their parents, who had unad-
visedly persecuted this servant of God. The precious
remains were laid in the church of the apostles, the
burying-place of the emperors and bishops, on the
27th of January, 438; on which day he is honored
by the Latins: but the Greeks keep his festival on the
13th of November. His ashes were afterwards carried to Rome, and rest under an altar which bears
his name in the vatican church. The saint was low
in stature; and his thin, mortified countenance bespoke
the severity of his life. The austerities of his youth,
his cold solitary abode in the mountains, and the
fatigues of continual preaching, had weakened his
breast, which occasioned his frequent distempers. But
the hardships of his exile were such as must have
destroyed a person of the most robust constitution.
Pope Celestine, St. Austin, St. Nilus, St. Isidore of
Pelusium, and others, call him the illustrious doctor
of churches, whose glory shines on every side, who
fills the earth with the light of his profound sacred
learning, and who instructs by his works the remotest
corners of the world, preaching everywhere, even
where his voice could not reach. They style him the
wise interpreter of the secrets of God, the sun of the
whole universe, the lamp of virtue, and the most
shining star of the earth. The incomparable writings

of this glorious saint, make his standing and most authentic eulogium.

In the character which St. Chrysostom has in several places drawn of divine and fraternal charity and holy zeal, we have a true portraiture of his holy soul. He excellently shows, from the words of our Lord to St. Peter, that the primary and essential disposition of a pastor of souls is a pure and most ardent love of God, whose love for these souls is so great, that he has delivered his Son to death for them. Jesus Christ shed his blood to save this flock, which he commits to the care of St. Peter. Nothing can be stronger or more tender than the manner in which this saint frequently expresses his charity and solicitude for his spiritual children. When he touches this topic, his words are all fire and flame, and seem to breathe the fervor of St. Peter, the zeal of St. Paul, and the charity of Moses. This favorite of God was not afraid, for the salvation of his people, to desire to be separated from the company of the saints, provided this could have been done without falling from the love of God; though he knew that nothing would more closely unite him forever to God, than this extraordinary effort of his love. The apostle of nations desired to be an anathema for his brethren, and for their salvation; and the prince of the apostles gave the strongest proof of the ardor of his love for Christ, by the floods of tears which he shed for his flock. From the same furnace of divine love, St. Chrysostom drew the like sentiments towards his flock, joined with a sovereign contempt of all earthly things; another distinguishing property of charity, which he describes in the following words: "Those who burn with a spiritual love, consider as nothing all that is shining or precious on earth. We are not to be suprised if we understand not this language, who have no experience of this sublime virtue. For whoever should be inflamed with the fire of the perfect love of Jesus Christ, would be in such dispositions with regard to the earth, that he would be indifferent both to its honors and to its disgrace, and would be no more concerned about its trifles than if he was alone in the world. He would despise sufferings, scourges, and dungeons, as if they were endured in another's body, not in his own; and would be as insensible to the pleasures and enjoyments of the world, as we are to the bodies of the dead, or as the dead are to their own bodies. He would be as pure from the stain of any inordinate passions, as gold perfectly refined is from all rust or spot. And as flies beware of falling into the flames, and keep at a distance, so irregular passions dare not approach him."

REMARKABLE ANECDOTES

APHORISMS AND EXAMPLES,

OF THE

EASTERN SOLITARIES.

Extracted from Ancient Ecclesiastical Writers.

From the Third Book of the Lives of the Fathers,
BY RUFINUS.

1. An ancient father said one day to his disciples, brethren, if we hate the repose of the present life, the pleasures of the body, the gratification of its appetites, and seek not the honor that is from man, the Lord Jesus will then give us the honor and glory of heaven, the repose of eternal life, and never ending joys with his angels.

2. An ancient father, who had many years led an anchoretical life in the heart of the wilderness, in the

practice of extraordinary abstinences and coi tinual labors, being one day visited by some of his brethren
after admiring his patience and perseverance, they
asked him how he was able to endure so many trials
and great sufferings as he was obliged to undergo in
that dry and frightful solitude? "O brethren," said
he, "all the labors and sufferings of the many years
I have been here are not comparable to one hour of
suffering in the flames of hell; wherefore, in order tc
escape them, we must cheerfully undergo the hardships and labors of the short time of our mortal life.
We must mortify ourselves here, that we may find
never-ending rest hereafter in the happy mansions of
the world to come."

3. The emperor Theodosius having heard that a
certain religious hermit lived a recluse and penitential
life in a small cell near the suburbs of Constantinople,
and being desirous to see this servant of God, he went
one day alone to his cell and knocked at the door.
The hermit having let him in, they, according to the
custom of the religious in their visits, first made their
prayer together, and then sat down. The emperor
inquired of him concerning the employment and
manner of living of the holy fathers in Egypt. They
all pray, said the hermit, for your salvation. Theodosius looked about to see what he had in his cell, and
discovering nothing but some dry bread in a basket,
he said: father, give me your benediction, and let us

refresh ourselves together. The hermit put some salt into water, and then soaked the dry bread in it, of which they made their meals together, and when they had done, he presented the emperor with a cup of water. Theodosius said to him : Do you know who I am ? God knows who you are, said the hermit. "I am Theodosius the emperor," said he, "and I came hither to be edified by you. O how happy are you solitaries, who being altogether free and disengaged from worldly cares and occupations, enjoy a calm and quiet life, having no other solicitude but for the salvation of your souls, nor any other thoughts but how to make yourselves worthy of the heavenly rewards of that life, and kingdom to come, that knows no end. But I, though born to the purple, and seated on the imperial throne, declare to you in truth, that I never sit down to my meals without having some cares upon my mind." Having said this, and testified a great deal of honor and esteem for the servant of God, he returned home. But the hermit suspecting, that in consequence of this visit from the emperor, a great number of all conditions, not excepting even the courtiers and senators, would be frequently coming to interrupt his devotion ; and being also apprehensive lest he should come at length to take a complacency in their isits, and in the honors they would show him, and thus fall, by degrees, into the nets of Satan, by pride and vain-glory, in order to secure himself from the

danger, he departed that very night, and made **the**
best of his way into Egypt, where he associated him-
celf with the holy fathers of the Egyptian deserts.

4. Amongst the many holy inhabitants of the
Egyptian deserts, there was an ancient anchoret named
Agatho, who was much admired for his extraordinary patience and humility. Some of the brethren,
with the design of putting his virtue to a trial, went
one day to his cell and complained of the scandal his
pride and self-conceit had given by his contempt of
others, setting them at nought, and taking the liberty
to censure and detract them, and all this, said they,
because, being yourself vicious and given to lewdness,
you think to disguise your own vices by charging
them upon others. The holy man heard all they
said without discovering the least emotion or disturbance of soul, or denying any part of the charge ; on
the contrary, casting himself at their feet, he confessed himself to be indeed a most grievous sinner, and
begged they would be so charitable as to intercede to
our Lord for a poor miserable wretch, loaded as he
was with so many crimes, to the end he might obtain
mercy and forgiveness for them through the assistance
of their prayers. But, said they, we must tell you
moreover, that some people say you are also a heretic.
O no, said the Saint, however wretched I am in other
respects, or how guilty soever I may be of innumerable other sins, I am not so great a wretch as to forfeit

my share in Jesus Christ by heresy; far be this thought from my soul! The brethren hereupon casting themselves at his feet, desired to know why he, who had suffered so many other false accusations, without the least emotion or resistance, showed so much horror and so great a repugnance at being accused of heresy? The man of God answered, that as to the other accusations, it was the part of humility to love to be despised, and be willing to pass for a grievous sinner; to bear also with reproaches and calumnies, after the example of Jesus Christ himself, who suffered in silence such treatment as this from the Jews for our instruction; but that there was a particular enormity and malignity in *heresy*, which is an obstinate opposition to the revealed truths of God, by means whereof the *soul* is separated in such manner from Jesus Christ, as to destroy *faith*, the very foundation of its salvation, and is given up as it were to the devil, without reserve; therefore, as no one ought to be willing to pass for an obstinate enemy of Jesus Christ, or of any of his revealed truths, so no one ought to be willing to pass for a heretic.

5. There was in a certain monastery of Egypt a monk named Eulalius, endued in an extraordinary degree with the grace of humility. As there were not wanting in that numerous community several lukewarm brethren, who had been guilty of frequent faults and negligences, particularly in breaking or de-

46

stroying the earthen vessels and other utensils of **the**
monastery, they were accustomed to lay all upon Eulalius, whom they found ever ready to bear the blame.
On these occasions the superiors often took him to task,
whilst he, instead of pleading *not guilty*, prostrated
himself before them, and begged pardon for his faults
and negligences. The rule of the monastery enjoined
penances for these faults, which he cheerfully underwent, even to the passing often two or three days together without eating. But as fresh accusations still
were brought against him, the ancient religious, who
were ignorant that he endured all this for the sake of
Christ, and for the exercise of his patience and humility, represented to the abbot, that as they found no
amendment in Eulalius, it became necessary to think
of taking some other course with him, since by his
negligences most of the utensils of the house were
already destroyed, and that there would be no keeping any thing whole in the monastery so long as he
remained amongst them. The abbot desired some
time to consider on the manner, and in the mean
while begging light of heaven to direct him, he learnt
from God in prayer the extraordinary merit, patience,
and humility of Eulalius, which his divine Majesty was
also pleased, not long after, to declare by a miracle, in
the presence of all the religious. Upon this the
brethren began to esteem him as a saint, and to honor
and praise him as such on all occasions, which became

so sensible a mortification to this humble servant of
God, that he heavily complained of his misfortune in
having now lost as he said, the treasure of humility,
which by the grace of Christ he had for so long a
time been laboring to acquire. At length, to fly from
all this honor and esteem, he withdrew himself privately by night from the monastery into a desert,
where he might be unknown to all men, and there
chose a lonesome cave for his habitation, in which he
spent the remainder of the days of his mortality, in
order to guard his humility from those dangers to
which it was before exposed in the midst of applause
and esteem.

6. A certain solitary having come one day to the
monastery of abbot Sylvanus, on mount Sinai, and
finding the brethren all at work, said to them : *Why
do you labor for the meat that perisheth?* did not
Mary choose the better part? The abbot turning to
his disciple Zacharias, bid him hand that brother a
book, and conduct him to an empty cell. When the
hour came at which the monks were accustomed to
take their meal, viz. about three in the afternoon, the
stranger was incessantly looking out, in expectation
that the abbot would send for him to the refectory ;
but finding that the hour had passed, and no one came
to call him, he went and asked the abbot if the monks
did not dine that day ? He told him, yes, they had
dined ; but that, as for his part, they had not sent for

him, because they understood he was a *spiritual* man, and had no need of *the meat that perisheth ;* whereas they, being carnal, and standing in need of food, were under a necessity of laboring for it ; but you have, said he, *with Mary, chosen the better part* by reading the whole day long, without requiring this *perishable* food The brother having begged pardon, and acknowledged his error, the abbot desired him to remember, that as Martha wanted the assistance of Mary, so Mary could not do alone, without the help of Martha.

7. Abbot Moses was accustomed to say, that as when a general besieges a city he endeavors to prevent any provisions being brought to the besieged, in order that through hunger and want the enemy may be obliged to deliver up their city ; so the man that desires to overcome his carnal passions, must starve them out by fasting and abstinence.

8. A certain religious man having received an injury from another, came to complain of it to one of the ancient fathers. The old man bid him, on this and the like occasions, to think with himself that the injury or affront was not levelled at him, but at his sins ; and advised him to sit down contented, and to say, *all this is for my sins.*

9. Another good brother, when any person affronted him, scoffed at him, or injured him, used to rejoice and to say : these are my friends who are giving me

an opportunity of advancing in virtue ; whereas they that extol and applaud us are rather our enemies according to that of Isaiah, iii. 12. : *O my people, they that call thee blessed, the same deceive thee, and destroy the way of thy steps.*

10. A brother having asked an ancient father to give him some short prescription by the observance of which he might be saved. The father told him the best prescription he could give for the security of his soul, was to overcome himself so far as to bear the greatest injuries and reproaches with meekness and silence.

11. St. Macarius used to say, *He that overcomes himself in all things is a monk indeed.* For if a person, whilst he corrects or rebukes another for his faults, suffers himself to be moved to anger, he is only gratifying his own passion. No one ought to run the risk of losing his own soul, whilst he pretends to save that of another.

12. The abbot Sylvanus, being asked by certain brethren to speak something for their edification, desired his disciple Zacharias to give them a lesson. The disciple taking off his outward habit, laid it upon the ground, and stamped with his feet upon it, saying : " No one can be a truly religious man who is not will ing to be trodden under foot in this manner."

13. Some of the brethren having extolled, in the hearing of St. Antony, the *virtues* of one of the monks,

the Saint, *putting him to a trial*, found that he could not bear an *injury ;* whereupon the man of God told him, that he resembled a building which had a beautiful front, but which lay open behind to thieves and robbers.

14. It was observed by one of the fathers, that all the labors of a monk are vain without humility ; for since humility, said he, is the forerunner of charity, as John the Baptist was the precursor of Christ, drawing all to him, so in like manner humility draws men to charity, that is, to God himself; *for God is charity,* 1 John iv.

15. St. Antony having seen one day in a vision the whole earth as a large field, covered on every side with the nets and snares of the enemy ; whereupon sighing, he cried out, who shall be able to pass over them, or escape them ? and immediately he heard a voice answering, *Humility alone can pass secure.*

16. A monk in a certain monastery having committed a fault, for which he was severely rebuked by the rest of the brethren, went away to St. Antony. The brethren having followed him thither in order to bring him back, they warmly upbraided him with his faults, in the presence of the Saint, which he, on his part, as warmly denied. The holy abbot Paphnucius, surnamed Cephala, happening to be present, put a stop to the contention, by the means of a parable : "Whilst I stood one day on the banks of a river, I

saw a man sunk into the mire up to his knees, when behold there came other men stretching out their hands, endeavoring to help him out; but instead of succeeding in their attempt, they pushed him further in, even up to the neck." St. Antony hearing the parable, and approving of the moral lesson it convey-ed, said of St. Paphnucius: "Behold a man who has the right notion of the way of reclaiming the faulty, and of saving their souls." The brethren presently took the hint, and begging pardon for their heat, re-ceived the brother in the tender bowels of the mercy of Jesus Christ.

17. St. Pemen, alias Pastor, gave it as an invariable rule to his disciples: "Never to do their own will, but rather humble themselves to do the will of their neigh-bors."

18. A certain anchoret, who dwelt in a cave not far distant from a religious community in great absti-nence and sanctity of life, being one day visited by some of the monks, they prevailed on him to eat be fore his usual time, and then asked him if it was no pain or trouble to him to be put out of his way, by eating contrary to his custom? "No," replied he, " nothing gives me pain or trouble but following my own will."

19. The holy abbot Agatho coming one day into the neighboring city to sell his work, found a certain stranger lying in a bye corner very sick, without any

one to take care of him ; the servant of God, on be·
holding so great an object of charity, instead of return·
ing back to the wilderness, hired a lodging in the city,
to which he carried the sick man, and attended on
him for the space of four months, working in the mean
time with his own hands, in order to procure for him
all necessaries, aid, and comfort; after which, the sick
man being now perfectly recovered, the Saint returned
back again to his cell.

20. An ancient servant of God, on seeing his disciple sick, bid him be of good comfort, and return thanks
to God for this visitation : " For," said he, " if thou
art but iron, the *fire* will serve to take the rust away
from thee ; and if thou art gold, it will refine thee, and
purify thee.   Resign thyself then, my dear brother ;
for since it hath pleased God to send thee this sick·
ness, who art thou that thou shouldest grieve or re-
pine at the accomplishment of his will ? O rather suffer all with patience and resignation, and let thy only
prayer be, that God would deal with thee according to
his pleasure."

21. An ancient religious, who was accustomed to be
visited with sickness, happening to pass one whole
year without any illness, he wept and grieved exceedingly, saying, " Lord, thou hast forsaken me, for thou
hast not once visited me this year." O what a just
notion he must have had of the inestimable value of
patient sufferings.

22 When the holy abbot Agatho was drawing near to his end, and had lain for the space of three days with his eyes fixed, in silence, some of the brethren touching him, said : "Father, where are you now?" He answered, "1 am standing before the judgment seat of God."—" Why then," said they, " are you afraid?" "According to the utmost of my power," replied he, " I have always endeavored to keep the commandments of my God ; but being a poor frail mortal, how do I know whether my works are pleasing to him or not?" "But do you not trust," said they, " that they are pleasing to him?" "I dare not trust to my works," said he, " in his sight ; for the judgment of God is very different from the judgment of men."

23. A certain brother having asked one of the fathers how the soul might attain to perfect humility : he answered, " by thinking only on her own evils, and not on those of others."

24. Nothing gives so much pleasure to the enemy, said the abbot Pemen, as when a person will not discover his temptations to his superior or director.

25. A certain father observed, that as the flies cannot come near a pot that is boiling hot, but only rest on such things as are neither hot nor cold, and there deposit their maggosts ; so the devils are kept at a distance by such religious as are quite fervent in the love and service of God, but have so great a power

over such as are but lukewarm, as to defile and cor·
rupt them with sin.

26. An ancient father gave the following lesson to
his disciple: " Think every day," said he, " that the
hour of thy death is at hand, and as if thou wert
already shut up in thy tomb, be not solicitous abou
this world. Let the fear of God continually abide
with thee. Believe thyself to be inferior to every one.
Speak no evil of any one because God knows all
things; and be at peace with all men, and the Lord
shall at all times give rest to thy soul."

27. Abbot John used to say, that a religious in his
cell ought to resemble one sitting under a tree; for as
the latter, on seeing any wild beast or serpent coming
towards him, climbs up the tree, that he may get out
of their reach; so the former, on perceiving any evil
thoughts approaching, ought to ascend up to God by
the tree of prayer.

28. Some of the brethren coming one day to visit
the holy abbot Lucius, he inquired of them what kind
of work, they followed? They answered; they did
not work, but, according to the Apostles, *prayed without ceasing.* "But do you not eat and sleep," said the
father, "and who prays for you then?" To which
having made no reply, "Now, I will tell you," said
he, "the manner in which I endeavor to *pray withou
ceasing,* and yet never fail to work with my hands.
Whilst I am making baskets, or cords, or the like, I

say to my God : Have mercy on me, O God, *according to thy great mercies ; and according to the multitude of thy tender mercies blot out my iniquity.* Thus, when I have finished my work, I am enabled to give some part of the price of it to the poor servants of Christ, to engage them thereby to pray for the forgiveness of my sins, even whilst I am eating or sleeping ; and thus they by praying for me, help to make my prayer continual, and without ceasing."

29. A certain young man, desirous to embrace a monastic life, was prevented from so doing for some time by his mother ; but as he still persevered in begging her to let him go, by often repeating that he was resolved to save his soul, she at length consented to his entering into a monastery. Being admitted to the habit, although an utter stranger to the spirit of religion, he led for many years a very tepid and negligent course of life. His mother having in the mean time died, and he soon after falling grievously sick, lay for some time in a trance, as if dead, in which he seemed to be carried before the judgment seat of God, where he met his mother amongst others expecting their sentence. " How now, my son," said she to him, " art thou also brought hither, to receive with us the sentence of damnation ? What is become of that specious determination of thine, which thou so often repeatedst, that thou wast *resolved* to save thy soul ?" The horror and confusion that oppressed him, upon

hearing this reproach from his mother, was so inexpressible, that he seemed to himself to stand, as it
were, upon the brink of hell, till he heard a voice, ordering that he should be sent back again, as not being
the person called for, and that such another of a
neighboring monastery, that was of the same name,
should be brought thither. Hereupon, having come
to himself, he related to those about him all he had
seen and heard, and desired that one of them would
instantly go to the neighboring monastery and inquire whether the brother alluded to was departed
this life, and being informed that he was just then
dead, they were confirmed in their belief of the truth
of what he had related. As to this young monk, no
sooner was he recovered from his sickness, than he
shut himself up in his cell, and applied himself with
such diligence to the care of his salvation, as to think
now of nothing else, but to weep night and day, and
do penance for his former negligences and sins; and
although some of the brethren advised him to be
more moderate in his tears and other penances, lest
the excess of his compunction might prove prejudicial
to his health, he nevertheless persevered in his penitential labors to the end, telling them upon these occasions: "If I could not bear the reproach which I
heard from my mother, how shall I be able to endure
the reproaches of Christ and his angels at the day of
judgment?"

80. A certain monk in the deserts of Egypt, having had a sister that followed a wicked course of life in the city, where she enticed many into sin, his brethren persuaded him to go in search of her, in order to reclaim her from her wickedness, and rescue her soul, as well as the souls of many others who were ensnared by her beauty, from the paths that lead to eternal perdition. When he came near the place where she dwelt, one who knew him, ran and told her that her brother was come from the desert to see her. Upon hearing this she immediately left her company, and going out with joy to meet him, offered to salute him ; but he keeping at a distance, earnestly besought her to have pity on her soul, expatiating on the dreadful state of life in which she was engaged, and the dismal consequences she had to apprehend for eternity, if she did not immediately return to God. This exhortation he delivered in so nervous and pathetic a manner, that, seized with dread and horror, she asked him, trembling, whether there remained any hopes of salvation for her, and whether it was not now too late for her to think of returning to God ? He assured her it was not, provided she would be quite in earnest in her application to the throne of divine mercy, by the practice of true penance. Hereupon, casting herself at his feet, she begged that he would take her along with him into the desert, where she might do penance for her sins. Go then, said he, and cover

your head (for she had run forth to meet him bareheaded), and then come along with me. O brother,
said she, let us make no delay; is it not better for me
to suffer the disgrace of going bareheaded, than to
enter any more into a house that has been the shop
of my iniquities? They therefore departed with speed
towards the desert, the brother preaching penance to
her on their way thither; till observing some of the
brethren coming towards them, he desired her to step
aside, and keep at some distance, for fear of any one's
taking scandal at seeing him in the company of a woman; for every one, said he, don't know that your are
my sister. She did so: and as soon as the brethren
had passed by, he went in search of her, and found
her lying dead on the ground, with her feet all bloody,
for she had walked the whole way barefoot. Having
lamented her death, he went and related all that had
happened to the ancient religious. Whilst these servants of God were at a loss what judgment they
should make with regard to her soul, dying as she
did, so shortly after so sinful a life, without any time
to do penance, one of them learnt by revelation, that
she had forsaken all she had in the world, and been
solicitous for nothing but the healing of the wounds
of her soul, in a word, as she had so bitterly wept, and
grievously lamented her sins, the divine goodness had
accepted her penance, and shown her mercy.

From the fifth Book of the Lives of the Fathers, translated from the Greek of an ancient ecclesiastical Writer into Latin, by Pelagius, *Deacon of Rome, who was made Pope, Anno* 558

31. WHEN the holy abbot John, surnamed the Dwarf, drew near his end, his disciples entreated him to leave them, by way of legacy, some short wholesome lesson of christian perfection, he sighed and said to them: "I never followed my own will, nor did I ever teach any other what I had not first practised myself.

32. Abbot Sisois being asked which was the best way to obtain peace and rest for the soul, he replied: "Be contemptible in your own eyes—cast pleasures behind your back—be free from all earthly cares, and you shall assuredly find rest."

33. Another holy man prescribed for this end the following precepts: "Pray incessantly to God that he would grant you compunction and humility;—think always on your own sins, and do not presume to judge others;—be subject and obedient to all;—avoid familiarity with women, boys, or heretics;—place no confidence whatever in yourselves;—restrain your tongue and your sensual appetite;—contend with no man;—contradict no one in discourse, and your mind shall be at peace."

34. A certain brother came to visit abbot Moses in the desert of Scete, in order to learn of him the way to perfection, " Go," said the Saint, " and keep thyself retired and recollected in thy cell, and thy cell shall teach thee all things."

35. Some brethren going from Scete to visit St. Antony, entered into a boat that was to convey them part of the way up the Nile, in which they found a strange old man, who was also going to St. Antony. Whilst they were entertaining each other, during their passage, with discourses upon different subjects, the old man sat by himself in silence and recollection. Finding, when they came to land, that the old man was also going to St. Antony, they went along with him. St. Antony, on their arrival, told them they had met with a good companion in that servant of God; and you, said he, father, addressing himself to the old man, have found them good company. "I believe," replied he, " that they are good; but having no door to their dwelling, whoever pleases goes into the stable, and takes out the beast to ride upon it;" alluding to their want of recollection, and setting no guard upon their tongue, but uttering whatever came uppermost in their mind.

36. An ancient religious seeing another laugh, said— " How can you laugh, since we must by and by appear before the great Lord of heaven and earth, to give a strict account of our whole lives?"

37. A certain gentleman came one day to the church of the wilderness of Scete with a bag of money, which he desired the priest, the superior, to distribute amongst the brethren. The priest told him they did not want it; but as the gentleman became very pressing, and would not be content except he would receive it, he put the money into a basket, and setting it in the entrance of the church cried out to the brethren: *if any one wants, let* him here *take what he wants:* but so far from touching it, some of them would not so much as look on it. The superior then addressing the gentleman, said: "our Lord, Sir has accepted of your offering, go now and give it to the poor; and thus he dismissed him, much edified with their disinterestedness."

38. Another brought a sum of money to a brother, who was a leper, saying: keep this for your own use, because you are old and infirm. The old man answered: "would you then deprive me, Sir, of my nursing father, who has fed me threescore years? Behold for so long a time, notwithstanding my infirmity, I have never been in want; for God has always provided for me, therefore I cannot distrust him now."

39. The brethren having desired one of the ancient fathers to remit something of his great labors and austerities, he answered: "believe me, my children, I am of opinion, that Abraham himself when he saw the greatness of the eternal rewards of heaven, was sorry

he had not labored more than he did whilst he remained here upon earth."

40. As a certain hermit, who dwelt in a cell near the wilderness, at the distance of twelve miles from any water, was one day going for water, he found himself so much exhausted and tired with the journey, that he began to blame himself for taking so much unnecessary pains, and to think of changing his abode, and building himself a cell near the spring. Whilst he had this thought in his mind, he heard one behind him numbering his steps; and turning about, he saw an angel, who told him he was commissioned from heaven to take an exact account of his laborious steps, which should all be hereafter rewarded. This vision encouraged the good old man, and made him not only give up his design of fixing his habitation near the water, but also determined him to remove his cell to a still further distance, since the divine goodness was pleased to reward all his steps in so bountiful a manner.

41. There was an ancient hermit in Thebais, who dwelt in a cave, together with a virtuous young man, his disciple. It was his custom to deliver an exhortation to the young hermit every evening for his instruction, direction, and progress in virtue and piety, and after spending some time together in prayer, the old man gave him his blessing, and sent him to bed. It happened one day, when the servants of God had en-

tertained some visitors with discourses of piety till a late hour, that after their departure, whilst he was making his exhortation, as usual, to his disciple, he fell fast asleep. The brother waited in expectation of the father's awaking, that they might make their prayer, according to custom, before he went to bed: but the old man slept on so sound, as not to awake till after midnight. In the mean time the young man, finding he slept so long, and being wearied and sleepy himself, was strongly tempted to leave him and retire to bed: but he resisted the temptation, and continued to remain with him. Shortly after the temptation returned, and became very troublesome to him; but he again got the better of it, and drove it away: and in this manner was he violently assaulted seven different times, but still overcame the temptation, and forced himself to stay till his master awaked. After midnight the father awaking, and finding the young disciple with him, asked him why he did not go to bed? Because, replied he, you did not discharge me. Why then, said the father did you not awake me? I could not presume, said he, to disturb you. Wherefore, it being now midnight rising up, they began their matins together, and when they had finished, the father sent him to take his rest. Whilst the old man was sitting afterwards by himself, he fell into a trance or ecstasy, when a stranger pointed out to him a glorious palace, in which was placed a throne, and over the throne

seven crowns, telling him that they were destined by
our Lord as a reward for the virtue and piety of his
disciple; and that as to the seven crowns, he had purchased them that very night. The father having asked
him in the morning what he had done in the night?
he answered, nothing particular; but as he insisted
upon his telling him all that had passed, even to his
very thoughts, he at length assured him he knew of
nothing whatever, except that he had been seven times
strongly tempted to leave him whilst he continued
asleep, and to retire to bed; but as he had not discharged him, according to custom, he had forced himself to stay : hence the father was given to understand,
that every victory over one's self purchases a crown
from God, and how much it imports to overcome ourselves, even in small matters.

42. St. Antony being told one day of a young religious man who had been already so far favored with
miraculous gifts, that the very wild beasts of the desert obeyed him. The Saint, apprehending some ostentation and pride in the manner of his proceeding,
said, he seems to resemble a ship richly laden, which
is in danger of being shipwrecked before it reaches the
haven. Not long after, the Saint being in company
with some of his disciples, began all on a sudden to
weep and lament, and being asked the reason, he exclaimed, Oh ! a great pillar of the church is just now
fallen ; go ye and look after such a one, naming the

young religious man. They went and found him in a most melancholy way, for having just then committed a mortal sin ; but he begged they would desire their holy father to obtain for him by his prayers, a reprieve of ten days, that in that time he might make satisfaction for his crime. But this was not granted him, for within five days he was called out of this life.

43. When a certain brother came one day to visit the holy abbot Serapion, he begged of him, according to the custom of the ancient religious in their visits, to give out the prayer which was to be made when they first met ; which he refused, saying he was a poor sinner, and unworthy to wear the religious habit. In like manner, when the Saint offered to wash his feet, according to the custom, he would not permit him, still alledging his great unworthiness. The holy man, after having entertained him at table with what his cell could afford, dismissed him with this charitable advice: "My son, if you desire to make due progress in religion, return to your cell, and there, attending to God and yourself, employ yourself in working with your hands ; for coming abroad in this manner is not so good for you as it would be to remain at home." The brother on hearing these words was so much disturbed and offended, as to discover his displeasure and resentment by the change of his countenance ; which the holy abbot observing, said to him : " A little while ago you said you was a poor sinner, and accuse I your-

self as one who were not worthy to tread upon the earth, how comes it then that you are so much disturbed at the charitable admonition I have given you? If you have a real desire to be humble, you must learn to bear patiently the things that others lay upon you, and not be ever saying reproachful things of yourself which you would not be willing another should believe of you." The brother having acknowledged his fault departed, highly edified with the lessons he received from the Saint.

44. When the holy abbot Moses being told that the judge of the province, who had heard of his eminent sanctity, was coming to visit him in his cell in the desert of Scete, the man of God to shun this visit left his cell, and retired towards the marsh. In his way he met the judge with his train, who not knowing him, inquired of him where the cell of the abbot Moses was? Why do you inquire, said he, after that worthless wretch? He is one that is void both of sense and religion. Whereupon the judge went to the church, and told the clergy that he came into the desert on purpose to visit abbot Moses, and to be edified by his conversation, but that he had met with an old man who had given him a vile character. Pray, sir, said they, what sort of a person was he who gave so bad a character of that holy man? A tall, black man, said the judge, with his habit very much worn. It was abbot Moses himself, said they, who spoke to you

of himself, to avoid being visited and honored by you.
Upon hearing of which the judge departed very much
edified with the Saint's humility. This was that same
Moses who had formerly been a captain of a band of
robbers, but who after his conversion became not only
an illustrious penitent, but so eminent in all virtue and
sanctity as to be raised to the dignity of a priest, and
superior of the holy monastery of Scete, and after his
death to be enrolled amongst the Saints. See the
Roman Martyrology, August twenty-eight.

45. A brother having committed a fault for which
he was expelled the convent of Abbot Elias, went to
Saint Antony on his mountain, and after remaining a
while with him he sent him back to the convent, but
the brethren refusing to receive him, he returned again
to Saint Antony. The Saint sent him back again the
second time with this message : " A ship that was cast
away at sea had lost all its cargo, but with much ado
the empty vessel has been drawn to the shore; and
would you, my brethren, after it has been thus brought
to land go and sink it entirely ? " The brethren understanding the meaning of the Saint presently complied, and received the brother again into their congregation.

46 Another brother had fallen into some sin, on
account of which the priest bid him go out of the
church ; whereupon the abbot Besarion, who was
present, rose up, and went out with him, saying, " I

also am a sinner as well as he." This was the great Besarion, of whose extraordinary sanctity and wonderful miracles frequent mention is made in ancient monuments, whose name is recorded in the Roman Martyrology amongst the Saints on the seventeenth of June.

47. A certain priest was accustomed to come from time to time to the cell of a hermit who lived in the wilderness, to celebrate mass and to administer to him the blessed sacrament, till at length it happened that the man of God heard an ill report concerning the priest, and accordingly the next time he came he shut the door against him and sent him away; but he had no sooner dismissed him than he heard a voice saying : " *Men have taken away the judgment that belongs to me, and have arrogated it to themselves.*" After which he was rapt in a kind of ecstasy or trance, in which he saw a golden well full of most clear and excellent water, with a chain and bucket of the same precious metal, and a leper drawing up some of this water, and pouring it out of the golden bucket into a clean vessel. Now he seemed extremely desirous to drink of it, and was only prevented by the repugnance he felt at seeing it drawn up by the leper.—Whereupon he thought he heard a voice which said to him : " Why dost thou not drink ? What harm has he done who has drawn the water, since he has done no more than filled the bucket, and then poured it out into the vessel ? " The

The hermit upon this returned to himself, and having reflected on the vision, called back the priest, and desired him to celebrate and consecrate for him as usual.

48. Some of the brethren went one day to consult St. Antony whether they ought to pay any regard to their dreams when they found them followed by the event, or to despise them as illusions of the devil? Now having had an ass with them who died by the way, as soon as they came to the Saint he was before hand with them, and asked them how their ass happened to die? How, father, said they, how did you know of the death of the ass? The devils, said he, showed it me in a dream. Upon this they told him the occasion of their coming, for that they had also often dreams which came to pass, and for fear of being deluded they desired his opinion concerning these matters. The Saint gave them full satisfaction on this head, assuring them by the example of the ass, that dreams being only tricks of the enemy to fill the mind with superstition, are by no means to be regarded.

49. The holy abbot Agatho being asked whether the mortification of the flesh by corporal labors and austerities, or the keeping a guard upon the inward man was of greater importance in a spiritual life, he answered: that man was like a tree, of which corporal labors and austerities were the leaves, but the regu

larity of the interior was the fruit: wherefore, as cur
principal care must be about the fruit: because it is
written, that *every tree, which doth not bring forth
good fruit, shall be cut up, and shall be cast into the
fire*, our chief solicitude must be about the interior.
yet we must not neglect the leaves of corporal exercises, since they are both an ornament and a covering
to protect the fruit.

50. The same holy Abbot used to say, that a man
who does not restrain the passion of anger, though
he were even to raise the dead to life, cannot be pleasing to God.

51. The holy abbot Pemen used to say, "Evil cannot be cast out by evil; wherefore if any one doth
evil to you do you good to him, that you may overcome his evil by your good." He was also accustomed to say : "He that is quarrelsome, or apt to murmur and complain, is no monk;—he that renders
evil for evil is no monk ;—he that is passionate is no
monk."

52. The same Saint said, self-will stands as a wall
of brass between man and God: wherefore he that
renounces his own will, may say with the Psalmist, Ps.
xvii. 30. *Through my God I shall go over the wall*,
and may arrive at the justice of God ; concerning
which it is written in the following verse, *as for my
God his way is undefiled*.

53. Abbot Abrahrn, who had been a disciple of

St. Agatho, having asked St. Pemen, "How it came to pass that the devils were always assaulting him? The devils, replied the Saint, don't oppose those who do their own wills; for our own wills are devils with respect to us, because they are always tempting us to follow them. But it is such, as like Moses and other saints, have got the better of their own wills that the devils impugn."

54. A certain brother complained to St. Pambo, that the wicked spirits would not suffer him to do good to his neighbors. Don't say so, said the Saint lest you charge our Lord with not being true to his word, for he has told us, Luke x. 19. *Behold I have given you power to tread upon serpents and scorpions, and upon all the power of the enemy.* 'Tis then your want of a good will, and not the wicked spirits which you ought to accuse on this occasion, for why don't you resist them, and tread them under your feet?

55. One having asked abbot Sisois, what can be the meaning, father, that these passions will not depart from me? The abbot answered, because by your irregular affections you keep within you what belongs to them; but if you give up all that is theirs, by mortifying your disorderly affections, they shall have no control over you, but shall depart from you.

56. An ancient father being asked, which was that *straight and narrow way that leads to life,* as is spoken

of Matt. vii ? answered, to do violence to our own
thoughts and inclinations, and to sacrifice our own
will to the will of God, and that such as do this may
say with the apostles, Matt. xix. *behold we have left
all things, and have followed thee.*

57. One of the brothers said to the abbot Sisois:
" I desire to keep a guard upon my heart ; " he replied, " how can you guard your heart, and preserve it
from dangers, if you suffer the gate of the tongue to
be always open ?" The same holy abbot used to say :
" That the great business of our pilgrimage is to keep
a guard upon our mouths."

58. Abbot Allois said: " Except a religious man
think in his heart that there is no one in the world but
God and himself, he will never enjoy true rest."

59. One of the ancients said : " As no one presumes
to offer violence to a person whilst he is at the side of
the emperor, so neither can Satan do any hurt to a
soul whilst it sticks close to God ; for it is written :
Approach to God, and he will approach to you,
James iv. 8. But because the poor soul is frequently
dissipated and forgets her God, the enemy has power
to drag her away into shameful passions."

60. One of the brothers told an ancient religious,
that he was not sensible of any conflict or war in his
soul.—" Oh," said the father, " it is because your soul
is like an open place, where every one comes in and
goes out at his pleasure without meeting with any re-

sistance on your part, or your ever taking any notice
of them; but if you kept the door shut, by guarding
against evil thoughts, you would quickly become sensible of the war they would wage against you."

61. Another ancient father said, that Satan had
three precursors who usually prepared the way for
him, and helped to introduce sin into the soul, viz.
forgetfulness of God, negligence, and *concupiscence.*

62. When the patriarch Theophilus visited the religious of mount Nitria, he asked the superior what
was the most important thing he had found out in
that way of life? The father answered: *to accuse
and reprehend myself without ceasing.* The prelate
replied, *there can be no way more safe.*

63. Abbot Mathos said, the nearer a man draws towards God, the more he perceives himself to be a sinner; thus when the prophet Isaias saw the Lord,
chap. vi. he immediately exclaimed, *Wo is me,—because I am a man of unclean lips—and I have seen with
my eyes, the King, the Lord of Hosts.*

64. St. Arsenius related as of another, though it
was thought himself was the person, that whilst one
of the ancient religious was sitting alone in his cell he
was called out by a voice that said to him: "Come,
and I will show thee the works of men." The person
that called him out, brought him first to a place where
he saw a negro cutting wood, and making a large bundle, which he tried to carry, but found 't too heavy;

whereupon instead of lessening the bundle he went to
cut more wood, and still continued to add to his burden, without offering to take anything away from a
load which even at the first was more than he could
carry. Having gone a little further, he perceived a
man standing by a lake drawing water and pouring it
into a vessel full of holes, through which the water ran
again into the lake. Afterwards he was brought to
another place where he saw a building like a temple,
with two men on horseback marching abreast, and
carrying a long pole together on their shoulders, with
which they endeavored to go into the temple, but as
they would not be put out of their way, nor stop, nor
turn the pole, so that one might pass in before the
other, they were both of them kept out, because the
length of the pole, and the manner they carried it,
would not suffer them to enter within the gate of the
temple. The person that showed him these things
told him, that these two men resembled such as pretend to carry the yoke of religion without renouncing
their pride ; and if they are not reclaimed, so as to
walk humbly in the way of Christ, they shall assuredly be excluded from God's eternal temple. He also
told him, that the man whom they saw cutting the
wood, represented worldlings loaded with sins, who instead of doing penance, or turning from their evil
ways, were, by adding sin to sin, continually increasing their burden ; and that the man who poured the

water into the vessel full of holes, resembled such as do many good works, but lose the fruit of them by mingling with them many that are evil. Wherefore every one ought to be watchful with regard to the unity and perfection of his works, that he may not be found hereafter to have labored in vain.

65. St. Arsenius also informs us, that there was in the wilderness a certain old man, who was wonderful in his actions, but simple in faith, so that being ignorant, he had an erroneous opinion with respect to the holy eucharist, saying, that the bread which we receive is not really the body of Christ, but only the figure of his body. Two of the ancient fathers, on hearing this, went to beg of him to lay aside so erroneous an opinion, and to believe with them and the universal church, that the eucharistic bread was indeed the body of Christ, and the chalice his blood, according to the truth, and not according to figure; because Christ himself had assured us, saying, *this is my body*, &c. But as the old man did not appear satisfied with what they said on this subject, it was agreed upon between them, that they should all three earnestly pray to God during the week with relation to the mystery, that the truth might be made manifest to him. On the following Sunday, having placed themselves together in the church, at the time of celebrating the sacred mysteries, there appeared to them a little child as it were lying upon the alta , and when the priest was going

to divide the sacramental bread, they saw an angel.
with a knife dividing the body of the child, and receiving his blood in the chalice ; and when they went
up to communion, whilst the other two received the
blessed sacrament in its usual form, the particle that
was given the old man appeared to be bloody flesh, at
which he was frightened, and exclaimed: "*I believe,
O Lord, that the consecrated bread is thy body, and
the chalice thy blood ;*" immediately what he was going to receive returned to the shape of bread according to the mystery.   Whereupon they all returned
thanks, and blessed God for his wonderful goodness,
in not suffering his servant to lose, by incredulity, the
fruit of so many years labor.

---

*Out of the Book of the Virtues and Miracles of the Reli-
gious of their own times, published under the Title of
" The Spiritual Meadow," by that holy man John Moschus, surnamed Eviratus, and his intimate friend and
individual companion, St. Sophronius*

66. An ancient religious, who dwelt in the monastery of the towers of Palestine, was so eminent in that
virtue, that all the monks were desirous of choosing
him for their abbot; but the old man begged to be

excused, saying : "Pardon me, reverend fathers, and suffer me to bewail my sins, I am not worthy to be intrusted with the care of souls ; that is an office only fit for such men as an Antony, Pachomius, or Theodore, and not for such a wretch as I am." But as the brethren still importuned him to accept of the superiority, and would hear of no excuse, he at length told them : "Let me pray for three days, that I may know the will of God ; and whatever he ordains that will I do." This he said on the Friday, and the Sunday morning following our Lord took him to himself.

67. Another religious man of the same monastery, an eminent servant of God, having died in the hospital of Jericho, when the brethren took his body from thence, and carried it to be buried in his own monastery, they perceived a bright star over his head, which accompanied them the whole way, and continued to be visible till the body was interred.

68. Another monk of the same monastery, whose name was Myrogones, who, by the austerity of his life, had fallen into a dropsy, when the brethren came to visit and comfort him under his sufferings, used to say to them :—"Good fathers, pray for me, that the inward man may not fall into a dropsy ; for as to this exterior infirmity, I make it my prayer to God that it may continue with me." The Patriarch of Jerusalem, Eustochius, hearing of this holy man, desired to be at the charges of furnishing him with all necessaries,

but the servant of God declined accepting his charita
ble offer, and only begged that he would pray for him,
that he might be delivered from the everlasting sufferings of the world to come.

69. A brother having desired the abbot Olympius,
priest of the monastery of St. Gerasimus, to give him
a word of instruction: "Fly," said he, "the conversation of heretics; put a restraint upon thy tongue, and
thy sensual appetite, and wheresoever thou art, say
always to thyself—I am a stranger and a pilgrim,"

70. One of the fathers of the laura of Cupatha related, as what he had heard from the person himself
to whom it happened, that when there was a war in
Africa, between the Romans and Moors, and the latter, in a certain engagement, had defeated the former,
and slain many of them, one of the Roman soldiers in
the flight, being closely pursued by a barbarian, whose
spear almost touched his back, prayed earnestly to our
Lord to deliver him, as he had delivered St. Thecla
out of the hands of her enemies, and promised, if he
escaped with his life, he would presently retire into the
desert, and dedicate himself wholly to the love and
services of God; when behold, looking back, he could
neither see the barbarian that pursued him, nor any
other enemy. Wherefore, to fulfill his promise, he
presently repaired to the laura of Cupatha, and had
already passed five and thirty years alone in a neighboring cave, in devotion and penance.

71. When John and Sophronius came to the monastery called Philoxene, near the town of Dade in Cyprus, they found there a monk, a native of Melitine, named Isidore, who passed his whole time in weeping and mourning. The brethren often desired that he would desist from his lamentations, and allow himself some rest and ease; but he would not hear of it, alledging that he was the most enormous sinner that ever had been since the creation. His history, which we had from his own mouth, was briefly to the following effect. Whilst he lived a married man in the world, both himself and his wife were followers of the heresy of Severus the Eutychian; but one day his wife visiting a catholic woman, her neighbor, went with her to receive the catholic communion. The husband being informed thereof, made what haste he could in pursuit of her, to prevent her so doing; but when he arrived he found she had just communicated. Upon which, in a great rage, he seized her by the throat, and obliged her to cast up the consecrated species, which he let fall into the dirt; when presently he perceived the sacred particle which he had abused, shining with brilliant rays of light. Two days after he saw a deformed black fellow, who said to him: "You and I are condemned to suffer the same punishment together;" and having asked him who he was, he answered: "I am the wretch who struck the Lord Jesus, the Maker of all things on his cheek at the time of his

passion." For this reason, said Isidore, I can never
leave off weeping. And now you have heard my history, I hope you will be pleased to pray for me.

72. Two ancient religious, travelling from Æga, in
Cilicia, to Tarsus, were obliged, by the heat of the day,
to go into an inn, where they found three young men
with a harlot in their company. The two religious
went and sat down by themselves; and when one of
them took out the holy gospel, and began to read, the
woman left her company, and came and sat down by
his side to hear him. The servant of God, in order
to drive her away, asked her how she could be so impudent as to come and sit by them? It is true, replied
she, I am a wretched sinner; but as our God and Saviour Jesus Christ did not prevent a sinful woman
from coming to him, why should you cast me off?
The woman that came to our Saviour, rejoined the
holy father, renounced her wicked way of life, and was
no longer a harlot. And I, said she, trust in Jesus
Christ, that from this very instant, by his divine grace,
I shall quit this sinful way, and never more be guilty
of the like sins. Firm in her resolution, she instantly
quitted the world with all she possessed, and went to
the nunnery near Æga, to which the two old men recommended her; "where," says my author, "I saw
her, being now an old woman of great prudence, and
learnt these things from her own mouth." Her name
was Mary.

73. A certain comedian of Tarsus in Cilicia, named Babylas, who led a very wicked life and kept two concubines, one called Cometa, and the other Nicosa, one day hearing in the church those words of the gospel, *do penance, for the kingdom of heaven is at hand,* (Matth. iii.) was so suddenly touched with an extraordinary compunction for his sins, that he resolved upon the spot to quit the world entirely, and to dedicate the remainder of his days to devotion and penance. This resolution, as soon as he returned home, he imparted to the two women, telling them that they might, if they pleased, divide his whole substance between them; but as for his part he was resolved to provide for the salvation of his soul, by renouncing the world from that very instant, and entering into religion. Both being greatly moved by his words, told him with one voice, and an abundance of tears, that as they had been partners with him in his sinful ways, and had borne him company whilst he was walking in the broad road to perdition, so they were also determined to accompany him in his conversion to God, and to enter with him upon the narrow way of eternal life; for why should you, said they, choose the better part for yourself, and leave us in the lurch? Wherefore Babylas went, and shut himself up in one of the towers belonging to the walls of the city; and the two women, after selling all their substance, and giving the price to the poor, made themselves also a cell in

the neighborhood, where they dedicated themselves to a recluse and penitential life. This man, says our author, I myself have seen, and was very much edified by his conversation ; for he was exceedingly humble, mild, and charitable

74. One of the fathers related a remarkable anec dote to us concerning St. Ephrem, the patriarch of Antioch :—that being very zealous and fervent in faith, he attempted the conversion of a famous monk who lived on a pillar in the neighborhood of Hierapo- lis, who had been tampered with by the Eutychian heretics, and seduced into their errors. This Stylite being obstinate against the remonstrances of the holy patriarch, to show how confident he was of the truth of his religion, made a proposal that a great fire should be kindled into which he and the patriarch should go together, and that they should abide by the faith of him who should come out of the flames without hurt. St. Ephrem told him, that although he had proposed a thing that far exceeded the strength of such a poor sinner as he acknowledged himself to be, however, that confiding in the mercies of his Saviour, and hop- ing by this means to bring about the salvation of a soul in error, he would agree to the proposal, and im- mediately he ordered a great quantity of wood to be piled up, which he himself set on fire, and then he desired the monk to come down from his pillar, that they might go hand in hand into the flames. But

.he heretic, who thought to have frightened the patriarch with his proposal, being dismayed at his courage
and resolution, would not come down.   The Saint then
going up to the fire, and taking off his stole, prayed
to our Lord Jesus Christ, who was pleased to be incar-
nate for the love of us, to make manifest on this occasion his divine truth; and when he had ended his
prayer, he cast his stole into the midst of the flames,
where it remained for the space of three hours, till all
the wood was consumed, and then it was taken out
whole and entire, without having been so much as
singed by the fire.   The Stylite, astonished at so evident a miracle, gave glory to God, and was converted
upon the spot to the Catholic Church, and was admitted by St. Ephrem to receive the holy communion
from his own hands.

75. St. Ephrem, who, before he was patriarch,
was count or governor of all the eastern district of
which Antioch was the capital, was very illustrious for
his alms-deeds and works of mercy.   In his time, the
city of Antioch was destroyed by an earthquake, which
calamity, amongst many other occasions of exercising
his charity, furnished him with that of employing a
number of workmen and laborers in repairing the public buildings of that city.   Now one of the fathers related to us, says our author, that on this occasion a
certain bishop privately withdrawing himself from his
see, and putting on a poor laborer's frock, came to An-

tioch, and there hired himself to serve the masons.
After some time the governor, in a vision by night,
saw this laborer lying asleep, and over his head a pillar of fire, which reached even up to the firmament.
He was the more astonished at the sight, because he
perceived nothing in the whole garb, or person of the
man, but what appeared mean and contemptible;
however, as he continued for many nights to see the
same thing, he sent for the laborer, and asked him
who or what he was?   He answered he was a poor
man, who endeavored to gain his little livelihood by
his work.   The count, not satisfied with this answer,
told him plainly he should not depart from him till he
had discovered the whole truth, and continued to conjure him in so pressing a manner to give him a more
particular account of himself, that at length, after requiring a solemn promise of secrecy, at least till he
should be dead, he told him: "I am a bishop, who
have for God's sake resigned my bishopric, and am
come hither as to a strange place, where no one might
know me; to mortify my flesh, employ myself in labor, and by the work of my hands to earn myself a
little bread.   Ask not my name, for that I must and
will conceal; but take care to multiply thy alms-deeds
and good works as much as possible, for before it be
long God will promote thee to the apostolic see of this
city, to feed the flock which Christ our true God has
purchased with his own blood.   Therefore, as I said,

be diligent in all the works of mercy, and always stand up zealously, and contend earnestly for the orthodox faith; for with such sacrifices as these God is best pleased." St. Ephrem hearing all this, glorified our Lord, who has many hidden servants in the world, known to himself alone.

76. The abbot Stephen related to us, that a certain monk, named Cyriacus, of the monastery of our holy father St. Sabas, being one day visited by his worldly friends, when they knocked at the door of his cell, he prayed to God that he might not be seen by them; then opening the door, he went out without their perceiving him, and remained abroad in the desert till he understood they were gone away.

77. The same abbot Stephen related to us the following extraordinary anecdote concerning father Julian the Stylite, who was illustrious for many miracles: the servant of God understanding that there was in his neighborhood a lion that did much mischief, called one day to his disciple Pancratius, and bid him go two miles to the south, and there, said he, thou shalt find the lion, to whom thou shalt say: "Julian, the poor servant of Jesus Christ, commands thee, in the name of the same Jesus Christ, the Son of God, who gives life to all things, to depart from this country." Pancratius having found out the lion, and spoken to it as the saint had ordered, the beast immediately obeyed, and was seen no more in that province.

78. Father Peter, a priest of the same monastery of St. Sabas, told us of another holy man, named Thaleleus, of the province of Cicilia, who had spent three score years in religion, in such perpetual compunction and devotion as to never cease from weeping and saying: "this present time is allowed us by divine mercy for repentance and penance, and O what a terrible account shall we have to give if we do not make good use of it!"

79. Three ancient religious men came one day to the cell of the holy abbot Stephen, priest of the monastery of the Æliotæ, to be edified by his conversation; but he keeping silence whilst they conversed on different subjects of piety, Father, said they, we came to you, in hopes of learning something, why don't you say something to us? "I beg your pardon," said he, "I really did not take notice of what you were speaking; for, to tell you the truth, I have nothing before my eyes, night or day, but our Lord Jesus Christ crucified." With this answer they departed not a little edified.

80. Abbot John, surnamed Molybin, related to us concerning the same holy priest Stephen, that being in his last illness obliged by his physicians to eat meat, a brother of his, a secular, but a very virtuous man, was shocked, and exceedingly grieved, that he who had lived so many years in such extreme abstinence and mortification, should, at the end of his life, fall to

the eating of flesh meat. In the midst of these thoughts he fell into an ecstasy, and saw in spirit one standing by reprehending him for being scandalized without cause at what his brother did through necessity, and by obedience. "But, (said he) if you desire to know the merit and glory of your brother, turn and see him." Upon which, turning about, he saw his brother fastened to the cross with our Lord: "Behold," said the person that appeared to him, "the happy state of your brother, and learn to glorify him who glorifies, in this manner, those that love him in truth."

81. Abbot Theodosius related of himself, that in his younger days, before he embraced a solitary life, he saw one day in an ecstasy, a peison shining brighter than the sun, who took him by the hand, and said :— "Come along with me; for thou must wrestle and fight for a crown." Whereupon he led him into a theatre that appeared immensely wide, and full of people; one part of whom were clothed in white, the other in black, and placed him in the centre. And here he saw a filthy negro of a gigantic size and strength, standing before him, with whom he was told he was to wrestle. He strove to excuse himself, alledging that no strength upon earth could be able to stand against such a monster; but the person that brought him thither said, you must wrestle with him. "Advance then courageously and attack him, and I will

stand by and assist thee, and give thee the crown of
victory." Upon this encouragement Theodosius seemed to himself to have entered the lists, and with the
help of his friend to have overthrown his adversary,
and received the crown; to the great joy of those that
were clothed in white, who gave praise and glory to
him who had given his servant the victory, whilst the
others in black were all confounded, and put to flight.
The same abbot Theodosius, as we learnt from his disciple, the abbot Cyriacus, spent thirty-five years in solitude, eating but once in two days, and observing a
perpetual silence. Of this, says John Moschus, I was
for some time an eye-witness, having lived during ten
years with him in the monastery.

82. When Sophronius and I, said John Moschus,
were at Alexandria, we went to visit abbot Palladius,
a true servant of God, superior of the monastery in
Lithosomenon, to learn of him some lessons of edification. "My children," said he, "our time here is
very short; let us then fight during this short time;
let us labor in earnest for the immortal goods of a
happy eternity. Behold the martyrs; look upon
those champions of heaven, and see how bravely they
have fought and conquered; what cruel torments they
have sustained; with what ardor of faith they have
gone through all the sufferings of the present life, and
thereby purchased an eternal and immense weight of
g.ory. To labor, therefore, to suffer, and to overcome,

with the help of our Lord, the tribulations of this life, is the way to prove ourselves true lovers of God. In the mean time he himself will remain with us; he will fight and conquer in and for us; he will alleviate by his divine grace all our labors and sufferings. Patience and Penitence must then be our exercises during the short time that is allowed us here, that so we may arrive at the honor and dignity of being the eternal temples of God." He added, that we should always set before our eyes him who *had not*, during his mortal life, *whereon to lay his head :* and that we should remember that the suffering of *tribulation*, according to St. Paul, Rom. v. *worketh patience, and patience trial, and trial hope, and hope confoundeth not*, &c. ; so that this is indeed the true way to dispose our souls for the kingdom of heaven. Wherefore, *my children*, said he, *let us love not the world, nor those things which are in the world*, 1 John ii. but let us keep a constant guard upon our thoughts, by recollection of spirit, which is the medicine of salvation.

83. We asked this holy man what had been the first occasion of his call to this monastic life? Upon which he related to us the following history : " There was," said he, " in my country (Thessalonica in Macedonia) an ancient religious man, named David, a native of Mesopotamia, who lived during the space of fourscore years shut up in a little cell by himself, at the distance of about three furlongs without the walls

of the city, in great sanctity and abstinence. Now it
happened, on account of the inroads of the barbarians,
that soldiers were placed round the walls of the city
to guard it at night from the attack of the enemy.
These guards observed one night flames of fire issuing
forth from the windows of the cell of the servant of
God, from whence they concluded that the barbarians
had been there, and had set fire to his cell; but to
their great astonishment, when they went out the next
morning to see what mischief had been done, they
found the old man safe and sound, and no mark of
fire in his cell. The following night they saw the
same fire again, which from that time continued to be
seen every. night for a long time after, even till the
death of the holy anchoret; and many of the citizens
often passed the night upon the wall on purpose to see
it. This I myself saw, not once, or twice, but many
times; upon which I said to myself, if God gives so
much glory to his servants in this world, how much,
thinkest thou, has he reserved for them in the world
to come; where *the just shall shine like the sun in
the kingdom of their Father.* This was the first occasion of my resolving upon taking the monastic habit,
and entering upon a religious course of life."

84. The same holy abbot told us of a soldier in
Alexandria, named John, who constantly observed the
following rule and order of life. Every day he came
early in the morning to the monastery, and sitting

down alone, clothed in hair-cloth, at the steps of the chapel of Saint Peter, employed himself in making baskets in silence and recollection, till the ninth hour of the day. In the mean time he used no other vocal prayer but this:—"*From my secret sins cleanse me, O Lord,* that when I pray I may not be confounded." This he repeated seven times in the day, and after each time continued recollected and silent for a whole hour. At the ninth hour he put off his hair cloth, and put on his military habit, and went to his station amongst the soldiers. With this man, said the father, I lived for eight years, and was much edified with his silence and his whole manner of life.

85. The same holy man told us one day, that the source of all heresies and schisms in the church was, loving God too little, and ourselves too much.

86. He also related to us the history of a certain merchant of Alexandria, a very religious, charitable, and hospitable man, who had a wife that was also a very pious, humble Christian, and a little daughter six years old. This man being called away by his affairs to Constantinople, was asked by his wife, at parting, to whose care and protection he would recommend her and her child during his absence? He answered, I recommend you to our blessed Lady, the mother of God. Having left behind with them only one servant man, a slave, the wretch, by the instigation of the devil, conceived the design of murdering his mistress and

her little daughter, and after rifling the house, to de-
camp with the spoils.   To put his diabolical plan in
execution, taking the kitchen knife with him, he attempted to go into the parlor where his mistress, with
her little girl, was sitting at her work ; but no sooner
had he come to the door than he was struck blind,
and withheld in such manner that he could neither go
forward nor backward.   At length he called to his
mistress to come out to him, whilst she, ignorant of
his case, replied, that if he wanted any thing he might
come in ; and although he called aloud again and
again, still she would not come, until at length, in a
fit of rage and despair, he stabbed himself.—His mistress hearing him fall, and seeing what he had done,
called in the neighbors, with whom came in also some
of the officers of justice, and finding him not quite
dead, they learnt from his own mouth the particulars
here mentioned, and glorified our Lord, who had in so
miraculous a manner preserved the life both of the
mother and the child, who were thus recommended
to the care of his Virgin Mother.

87. The same Palladius related also to us another
remarkable history, which he learnt from a master of
a ship, to the truth whereof himself was a witness.   A
widow, named Mary, had made away with two of her
own children, in order to recommend herself to a man
with whom she was in love, but who refused to marry
her on account of her children.   But when she had

secretly perpetrated this crime, and had signified to the man that her children were now removed out of the way, he conceived so great a horror for her, that he declared, with a solemn oath, he would never marry her on any account whatsoever. Being thus disappointed, and apprehending lest her guilt being divulged, she should fall into the hands of justice, and be put to death, to withdraw herself as far as possible from the danger, she went on board the vessel belonging to the captain above mentioned. But although she thus fled from the justice of man, she could not escape the justice of God; for when they had set sail, and were advanced into the deep, the ship all on a sudden stood still, so that for many days they could neither go forward nor backward, though they saw other ships, not far distant from them, sailing various courses, and going on with prosperous gales. All were in the utmost consternation at seeing themselves stand thus immovable in the midst of the sea, (for there were many passengers on board), but particularly the master of the ship, whose all was at stake, being in the greatest perplexity of mind, with the utmost fervor begged that God would send them a deliverance. At length in his prayer he heard a voice, saying : " Put Mary out of the vessel, and you shall have a good voyage." As he did not comprehend what the meaning of this could be, nor knew who this Mary was, and therefore was dubious what was to be done the voice said to him again : " Put Mary, I say, out of your ship, and all shall go well with you." Upon this he called out *Mary, Mary ;* and upon her an- swering to her name, he desired to speak to her apart, and told her he was afraid, that on account of his sins, they were all going to perish. O no, Sir, said she, fetching a deep sigh, it is rather on account of my sins ; for there is no crime of which I have not been guilty, and immediately told him the history of the murder of the children. He then proposed to her, as it were in order to know whether it was for his own, or for her sins, that the ship was stopped in her course, that the boat should be let down, and that he should first descend into the boat to see whether the ship would then advance, and if not, then he should return into the ship, and she should go down into the boat. The captain went down first, according to his proposal, into the boat, but still the ship and boat remained immovable ; but no sooner had he come back, and she gone down out of the ship, than the boat immediately turning round five times, went down with her to the bottom and was never seen more. Immediately the ship sprang forward, and continued to advance with such unusual speed, as to sail in three days and a half a voyage which otherwise must have cost them fifteen days.

88. As another instance of the justice of God often overtaking the wicked even on this side of eternity,

our author relates how he and Sophronius, sheltering themselves one day at noon from the violence of the heat of the sun, under the shade of a place called Te-trapylon, where the Alexandrians say the bones of the prophet Jeremias were deposited, they found there three blind men sitting, and heard them relating to each other the manner how they became blind. The first said, that being a sailor, he was struck blind by lightning at sea ; the second, that he had lost his eyes by the fire, working in a glass-house ; but the third made a sincere confession, that being an idle young fellow, and averse to labor, he begun to take to pilfer-ing ; and that seeing one day a man carried to be buried in rich clothes, and deposited in a monument behind St John's church, he had watched his oppor-tunity, and going into the monument, stripped the corpse of the clothes ; but that when he was about to take away the linen which was next to the body, the corpse, by some supernatural power, sat up, and fixing its nails in his eyes, plucked them out : "And thus," concluded he, "wretched I, in great anguish and des-olation, quitting all that I had taken, fled out of the monument ; and this is the true history of my blind-ness." This account which these two servants of God heard from the mouth of the blind man himself, they committed to writing, as a warning to sinners not to think, even in their most private sins, to escape the notice of the justice of God.

89. No less remarkable in this kind is the history which the same holy men learnt from abbot John, superior of a monastery near Antioch, with relat'on to a young man who had presumed to strip the dead corpse of a maiden gentlewoman. When he was going out of the monument laden with the spoil, she held him fast, and would not suffer him to stir, till he had restored all he had taken. Hereupon he made a solemn promise to renounce his wicked course of life, and to enter forthwith into religion ; and being as good as his word, he went immediately to abbot John, and with the greatest marks of compunction besought him, for the love of God, to receive him into his monastery. When the abbot inquired into the cause of that excessive grief and anguish wherein he saw him, he related to him the whole matter of fact as above. The abbot after having comforted him, received him into the monastic habit, and appointed a cavern in the mountain for his cell, where, at the very time my authors heard from him this history, which happened but a little while before, the young man was actually doing penance for his sins, and serving our Lord with great fervor and piety.

90. Sophronius and John Moschus having one day visited a holy anchoret, who had his cell at the distance of eighteen miles from Alexandria, they begged of him to give them some lessons for their instruction and edification. "My children," said he, "you do

well in renouncing the world, in order to secure your salvation. Go then and remain in your cells;—be sober and watchful; keep yourselves quiet;—be silent and pray without ceasing, and I trust in God that he will there enlighten your souls, and instruct you in the science of the Saints." He said again, " My children, if you desire to be safe, flee from the company of men, and be not of the number of those that run gadding about from house to house, or from place to place, for the sake of worldly interest or empty glory, and thus fill their souls with nothing but vanity. Let us flee, my children, let us flee, for the time is near at hand." Again he said; " Alas, alas! how bitterly shall we repent our not being sincere penitents now? Our misery is so great, that when we are praised we are puffed up, and when we are dispraised we are quite dejected: the former suggests to us poor wretches, pride and vain glory; the latter depresses us with sadness and anguish. Now there can no good be found where either sadness or vain glory resides." He said again, " the devils make it their business, when they have drawn a soul into sin, to strive to cast her headlong into dejection and despair, that so they may complete her ruin. They are always plotting against the poor soul, and saying, *when shall she die, and her name perish?* but let the soul that is sober reply with confidence in God, *I shall not die, but live, and declare the works of the Lord.* And if they should say

to her again, *Get thee away from hence to the mountain like a sparrow,* let her reply, behold *my God and
my Saviour, he is my protector, I will not go hence."*
He also said: "keep a guard at the gate of your
hearts, and let no stranger in, but diligently inquire,
Art thou one of ours, or of our adversaries!"
Jos. v.

91. We went also to the abbot John of Petra, and
desired a word of instruction from him. This good
father recommended continual mortification and poverty of spirit to us, in such a manner as to love to be
stript of all earthly things; and to this purpose he re
lated to us that when he was a young man, and abode
in the desert of Scete, one of the religious of that
place being ill, had occasion for a small quantity of
vinegar, but that so great was their poverty and abstinence, that a single drop could not be found in all
the four monasteries, although they contained at that
time no less than three thousand five hundred fathers.

92. John the Cicilian, abbot of Raithu, used to inculcate the following lessons to his brethren: "My
children, as we have fled from the world, by entering
into religion, let us also flee from the flesh, and all its
passions and concupiscences. Let us walk in the steps
of our fathers and holy founders who first inhabited
this place, and led such strict and mortified life with
so much silence and recollection. O, my children, let
us not be so unhappy as to defile this place by our sins,

which our fathers have taken so much pains to cleanse
and purify from the evil spirits and their works of
darkness." He also told them for their encouragement, that when he came thither first he found aged
monks who had spent seventy years in that place,
living the whole time upon nothing but herbs and
dates; and that for his own part he had now been
seventy-six years there, and had gone through many
a conflict, and a great variety of molestations and
temptations from the spirit of darkness. This was the
same abbot of Raithu to whom Saint John Climacus
dedicated his *Ladder of Paradise*.

93. We went also to visit abbot John the Persian,
who recounted to us the following anecdote concerning Gregory the great, the most blessed bishop of
Rome. "When I went," said he, " to Rome, to venerate the sepulchres of the holy apostles Peter and
Paul, and was one day standing in the midst of the
city, they told me that the Pope was about to pass
that way. Upon which I thought I would stop and
cast myself at his feet, to show reverence to him and
crave his blessing ; but when he came near and saw
me ready to pay him that veneration, I call God to
witness that he first prostrated himself upon the
ground before me, and would not rise again till he
saw me get up: then saluting me with a wonderful
humility, he put three pieces of money into my hand,
and gave orders to his people that I should be supplied

with every necessary, which gave me occasion to glorify God for the exceeding great humility, mercy, and
unbounded charity, which he had bestowed upon this
his servant."

94. Abbot Andrew, superior of a monastery near
Alexandria, related to us, that whilst in his youth he
was going from Alexandria into Palestine, with nine
others in his company, one of the number, who was a
Jew, named Theodore, was taken ill with a violent fever in the desert through which they were obliged to
pass.   The rest of the company pitying his case, afforded him what comfort they could, and led him forward in hopes of being able to reach some town or
village where he might meet with refreshment, but
the vehement heat of the sun, joined with the fatigue
of the journey, and the excessive thirst he endured,
would not suffer him to go any farther : in a word,
he was brought to that extremity of weakness and debility, that there were now no hopes left of his life, so
that his companions fearing lest the same should be
their own case if they did not make the best of their
way out of the burning desert, thought of leaving him,
since they could no longer be of any service to him.
Seeing them about to depart from him, he conjured
them for Christ's sake not to suffer him to die without
baptism, since he ardently desired to die a Christian.
They answered, that there was not one amongst them
who could baptize him, as this sacrament could not

by any means be administered without water, which could not possibly be had in those burning sands; but as he still persevered in begging and praying with many tears, that they would not be so cruel as to suffer him to die without making him a Christian, one cf the company, inspired as we may believe from heaven, desired the rest to lift and hold him up, for he was not able to stand by himself, when filling both his hands with sand, he poured it upon his head at three effusions, repeating at the same time the form of words used by the Church in the administration of baptism, to which all the company answered, *Amen*. When behold, "As God is my witness, brethren," said the abbot to us, "the man who was dying before was so suddenly and perfectly healed, and strengthened by Christ our Lord, that there remained in him not the least signs of illness, or weakness, or of having suffered any thing whatsoever: but, on the contrary, he appeared to possess a sound, strong, and florid countenance, and performed the remainder of the journey through the desert with such wonderful alacrity, as to be always the foremost of the company." The abbot also related, how that as soon as they entered into Palestine and came to the city of Ascalon, they carried the convert to the holy bishop Dionysius, recounting to him all that had happened, and his miraculous cure upon his being baptized with the sand. The good prelate glorified our Lord for his goodness and mercy shown on this occasion; but after consulting with his clergy, he concluded that as neither scripture nor tradition allow of the administering baptism otherwise than in water, the man ought to be baptized in water as the Church prescribes; and for greater solemnity he sent him away to the banks of the Jordan, that he might be baptized in the same font wherein our Lord himself was baptized.

95. When we were in the isle of Samos, Lady Mary, the venerable and charitable matron, mother of the courtier Paul, related to us that whilst she resided at Nisibis, in Mesopotamia, there lived in that city a very pious christian woman who was married to a pagan husband, but a well-meaning simple man. Being low in their circumstances, they had only a small sum of about fifty pieces of silver by them, which the husband designed to put out to use. The wife told him the best way he could put his money out was to give it to Jesus Christ, the God of the Christians, for that no one gave such good interest for money as he did, for that he would even return the principal double. Having asked her where he could find this God of the Christians, that he might put out his money into his hands, she led him to the church porch, and there showing him a number of poor people, told him that whatever was given to the poor the God of the Christians would accept of as given to himself, and repay it with interest; whereupon without hesitation he

cheerfully distributed the whole sum amongst the poor. After a lapse of three months, finding himself in some straits, he told his wife that the God of the Christians seemed not to take any notice of the debt, now that he stood in want of money; but she, strong in faith, bid him go to the place where he had lent him the money, and no doubt he should be paid. Accordingly he went to the church, where he saw the poor to whom he had given the money, but met with no one that offered to reimburse what he had lent them, or pay him any interest. At length, whilst he was considering within himself what he should do, or to whom he was to address himself, he saw a piece of silver lying at his feet, which he took up, and having carried it home, his wife told him that the God of the Christians, who, without being seen by us, disposes of all things, and provides for the whole world, had sent him that piece of money, and desired him to go and buy with it what they wanted for that day, assuring him that he would not fail to provide for them also for the time to come. Having gone to market with the money, he bought some bread and wine, and a fish, which he gave to his wife to dress for their dinner, when behold upon opening the fish she found in its entrails a precious stone of admirable beauty, which she showed to her husband, and he, without knowing the value of it, carried it to a jeweller to sell. The jeweller at first sight bid him five pieces of silver for it. "What," says he to himself, "so much as that?" supposing the man not to be serious. The jeweller then bid him ten pieces; but he still thinking him to be in jest, as he had no idea of the value of the stone, stood silent; but when he offered him twenty, then thirty, and afterwards forty, and had at length rose to fifty pieces of silver, he began to be convinced that the jewel was worth a great deal more, and stood out for a higher price. The jeweller advancing gradually, at last offered him three hundred pieces of silver, which he agreed to take, and carried the money home to his wife. From thence she took occasion to represent to him how liberally he had been dealt with by the God of the Christians, and how kind and how bountiful he must be, who for the fifty pieces of silver he had lent to him three months before, had returned him in so short a space of time, three hundred. This wonderful event was immediately followed by the conversion of the man, who ceased not afterwards to glorify God for his infinite goodness, and to hold himself highly indebted to the wisdom and piety of his religious wife, who had been the happy instrument by which he was brought to the knowledge of the saving religion of Jesus Christ.

96. When we were at Alexandria, in the days of the holy patriarch Eulogius, the cotemporary and intimate friend of St. Gregory the Great, we met with Leontius of Apamea, a most religious and faithful

man. who lived for many years at Cyrene, and came
to b? consecrated bishop of that see, fiom whom we
heard the following history : In the days of the patriarch Theophilus, a famous philosopher, called Synesius, was made bishop of Cyiene, who had an intimate
friend, a philosopher also, whose name was Evagrius.
This man, being a pagan, was very averse to the christian religion, to which the holy prelate would gladly
have brought him over ; he particularly objected
against the articles of the resurrection of the dead, and
of the eternal iewards and punishments of the world
to come. Synesius, however, was not discouraged
with the resistance he met with, and did not desist
from using all the means in his power for the conversion of his old friend, till the grace of God blessing
his endeavors, Evagrius at length determined to embrace the christian faith, and was baptized with his
whole family. Some time after he brought a bag of
three hundred pieces of gold to the bishop, and put it
in his hands for the use of the poor, desiring he would
be pleased to give him a note under his own hand,
that Christ would repay him in the world to come,
with which proposal Synesius readily complied. Eva·
grius some years after fell il. of a distemper, of which
he died ; and being near h's end, he gave the bishop's
note of hand to his sons, desiring it might be buried
with him. The sons, according to his desire, put the
note into the hand of the father's corpse, and buried

him with it. Three nights after Evagrius appeared to Synesius in his sleep, and bid him go to the monument where his body lay, in order to receive back his note, for that the whole had been repaid to him; and that in testimony thereof, he should find an acquittance, written by his (Evagrius's) own hand. The bishop next morning sent for the young men, asked them if they had not buried some paper with their father? They acknowledged that at his request they had, but that no one besides themselves knew any thing of the matter. Then taking them along with him, together with his clergy, and the principal men of the city, he ordered the tomb to be opened in their presence, where they found the philosopher lying, with the paper in his hand, which when they had taken from thence and opened, they saw at the bottom an acquittance, which appeared to be newly written, in Evagrius's own hand, whereby he acknowledged that he had received the contents, and was fully satisfied for the whole sum which he had given by the hands of Synesius to Jesus Christ our God and Saviour. This note and acquittance, as the same Leontius assured us, is kept to this day in the treasury of the church of Cyrene, and is always, in a special manner, recommended to the care of the treasurer of that cathedral.

97. One of the fathers related to us, that being at Constantinople upon some necessary business, whilst

he was sitting one day in the church, a gentleman of
condition came up, and saluting him, desired to sit
down by his side to hear from him some lessons for
the good of his soul. The father told him that if he
made a good use of the things of the earth, it would
be a great means to bring him to heavenly goods
"Father," said he "you are in the right; and that
man is truly happy who places his confidence in God,
and commits himself wholly to his providence. My
father, who was a gentleman of distinction and opu-
lence, but a great alms-giver, who distributed large
sums of money to the poor, asked me one day, after
giving me an account of all his worldly wealth, whether
I chose that he should reserve it to bequeath wholly
to me at his death, or whether he should dispose of it
in the manner he had begun, by giving it to Christ by
the hands of the poor, and to leave me Christ for my
guardian and trustee. I told him I was very well satisfied with his disposing of his worldly substance in
charity, and that I chose Christ before all worldly
riches, which quickly pass away; they are with us to-
day and gone to-morrow, but Christ remains for ever.
After this, my father became so liberal in his alms,
that at his death he left me very poor, but not without
the utmost confidence in Christ, to whose care he had
committed me. There happened to be at this time
another gentleman of distinction in the city, exceeding
rich, who was married to a very pious christian lady,

who greatly feared our Lord. This worthy couple had one only daughter to inherit all their substance; and as she was now marriageable, the wife proposed to her husband, that instead of giving her in marriage to some rich nobleman, who, if he were not a servant of God, might make her miserable, they should rather look out for some virtuous humble man that feared God, and would both love and cherish her, and go hand in hand with her to heaven; for riches they wanted none for her, having a large fortune to give her; and therefore virtue and happiness was all they had to seek for. The husband being of the same way of thinking, bid her go to church and recommend the matter earnestly to God; and after praying, with all possible fervor, then address herself to the first person whom God should send into the church, as to the man designed by providence to be the husband of their daughter. Having accordingly gone to church, after she had finished her prayers, she sat down; and, as providence had ordered it, I was the first that entered. As soon as she perceived me, she sent her servant to call me, and having inquired of me who or whence I was? I told her I was a native of this city, and the son of such a one. What, said she, of that gentleman who gave away all his estate in alms? Yes, replied I, of the same. Are you married, said she? I answered, no· and told her all my father had said, when he left me Christ for my guardian and trustee.

Hereupon she glorified God, and told me that my good guardian had provided both a wife and a plentiful estate for me, and wished me to use them both with the fear of God. Thus I received both her daughter and all her worldly substance; and I pray God that I may walk to the end of my life in the footsteps of my father."

98. Another of the fathers related to us concerning a certain lady of the first quality, who, after visiting the holy places, and performing other devotions in Jerusalem, went down to Cesarea to fix her abode in that city. Here she desired the bishop to place some religious woman with her, who might teach her humility and the fear of God. The bishop made choice of a virtuous, humble maid, whom he recommended to her for that purpose. After some time he asked her how she liked the companion he had placed with her? She is good, said she, but is of no great service to my soul; for she is so exceedingly humble, that she lets me do whatever I please, and never contradicts me. Upon this the bishop sent a woman of a more rough and untowardly disposition to her, who failed not to afford the good lady frequent opportunities of exercising her patience, as well as her humility and charity, in bearing with her sour temper, her unruly tongue, her perpetual contradictions and reproaches. After some time the bishop again desired to know how she liked her new companion? She answered,

that she had reason to be contented with her, because she was of essential service to her soul, by teaching her patience, meekness, and humility, which are best learnt in the school of reproaches and contradictions.

99. Another told us, that there happened to be a dispute between two neighboring bishops upon affairs relating to their respective dioceses, which was like to turn out very much to the prejudice of the weaker of the two, because his antagonist was a politica man, and one that had great power and interest. Wherefore, being sensible of his danger, he assembled one day all his clergy, and told them he had found out an expedient, by means of which, through the grace of Christ, he made no doubt but they should gain their cause and overcome their adversary. They could not comprehend how this could possibly be, considering the power and the craft of the man with whom they had to contend. Well, said he, stop a little, and you shall see the goodness of God. On such a day they celebrate the feast of the holy martyrs with great solemnity in that diocese, therefore you shall accompany me thither, and provided you imitate me in whatever I shall then do, we shall certainly carry our cause. Having assured them they would, on the day appointed they all followed him to the neighboring city, although ignorant of the means whereby he intended to overcome his adversary. At their arrival they found the whole people assembled, with their

bishop and his clergy; when, without a moment's hesitation, the humble prelate advanced, his clergy all following him, and, together with them prostrated himself at the feet of the other bishop, saying : *Forgive us, my good lord, we are all of us your servants.* The other, struck with astonishment at such profound humility, and at the same time touched with compunction, God changing his heart, fell also down upon his face, and taking hold of the feet of his fellow bishop, cried out : *It is you that are both my Lord and my father* : and from that moment their dispute was happily terminated, and they ever after lived in perfect concord and mutual charity. Thus the good prelate, by his humility, gained both his cause and the heart of his adversary, and told his clergy upon the occasion, that this was the true way to overcome their enemies.

100. A certain brother being assaulted with sadness, applied to one of the fathers, asking what he should do to prevent his thoughts from continually suggesting to him, that he was but losing his time in religion, and could never be saved? "Brother," said the father, "whatever you do, never think of going back to the world which you have renounced. If we cannot arrive at the land of promise, it is better for us to die in the wilderness, than to return into Egypt."

101. Gregory, the Governor of the province of

Africa, a good Christian and great lover of the poor
and the religious, related to us the following history
which happened in our times in his native country,
the district of Apamea in Syria.   There is in that part
of the world a place called Gonagus, forty miles distant from the city of Apamea, in the neighborhood of
which some country boys, by the way of play took
upon themselves to mimic the sacrifice of the mass and
the holy communion, according to what they had seen
done by the priests in the church.   For this purpose
they appointed one of their number to officiate as
priest, and two others to assist as deacon and sub-dea-
con ; and making a large stone, in the middle of the
field, serve for an altar, they placed some bread and
some wine in an earthen cup upon it.   Then he that
personated the priest, having his two ministers on
each hand of him, recited the words of the sacred oblation and consecration, which he had learnt by heart,
by being near the altar, as in some places the priests
recited them aloud, and proceeded in the mass till towards the end of the canon ; but before they came to
the breaking of the bread and the communion, a fire
descended from heaven, which instantaneously con
sumed both all they had set upon their altar, and the
stone itself, so as to leave no mark or trace of them
remaining.   Upon which they all fell to the ground,
half dead with the fright, and for some time could
neither recover speech or motion.   In this condition

they were found by their friends and carried home; to whom, as soon as they were able to speak, they recounted all that had happened, whilst the marks of the fire, in the place where it fell, plainly demonstrated the truth of what they related. The bishop of Apamea, on hearing of this extraordinary event, came out with all his clergy, and took cognizance of the whole matter upon the spot, by first examining the boys, and then viewing the footsteps of the fire, and in the conclusion caused a monastery to be built and a church erected in the field, the altar of which he fixed in the very spot where the fire had fallen. As to the boys, he placed them all in religious houses, one of whom afterwards became a monk in the said monastery, where Gregory, the governor, who related to us this wonderful history, saw him, and knew him

www.ingramcontent.com/pod-product-compliance
Ingram Content Group UK Ltd.
Pitfield, Milton Keynes, MK11 3LW, UK
UKHW020827230425
5580UKWH00023B/1033

9 781017 713343